THE TYNDALE
NEW TESTAMENT COMMENTARIES

LEON MORRIS

General Editor

*Dedicated to
my wife Rosemary
in deep appreciation
for her love and companionship*

THE GOSPEL ACCORDING TO JOHN

An Introduction and Commentary

Colin G. Kruse

William B. Eerdmans Publishing Company
Grand Rapids, Michigan / Cambridge, U.K.

First published in 2003 by Inter-Varsity Press
38 De Montfort Street, Leicester LE1 7GP, England

This edition published 2004 in the United States of America by
Wm. B. Eerdmans Publishing Company
255 Jefferson Ave. S.E., Grand Rapids, Michigan 49503 /
P.O. Box 163, Cambridge CB3 9PU U.K.
www.eerdmans.com

Printed in the United States of America

09 08 07 06 05 04   7 6 5 4 3 2 1

Library of Congress Cataloging-in-Publication Data

ISBN 0-8028-2771-3

CONTENTS

GENERAL PREFACE

The original *Tyndale Commentaries* aimed at providing help for the general reader of the Bible. They concentrated on the meaning of the text without going into scholarly technicalities. They sought to avoid 'the extremes of being unduly technical or unhelpfully brief'. Most who have used the books agree that there has been a fair measure of success in reaching that aim.

Times, however, change. A series that has served so well for so long is perhaps not quite as relevant as it was when it was first launched. New knowledge has come to light. The discussion of critical questions has moved on. Bible-reading habits have changed. When the original series was commenced it could be presumed that most readers used the Authorized Version and one's comments were made accordingly, but this situation no longer obtains.

The decision to revise and update the whole series was not reached lightly, but in the end it was thought that this is what is required in the present situation. There are new needs, and they will be better served by new books or by a thorough updating of the old books. The aims of the original series remain. The new commentaries are neither minuscule nor unduly long. They are exegetical rather than homiletic. They do not discuss all the critical questions, but none is written without an awareness of the problems that engage the attention of New Testament scholars. Where it is felt that formal consideration should be given to such questions, they are discussed in the Introduction and sometimes in Additional Notes.

But the main thrust of these commentaries is not critical. These books are written to help the non-technical reader understand the

Bible better. They do not presume a knowledge of Greek, and all Greek words discussed are transliterated; but the authors have the Greek text before them and their comments are made on the basis of what the originals say. The authors are free to choose their own modern translation, but are asked to bear in mind the variety of translations in current use.

The new series of *Tyndale Commentaries* goes forth, as the former series did, in the hope that God will graciously use these books to help the general reader to understand as fully and clearly as possible the meaning of the New Testament.

LEON MORRIS

Publisher's note:

We regret that, because of poor health, Leon Morris was unable to fulfil his editorial role for this volume, and are grateful to Andreas Köstenberger of Southeastern Baptist Theological Seminary for his willingness to read and comment on the manuscript.

AUTHOR'S PREFACE

In 1999 I completed work for a commentary on the Letters of John (Pillar New Testament Commentary series); work that involved me in reflection upon the parallels between those Letters and the Gospel of John. Thereafter, I was keen to do further work on the Gospel of John, and was therefore pleased when the invitation came from Inter-Varsity Press to contribute a commentary on this Gospel for the revised Tyndale New Testament Commentary series. My commentary will replace one written by the late Professor Tasker, and I hope it proves to be a worthy successor to his commentary.

Many different people have helped me in one way or another in the preparation of this commentary, and I want to express my thanks to them all. The Council of the Bible College of Victoria gave me study leave in the second half of 2001. Without that leave I could not have completed the commentary on time. The greater part of my study leave was spent at Tyndale House, Cambridge, where my wife and I enjoyed the support and encouragement of the Warden, Dr Bruce Winter, and Mrs Lyn Winter, as well as other scholars and Ph.D. students working there at that time. My colleagues at the Bible College of Victoria, Dr Darrell Paproth, Dr Ted Woods, and especially Dr Greg Forbes, read and commented helpfully on parts of the manuscript. Dr Philip Duce, the Theological Books Editor of Inter-Varsity Press, and Dr Andreas Köstenberger provided helpful comments on the entire manuscript.

Few people write commentaries today without profiting from the work of others, and this has certainly been true in my case. I have learned much from many scholars from different traditions. It is not possible nor desirable in a commentary of this size and

9

intended for general readership to acknowledge all those from whose work I have benefited nor to interact with the work of those from whom I differ. However, people who know the field will recognize my indebtedness to other scholars at many points in the commentary. There are many substantial commentaries on the Gospel of John, and in the preparation of this commentary I have made use of a good number of them. Again and again, however, I found the commentary written by Professor Don Carson treated most helpfully the issues raised by the text of the Gospel of John, and I want to express particular appreciation for his work.

This book is affectionately dedicated to my wife, Rosemary, in deep appreciation for her love and companionship over many years, which I hope will continue for many years to come.

The writing of this commentary has been a rich experience for me. I have seen afresh something of the glory of Jesus Christ, the Word made flesh and full of grace and truth, whom the evangelist so skilfully portrays. As the commentary goes out, it is my prayer that it will enable readers to understand the Gospel of John better, and by so doing to know better the only true God whose glory, grace and truth were revealed in the person and ministry of Jesus. To know this God and Jesus Christ whom he sent is to experience eternal life (Jn. 17:3).

COLIN G. KRUSE

CHIEF ABBREVIATIONS

1QS	*Community Rule / Manual of Discipline*
1QSa	*Rule of the Congregation*
4QFlor	*Florilegium*
4QpsDan	*Pseudo-Daniel*
AB	Anchor Bible
ABD	*Anchor Bible Dictionary*, 6 vols., edited by D. N. Freedman (Doubleday, 1992)
ABR	*Australian Biblical Review*
AV	Authorized Version
BAGD	W. Bauer, W. F. Arndt, F. W. Gingrich and F. W. Danker, *Greek-English Lexicon of the New Testament and Other Early Christian Literature* (University of Chicago Press, ²1979)
BSac	*Bibliotheca sacra*
CD	*Damascus Document*
DJG	*Dictionary of Jesus and the Gospels*, edited by J. B. Green, S. McKnight and I. H. Marshall (InterVarsity Press, 1992)
ET	English translation
Gk.	Greek
Heb.	Hebrew
IBS	*Irish Biblical Studies*
IVPNTC	Inter-Varsity Press New Testament Commentary

JBL	*Journal of Biblical Literature*
JTS	*Journal of Theological Studies*
Lat.	Latin
lit.	literally
LXX	Septuagint (Greek translation of the Old Testament)
NCB	New Century Bible
NEB	New English Bible
NIBCNT	New International Biblical Commentary on the New Testament
NICNT	New International Commentary on the New Testament
NIV	New International Version
NRSV	New Revised Standard Version
NT	New Testament
OT	Old Testament
PNTC	Pillar New Testament Commentary
REB	Revised English Bible
RSV	Revised Standard Version
RV	Revised Version
SBT	Studies in Biblical Theology
SEÅ	*Svensk exegetisk årsbok*
SNTSMS	Society for New Testament Studies Monograph Series
Str-B	H. L. Strack and P. Billerbeck, *Kommentar zum Neuen Testament aus Talmud und Midrasch,* 6 vols. (Beck, 1922–61)
TynBul	*Tyndale Bulletin*
WBC	Word Biblical Commentary

Note: Philo and Josephus are cited from the Loeb Classical Library, Justin Martyr from The Ante-Nicene Fathers, and the Mishna from Danby's translation.

SELECT BIBLIOGRAPHY

COMMENTARIES

Barrett, C. K., *The Gospel according to St John* (SPCK, ²1978).

Beasley-Murray, G. R., *John*, WBC 36 (Word Books, 1987).

Brown, Raymond E., *The Gospel according to John*, 2 vols. AB 29, 29A (Doubleday, 1966, 1970).

Bultmann, Rudolf, *The Gospel of John: A Commentary* (Basil Blackwell, 1971).

Carson, D. A., *The Gospel according to John* (IVP/Eerdmans, 1991).

Kruse, Colin, G., *The Letters of John*, PNTC (Eerdmans/Apollos, 2000).

Lindars, Barnabas, *The Gospel of John*, NCB (Oliphants, 1972).

Michaels, J. Ramsey, *John*, NIBCNT (Hendrickson, 1989).

Moloney, Francis J., *The Gospel of John*, Sacra Pagina 4 (Liturgical Press, 1998).

Morris, Leon, *The Gospel of John*, NICNT (Eerdmans, 1971).

Schnackenburg, Rudolf, *The Gospel according to St John*, 3 vols. (Crossroad, 1990).

Westcott, B. F., *The Gospel according to St John: The Greek Text with Introduction and Notes*, 2 vols. (Eerdmans, repr. 1967).

Whitacre, Rodney A., *John*, IVPNTC (IVP, 1999).

Witherington, Ben, III, *John's Wisdom: A Commentary on the Fourth Gospel* (Westminster/John Knox Press, 1995).

OTHER WORKS

Ashton, J., *The Interpretation of John* (SPCK, 1986).

Bailey, Ken, 'The Shepherd Poems of John 10: Their Culture and Style', *IBS* 15 (1993), pp. 2–7.

Barrett, C. K., *Essays on John* (SPCK, 1982).

Bauckham, Richard, ed., *The Gospel for all Christians: Rethinking the Gospel Audiences* (T. and T. Clark, 1998).

Beasley-Murray, G., *Gospel of Life: Theology in the Fourth Gospel* (Hendrickson, 1991).

Blomberg, Craig L., *The Historical Reliability of John's Gospel* (Apollos, 2001).

Brown, Raymond E., *Community of the Beloved Disciple* (Paulist Press, 1979).

Bultmann, Rudolf, *Theology of the New Testament*, 2 vols. (SCM Press, 1955).

Burge, G., *Interpreting the Gospel of John* (Baker Book House, 1992).
——— *The Anointed Community: The Holy Spirit in the Johannine Tradition* (Eerdmans, 1987).

Caragounis, C. C., 'Jesus, his Brothers and the Journey to the Feast (John 7:8–10)', *SEÅ* 63 (1998), pp. 177–187.

Culpepper, R. Alan, *Anatomy of the Fourth Gospel: A Study in Literary Design* (Fortress Press, 1983).

Danby, Herbert, *The Mishnah. Translated from the Hebrew with Introduction and Brief Explanatory notes* (Oxford University Press, 1933).

Derickson, Gary W., 'Viticulture and John 15:1–6', *BSac* 153 (1996), pp. 44–48.

Dodd, C. H., *Historical Tradition in the Fourth Gospel* (Cambridge University Press, 1963).
——— *The Interpretation of the Fourth Gospel* (Cambridge University Press, 1953).

Fortna, Robert T., *The Fourth Gospel and its Predecessor: From Narrative Source to Present Gospel* (T. and T. Clark, 1989).
——— *The Gospel of Signs: A Reconstruction of the Narrative Source Underlying the Fourth Gospel*, SNTSMS 11 (Cambridge University Press, 1970).

Gardiner-Smith, P., *St John and the Synoptics* (Cambridge University Press, 1938).

Green, J. B., McKnight, S., and Marshall, I. H., eds., *Dictionary of Jesus and the Gospels* (InterVarsity Press, 1992).

Hengel, Martin, *The Johannine Question* (SCM Press/Trinity Press

International, 1989).

Jackson, Howard M., 'Ancient Self-referential Conventions and their Implications for the Authorship and Integrity of the Gospel of John', *JTS* 50.1 (1999), pp. 1–34.

Josephus, Books I–VII, Loeb Classical Library, vols. 186, 203, 210 (Harvard University Press, 1926, 1927, 1928).

Koester, Craig R., '"The Saviour of the World" (John 4:42)', *JBL* 109 (1990), pp. 665–680.

Köstenberger, A. J., *Encountering John* (Baker Book House, 1999).

Kysar, Robert, *John: The Maverick Gospel* (Westminster/John Knox Press, rev. ed. 1993).

Marshall, I. Howard, *Last Supper and Lord's Supper* (Paternoster Press, 1980).

———— 'Son of Man', in Green, McKnight and Marshall, *Dictionary of Jesus and the Gospels* (InterVarsity Press, 1992), pp. 775–781.

Martyn, J. Louis, *History and Theology in the Fourth Gospel* (Abingdon Press, ²1979).

———— *The Gospel of John in Christian History* (Paulist Press, 1978).

Metzger, Bruce M., *A Textual Commentary on the New Testament* (German Bible Society, ²1994).

Morris, L. L., *Studies in the Fourth Gospel* (Paternoster Press, 1969).

Murphy-O'Connor, Jerome, *The Holy Land: An Archaeological Guide from Earliest Times to 1700* (Oxford University Press, 1980).

Neill, Stephen, and Wright, Tom, *The Interpretation of the New Testament 1861–1986* (Oxford University Press, ²1988).

Pryor, John W., *John: Evangelist of the Covenant People. The Narrative and Themes of the Fourth Gospel* (Darton, Longman and Todd, 1992).

Riesner, Rainer, 'Bethany beyond the Jordan (John 1:28). Topography, Theology and History in the Fourth Gospel', *TynBul* 38 (1987), pp. 29–63.

Robinson, J. A. T., *Redating the New Testament* (SCM Press, 1976).

———— *The Priority of John* (SCM Press, 1985).

———— *Twelve New Testament Studies*, SBT 34 (SCM Press, 1962).

Smalley, Stephen S., *John: Evangelist and Interpreter* (Paternoster Press, 1978).

The Ante-Nicene Fathers. Translations of the Writings of the Fathers down to A.D. 325. Vol. 1: *The Apostolic Fathers, Justin Martyr, Irenaeus*, edited by Alexander Roberts and James Donaldson (Eerdmans, repr. 1975).

INTRODUCTION

I. OVERVIEW

The Fourth Gospel has brought inspiration and comfort to countless generations of Christians, while providing scholars with many challenges. Those who study it seriously reap great rewards. The content of this Gospel is as follows:

- A prologue (1:1–18), which describes the pre-existent Word (Logos) who was with God in the beginning, was the agent of creation, and was then incarnate in the person of Jesus. (By commencing his Gospel in this way the evangelist ensures that his readers know the true identity of his main character.)
- A long section describing Jesus' work in the world (1:19 – 12:50), which includes signs and extended discourses through which he revealed God the Father and offered the gift of eternal life to all who believed.
- Another long section, which relates Jesus' return to the Father (13:1 – 20:31). It includes Jesus' preparation of the disciples for life without his physical presence, his prayer for himself and his disciples, followed by his betrayal, arrest, trials, crucifixion and post-resurrection appearances.
- An epilogue (21:1–25), which describes yet another post-resurrection appearance during which Jesus recommissioned Peter, predicted the nature of Peter's death, and made veiled comments about the fate of the beloved disciple.

II. DISTINCTIVE FEATURES OF THE FOURTH GOSPEL

The Gospel of John is unique in a number of ways. It alone speaks of the Logos who was with the Father in the beginning, who came down from heaven, incarnate in the person of Jesus. In this respect it is unlike Mark's Gospel, which begins its story of Jesus with the ministry of John the Baptist, or the Gospels of Matthew and Luke, which begin their accounts with the story of Jesus' birth. In the Fourth Gospel Jesus' message is presented mainly in terms of eternal life and resurrection, whereas the Synoptic Gospels highlight his preaching of the kingdom of God. In the Fourth Gospel Jesus' teaching is frequently presented in long conversations, extended discourses and debates. This is in contrast to the Synoptic Gospels, in which Jesus' teaching is more often found in parable form or in short pithy sayings. The Fourth Gospel has no account of Jesus' baptism by John or his temptation, his exorcisms, his transfiguration or the institution of the Lord's Supper, all of which feature in the Synoptic Gospels. Outstanding in the Fourth Gospel is the extensive teaching about the Holy Spirit, which stands in contrast to the paucity of Jesus' teaching on this subject in the Synoptic Gospels. These are but a sampling of the distinctive features of the Fourth Gospel

III. THE FOURTH GOSPEL AND THE LETTERS OF JOHN: A SCENARIO

There is a striking similarity between the language of the Fourth Gospel and the letters of John, so a *prima facie* case exists for positing the same basic authorship for all four documents (the question of the authorship of the Fourth Gospel is discussed in more detail below). A possible scenario for the production of and interrelationship between the Gospel and the three letters is offered below. It represents one possible reconstruction that depends upon certain assumptions concerning historical and literary matters, and is only as good as those assumptions. Nevertheless, it provides a working hypothesis to begin a study of the Fourth Gospel and may be modified if that proves necessary.

The beloved disciple (identified as the apostle John) lived in

Ephesus and was an esteemed figure in a group of churches in relationship with the church at Ephesus. These churches are referred to by scholars today as the 'Johannine community'. The beloved disciple produced an early form of the Fourth Gospel, in which the life and teaching of Jesus were depicted primarily to show readers that Jesus was the Christ and to encourage them to believe in him and so experience eternal life (20:30–31). He may have had secondary purposes, including the aim to encourage Jewish believers being persecuted by their unbelieving Jewish kinsfolk.

Sometime after the writing of the early form of the Gospel, disagreement arose in the parent church in Ephesus concerning the nature of Christ, the necessity of his atoning sacrifice, and the behaviour expected of those who claim to know God. This disagreement became so sharp that it resulted in the secession of a number of the members, who then proceeded to propagate their aberrant beliefs among those remaining in the Johannine community. This caused deep uncertainty in the community. Therefore, the beloved disciple wrote 1 John to expose the errors of the secessionists and to reassure the remaining members that they were in the truth, that they knew God, and that they were recipients of eternal life. First John was sent as a circular letter around the churches of the Johannine community. As a follow-up to this circular letter the beloved disciple wrote 2 John, which was addressed to one of these churches and its members ('the elect lady and her children') to warn them about the secessionist missionaries and to urge them not to give hospitality to them and thereby endorse their erroneous teaching. Third John was written as a further follow-up and was addressed to an individual, Gaius, who was a member of one of these churches. It commends him for giving hospitality to faithful missionaries who had gone out from the parent church, and complains about one Diotrephes who refused to do so.

Following the writing of these three letters, it appears that the beloved disciple died and others edited his Gospel and included their testimony to the trustworthiness of his work (see 21:20–24). It is this edited version of the Gospel that was included in the NT canon.

IV. COMPOSITION OF THE FOURTH GOSPEL

The authors of Matthew and Luke probably made use of Mark's Gospel and another source, which scholars call Q, as well as other material known only to themselves. The question naturally arises whether in writing the Fourth Gospel the evangelist made use of sources as well. He knew the Synoptics (see commentary on 3:24; 11:2) but did not make extensive use of them. Only 8% of the Synoptic material has parallels in the Fourth Gospel, and even these parallels are not close. There are indications within the text of the Fourth Gospel that the evangelist may have made use of other sources in composing his Gospel. There are a number of rough transitions (called *aporias*) in the Gospel that may reflect the weaving together of material from various sources. For example: (1) The prologue (1:1–18) has a distinctive poetic style of its own, and if it were omitted, then the story of Jesus would begin with the ministry of John the Baptist as it does in Mark's Gospel; (2) chapter 5 describes events and a debate that took place when Jesus was in Jerusalem, and then, without any indication that Jesus returned from Jerusalem to Galilee, we are told abruptly in 6:1 that 'Jesus crossed to the far shore of the Sea of Galilee'; (3) in 11:2 Mary is described as 'the same one who poured perfume on the Lord and wiped his feet with her hair', but the story of this act of devotion does not appear until chapter 12; and (4) in 14:31, following the first part of the farewell discourse, Jesus says to his disciples, 'Come now; let us leave,' but there is no hint of any movement in what follows; this only comes in 18:1. These *aporias* suggest that the evangelist may have made use of sources in composing his Gospel. One such source, it has been suggested, was a Gospel of Signs (see p. 35 below).

V. PURPOSE AND READERSHIP

The purpose for the writing of the Fourth Gospel is stated in 20:30–31: 'Jesus did many other miraculous signs in the presence of his disciples, which are not recorded in this book. But these are written that you may believe that Jesus is the Christ, the Son of God, and that by believing you may have life in his name.' Those needing to be convinced that Jesus is the Christ were unbelieving Jews; the messiahship of Jesus was not an issue for Gentiles. Seeing that the Gospel was probably written originally in Greek, we may say it was intended primarily for unbelieving Greek-speaking Jews.

There are notable variant readings in 20:31, where the word 'believe' is found. One variant uses the aorist subjunctive (*pisteusēte*) while the other has the present subjunctive (*pisteuēte*). It has been argued that the aorist subjunctive denotes initial belief, whereas the present subjunctive denotes ongoing belief. If this distinction is accepted the adoption of the aorist subjunctive would support an evangelistic purpose for the Gospel (*i.e.* to bring about initial belief), while the adoption of the present subjunctive would indicate an edificatory purpose (*i.e.* to urge people to continue to believe). However, this whole approach is questionable, for the actual use of Greek tenses does not support this sort of distinction. In the Fourth Gospel itself the aorist tense of the verb 'to believe' is used to denote both initial and continuing belief (*cf. e.g.* 1:7; 7:39), and the present tense likewise is used to denote both continuing and initial belief (*cf. e.g.* 6:35; 1:12).

A comparison of 20:31 with 1 John 5:13, especially if 1 John was written by the same author, supports an evangelistic purpose for the Gospel as opposed to a clear edificatory purpose for the letter:

John 20:31: 'But these are written that you may believe that Jesus is the Christ, the Son of God, and that by believing you may have life in his name.'

1 John 5:13: 'I write these things to you who believe in the name of the Son of God so that you may know that you have eternal life.'

If the evangelist intended his Gospel to be primarily edificatory, he could have made his intention a lot clearer by expressing himself along the lines of 1 John 5:13.

More than anything else, it is the emphasis of the Fourth Gospel upon the need to believe in Jesus and the stories of people who did so that suggest its primary purpose is evangelistic. John the Baptist testified to the light 'so that through him all men might believe' (1:7; *cf.* 10:40–42). The evangelist says Jesus gave the right to become children of God to all who believed in him (1:12) and stresses that those who believe receive eternal life (3:15–16, 36) and escape condemnation (3:18). Jesus promised eternal life to those who believed in him (5:24; 6:40, 47) and prayed for those who would believe through his disciples' preaching (17:20).

There are many examples of people who met Jesus, heard his word and believed in him: Nathanael acclaimed Jesus as the Son of God and the King of Israel (1:47–51), the Samaritan villagers acknowledged Jesus as the Saviour of the world (4:29, 39–42), his disciples (6:69; 16:30–31), the man born blind (9:35–38) and Martha (11:27) all put their faith in him, and Thomas acclaimed Jesus as 'my Lord and my God' (20:28), after which Jesus pronounced a blessing upon those who, unlike Thomas, would not see yet would believe (20:29).

There are just as many examples of people who believed in Jesus when they witnessed the miracles he performed: his disciples believed when they saw him turn water to wine in Cana (2:11), the royal official believed when he saw his son healed by the word of Jesus (4:53), the crowds in Jerusalem believed when they saw the many signs Jesus did there (7:31), many Jews believed when they saw Jesus restore Lazarus to life or heard that he had done so (11:45; 12:11), and many Jewish leaders believed secretly when they saw his miracles (12:37–43).

Finally, the editors who shaped the final form of the Gospel added their comments in support of the truthfulness of the Gospel to encourage readers to put their faith in Jesus (19:35; 21:24). The cumulative effect of all this indicates that the primary purpose of the Gospel is evangelistic: to bring people to faith in Jesus.

However, while this appears to be the primary purpose of the Fourth Gospel, it is not the only one. Many secondary purposes can and have been suggested. The most important is to encourage and edify those who already believe. In particular, one aim of the evangelist seems to have been to strengthen Jewish believers who were being persecuted by their unbelieving kinsfolk by showing that Jesus himself had suffered similar persecution, and that he had warned his disciples that they would experience the same. Nowhere is the aim of encouraging readers more evident than in Jesus' farewell speech in chapters 13 – 16. Here Jesus prepares his disciples for life without his physical presence when he returns to the Father. He exhorts them to carry out humble, sacrificial service for one another and to love one another as he loved them. He tells them to remain in him and in his love by obedience to his commands. He promises another Counsellor, the Holy Spirit, will come to be with them, to teach and guide them, to bear his witness to the world along with theirs. He warns them of the hostility they will encounter from the world when he has returned to the Father, and bequeaths to them his peace.

Other secondary purposes have been suggested, some more likely than others. These include (1) to supplement (likely) or supersede (unlikely) the Synoptic Gospels; (2) as a polemic against followers of John the Baptist (unlikely) – while John is repeatedly portrayed as less than Jesus, he is nevertheless consistently depicted positively as a faithful witness; (3) to encourage members of the Johannine community in their struggle with the synagogue (possible) – but the Gospel appears to have been intended for an audience wider than just the Johannine community; (4) as a polemic against 'the Jews'[1] (unlikely) – at the most this could only refer to those Jews opposed to Jesus and can in no way be applied to all Jews then or now; (5) to combat Gnosticism (unlikely) – while there is a stress on Jesus' incarnation and real humanity that could serve to combat Gnosticism, those places where Jesus' real humanity is implied do not appear to be polemically intended, as corresponding passages in the Letters of John are (1 Jn. 4:2; 2 Jn. 7); (6) to deal with the problem created by a delayed parousia (unlikely) – some see the promise of the Counsellor as a response to the delayed parousia, but this promise is better seen as preparation of the disciples for life without Jesus' physical presence, and in any case the hope of Jesus' second coming is still retained; (7) to correct attitudes towards the sacraments, either by providing a basis in the gospel tradition for later practices of the church or to combat their overemphasis and abuse in the church (unlikely) – while later Christians might detect what they think are sacramental allusions, it is hard to demonstrate that the evangelist's intention was sacramental in the passages concerned (*e.g.* 3:5; 6:51–58).

---

[1]See '"The Jews" in the Fourth Gospel', pp. 49–50.

VI. AUTHORSHIP

In the scenario provided above it was assumed that the beloved disciple, identified as the apostle John, was responsible for producing the original form of the Fourth Gospel. Such a view is not universally accepted and therefore needs to be examined in the light of the testimony of the early church fathers (external evidence) and the information that may be gleaned from the Fourth Gospel itself (internal evidence).

A. EXTERNAL EVIDENCE

The testimony of early Christian tradition is that the apostle John spent the latter years of his life in Ephesus, the capital of the Roman province of Asia. There he wrote and published the Fourth Gospel, which he sent to the churches of Asia. He died and was buried in Ephesus. This tradition rests upon various testimonies of early church fathers, which are set out in (roughly) chronological sequence below.

First, there is the testimony of Papias (*c.* AD 60 – 140), Bishop of Hierapolis in the Roman province of Asia. Papias' own writings survive only in fragmentary quotations in the works of Irenaeus and Eusebius. Irenaeus (*d.* AD 202), bishop of Lyons and native of the Roman Province of Asia, describes Papias as 'the hearer of John and a companion of Polycarp' (*Against Heresies* v.33.4). The Anti-Marcionite Prologue to the Fourth Gospel, found in about forty manuscripts of the Vulgate, and believed to have been written in the latter half of the second century AD, describes Papias in similar fashion as 'the dear disciple of John' and ascribes to the apostle John the authorship of the Fourth Gospel.

Second, Clement (*c.* AD 150–215), who became head of the catechetical school in Alexandria in AD 190, records the tradition which associates the apostle John with Ephesus, saying that he returned to that city from the Isle of Patmos after the death of the tyrant (usually identified with the emperor Domitian [AD 81–96]) (*The Rich Man's Salvation* 42). Clement attributed the writing of the Fourth Gospel to John the apostle in the oft-quoted words which imply that the apostle knew the Synoptic Gospels, but chose to compose a 'spiritual gospel' to complement the bare facts they had already made known (cited by Eusebius, *Ecclesiastical History* vi.14.7).

Third, part of a letter written about AD 190 by Polycrates, bishop of Ephesus, which refers to the burial place of John in Ephesus, is preserved by Eusebius (*Ecclesiastical History* iii.31.1–3). There are some problems with Polycrates' testimony (which includes statements confusing Philip the apostle with Philip the evangelist); however, his claim that John was buried in Ephesus is corroborated by Eusebius' own affirmation that the story about there being tombs for two Johns in Ephesus was true (*Ecclesiastical History* iii.39.6).

Fourth, the Muratorian Canon, written about AD 180–200 and associated with the city of Rome, affirms that the apostle John was the author of the Fourth Gospel:

> The fourth of the gospels, that of John, (one) of the disciples. When his fellow-disciples and bishops urged him, he said: Fast with me from today for three days, and what will be revealed to each one let us relate to one another. In the same night it was revealed to Andrew, one of the apostles, that whilst all were to go over (it), John in his own name should write everything down.

Fifth, The clearest affirmation of the writing of the Fourth Gospel by the apostle John was made by Irenaeus. In a passage where he claims to have known Polycarp, who in turn knew John the apostle, he states that John the apostle lived among the believers in Ephesus until the time of Trajan (AD 98–117) (*Against Heresies* iii.3.4). He asserts further, 'John, the disciple of the Lord, who also had leaned upon His breast, did himself publish a Gospel during his residence at Ephesus in Asia' (*Against Heresies* iii.1.1). In another place he says:

> The Gospel, therefore, knew no other son of man but Him who was of Mary, who also suffered; and no Christ who flew away from Jesus before the passion; but Him who was born it knew as Jesus Christ the Son of God, and that this same suffered and rose again, as John, the disciple of the Lord, verifies, saying: 'But these are written, that ye might believe that

Jesus is the Christ, the Son of God, and believing ye might have eternal life in His name.' (*Against Heresies* iii.16.5)

Sixth, Dionysius, bishop of Alexandria (*d. c.* AD 265), a person of critical independence in matters relating to the Bible, while denying the common authorship of the Fourth Gospel and Revelation, affirmed that John the apostle was the author of the Fourth Gospel:

I do not, therefore, deny that he [the author of Revelation] was called John and that this was the writing of one John, and I agree that it was the work, also, of some holy and inspired man. But I would not easily agree that this was the apostle, the son of Zebedee, the brother of James, who is the author of the Gospel, and the general (catholic) epistle that bears his name. (Cited in Eusebius, *Ecclesiastical History* vii.25.6ff.)

From these various quotations from early church fathers it is clear that the apostle John was believed to be the author of the Fourth Gospel. Questions were very early raised concerning the authorship of Revelation, but there were no questions raised about the apostolic authorship of the Fourth Gospel. However, there are matters which caution us from too easily embracing these traditions: (1) the NT itself says nothing about John residing in Ephesus; (2) Ignatius who wrote to the church at Ephesus in the early years of the second century never refers to John, though he does mention the church's connection with Paul (Ignatius, *Letter to the Ephesians* xii. 2); (3) Mark 10:39 could be taken as a prophecy that John as well as James was to be martyred, and there are ancient martyrologies that speak of both apostles suffering martyrdom at the same time. However, against both the silence of Ignatius and the questionable testimony of the martyrologies must be placed the strong testimony of both Irenaeus and Eusebius especially in support of John the apostle as the author of the Fourth Gospel.

B. INTERNAL EVIDENCE

The Fourth Gospel itself does not disclose the name of its author. In this respect it is the same as the other three canonical Gospels (the titles that appear in the NT today were added by early editors of the NT canon). However, in the Fourth Gospel we find the following statement: 'This is the disciple who testifies to these things and who wrote them down. We know that his testimony is true' (21:24). This statement is found in the epilogue and contains the testimony of others ('we') to the truthfulness of the things written by the beloved disciple. The beloved disciple is mentioned five times in the Gospel (13:23; 19:26; 20:2; 21:7, 20). Also in several places mention is made of 'the other disciple' or 'another disciple' (18:15, 16; 20:2, 3, 4, 8), who is identified as the beloved disciple in 20:2. Can the beloved disciple be identified more explicitly?

The Fourth Gospel mentions the Twelve (*i.e.* the twelve disciples whom Jesus chose) four times (6:67, 70, 71; 20:24). We may infer that the beloved disciple was one of the Twelve, because he was present at the Last Supper, and other Gospels indicate that Jesus celebrated this supper with the Twelve and apparently the Twelve only (Mt. 26:20; Mk. 14:17). The Fourth Gospel mentions five of the Twelve by name: Simon Peter (1:40–42, 44; 6:8, 68; 13:6, 8–9, 24, 36–37; 18:10–11, 15–18, 25–27; 20:2–4, 6; 21:2–3, 7, 11, 15–17, 20–21), Andrew (1:40, 44; 6:8; 12:22), Philip (1:43–46, 48; 6:5, 7; 12:21–22; 14:8–9), Thomas (11:16; 14:5; 20:24, 26–28; 21:2) and Judas Iscariot (6:71; 12:4; 13:2, 26, 29; 18:2–3, 5). It refers to 'the sons of Zebedee' (21:2) without mentioning their names (their names were, of course, James and John: Mt. 4:21; 10:2; Mk. 1:19; 3:17; 10:35; Lk. 5:10). That the apostle John is not mentioned by name in the Fourth Gospel leaves open the possibility, but does not prove, that he was the beloved disciple and therefore the Gospel's anonymous author.

Theoretically, however, the author could have been any of the Twelve not mentioned by name in the Fourth Gospel, excluding of course Judas Iscariot. However, other considerations narrow the field. That the disciple who wrote these things came to be known as the beloved disciple and was the one who reclined next to Jesus at the Last Supper suggests he enjoyed some intimacy with him. The Synoptic Gospels indicate that of the Twelve, Jesus chose three, Peter, James and John, to be present at the raising of Jairus' daughter (Mk. 5:37; Lk. 8:51), to witness the transfiguration (Mt. 17:1; Mk. 9:2; Lk. 9:28), and to be with him during his agony in Gethsemane (Mk. 14:33). It was also Peter, James and John who asked Jesus for an explanation concerning the time of fulfilment of his prophecy concerning the destruction of the temple (Mk. 13:3). It is highly likely that one of these three intimates of Jesus was the one who became known as the beloved disciple. It is unlikely to have been Peter, as he is frequently mentioned by name in the Fourth Gospel. It could be either of the sons of Zebedee, for neither of these disciples is mentioned by name. However, it is unlikely to have been James, as he was martyred very early on (Acts 12:1–2). There is, therefore, a *prima facie* case for identifying the beloved disciple as the other son of Zebedee, the apostle John. As this is also the consistent testimony found in the writings of early church fathers, it is hard to pass by this conclusion, despite widespread reluctance to accept it by many, but by no means all, modern scholars.

To recognize the apostle John as the author of the Fourth Gospel does not mean that the Gospel in the form we have it today came entirely from his hand. The epilogue contains the testimony of others to the truthfulness of what the beloved disciple wrote (21:24), a testimony that appears to have been added by others after the apostle John had died. This is implied by the incident related in 21:20–23:

> Peter turned and saw that the disciple whom Jesus loved was following them . . . When Peter saw him, he asked, 'Lord, what about him?' Jesus answered, 'If I want him to remain alive until I return, what is that to you? You must follow me.' Because of this the rumour spread among the brothers that this disciple would not die. But Jesus did not say that he would not die; he only said, 'If I want him to remain alive until I return, what is that to you?'

Jesus' words to Peter concerning the beloved disciple gave rise to a rumour in the early church that this disciple would not die before the Lord came again. The need to scotch such a rumour would have become pressing if the beloved disciple had died, and people's faith was being unsettled by the apparent failure of Jesus' word to be fulfilled. Hence the epilogue insists, 'Jesus did not say to him that he would not die, but, "If it is my will that he remain until I come, what is that to you?"' This suggests that the epilogue was written by others after the death of the beloved disciple. It is also possible that they made other editorial additions to the Gospel, including the testimony to the truthfulness of the beloved disciple found in 19:35. Perhaps the anonymous self-references made by the author found in the original form of the Gospel, expressions such as 'the other disciple' or 'another disciple' (18:15, 16; 20:2, 3, 4, 8), were explained as, or supplemented by, references to the beloved disciple by later editors of the Gospel. If this were the case, references to the beloved disciple need not reflect egocentrism on the part of the original author, but rather the attitude of a later generation of Christians to him and his special relationship to Jesus.

C. REASONS FOR FREQUENT REJECTION OF APOSTOLIC AUTHORSHIP

Despite the fact that a reasonable case can be made for regarding the apostle John as the author of the (original form of the) Fourth Gospel from both external and internal evidence, there is widespread rejection of this conclusion for other reasons. Some of these are listed below, together with brief comments on their viability:

1. Much of what is found in the Synoptic Gospels is missing from the Fourth Gospel, which belies the fact that its author was one of the Twelve – yet John may have had his own reasons for the selection of material for inclusion in his Gospel.

2. As a Galilean fisherman John would be uneducated, possibly illiterate, and not sophisticated enough to produce this Gospel – however, young Jewish boys were normally taught to read and write, and Greek was used extensively in Jesus' world. Also, a long ministry in various parts of the empire would enable John to obtain a working knowledge of that language. It is noteworthy that the Greek of the Fourth Gospel is the simplest in the NT, not surprising if the author's mother tongue was Aramaic.

3. A Galilean fisherman would not have been sufficiently well known in Jerusalem and to the family of the high priest to gain access to his courtyard and feel secure there when Jesus was on trial (18:15–16). This is a more substantial objection, but it needs to be

noted that John's father Zebedee was not a poor fisherman but one who owned his own boat and had hired hands, as well as his sons, to help operate his business. It is reasonable that such a family would have connections with the high priestly family in Jerusalem.

4. The Synoptic Gospels say that all the disciples forsook Jesus and fled when he was arrested, but the Fourth Gospel says the beloved disciple, identified as John, followed him to the high priest's courtyard and later stood by him at the cross. Such a problem is not insurmountable. John's initial reaction, like that of the other disciples, might have been to flee when Jesus was arrested, but then he could have recovered himself and followed him to the high priest's house, and later to the cross.

5. The author of this Gospel shows an intimate knowledge of the geography of Jerusalem and Judea, something one would not expect from John who was a Galilean – but Galilean Jews went on frequent pilgrimages from Galilee through Samaria and Judea to Jerusalem and would therefore have a good knowledge of the geography of Judea and Jerusalem. Also, John, as one of the Twelve, accompanied Jesus on his five journeys to Jerusalem, and these trips would have reinforced his geographical knowledge.

These are the more significant objections,[1] but none of these or others seems sufficiently compelling to force one to reject the evidence of the early church fathers and the Gospel itself in favour of identifying the apostle John as the author of the original form of the Fourth Gospel. In the commentary that follows, this is the position assumed, though out of respect for the author's desire for anonymity he is referred to simply as 'the evangelist'.

VII. DATE AND PLACE OF WRITING

By the end of the nineteenth century the dominant view in scholarly circles was that the Fourth Gospel was written in the latter half of the second century AD in order to present the gospel message in

---

[1]These and others are discussed in more detail in Blomberg, pp. 31–41.

Hellenistic terms. Such a position is now untenable in the light, especially, of the discovery in 1920 of the papyrus $\mathfrak{P}^{52}$ (a small fragment containing five verses from Jn. 18) dated to the early part of the second century AD, and arguably the earliest known portion of the NT. This suggests that the Fourth Gospel was written, at the latest, in the final decade of the first century, and certainly not the latter half of the second century as previously argued.

While the latest possible date for the writing of the Fourth Gospel is now generally recognized as the last decade of the first century, there are widely divergent opinions concerning the actual date of composition. Robinson claimed that the Fourth Gospel was written as early as the 60s, before the destruction of Jerusalem in AD 70.[1] He mounted a strenuous defence of the antiquity of the Fourth Gospel, arguing that it predated the other three canonical Gospels.[2] The arguments for such an early date are largely arguments from silence, notably that there is no mention of the destruction of the temple in AD 70. However, if the Fourth Gospel was written in the late 80s or 90s the destruction of the temple would have occurred some 20 to 30 years before, long enough ago for it not to have required any comment. Some support an early date by arguing that the evangelist did not know the Synoptic Gospels and therefore could have written his Gospel before them. However, there are indications that the evangelist did know the Synoptics even though he chose to incorporate little of the Synoptic tradition in his own Gospel. Accordingly, we would need to date the writing of the Fourth Gospel after, not before, the writing of the Synoptics.

According to early church tradition, John the apostle wrote this Gospel while resident in Ephesus. Clement of Alexandria says John *returned* to Ephesus after the death of the tyrant (Domitian, emperor from AD 81–96), and Irenaeus says he remained there until the time of Trajan (emperor from AD 98–117). Unfortunately, there is no information about the time John first took up residence in Ephesus. According to the Muratorian Canon there was collaboration between John and other disciples of the Lord of whom only the apostle Andrew is specifically mentioned. Even if this tradition is

---

[1]Robinson, *Redating New Testament*, pp. 310–311.
[2]Robinson, *Priority of John*, pp. 33–35.

reliable we have no information about Andrew being in Ephesus nor of the time of his death, traditionally held to have been by crucifixion in Achaia.

The fact that early church traditions mention John's residence in Ephesus continuing through to the time of Trajan (AD 98) has led to the conclusion that the Fourth Gospel was probably written quite late, in the 80s or 90s. However, those traditions do not actually specify the time of writing, only the extent of his period of residence in Ephesus. In the absence of further information a date of writing in the 80s or 90s is reasonable. Ephesus as the place of writing appears to be quite secure in early church traditions.

VIII. HISTORICAL RELIABILITY

Beginning in the eighteenth and nineteenth centuries, serious questions were raised concerning the historical reliability of the Fourth Gospel. A number of factors contributed to this. First, there are the significant differences between the portrayal of Jesus' life and ministry in the Synoptic Gospels and the Fourth Gospel. Many of the significant events recorded in the Fourth Gospel (*e.g.* the dialogue with Nicodemus, the conversation with the woman of Samaria, the raising of Lazarus, and Jesus' farewell speeches to his disciples in chs. 13 – 17) have no counterparts in the Synoptic Gospels. The Synoptic Gospels record only one journey by Jesus to Jerusalem in the period of his ministry, whereas the Fourth Gospel records five such journeys. The Fourth Gospel places the cleansing of the temple at the beginning of Jesus' ministry, whereas the Synoptic Gospels all locate it at the end. In the Synoptic Gospels Jesus' teaching is presented mostly in short pithy sayings and with frequent use of parables, but in the Fourth Gospel it takes the form of long conversations or extended discourses. In the light of these differences it is asserted that if the evangelist knew the Synoptic Gospels (and there are indications that he did), then these significant divergences from the Synoptics make the historical reliability of the Fourth Gospel suspect.

Second, the language of the Fourth Gospel is strikingly similar to that of the Letters of John. Even the way Jesus speaks is similar to the style of the author of the Letters of John. Further, it is argued that the language of the Fourth Gospel is Hellenistic, that the Gospel was produced in a Greek community and is to be dated in the second half of the second century AD. Therefore, it could not have been written by one of Jesus' disciples.

As a result of observations such as these, the dominant scholarly view by the end of the nineteenth century was that the Synoptic Gospels, not the Fourth Gospel, are to be regarded as primary evidence for the life of Jesus. The Fourth Gospel's contribution is theological rather than historical, its cultural background is Hellenistic rather than Jewish, and it was written in the latter half of the second century to express the gospel message in terms compatible with Greek philosophy. Despite exhaustive reviews of the evidence, like that conducted by B. F. Wescott,[1] which challenged this view, it continued to dominate scholarly work on the Fourth Gospel throughout the nineteenth century.

A number of factors emerging in the twentieth century changed the direction of the study of the Fourth Gospel and gave rise to greater respect for its historical reliability. First, Israel Abrahams, Reader in Rabbinics at the University of Cambridge and an Orthodox Jew, told the university's theological society, 'To us Jews, the Fourth Gospel is the most Jewish of the Four.'[2] Such a statement can be supported by the many references and allusions to the OT found in the Fourth Gospel (e.g. ch. 10 / Ezk. 34; 3:14 / Nu. 21:9), the intimate knowledge of Jewish festivals and their symbolism reflected in Jesus' discourses (Tabernacles / ch. 7; Dedication / 10:22–39), and Jesus' use of rabbinic arguments in his debates with 'the Jews' (e.g. 5:31–47).

Second, the discovery of the Dead Sea Scrolls beginning in 1947 provided first-hand documentation of an Orthodox Jewish community whose occupation of the site known today as Qumran covered the period of Jesus' ministry. These documents use language similar to that found in the Fourth Gospel, in particular dualistic language (life/death, light/darkness etc.), which had theretofore been regarded as emanating from second-century Hellenistic sources.

Third, the accuracy of the evangelist's references to the

[1]Westcott, pp. v–xl.   [2]Cited in Neill and Wright, p. 338.

customs, culture and geography of first-century Palestine have been recognized. For example, he accurately portrays Samaritan beliefs and outlook in chapter 4, and his reference to the five covered colonnades of the Pool of Bethesda in 5:2, long thought to be unhistorical, has been verified by archaeological work.

The undeniable differences between the Synoptic Gospels and the Fourth Gospel are best accounted for by recognizing that the evangelist worked largely independently of the Synoptics. In 1938 Percival Gardiner-Smith argued that the evangelist did not even know the Synoptics and therefore could not have been guilty of embellishing them.[1] Dodd's statements are more balanced: 'The *prima facie* impression is that John is in large measure at any rate, working independently of other written gospels';[2] 'Behind the Fourth Gospel lies an ancient tradition independent of the other gospels, and meriting serious consideration as a contribution to our knowledge of the historical facts concerning Jesus Christ.'[3] Robinson publicized these developments referring to a 'new look' on the Fourth Gospel.[4] Smalley sums up the implications of the 'new look': 'We can now reckon seriously with the possibility that the Fourth Gospel, including John's special material, is grounded in historical tradition when it *departs* from the synoptics *as well as* when it overlaps them.'[5] Not all scholars have gone along with these trends, but the Jewishness of the Fourth Gospel is widely recognized, and its claims to historical reliability are being taken more seriously. But in some ways the historical debate has been overtaken by other concerns related to the interpretation of the Fourth Gospel.

IX. RECENT TRENDS IN THE INTERPRETATION OF THE FOURTH GOSPEL

Three trends are discernible in recent studies of the Fourth Gospel, and in each case particular scholars have been involved in the pioneering work.

[1]Gardiner-Smith, pp. 96–97; cited in Smalley, p. 14.
[2]Dodd, *Interpretation of Fourth Gospel*, p. 449.
[3]Dodd, *Historical Tradition in Fourth Gospel*, p. 423.
[4]Robinson, *Twelve New Testament Studies*, pp. 94–106.
[5]Smalley, p. 29.

A. A GOSPEL OF SIGNS

Robert Fortna, taking note of the rough transitions (*aporias*) in the Fourth Gospel, has reconstructed what he believes was the original Gospel of Signs used by the evangelist in his composition of the Fourth Gospel.[1] The content of Fortna's Gospel of Signs consists roughly of (1) an introduction, including exordium (1:6–7), the Baptist's Testimony (1:19–34), and the conversion of the first disciples (3:23–24; 1:35–50); (2) the Signs of Jesus, including water turned to wine (2:1–11), a nobleman's son healed (2:12a; 4:46b–54), a miraculous draught of fish (21:2–14), the multitude fed (6:1–14), interlude: walking on water and a miraculous landing (6:15b–25), a dead man raised and a conversation with a Samaritan woman (11:1–5; 4:4–42; 11:17–45), a man blind from birth healed (9:1–8), and a thirty-eight-year illness healed (5:2–14); (3) the death and resurrection of Jesus including the cleansing of the temple and death plot (2:14–19; 11:47–53), the anointing at Bethany (12:1–8), the triumphal entry (12:12–15), the Last Supper (fragments of sources scattered in chs. 12, 13, 14 and 16), the arrest (18:1–12), Jesus in the high priest's house (18:13–28a), the trial before Pilate (18:28b–38; 19:15; 18:39–40: 19:6–16a), the crucifixion and burial (19:16b–38; 3:1; 19:39–42), the resurrection (20:1–20), and the peroration (20:30–31). Fortna argues that the purpose of the Gospel of Signs, stated explicitly in 20:30–31, was to show potential Jewish converts that Jesus is the Messiah. The way many of the accounts of Jesus' signs finish with statements that people 'believed in him' indicates that the Gospel of Signs was not just a mere collection of stories but a 'missionary tract' with a unifying purpose: to bring people to faith in Jesus. It was the combining of the Gospel of Signs with material from other sources by the evangelist that accounts for the *aporias*. While it is likely that the evangelist made use of sources, both oral and written, in the composition of his Gospel, Fortna's suggestion concerning a pre-existing Gospel of Signs remains just an interesting conjecture.

---

[1]Fortna, *Gospel of Signs; Fourth Gospel and its Predecessor.*

B. A TWO-LEVEL DRAMA

J. Louis Martyn, building upon Fortna's hypothesis concerning an underlying Gospel of Signs, seeks to identify the influences that caused the evangelist to make the additions to this work, thus producing the Fourth Gospel as we know it.[1] Martyn suggests that the conflict between the church and the synagogue (*i.e.* between Jews who believed in Jesus and those who did not) prompted the evangelist to add extra material to the Gospel of Signs. As it now stands, the Fourth Gospel functions as a two-level drama. On one level it recounts events in the life and ministry of Jesus. At another level, and this is the more important of the two, it reflects the experience of Jews the evangelist knew in the town in which he lived: believing Jews, unbelieving Jews, and Jews who secretly believed. The man born blind plays the part, not only of a Jew healed by Jesus, but also reflects the experience of Jews of a later time who were expelled from the synagogue because of their allegiance to Jesus as Messiah. The references to threats of excommunication for any who believed in Jesus (9:22; 12:42; 16:2) reflect the attitude of unbelieving Jews, not only in Jesus' day, but also at the time the evangelist wrote. Nicodemus' three appearances in the Gospel (3:1–15; 7:50–52; 19:38–42) and the reference to the leaders who believed in Jesus but were afraid to confess their belief openly (12:42–43) reflect the experiences of secret Jewish believers both in Jesus' time and those who lived in the town and at the time in which the evangelist wrote his Gospel.

The implications of this approach are that the Fourth Gospel in its final form addresses problems experienced in the Johannine community; it was not intended as an evangelistic tract as was the hypothetical Gospel of Signs. However, if more recent claims that the Gospels were intended for all Christians, not just a particular community, are true,[2] then reading the Fourth Gospel largely as a message addressed to the Johannine community and reflecting its struggles might not be the best way to approach this Gospel.

---

[1]Martyn, *History and Theology.*   [2]See Bauckham.

C. NARRATIVE CRITICISM

R. Alan Culpepper advocates another way of reading the Fourth Gospel; one that neither seeks to identify the sources used, nor attempts to uncover historical facts about Jesus or the Johannine community. Instead, the Gospel is studied as a literary production, making use of the insights of modern narrative theory and literary criticism.[1] The focus of his study is upon the way the real author transmits his story to the real reader. This involves an implied author/narrator and an implied reader/narratee. The story itself has its own narrative time, plot and characters. Explicit commentary is added when the implied reader is judged to need extra information (*e.g.* concerning what is really going on or what the characters in the story are thinking and feeling). Implicit commentary is provided through symbolism and irony, something the implied reader is expected to understand. Culpepper's approach helps today's readers to understand the narrative of the Fourth Gospel, and should be used along with other critical tools in the study of the Fourth Gospel. For Culpepper, however, truth is not dependent upon the historical reliability of the storyline. A novel can convey 'truth' even if it is fictional. He says the Gospel should not be used as a window into the life of Jesus or the Johannine community but as a mirror in which we see ourselves reacting, learning and discovering what the narrative gives us. However, to read the Fourth Gospel in this way, without taking cognizance of its claims to historical reliability and the credibility of the eyewitnesses, opens the door to excessive subjectivity.

X. THEOLOGY OF THE FOURTH GOSPEL

A. GOD THE FATHER

God, referred to more often as the Father and addressed once by Jesus as 'Holy Father' (17:11), existed in the beginning (1:1, 2), has never been seen by any human being apart from Jesus (1:18; 6:46), has life in himself (5:26), and raises the dead (5:21). To know him

---

[1] See Culpepper.

is eternal life (17:3). He is 'spirit' and seeks those who will worship 'in spirit and truth' (4:23–24). The Father spoke in ancient times to Moses (9:29), and in latter times sent John the Baptist to testify to his Son (1:6).

He has one unique and only Son (3:16, 18), upon whom he has placed his seal of approval (6:27), and to whom he has given power over all things (3:35; 13:3; 16:15) including responsibility for judgment (5:22). The Father loves the Son (3:35; 5:20; 10:17; 15:9; 17:24), glorifies him (8:54; 12:28; 13:31–32; 17:5) and testifies to him (5:37; 8:18). The Father is one with the Son (14:7, 9–11, 20) yet greater than him (14:28). He teaches him (8:28), sends him into the world (3:16, 17, 34; 5:36, 37; 6:57; 8:42; 10:36; 14:24; 20:21), works through him (5:17–19; 10:32) and tells him what to do (10:18; 12:49–50; 18:11). Those whom he has given to the Son (6:37; 10:29; 17:24) he teaches and draws to the Son (6:44–45, 65). The Father sends the Counsellor, the Holy Spirit, to the disciples in answer to Jesus' prayer (14:16, 26; 15:26).

The Father loves the people of the world and gave his Son so that they might have eternal life (3:16). He requires that they should believe in his Son (6:29) and his wrath rests upon those who reject his Son (3:36). Those who believe in the Son are born of God (1:13), are the recipients of his special love (16:27) and become his children (1:12–13; 20:17).

B. JESUS THE SON

The Fourth Gospel is overwhelmingly rich in Christological statements. Jesus is portrayed supremely as the Son of God (see commentary on 1:34) who reveals the Father, but there are many other ways in which he is described. It is difficult to classify and present them all. One way of doing so is to note the evangelist's comments in his own name first, then what he has the various characters within his narrative say about Jesus, and finally what he has Jesus say about himself.

The evangelist's comments: the evangelist describes Jesus as the Logos who existed from the beginning in close relationship to God. The Logos may be said to be God, was the agent of creation, and is the light of all people (1:1–4). He was incarnate in the person of Jesus and revealed the Father's glory, full of grace and truth (1:14). Jesus is the 'the only Son, who is close to the Father's heart' (1:18 NRSV), something reflected in the evangelist's many references to Jesus as the Son of God (3:16, 17, 18, 35; 5:18). He also speaks of Jesus as the Son of Man who descended from heaven, and who will be lifted up, as the serpent was in the wilderness (3:13, 14–15). He is the one from above, sent into the world by God and who will return to God (3:31, 32, 34; 13:1, 3). He is the king of Israel who comes to Zion sitting on a donkey's colt (12:14–15), and is described as a king in Pilate's inscription (19:19). He is the one who utters the divine 'I am' when the temple police try to arrest him, causing them to fall backwards to the ground (18:6). The evangelist says he composed his Gospel so that his readers might come to believe that Jesus is the Messiah, the Son of God (20:31). Alongside all this emphasis upon Jesus' exalted status the evangelist also notes things that reflect Jesus' human frailty, thereby confirming the fact that the Logos became flesh: he was tired from his journey into Samaria (4:6), he wept at the tomb of Lazarus (11:35), and from his pierced side blood and water flowed (19:34)

The witness of various characters in the narrative: John the Baptist hails Jesus as the Lamb of God who takes away the sins of the world (1:29, 36), the one upon whom the Spirit rested and who baptizes in the Spirit (1:32, 33), and declares that Jesus surpasses him (1:30). Above all, John testifies, Jesus is the Son of God (1:34). Andrew tells Peter that he has found the Messiah (1:41), the blind man says Jesus is a prophet (9:17), Nathanael addresses him as the King of Israel (1:49), the Samaritans acknowledge him as the Saviour of the world (4:29, 41–42), Peter and the other disciples say they have come to believe that he is the Holy One of God (6:69), the blind man comes to believe in Jesus as the Son of Man (9:35, 38). The culminating confession is that found in the words of Thomas: 'My Lord and my God' (20:28). Exposed to Jesus' words and works Jewish people ask whether he is in fact the Messiah (7:26, 31), or the prophet (7:40). At his triumphal entry they hail him as King of Israel (12:13), but their leaders reject this identification (19:12, 21). The leaders recognize the implications of Jesus' teaching, but reject his claims: he is not the Son of God (19:7), and he is not equal to God (10:33). Pilate consistently refers to Jesus (satirically?) as the king of the Jews (18:39; 19:14, 15, 21–22).

The testimony of Jesus himself: the most abundant expressions of Christological data in the Fourth Gospel are those the evangelist places on the lips of Jesus. Jesus refers to himself as the Son of Man upon whom the angels of God ascend and descend, who has received authority to execute judgment, who gives the bread of life, who will ascend to where he was before, who will be 'lifted up' by the Jews, and who is glorified in his passion when God himself is also glorified in him (1:51; 5:27, 28; 6:27, 62; 8:28; 9:35, 37; 13:31). Some forty times Jesus speaks to or of God as his Father, thus presenting himself as the Son of God. About eleven references imply that heaven is Jesus' home; he is the one from heaven. In 4:26 Jesus states explicitly that he is the Messiah. Some twenty-one times Jesus speaks of himself as the one sent by the Father. Seven times he speaks of himself as the one who gives eternal life. He is the one to whom the Scriptures bear witness (5:39, 46). In chapter 6 he refers to himself eleven times as the bread of life which came down from heaven. In 8:12 he declares himself to be the light of the world. He is the one who makes known the truth (8:31–32, 40). He claims to be the pre-existent one, having existed before the patriarch Abraham (8:58). Using the 'I am' + predicate formula seven times, Jesus reveals himself as the bread of life, the light of the world, the gate of the sheep, the good shepherd, the resurrection and the life, the way the truth and the life, and the true vine (6:35, 48; 8:12; 10:7, 11, 14; 11:25; 14:6; 15:1). Jesus uses the absolute 'I am' formula in a way that seems to imply divinity, especially in the great controversy with the Jews (8:58) and when arrested in the garden (18:6). Jesus deliberately accepts the disciples' recognition of him as Teacher and Lord (13:13, 14). Jesus, by his actions, presents himself as the bestower of the Spirit (20:22). Alongside all this there are statements of Jesus in which he expresses something of his human frailty: his heart is troubled at the prospect of the cross (12:27), his spirit is troubled at the prospect of betrayal (13:21) and he thirsts on the cross (19:28).

C. THE HOLY SPIRIT

The difference between the Synoptic Gospels and the Fourth Gospel is quite marked in respect of Jesus' teaching concerning the

Holy Spirit. The Synoptics say a lot about the role of the Spirit in the life and ministry of Jesus, but contain few references to Jesus' own teaching about the Spirit. The Fourth Gospel, by way of contrast, contains many sayings and some lengthy discourses of Jesus concerning the Spirit, notably in the Last Supper farewell discourses.

The Spirit and Jesus' own ministry: in the Fourth Gospel Jesus is proclaimed by the Baptist as the one upon whom the Spirit descended and remained (1:32), possibly distinguishing Jesus from the prophets upon whom the Spirit came sporadically. Unlike John who baptized only with water, Jesus baptizes with the Spirit (1:26, 32–33). Jesus speaks the words of God and what he says is trustworthy because God has given him the Spirit 'without limit/measure' (3:34), possibly again distinguishing Jesus from the prophets to whom the Spirit may be said to have been 'measured'. Jesus' glorification (death and subsequent exaltation) was the necessary precursor to the bestowal of the Spirit upon his followers (7:39).

The Spirit and the disciples: only those who are born from above by the mysterious work of the Spirit can see/enter the kingdom of God (3:3, 5). The words of Jesus, which are spirit and life (6:63), mediate this birth from above. Jesus refers to the Spirit as living water that wells up to eternal life within those who believe (4:14) and flows from him through them (7:38). Jesus foreshadowed a time when people's worship would be in Spirit and truth (4:23–24). In the Last Supper discourses Jesus promised his disciples another Counsellor after his departure, one who would be with them forever (14:15). The Counsellor is identified as 'the Spirit of truth', who will be in them (14:16–17), teach them and remind them of all that Jesus taught them (14:26), bear his witness to Jesus alongside the witness of the disciples (15:26–27), prove the world guilty in respect of sin, righteousness and judgment (16:7–11), and will also guide the disciples into all truth, declaring things to come (16:12–15) (see Additional Note: The *Paraklētos*, pp. 303–306).

D. ESCHATOLOGY

One noticeable difference between the Synoptic Gospels and the Fourth Gospel is the emphasis on futurist eschatology in the former and the lack of emphasis upon it in the latter. The Fourth Gospel places significant emphasis upon realized eschatology, *i.e.* blessings normally thought to be realized only in the future can be experienced in the present. Thus those who believe already have eternal life (3:36; 4:14; 5:24; 6:47, 54), have passed from death to life (5:24), have received the promised Spirit (7:39; 14:16–18, 26; 16:13) and have escaped condemnation/judgment (3:18; 5:24). Yet alongside the realized eschatology in the Fourth Gospel are also traces of futurist eschatology. Jesus speaks of the 'last day' when he will raise up those who believe in him (6:39–40), a time 'when all who are in their graves will hear his voice and come out – those who have done good will rise to live, and those who have done evil will rise to be condemned' (5:28–29). Jesus also promised his disciples that although he was shortly to leave them the purpose of his leaving was to prepare places for them in the presence of God, and that he would come back to take them to be with him there (14:1–3).

Bultmann argued that the evangelist's eschatology was essentially realized and that later Christians introduced futurist elements, thus spoiling what the evangelist himself wanted to say.[1] Others have argued that while the evangelist's eschatology was realized, he preserved futurist elements in his Gospel, a sign that he was being true to his sources even when they conflicted with his own position. He wanted his readers to stop thinking about the future and concentrate on the blessings of the present, to enjoy the eternal life that was theirs in the here and now, and to realize that judgment was not future, but determined by one's response to the message of the gospel here and now. They should stop thinking about Jesus' coming again at the end of the age, realizing that he comes to them now in the person of the Holy Spirit.

However, the tension between realized and futurist eschatology is a common feature in the NT, and its presence in the Fourth Gospel should not be regarded as unusual. The evangelist is not only being faithful to his sources by retaining references to futurist eschatology, but also faithful to the teaching of Jesus, which holds in tension the 'already and the not yet'.

[1]Bultmann, *Theology of New Testament*, vol. 2, pp. 37–40.

E. ETERNAL LIFE / SALVATION

The major category employed to depict salvation in the Fourth Gospel is life / eternal life. God the Father is the source of eternal life and he has given the Son also to have life in himself (5:26). The literal meaning of 'eternal life' is the life of the age (to come), but with the coming of Christ it is something that may be experienced in part in the present age and will be consummated in the resurrection (5:24).

Eternal life, as it is experienced by humans, is defined as knowing God through Jesus Christ (17:3). This knowledge involves a relationship with God, which on the human side is expressed in obedience and fellowship. Jesus employs three primary metaphors to depict the human experience of eternal life: being born of the Spirit (3:3–8), having one's thirst quenched by the water of life (4:14; *cf.* 7:37), and having one's hunger satisfied by the bread of life (6:35). Eternal life for those who believe was obtained at the cost of Jesus' own life (6:51; 10:11, 15), and is mediated to them through the word of Jesus (5:24; 6:63, 68). For a fuller discussion see Additional Note: Eternal life, pp. 111–113.

F. WITNESS

There are forty-seven uses of witness terminology in the Fourth Gospel (either the verb *martyreō* or the noun *martyria*), all but three of which involve testimony to Jesus, or Jesus' own testimony. There are seven witnesses to Jesus in the Fourth Gospel: (1) John the Baptist (1:7–8, 15, 19, 32, 34; 3:26; 5:32–34); (2) other humans – including the Samaritan woman (4:39), the Jewish crowd (12:17) and his own disciples (15:27); (3) Jesus himself (3:11, 32–33; 7:7; 8:13–14, 18; 18:37); (4) Jesus' works (5:36; 10:25); (5) God the Father (5:37; 8:18); (6) the Scriptures (5:39); and (7) the Holy Spirit (15:26).

'Witness' is a forensic term. A witness (*martys*) is one who knows the truth and can testify to it in a court of law. Many times the witness motif in the Fourth Gospel carries the idea of the lawsuit, something that has its background in Yahweh's lawsuit against Israel (Is. 43 – 48). A significant proportion of the witness terminology occurs in contexts in which God, incarnate in Jesus Christ, has

43

a controversy with the 'world', incarnate in 'the Jews' (*i.e.* Jewish leaders who epitomize the world in its opposition to God). The majority of uses of witness terminology are found in chapters 5 – 12, which record the great controversy between Jesus and 'the Jews'.

During his ministry on earth Jesus was the main witness to the truth. Following his glorification that role was taken over by the Counsellor, the Holy Spirit, who acts as Jesus' advocate. The disciples also function as witnesses to Jesus in the world alongside the Counsellor (15:26–27; 16:8–11). On the last day the words Jesus spoke while in the world will function as a witness against those who rejected his message (12:48)

The witness theme of the Fourth Gospel relates primarily to the overall purpose of the Gospel, *i.e.* to promote belief in Jesus. However, it is also a reminder that the Christian faith does not rest upon subjective experience but historical fact for which reliable testimony is available (Jn 19:35; 21:24; and 1 Cor. 15:1–8). This explains the stress upon eyewitnesses in the NT (Jn 1:14–15; 19:35; 21:24; 1 Cor. 15:1–8; 2 Pet. 1:16–18; 1 Jn 1:1–4). That the witness theme in the Fourth Gospel emerges most predominantly in the context of controversy and denials of Jesus' claims is a reminder that witness to Christ in our own day may have to be given in similar circumstances, and that believers should not be overawed by the doubt and disbelief they encounter. As Jesus' witness led to persecution and death, and the witness of his disciples attracted the same, so too believers today may face opposition and rejection if they act as witnesses for Jesus Christ.

G. FAITH AND SIGNS

When the Jewish crowd asked Jesus what they must do to do the works God requires, he replied, 'The work of God is this: to believe in the one he has sent' (6:29). Faith, belief in Jesus, is what the Fourth Gospel is all about. It was written to bring about faith (20:31), and as its story unfolds numerous examples are given of people who responded in faith to Jesus (see comments on the purpose of this Gospel, pp. 20–23).

Exemplary faith responds immediately to Jesus' word. Examples of such faith are seen in the response of the mother of

Jesus (2:5), the servants at the wedding feast in Cana (2:7–8), the Samaritan townspeople (4:41), the royal official who sought healing for his son (4:49–50), and the man born blind (9:35–38). These all responded in faith to Jesus' word.

Some people responded with faith when they saw the signs/miracles that Jesus performed (2:11, 23; 7:31; 11:45; 12:9–11), while others who witnessed his miracles still refused to believe (12:37). Sometimes the faith of those who 'believed' because of his miracles was inauthentic (2:23–25; 8:30–47).

Jesus' attitude to the role of miracles as a basis of faith is complex. On the one hand, he upbraided those who would not believe unless they saw signs and wonders (4:48), and on the other hand, he urged those who were having difficulty accepting what he said to consider the signs he performed so that they might believe (10:38; 14:11). He criticized those who saw only the miraculous event while failing to see its true significance (6:26). The evangelist describes seven miraculous signs performed by Jesus so that those who read about them might believe (20:31). It is perhaps true to say that miraculous signs have a role in stimulating faith when those who witness the signs perceive their significance, but that signs-based faith should develop into implicit faith based upon Jesus' word alone.

H. LOVE AND OBEDIENCE

Love and obedience are important and related themes in the Fourth Gospel. The Father loves the Son (15:9; 17:23–24, 26) and because of this love he has placed everything in his hands (3:35). The Father's love for the Son is called forth by the Son's obedience to him (15:10), especially his obedience in laying down his life (10:17). The Father's love for Jesus' disciples is also emphasized. He loves those who love (14:21) and obey (14:23) his Son just as he loves the Son himself (17:23). The Father loves the world, something demonstrated by giving his one and only Son so that those who believe in him might not perish but have eternal life (3:16).

The Son's love for the Father is seen in his doing exactly what the Father commanded (14:31). Jesus loves his disciples (14:21;

15:12) as the Father loved him (15:9). He showed them the full extent of his love by washing their feet (13:1) and what that symbolized (his sacrificial death on their behalf). 'Greater love has noone than this, that he lay down his life for his friends' (15:13).

Love is expected from Jesus' disciples. They are to show their love for Jesus by obeying his commands (14:15), in particular his command that they love one another (13:34–35). Peter is to show his love for Jesus by taking care of Jesus' 'sheep' (21:15–17).

I. THE CHURCH

There is a lot in the Fourth Gospel concerning the believer's individual relationship with Christ, and the importance of the individual's obedience to his commands. On first reading there appears to be little interest in the church or its ministry in this Gospel. For example, Jesus' words to Peter at Caesarea Philippi about the foundation of the church and his instructions about church discipline found in Matthew 16:17–19; 18:15–20 have no counterparts in the Fourth Gospel. Does this mean the evangelist was not interested in the people of God as a community or, in other words, did he have no theology of the church? On the surface of things this might appear to be so.

Despite appearances, however, there are many places in the Fourth Gospel where the idea of a church/community is implied. The evangelist speaks of the community among whom the new $š^e\underline{k}înâ$ dwells (1:14), the bride of Christ (3:27–30), those given by God to Christ as his own (17:2, 6), those in whom the promises to Israel concerning the Spirit find fulfilment (7:37–39), the flock of God (10:1–21), the dispersed people of God gathered into one (10:16), a community among whom mutual service, even lowly service, is carried out (13:12–17), those who will be gathered around Christ in the heavens (14:1–3), the community among whom the Spirit dwells (14:15–17), branches in the vine (15:1–17), a community among whom Peter was appointed to feed Christ's 'sheep' (21:15–17), and where the false rumour about the disciple whom Jesus loved not dying before Jesus returned spread (21:20–23). So, despite the emphasis upon the individual's relationship with Christ, there are in the Fourth

Gospel many allusions to the community character of the people of God.

There are few allusions to church order or official ministry in the Fourth Gospel. The word 'apostle' is not used. However, Peter is commissioned for a pastoral role *vis-à-vis* Christ's 'sheep' (21:15–17) and the disciples are to have a role in Christian mission (4:35–38; 13:20; 20:21–23).

There are places in the Fourth Gospel which suggest that the church is understood to be God's new covenant community. Pryor notes, for example, that (1) just as Israel was the flock of Yahweh, so now believers are God's flock cared for by Jesus, the 'Good Shepherd' (10:1–18); (2) just as the presence of God among the tribes of Israel was a sign of their covenant relationship with him, so the 'tabernacling' of the incarnate Christ among his disciples is a sign of their covenant relationship with God (1:14); (3) just as Israel was chosen by God to be his people and became the object of his special love, so too the disciples are chosen by Christ (15:16) and are the objects of his special love (13:1); and (4) just as God promised to breathe new life into Israel (Ezk. 37) so too Jesus breathed on his disciples and said, 'Receive the Holy Spirit' (20:21–23).[1]

It has sometimes been suggested that the Fourth Gospel's ecclesiology is sectarian. On the one hand, it emphasizes the need for love among the band of disciples, while, on the other hand, it speaks of the hatred of the world towards this band. Does this reflect a fortress mentality characteristic of a sectarian movement – the way the evangelist's community understood itself *vis-à-vis* the synagogue? Such a view is based upon modern definitions of a sect in terms of a community's self-perception over against the world. But this modern definition does not fit the context of first-century Judaism in which there was widespread adherence to core values, despite the existence of splinter groups (sects). The identity of these sects was defined, not over against the world, but *vis-à-vis* the other Jewish sects. Further, the love/hate motif in the Fourth Gospel does not reflect a sectarian attitude. Sects are inward looking, but the Fourth Gospel is outward looking and missiological. There is in the Fourth Gospel also an emphasis

[1]Pryor, pp. 157–158.

upon God's love for the world (3:16), those who are still to be gathered into God's people (10:16), and the disciples' witness in the world (15:27; 20:21). The warnings, then, about the world's hatred reflect not a fortress mentality on the part of the evangelist or his community but a realism about the experiences of those who are to be involved in mission.

J. SACRAMENTALISM

The Fourth Gospel contains no account of Jesus' baptism by John, nor of the institution of the Lord's Supper, and this raises the question of the evangelist's attitude to the sacraments. Bultmann argued that the evangelist was critical of, or at least reserved in his attitude towards sacraments, so deliberately omitted reference to them in his Gospel. Eventually, however, the Gospel was revised by a rather traditional Christian who was responsible for the sacramental allusions now found in the Fourth Gospel, in particular, adding 'water and' at 3:5, and references to eating Jesus' flesh and drinking his blood in 6:51–58.[1]

Others argue that the evangelist neither opposed nor endorsed the sacraments, but sought to revise his readers' understanding of them. So the bread of life discourse (ch. 6) and the footwashing scene (ch. 13) reinterpret the meaning of the Lord's Supper. Baptism is reinterpreted as meaningful for rebirth only through the gift of the Spirit (3:5). Still others argue that originally the Fourth Gospel did not mean to ignore the sacraments, but rather to leave them at an implicit rather than explicit level. Later editors 'helped' the Gospel say more clearly what they were confident the evangelist wanted to say. A third revisionist view suggests that originally the Johannine church knew nothing of the sacraments, being out of the mainstream of early church development – it was neither pro-sacramental, nor anti-sacramental, but asacramental. However, after the Gospel was circulated to a wider community, words and phrases were added to make it more sacramental. These were not revisions to bring out what was implicit, but additions at points where the author was neutral.

---

[1]Bultmann, *Theology of New Testament*, vol. 2, pp. 58–59.

Other interpreters see deliberate sacramental allusions in 2:1–11 (water turned to wine in Cana), 3:5 (born of water and spirit), 6:1–14 (feeding of the multitude), 6:51–59 (Jesus' discourse about eating his flesh and drinking his blood), 13:1–7 (Jesus' words to Peter during the footwashing), and 19:34 (water and blood flow from Jesus' side). Accordingly, Barrett says, 'there is more sacramental teaching in John than in the other gospels'.[1] Brown argues that we are indebted to the Fourth Gospel for most of our understanding of the sacraments, in particular to 3:5; 4:13–14; and 7:37–39 for our understanding of baptism, and to 2:1–11; 6:32, 57; 15:1–10 and 19:34 for our understanding of the Eucharist.[2]

Others have noted what they believe is the fundamental sacramentality of the Fourth Gospel. Kysar argues that in the Fourth Gospel faith grows out of sensory experience (signs, seeing and hearing) and this is analogous to the use of water, bread and wine in the sacraments.[3] Smalley says that the Fourth Gospel makes extensive use of symbolism, inviting readers to look beyond the material to the spiritual, and also that it moves from the symbolic to the sacramental: '*symbol* evokes and *represents* that which is spiritual and divine, but *sacrament* actually *conveys*, through the material elements involved, what is spiritual and divine'.[4]

Finally, there is an approach Carson calls metaphorical non-sacramental. One does not deny that Christian readers might detect, for example, overtones of the Eucharist in chapter 6, but insists that the chapter is primarily metaphorical and Christological.[5] Eating the flesh and drinking the blood of Christ is a heavily metaphorical way of speaking about belief in Christ, not about participation in the Eucharist. Such an approach seems more in keeping with the overall message of chapter 6 (see commentary on 6:25–59, especially on 6:40, 54).

K. 'THE JEWS' IN THE FOURTH GOSPEL

There are many references to 'the Jews' in the Fourth Gospel, and these must be interpreted with great care lest it be assumed 'the

---

[1]Barrett, *Gospel*, p. 82.   [2]Brown, *Gospel*, AB 29, p. cxiv.
[3]Kysar, pp. 122–126.   [4]Smalley, pp. 204–210.   [5]Carson, pp. 276–280.

Jews' are always the enemies of Jesus, and fuel is added to the fires of anti-Semitism.

There are seventy-one references to 'the Jews' in sixty-seven verses in the Fourth Gospel. Of these sixty-seven verses, three are references to Jews who believe in Jesus, twenty-nine depict 'the Jews' in a neutral fashion (neither as enemies nor as friends of Jesus), and another four depict Jewish leaders in a neutral way. On the other hand, eight verses depict Jewish people hostile towards Jesus and another twenty-three depict their leaders as hostile towards him. The use of the term 'the Jews' in the Fourth Gospel, then, is quite varied. The majority of negative references to 'the Jews' refer to the Jewish leadership who were antagonistic towards Jesus. This is balanced by a number of references to Jews who believe in Jesus. Jesus' disciples were Jews. Jesus himself insisted that 'salvation is of the Jews'. Nowhere does the evangelist imply that all Jews were antagonistic towards Jesus.

It is important to recognize that not all criticisms of things Jewish are anti-Semitic. There is a long tradition of internal self-criticism among Jewish people, *i.e.* intra-Jewish polemic (*e.g.* the prophets of the OT strenuously criticized their own people when they forsook the covenant). There are also criticisms of Jewish religion that are not anti-Semitic, any more than criticism of Hinduism is anti-Indian. Only criticisms of the Jewish race can properly be called anti-Semitic. It is therefore unjustified to brand the fourth evangelist as anti-Semitic. He is a Jew writing primarily for Jews. The way he writes the story of Jesus may reflect tensions between believing and unbelieving Jews, between those who followed Jesus Messiah and those who remained committed to Pharisaic tradition. In that case, what is reflected in the Fourth Gospel would not be anti-Semitic, but intra-Jewish tension. However, the Fourth Gospel was not written to attack Jews, but to commend Jesus as the Christ to them. Its negative references to 'the Jews' must never be taken to refer to all Jews in Jesus' day, and even less so to all Jews of all times.

XI. STRUCTURE OF THE FOURTH GOSPEL

The way the Fourth Gospel is structured is unique. As mentioned in the overview, it comprises four parts:

• Prologue (1:1–18);
• Jesus' work in the world (1:19 – 12:50);
• Jesus' return to the Father (13:1 – 20:31);
• Epilogue (21:1–25).

Related to this structure is the important theme of Jesus' 'hour/time'. Throughout Jesus' work in the world (1:19 – 12:50) readers are told repeatedly that Jesus' 'hour' had not yet come (2:4; 7:30; 8:20), but then, when the time for his return to the Father arrived, the readers are told that his 'hour' has now come (12:23, 27), and this realization dominates the Book of Glory (13:1; 16:32; 17:1). Virtually all interpreters of the Fourth Gospel recognize this overall structure, but when it comes to more detailed analysis there are differing opinions.

In respect of Jesus' work in the world (1:19 – 12:50) one popular approach is to see 1:19–51 as an introduction to Jesus' ministry, then 2:1 – 4:54 is an independent unit beginning and ending with Jesus performing a miracle in Cana in Galilee. The next long section, 5:1 – 10:42, is arranged around Jewish festivals (*cf.* 5:1; 6:4; 7:2; 10:22), and then 11:1 – 12:50 functions as a bridge concluding the account of Jesus' ministry in the world and preparing readers for the third major section of the Gospel, his return to the Father (13:1 – 20:31). One problem with this approach is that to identify a 'Cana to Cana' unit one has to make too much of the fact that two miracles happened to be performed in Cana, not something the evangelist makes much of in his account. Another problem is that the structuring of 5:1 – 10:42 around the Jewish festivals fails to recognize that throughout the Gospel, and not only in 5:1 – 10:42, the evangelist consistently uses Jewish festivals and Jesus' movements in relation to them as chronological markers (2:13, 23; 3:22; 4:4, 43; 5:1; 6:4; 7:2, 10, 14, 37; 10:22, 40; 11:55; 12:1, 12, 20; 13:1; 18:28; 19:31, 42). It is probably best, then, to treat 1:19 – 12:50 as one long presentation of Jesus' ministry in the world, marked by signs and public discourses, and this is reflected in the analysis below.

In respect of Jesus' return to the Father (13:1 – 20:31), there is little debate about the fact that it falls easily into three sections: the Last Supper with the farewell discourses and Jesus' prayer (13:1 – 17:26), the passion narrative (18:1 – 19:42) and the resurrection narrative (20:1–31).

ANALYSIS

I. PROLOGUE (1:1–18)
  a. *The Word as he was in the beginning (1:1–5)*
  b. *The ministry of John (the Baptist) (1:6–8)*
  c. *The true light comes into the world (1:9–11)*
  d. *Those who receive the Word become children of God (1:12–13)*
  e. *The coming of the Word into the world (1:14)*
  f. *The testimony of John (the Baptist) (1:15)*
  g. *The Word makes the Father known (1:16–18)*

II. JESUS' WORK IN THE WORLD (1:19 – 12:50)
  a. *John the Baptist bears witness to Jesus (1:19–34)*
    1. *John's testimony to 'the Jews' of Jerusalem (1:19–28)*
    2. *John's testimony to Jesus as the Lamb of God (1:29–34)*
  b. *Early disciples follow Jesus (1:35–51)*
    1. *John's disciples follow Jesus (1:35–39)*
    2. *Andrew brings Peter to Jesus (1:40–42)*
    3. *Jesus calls Philip and Philip brings Nathanael to Jesus (1:43–51)*
  c. *The wedding feast at Cana (2:1–12)*
  d. *Jesus goes up to Jerusalem for Passover (2:13–25)*
    1. *Cleansing the temple (2:13–22)*
    2. *Jesus and those who 'believed' (2:23–25)*
  e. *Jesus and Nicodemus (3:1–21)*
    1. *Jesus' conversation with Nicodemus (3:1–15)*
    2. *The evangelist's comments (3:16–21)*
  f. *The ministries of John the Baptist and Jesus (3:22–36)*
    1. *The overlapping ministries of Jesus and John (3:22–24)*

COMMENTARY

I. PROLOGUE (1:1–18)

Unlike the other Gospels, which commence their story about Jesus either with the ministry of John the Baptist (Mark) or stories about Jesus' birth (Matthew and Luke), the Gospel of John begins with the pre-existent Logos, who became incarnate in Jesus. The Prologue introduces this one to the readers before the story proper begins so that they will know the true identity of the central character. Barrett, speaking of 1:1 says, 'John intends that the whole of his Gospel shall be read in the light of this verse. The deeds and words of Jesus are the deeds and words of God; if this be not true the book is blasphemous.'[1]

The Prologue also introduces the main themes that are to appear throughout the Gospel: Jesus' pre-existence (1:1a/17:5), Jesus' union with God (1:1c/8:58; 10:30; 20:28), the coming of life in Jesus (1:4a/5:26; 6:33; 10:10; 11:25–26; 14:6), the coming of light in Jesus (1:4b, 9/3:19; 8:12; 12:46), the conflict between light and darkness (1:5/3:19; 8:12; 12:35, 46), believing in Jesus (1:7, 12/2:11; 3:16, 18, 36; 5:24; 6:69; 11:25; 14:1; 16:27; 17:21; 20:25), the rejection of Jesus (1:10c, 11/4:44; 7:1; 8:59; 10:31; 12:37–40; 15:18), divine regeneration (1:13/3:1–7), the glory of Jesus (1:14/12:41; 17:5, 22, 24), the grace and truth of God in Jesus (1:14, 17/4:24; 8:32; 14:6; 17:17; 18:38), Jesus and Moses/the law (1:17/1:45; 3:14; 5:46; 6:32; 7:19; 9:29), only Jesus has seen God (1:18/6:46), and Jesus' revelation of the Father (1:18/3:34; 8:19, 38; 12:49–50; 14:6–11; 17:8).

The Prologue functions as an introduction to the Fourth Gospel,

---

[1]Barrett, *Gospel*, p. 156.

much as an overture functions as an introduction to an opera. Or, to change the imagery, the Prologue is like the foyer of a theatre, where various scenes from the drama to be enacted inside are placarded. It appears to have been carefully crafted with a chiastic structure, which can be best seen by setting out its content as follows:

a. In the beginning was the Word,
and the Word was with God,
and the Word was God.
He was with God in the beginning.
Through him all things were made;
without him nothing was made that has been made.
In him was life,
and that life was the light of men.
The light shines in the darkness,
but the darkness has not understood it.

   b. There came a man who was sent from God;
     his name was John.
   He came as a witness to testify concerning that light,
     so that through him all men might believe.
   He himself was not the light;
     he came only as a witness to the light.

      c. The true light was coming into the world
        that gives light to every man
      He was in the world,
        and though the world was made through him,
      the world did not recognize him.
      He came to that which was his own,
      but his own did not receive him.

         d. Yet to all who received him,
           to those who believed in his name,
         he gave the right to become children of
           God –
           children born not of natural descent,
           nor of human decision
           or a husband's will,
           but born of God.

c^1. The Word became flesh
and made his dwelling among us.
We have seen his glory,
 the glory of the One and Only,
 who came from the Father,
full of grace and truth.

b^1. John testifies concerning him.
 He cries out, saying,
 'This was he of whom I said,
 "He who comes after me has surpassed me
 because he was before me."'

a^1. From the fullness of his grace
we have all received
 one blessing after another.
For the law was given through Moses;
grace and truth came through Jesus Christ.
No-one has ever seen God,
but God the One and Only,
 who is at the Father's side,
has made him known.

In this chiastic structure the first and last paragraphs (*a* and a^1), the second and second last paragraphs (*b* and b^1), and the third and third last paragraphs (*c* and c^1) all correspond to one another. So in paragraph *a* the Word is introduced as the one who was in intimate relationship with God and who came as light into the world (to make God known). This has its counterpart in paragraph a^1, where the Word made flesh is described as the one who is 'at the Father's side' and who has made him known. Paragraph *b* speaks of John (the Baptist) who came to bear witness to the light, and this corresponds to paragraph b^1, where once again John's witness to Christ is the subject. Paragraph *c* speaks about the true light coming into the world and this has its counterpart in paragraph c^1, where we are told that the Word became flesh and dwelt among us. Later paragraphs, while having clear parallels with their corresponding earlier paragraphs, do not just repeat what was said in those earlier paragraphs; rather, using different terminology, they extend it.

Within chiasms it is generally the central paragraph that contains the most significant statement. Paragraph *d* stresses that the purpose for the Word becoming flesh and bringing life and light into the world was that those who receive him, those who believe in his name, might become children of God. This corresponds to the stated purpose of the Gospel: 'Jesus did many other miraculous signs in the presence of his disciples, which are not recorded in this book. But these are written that you may believe that Jesus is the Christ, the Son of God, and that by believing you may have life in his name' (20:30–31).

The Prologue introduces the reader to the 'Word' (Logos). Though the idea of the Word/Logos sounds strange in modern ears, it would have resonated with ancient readers of the Gospel, whether Jew or Gentile. Parallels can be found (1) in the OT ideas of God's creative and sustaining word, the word of God spoken through the prophets, later Jewish personification of wisdom as the agent of God in creation; (2) in Stoic ideas of the logos as divine reason pervading and giving order to creation and relieving human ignorance; (3) in Philo's writings where the word logos is used extensively to denote the mind of God, the agent of creation and the mediator between God and the creation; (4) in rabbinic speculation in which the logos was identified with the pre-existent Torah; and (5) in the Gnostic writings in which a heavenly emissary bridges the spiritual and material worlds. All these parallels reveal that when the evangelist chose to identify Jesus as the Logos, he was using a term in wide circulation, but which meant different things to different people. More important than these parallels for our understanding of the Word/Logos is what the evangelist himself says about him in the Prologue.

A. THE WORD AS HE WAS IN THE BEGINNING (1:1–5)

This opening paragraph of the Prologue (*a*) describes the person and work of the Word in a number of brief but highly significant statements.

1. The first statement, *in the beginning was the Word*, echoes the opening words of Genesis, 'In the beginning God created the heavens and the earth . . .' (Gn. 1:1). As God was in the beginning prior to the creation of the world, so too was the Word. This implies something to be stated explicitly shortly: that the Word partakes of divinity.

The second statement, *and the Word was with God,* is susceptible to two interpretations. It may simply mean that the Word was with God in the beginning, just as Proverbs 8:27–30 says Wisdom was with God at creation. Alternatively, it could mean that the Word was faced towards God,[1] in intimate relationship with God. The final paragraph of the Prologue (*a¹*), which balances this first paragraph and extends its meaning, makes just this point when it describes the Son (= the Word) as the one 'who is close to the Father's heart'.

The third statement, *and the Word was God,* on first reading might suggest a unitarian understanding of God, the Word being simply equated with God. But the original language (*kai theos ēn ho logos*) will not allow such an interpretation.[2] To read the text in that way also overlooks the stress on the relationship existing between the Word and God (being 'with God' and being 'close to the Father's heart'). Relationship implies different persons, and this moves us away from unitarianism (one God, one person) towards trinitarianism (one God, three persons – Father, Son [= the Word] and Spirit). As the Fourth Gospel unfolds it becomes clear that this is what is intended. Jesus, the Word incarnate, claims to be one with God, but that involves being in relationship with God. So when the Prologue says 'the Word was God' it is not saying that the Word and God constitute an undifferentiated unity, but rather it is saying, in words aptly coined by Moloney, 'what God was the Word also was'.[3]

2. Two key ideas stated separately in verse 1 are brought together and repeated in verse 2: *He was with God in the beginning,*

---

[1]The preposition used (*pros*) has as one of its meanings 'orientation towards' someone or something.

[2]Barrett explains it succinctly: '*Theos,* being without the article, is predicative and describes the nature of the Word. The absence of the article indicates that the Word is God, but is not the only being of whom this is true; if *ho theos* had been written it would have been implied that no divine being existed outside the second person of the Trinity' (*Gospel*, p. 156).

[3]Moloney, p. 35.

i.e. the Word was in intimate relationship with God and he was in that relationship at the very beginning.

3. The evangelist explains the work of the Word in the beginning: *Through him all things were made; without him nothing was made that has been made.* Genesis 1:1–31 tells how God brought the universe into being by his creative word. The evangelist picks this up when he says that it was 'through' the person of the Word that God brought all things into being, or, putting it negatively, without his agency God brought nothing into being. This teaching is also found in Colossians 1:16–17 and Hebrews 1:2.

4. Further explaining the role of the Word in creation, the evangelist says, *In him was life, and that life was the light of men.* Because the Word shares in deity, he shares in the life of God (*cf.* 5:26). The evangelist does not make clear how the divine life in the Word illuminated human beings. Some suggest it relates to our creation in the image of God so that we participate in the light of reason in a way lesser created beings do not. Others suggest it refers to the light of general revelation, whereby the character of God is reflected in creation itself to be understood by human beings (*cf.* Rom. 1:19–20).

5. The first paragraph concludes with the statement *The light shines in the darkness, but the darkness has not understood it.* Again the allusion is to the Genesis creation account in which darkness covered the face of the earth. God said, 'Let there be light' (Gn. 1:3), and the darkness gave way to the light. The evangelist, while alluding to Genesis, foreshadows the coming of the light of God into the world in the person of the incarnate Word. Through him light shone among the Jewish people. He entered their 'darkness', and 'the darkness has not understood it'. The verb which the NIV translates as 'understood' (*katelaben*) could also be rendered 'overcame' (NRSV). This is in line with the way the verb is used elsewhere in John (8:3–4; 12:35). Understood in this way the evangelist is foreshadowing the repeated futile attempts of 'the Jews' to extinguish the light, Christ.

B. THE MINISTRY OF JOHN (THE BAPTIST) (1:6–8)

6. Paragraph *b*, which focuses upon the ministry of John, begins, *There came a man who was sent from God; his name was John*. Unlike other Gospels (*cf.* Mt. 3:1; 14:2; Lk. 7:20, 33), the Fourth Gospel never uses the expression 'John the Baptist'. It does not need to, because no other John is mentioned in this Gospel. John, the son of Zebedee, one of the Twelve, is not mentioned by name.

The evangelist describes John as a man 'sent from God'. He is thus depicted as a prophet. Frequent reference is made in the OT to prophets being sent by God (2 Ch. 24:19; 25:15; Je. 7:25; 25:4, 5; 28:9; 35:15; 44:4; Baruch 1:21). The Jewish crowds regarded John as a prophet (Mt. 21:26/Mk. 11:32/Lk. 20:6), and that is how Jesus also described him (Mt. 11:9/Lk. 7:26).

7. John's role is described: *He came as a witness to testify concerning that light, so that through him all men might believe*. John's role was to bear witness to the light that came into the world through the Word. In the Synoptic Gospels John appears as one who preaches repentance and baptizes those who heed his call. In the Fourth Gospel, however, there is no mention of his preaching of repentance, nor any actual descriptions of his baptizing ministry (neither his baptizing of the crowds nor his baptizing of Jesus, even though there are references to the fact that he did both). The reason for this might be that the evangelist wanted to emphasize John's role as witness. The purpose of John's witness, though sadly not its result, was 'so that through him all men might believe [in Christ]'.

8. After saying John came as a witness to the light, the evangelist adds, *He himself was not the light; he came only as a witness to the light*. Why he felt it necessary to add this statement has been the subject of speculation. Acts 19:1–4 reports that when Paul came to Ephesus on his third missionary journey:

> There he found some disciples and asked them, 'Did you receive the Holy Spirit when you believed?'
> They answered, 'No, we have not even heard that there is a Holy Spirit.'

So Paul asked, 'Then what baptism did you receive?'
'John's baptism,' they replied.
Paul said, 'John's baptism was a baptism of repentance. He told the people to believe in the one coming after him, that is, in Jesus.'

It has been suggested that the reason the evangelist says that John 'was not the light' is that when he wrote his Gospel there were still people in Ephesus who were disciples of John, and the evangelist wanted them to know that it was Jesus who was 'the light', not John. Some have even said that there is an anti-Baptist polemic in the Fourth Gospel, but this is going too far. This Gospel repeatedly portrays John positively as a faithful witness to Christ (*e.g.* 10:41) and the evangelist's main reason for including so many references to John (6–9, 15, 19–37; 3:22–30; 4:1–2; 5:31–36; 10:40–42) was that he might add to the strength of the witness concerning Christ. John 'was not the light', but he was an important witness to the light.

C. THE TRUE LIGHT COMES INTO THE WORLD (1:9–11)

9. This third paragraph (*c*) opens with the words *The true light that gives light to every man was coming into the world*. The phrase 'coming into the world' (*erchomenon eis ton kosmon*) could refer either to 'the light' (so NIV, treating *erchomenon* as a neuter) or to 'every man' (so AV, treating *erchomenon* as masculine). The NIV alternative is to be preferred because the following verses (10–13) speak about the reception accorded to true light when it came into the world.

The evangelist uses the word 'true' (*alēthinos*) in several other places to denote what is true or genuine (4:23: 'true worshippers', 6:32: 'true bread', 15:1: 'true vine', 17:3: 'the true God'), and he uses it here to stress that the Word, not John, was the 'true light'. The evangelist does not say *how* the true light was coming into the world; readers must wait till 1:14 to find that out. What he does say here is that the true light 'gives light to every man'. As this Gospel unfolds we find that the Word incarnate in Jesus Christ is 'the light of the world', and that through his person and teaching

65

he brought the light to bear upon all those with whom he came into contact. The next two verses indicate that though he brought light into the world it was not welcomed by many of those who witnessed it.

10–11. Looking back on the time when the Word came into the world, the evangelist says, *He was in the world, and though the world was made through him, the world did not recognize him.* The Word was the agent of God in creation (3), so it may be said 'the world was made through him'. There is a great irony here, for the Word came into the world he had made and yet the people of the world did not know him. This tragic irony is deepened in verse 11: *He came to that which was his own, but his own did not receive him.* When the evangelist says 'he came to that which was his own', he uses an expression, *eis ta idia*, found in two other places in the Gospel, where it means 'to one's own place/home' (16:32; 19:27). However, it is used in 1:11, not in the sense that he came to his own home, which would mean heaven, but into the world that was created through him and was therefore his property. When he says that 'his own (*hoi idioi*) did not receive him', he means the Jewish people by and large did not receive him. The rejection of the Word/Jesus is a recurring theme throughout the Gospel.

D. THOSE WHO RECEIVE THE WORD BECOME CHILDREN OF GOD (1:12–13)

Unlike the previous three paragraphs of the Prologue, this fourth paragraph (*d*) does not have a corresponding one balancing it in the chiastic structure of 1:1–18. Verses 12–13 stand at the centre of the chiastic structure and therefore receive the greatest emphasis. In fact, what is said in these verses encapsulates the purpose of the Gospel as a whole: that those who encounter the Word/Jesus through this Gospel might believe in him and become children of God, enjoying the eternal life that is the portion of those who believe.

12. Turning his attention from those who did not receive the Word to those who did, the evangelist says, *Yet to all who received*

*him, to those who believed in his name, he gave the right to become chil-
dren of God*. To 'receive' him means, as this verse indicates, to
believe in his name. To believe in a person's name is to believe
in the person, because the name stands for the person. Receiving
him involves accepting the teaching and revelation of God he
brought. Repeatedly this Gospel speaks about those who
receive or do not receive Jesus' testimony (3:11, 32–33; 5:34;
12:48; 17:8). To those who received him he gave the 'right to
become children of God'. The word translated 'right' (*exousia*)
can mean either 'power' or 'right', and it is used in both senses
in this Gospel (1:12; 5:27; 10:18; 17:2; 19:10–11). Here in 1:12 the
NIV renders it 'right', while the NRSV opts for 'power'. The NIV's
rendering, 'the right', is to be preferred, for it is Jesus as the
Word who gives the right to become children of God. The next
verse, 1:13, says 'the power' to do so comes from God.

When the evangelist describes those who believe as 'children'
of God, he uses the word 'child' (*teknon*). He reserves the word
'son' (*huios*) for Jesus himself. In this way he maintains a distinction between Jesus as the 'Son' of God, and believers as 'children'
of God. In this respect the evangelist differs from the apostle Paul,
who is willing to speak of believers as 'sons [and daughters]' of
God (Rom. 8:14, 19; 9:26; 2 Cor. 6:18; Gal. 3:26; 4:6–7).

13. Those who believe are further described as *children born not
of natural descent, nor of human decision or a husband's will, but born
of God*. A person has to be 'born' to be a child of God. But this birth
is 'not of natural descent' (lit. 'of bloods'). In the ancient world
procreation was understood to take place through the mixing of
bloods (of the father and the mother). Here it is denied that
natural procreation is the way people become children of God.
This is reinforced by the words that follow, which deny that children of God are born 'of human decision' (lit. 'of the will of flesh
[*sarx*]) or of a husband's will'. In John the word 'flesh' (*sarx*) often
means 'human being' (1:14; 3:6; 8:15; 17:2), so to be born of 'the
will of the flesh' means to be born because of the desires of human
parents as the NIV indicates. Those who become children of God,
the evangelist says, are 'born of God'. In this context he does not
offer any explanation of what this means. For that we must wait
until chapter 3, where Jesus speaks to Nicodemus about being

67

born of the Spirit, something as mysterious as the wind, and yet occurs in conjunction with belief in Jesus.

E. THE COMING OF THE WORD INTO THE WORLD (1:14)

This fifth paragraph (*c'*) balances the third paragraph (*c*), and explains *how* the Word came into the world: *The Word became flesh.* He entered the world by becoming flesh (*sarx*), *i.e.* by becoming human. The Word did not cease to be the Word, but in the incarnation he changed his mode of being the Word. How the Word who 'was God' could become human is not explained. This became the subject of much debate in the early centuries of the church. However, the evangelist was not interested in explaining *how* the Word became human. He was more concerned to explain what the consequences of this were. The first of these was that he *made his dwelling among us*. The expression 'made his dwelling' translates one word (*eskēnōsen*), which, rendered literally, means 'pitched a tent' or 'tabernacled'. The allusion is to the time when God's presence was localized in the tabernacle in the midst of the camp of Israel (Ex. 40:34–38). The evangelist is saying that the Word becoming flesh and living among us is like God tabernacling among the tribes of Israel, or, put in other words, the presence of God was localized in Jesus the incarnate Word.

The second consequence of the of the Word becoming human is that the evangelist could say *we have seen his glory*. The reference to 'glory' is also an allusion to God's presence in the tabernacle. Exodus 40:34–35 tells us that when Moses completed the construction of the tabernacle, 'Then the cloud covered the Tent of Meeting, and the glory of the LORD filled the tabernacle. Moses could not enter the Tent of Meeting because the cloud had settled upon it, and the glory of the LORD filled the tabernacle.' As the glory of God was once present in the tabernacle, so it was now present in the Word made flesh. Moreover, the evangelist, including himself among the eyewitnesses, says 'we have seen his glory', and then describes two aspects of the glory they saw. First, it was *the glory of the One and Only, who came from the Father*. He uses a special word (*monogenēs*) when he describes the Word as 'the One and Only'. It stresses the uniqueness of the Word who came from the Father (see Additional Note: *Monogenēs*, pp. 70–71). The evangelist indicates here, as he stresses repeatedly throughout the Gospel, that this unique one whose glory they saw came 'from the Father' into the world (5:36, 37, 43; 6:42, 57; 8:16, 18, 42; 12:49; 13:3; 14:24; 16:28; 17:21, 25; 20:21). He was the one who came 'from above' (3:31) and as such was the only one who could make the Father known (18).

Second, the glory the eyewitnesses saw was *full of grace and truth*. The expression 'grace and truth' (*charis kai alētheia*) is found only twice in the NT, here and in 1:17. It is almost certainly the evangelist's rendering of a similar expression 'kindness and faithfulness' (*eleos kai alētheia*) that is used frequently in the LXX as a translation of the Hebrew expression *ḥesed we'ĕmet* (*e.g.* Jos. 2:14; 2 Sa. 2:6; 15:20; Pss. 24:10 [ET 25:10]; 60:8 [ET 61:7]; 83:12 [ET 84:11]; 84:11 [ET 85:10]; 88:15 [ET 89:14]). The expression is used in Exodus 34:6–7, a passage in which God makes his glory known to Moses: 'And he passed in front of Moses, proclaiming, "The LORD, the LORD, the compassionate and gracious God, slow to anger, abounding in love and faithfulness (*ḥesed we'ĕmet*), maintaining love to thousands, and forgiving wickedness, rebellion and sin."' The 'love and faithfulness' that constituted the glory of God proclaimed to Moses is now found in the Word incarnate. What was *proclaimed* to Moses by the Lord as he passed by has now been *seen*, embodied in the incarnate Word, by the eyewitnesses.

The word 'grace' (*charis*), which the evangelist uses as his equivalent for the Hebrew, *ḥesed*, is found in only three places in John, all of them in the Prologue (14, 16, 17), and all of them in descriptions of the Word become flesh. Central to the glory of God revealed in the incarnate Word is his grace. As the Gospel of John unfolds, the grace of the Word incarnate in Jesus is seen again and again: he provides abundance of wine at the wedding feast of Cana (2:1–12), heals the official's son (4:43–54), causes the lame man at the Pool of Bethesda to walk (5:19–30), feeds the five thousand (6:1–15), gives sight to the man born blind (9:1–6), and restores Lazarus to life (11:38–44). His grace is seen most importantly in laying down his life for his people (10:11, 15), in giving eternal life (4:14; 6:27; 10:28; 17:2) and sending the Holy Spirit to those who believe (15:26; 16:7).

The Hebrew word *'ĕmet*, for which the evangelist substitutes the Greek word *alētheia*, translated 'truth', has the root meaning of 'reliability'. God is reliable both in his words and actions. He can be depended upon to carry out what he promises, and his words are always true. When the evangelist says the Word incarnate was 'full of grace and truth', he is affirming that the reliability of action and word predicated of God may also be predicated of the Word. The Word is reliable and truthful, he speaks the truth (8:45–46), testifies to the truth (18:37), and embodies the truth about God and his plan for salvation (14:6).

Additional Note: *Monogenēs*

The word *monogenēs*, rendered 'the One and Only' in 1:14 by the NIV, is in some other translations rendered 'only begotten'. That the word should be translated as 'the One and Only' is confirmed by its usage elsewhere in the NT, where it is found a total of nine times. It is found three times in the Gospel of Luke: once to describe the 'one and only son' of the widow of Nain (Lk. 7:12), once to describe the 'one and only daughter' of Jairus (Lk. 8:42), and once to describe the 'one and only son' of the man who sought Jesus' help for his demon-possessed boy (Lk. 9:38). It is found once in Hebrews, where Isaac, whom Abraham was about to sacrifice, is described as his 'one and only' son (Heb. 11:17) – in Abraham's case his one and only son by Sarah. In each of these cases the expression is used to add poignancy to a story by highlighting the fact that it was the person's 'one and only' child who was in dire need, was threatened or had died. The stress is not upon the fact that the person was begotten of the father or mother concerned but upon the fact that the father or mother had only one child and that that child was the one who was so sadly affected. It is found once in 1 John 4:9, where the author emphasizes the fact that the one whom God sent into the world was his 'one and only' Son. Once again the emphasis is not that Jesus was 'begotten' of God but that God had only one Son, and this 'one and only' Son he sent into the world that 'we might live through him'.

In the Gospel of John *monogenēs* is used in three other places and in each case it is used in relation to Jesus as God's Son. In 1:18 we are told that 'No-one has ever seen God, but God the One and Only (*monogenēs*), who is at the Father's side, has made him known.' And in 3:16 we find, 'For God so loved the world that he gave his one and only (*ton monogenē*) Son, that whoever believes in him shall not perish but have eternal life.' Finally, in 3:18 we read, 'whoever does not believe stands condemned already because he has not believed in the name of God's one and only (*monogenous*) Son'. In each case *monogenēs* denotes not that the Son was 'begotten' of the Father but rather his uniqueness as the 'One and Only' Son of God.

F. THE TESTIMONY OF JOHN (THE BAPTIST) (1:15)

This verse constitutes the sixth paragraph (*b¹*) of the Prologue, which balances the second paragraph (*b*). In paragraph b we are told that John was sent from God to bear witness to the light, though it is stressed that John himself was not the light. In this paragraph (*b¹*) the evangelist explains the content of John's testimony: *John testifies concerning him. He cries out, saying, 'This was he of whom I said, "He who comes after me has surpassed me because he was before me."'* To indicate that John was making an important public proclamation the evangelist uses the verb 'to cry out' (*krazō*) as he does in three places later in the Gospel when introducing important public declarations (7:28, 37; 12:44). John refers to Jesus as the one 'who comes after me', referring to the fact that Jesus' ministry began after his. The Fourth Gospel does mention a period in which the ministries of Jesus and John overlapped (3:22–24),[1] but essentially John's ministry was preparation for the ministry of Jesus, which was to follow. In this sense John could say 'He . . . comes after me'.

Even though John's ministry preceded that of Jesus, John emphasized that 'he who comes after me has surpassed me because he was before me'. He said the reason why Jesus surpassed him was 'because he was before me'. This cannot mean that Jesus surpassed John because he was older than him. The indications from the Gospel of Luke are that the reverse was the case: Jesus was six months younger than John (Lk. 1:24–31).

[1]The Synoptic Gospels speak of Jesus' public ministry taking place after John had been thrown into prison (Mt. 4:12; Mk. 1:14); only John's Gospel lets us know that there had been an earlier ministry of Jesus, which overlapped John's ministry.

The statement that Jesus was 'before' John could be read in the light of the opening verses of the Prologue (1:1: 'in the beginning was the Word'), suggesting that Jesus was 'before' John because of his pre-existence as the Word. While the NEB interprets 1:15 in this way ('before I was born, he already was'), there are no indications that John was aware of Jesus' pre-existence as the Word. It may be that John meant only to say that Jesus 'surpassed him' because he was always greater than him (even though he was born six months later). The evangelist may have introduced a note of ambiguity into the way he has reported John's words so that his readers will recognize that John spoke better than he knew. Later in the Gospel the evangelist points out that Caiaphas spoke better than he knew when he said 'it is better for you that one man die for the people than that the whole nation perish' (11:50–52), as did Pilate when he insisted on referring to Jesus as 'the King of the Jews' (18:39; 19:14–15, 19, 21–22).

G. THE WORD MAKES THE FATHER KNOWN (1:16–18)

The last paragraph (a^1) of the Prologue balances the opening one (a). It does in part pick up themes from paragraph c^1 when it speaks of receiving of the fullness of the grace of the Word and the relationship of that grace to the grace of God that came through Moses. But paragraph a^1 returns to the themes of the opening paragraph when it speaks of the Word being at the Father's side and making him known.

16. In verse 14 the evangelist spoke about seeing the glory of the incarnate Word, a glory that was 'full of grace and truth'. Here in 1:16 he speaks not about seeing that grace but of receiving it: *From the fullness of his grace we have all received one blessing after another.* Using the first-person plural, 'we', the evangelist identifies himself with others, and so we hear the testimony of the first witnesses coming down to us across the centuries. They experienced 'the fullness of his grace' as 'one blessing after another' (*charis anti charitos*), which literally translated would read 'one blessing instead of another', or 'one blessing replacing another'.

17. What the witnesses meant by 'one blessing after another' is explained by the words *For the law was given through Moses; grace and truth came through Jesus Christ.* The blessing replaced was the law given by God to Israel through Moses. What replaced it was the grace and truth, the kindness and faithfulness of God, that came through the Word incarnate. But what, exactly, was the grace that these people experienced and of which they bore witness? Taking our cue from this Gospel we could say at least that they witnessed the miracles Jesus performed. His disciples probably drank some of the wine Jesus provided at the wedding feast in Cana (2:1–11), they probably ate some of the food he miraculously provided for the hungry crowds (6:5–13) and they were saved from a violent storm when he brought their boat safely to shore (6:16–21). But probably much more than this is intended. They received of his grace as they saw the Father revealed in his Son, when Jesus laid down his life for them, when they experienced the gift of eternal life that Christ makes available to all who believe, and when their ascended Lord fulfilled his promise to send them another Paraclete, the Holy Spirit, to be with them for ever.

It is noteworthy that it is only here in verse 17 in the final paragraph (*a¹*) of the Prologue that the Word is identified as Jesus Christ. Everything that precedes is predicated of the Word, but here we discover that the Word was incarnate in Jesus Christ.

18. The grace and truth that came through Jesus far surpassed the blessing of the law given through Moses. One of these surpassing features was the unparalleled revelation of the Father that he brought: *No-one has ever seen God, but God the One and Only, who is at the Father's side, has made him known.* The words 'no-one has ever seen God' remind us of the invisibility of God, an important theme in the Fourth Gospel (*cf.* 5:37; 6:46). Significant in this context, where Moses and Jesus are compared, is the fact that when Moses asked to see God's glory he was told, 'I will cause all my goodness to pass in front of you, and I will proclaim my name, the LORD, in your presence . . . But you cannot see my face, for no-one may see me and live' (Ex. 33:19–20). Clearly, the revelation of God that came through Jesus Christ far surpassed the revelation that came through Moses, precisely because Moses did not see God – only Jesus has seen God and is therefore able to make him known.

73

Jesus is described here as 'God the One and Only (*monogenēs*)'.[1] This description is striking. It differs from other statements that use *monogenēs* in relation to Jesus to describe the uniqueness of his status as the one who came from the Father (14) or as the Son of God (3:16, 18). This verse speaks of Jesus as 'God the One and Only' and echoes the opening paragraph (*a*) of the Prologue, which says 'the Word was God'.

The word used for the Father's 'side' is *kolpos*. In the LXX this means a person's 'bosom' or 'lap' and is used of both males and females in relation to the affection, care and protection of a parent for a child. *Kolpos* is used again in 13:23 to depict the disciple whom Jesus loved 'reclining next to him' (*en tō kolpō*). The words 'who is at the Father's side', then, highlight the intimate relationship Jesus had with the Father and echo the description of the Word in the first paragraph (*a*) as the one who 'was with God'. It is because of his intimate relationship, as well as his being the only one who has ever seen God, that Jesus can make him known.

The word used for 'making known' is *exēgeomai*, which means to 'set forth in great detail' or 'expound'. Its cognate is *exēgēsis*, which in its anglicized form is used to mean 'exegesis'/'exposition'. The evangelist is saying, then, that the Word (Jesus), being God the one and only, at the Father's side, the only one who has seen God, has 'expounded' him, made him known, through his person, words and works.

II. JESUS' WORK IN THE WORLD (1:19 – 12:50)

Following the Prologue comes the second major section of the Fourth Gospel, Jesus' work in the world (1:19 – 12:50), sometimes called the Book of Signs because it includes reports of seven signs/miracles that Jesus performed. The description of Jesus' work in the world brings with it the description of the ministry of his relative John the Baptist (1:19–34) and the calling of Jesus' early disciples (1:35–51), events that took place over a four-day period (1:29, 35, 43).

---

[1] There is a variant that reads the 'one and only Son' (*monogenēs huios*), instead of 'God the one and only' (*monogenēs theos*), but the latter has stronger manuscript support.

A. JOHN THE BAPTIST BEARS WITNESS TO JESUS (1:19–34)

1. John's testimony to 'the Jews' of Jerusalem (1:19–28)

19. The evangelist begins his account of John's ministry, *Now this was John's testimony when the Jews of Jerusalem sent priests and Levites to ask him who he was.* This verse contains the first of many references to 'the Jews' in this Gospel. While some of these references are neutral and others positive, many have negative connotations and denote Jesus' adversaries among the Jewish leadership of the day. Great care needs to be exercised by modern readers in their interpretation of these references so as not to misconstrue them (see ' "The Jews" in the Fourth Gospel', on pp. 49–50). The evangelist identifies 'the Jews' here specifically as 'the Jews of Jerusalem', almost certainly referring to members of the Jewish Sanhedrin, or ruling council. Part of their responsibility was to assess the genuineness or otherwise of those claiming to be prophets or the Messiah. So they sent 'priests and Levites' to question him. The Levites' normal role was to support the priests in temple worship and to act as temple police. In this latter capacity, perhaps, they accompanied the priests to question Jesus.

20. The evangelist describes John's response: *He did not fail to confess, but confessed freely, 'I am not the Christ.'* John the Baptist's testimony is a disclaimer and the evangelist places very strong emphasis upon the disclaimer by the ponderous way he words it (lit. 'he confessed, and he did not deny, and he confessed, "I am not the Christ" ').

21. The priests and Levites were puzzled by John's response. They probably expected him to claim to be the Messiah as others had done before him and were to do after him (Mt. 24:24; Mk. 13:22; Acts 5:33–39; 21:37–39). *They asked him, 'Then who are you? Are you Elijah?' He said, 'I am not.' 'Are you the Prophet?' He answered, 'No.'* The priests and Levites were asking John whether he claimed to be one of the two great figures whose coming in the last days was predicted in the OT, Elijah or 'the Prophet'.

In Malachi 4:5 the Lord says to Israel, 'See, I will send you the prophet Elijah before that great and dreadful day of the LORD

75

comes.' First-century Jews were looking for the coming of this Elijah figure (Mt. 16:14; Mk. 6:15; 8:28; Lk. 9:8, 19). The teachers of the law were saying that the Elijah figure must come before the arrival of the messianic age, a teaching with which Jesus agreed (Mt. 17:10–11; Mk. 9:11–12). When Jesus uttered his cry of dereliction on the cross, Jewish onlookers thought he was calling upon Elijah and waited to see whether he would come to Jesus' aid (Mt. 27:47, 49; Mk. 15:35, 36). When the priests and Levites asked John, 'Are you Elijah?' he answered, 'I am not.' This is puzzling because John is elsewhere explicitly identified as the Elijah who was to come. The angel who appeared to Zechariah, John the Baptist's father, told him that his son would 'go on before the Lord, in the spirit and power of Elijah' (Lk. 1:17), and Jesus himself identified John as the Elijah who should come (Mt. 11:14; 17:12; Mk. 9:13). Jesus apparently had a greater view of John's importance than he did.

When John denied that he was Elijah, the priests and Levites asked, 'Are you the Prophet?' Moses had told the Israelites, 'The LORD your God will raise up for you a prophet like me from among your own brothers. You must listen to him' (Dt. 18:15, 18–19). First-century Jews were looking for the fulfilment of this promise (cf. 6:14; 7:37–40). Early Christian preachers also referred to 'a prophet' (Acts 7:37) and explicitly identified Jesus as the one in whom the promise found fulfilment (Acts 3:19–23). It is not surprising, then, that when John was asked if he was the Prophet, he replied, 'No.'

22–23. The priests and Levites needed to bring back a report to 'the Jews of Jerusalem' who sent them, so when John refused to accept any of their categories of identification, *Finally they said, 'Who are you? Give us an answer to take back to those who sent us. What do you say about yourself?'* To this question *John replied in the words of Isaiah the prophet, 'I am the voice of one calling in the desert, "Make straight the way for the Lord."'* John described himself in words drawn from Isaiah 40:3, where the prophet, announcing deliverance for Jewish exiles in Babylon, called for the preparation, metaphorically speaking, of the road to be used by the exiles on their way back to Jerusalem. John saw himself, like Isaiah did, as a voice calling in the desert, in John's case calling upon people to 'make straight the way of the Lord', *i.e.* to ready themselves for the coming of the Messiah.

24–25. *Now some Pharisees who had been sent questioned him.* Following John's exchange with the priests and Levites, some Pharisees took up the interrogation. The Pharisees were the most influential sect of the Jews in the time of Jesus. Here they are described as people 'who had been sent', *i.e.* they were included among those sent by the Sanhedrin to assess and report on John's ministry. They asked John, *Why then do you baptize if you are not the Christ, nor Elijah, nor the Prophet?* There are no accounts of John actually baptizing people in the Fourth Gospel. In this respect this Gospel differs from the Synoptics. Nevertheless, such a ministry is assumed and alluded to in numerous places (25, 26, 28, 31, 33; 3:23; 4:1; 10:40). Why did the Pharisees question John about his baptizing ministry? Baptism was not unknown among the Jews. It was self-administered by Gentiles who became Jewish proselytes (and by members of the Qumran sect for ritual cleansing). But John himself was administering the baptism and those he baptized were already Jews.

The way the Pharisees put their question suggests they thought it appropriate for John to baptize if he was the Christ, Elijah or the Prophet. However, the OT says nothing about baptism in connection with any of these figures. Perhaps their question simply reflects an attitude that if John did not claim to be a figure of importance he had no business baptizing people.

26–27. John did not answer the Pharisees' challenge to his baptizing ministry. Instead, he focused attention upon the one to whom had had been commissioned to bear witness: *'I baptize with water,'* John replied, *'but among you stands one you do not know.'* There is some irony in John's words. His interrogators wanted to know if he was the Christ, but they were asking the wrong person, for the Christ was already among them and they did not recognize him. John then identified him: *He is the one who comes after me.* He came after John in the sense that his ministry largely followed John's ministry. John indicated that Jesus was far superior to him when he said of him, *the thongs of whose sandals I am not worthy to untie.* In first-century Judaism, the task of removing sandals and washing feet was carried out by servants. Normally, a Jewish servant would not be asked to do this, the task being assigned preferably to Gentile servants. By saying that he was not worthy to untie Jesus' sandals, John was making a clear statement about the dignity of the Christ, which far surpassed his own.

28. The evangelist concludes his description of the exchange between John and the priests and Levites, and then the Pharisees, with the words *this all happened at Bethany on the other side of the Jordan, where John was baptizing*. This statement includes a puzzling reference to 'Bethany on the other side of the Jordan, where John was baptizing'. The other side of the Jordan is usually taken to mean the eastern side, a long way from the Bethany we read of elsewhere in the Fourth Gospel, which was located near Jerusalem (11:1, 18; 12:1). This problem was recognized very early in the history of the church, and is reflected in the variant readings preserved in a number of Greek manuscripts, which substitute Bethabara for Bethany. Bethabara is located 19 miles east of Jerusalem on the Jordan River about 6 miles to the south-east of Jericho. Both Origen and Chrysostom favoured this reading, but it is supported by few manuscripts and is not found in the older and more reliable manuscripts. Another possibility is that the Bethany of 1:28 is to be identified with Batanea, an area in the north-east of the country, but this places the site of John's baptizing ministry a long way from its traditional location. Efforts to locate a Bethany on the east of the Jordan closer to Jericho have not proved successful. The evangelist's geographical references that can be verified have proved accurate and he deliberately distinguishes this Bethany from the one on the Mount of Olives near Jerusalem. We cannot rule out the possibility that he is referring to another Bethany east of the Jordan, known to him but unknown to us.[1]

2. John's testimony to Jesus as the Lamb of God (1:29–34)

29. After John's interrogation by priests, Levites and Pharisees, the evangelist tells us, *The next day John saw Jesus coming towards*

[1] For a full discussion, see Riesner, pp. 29–63.

him and said, 'Look, the Lamb of God, who takes away the sin of the world!' The Fourth Gospel does not record, as the Synoptic Gospels do, the baptism of Jesus by John. However, the coming of Jesus mentioned in this verse was not his coming for baptism, because, as 1:32-33 implies, John had already witnessed the descent of the Spirit upon Jesus when he had baptized him. John already knew who Jesus was, and therefore said to those around, 'Look, the Lamb of God, who takes away the sin of the world!' Christian readers of the Fourth Gospel naturally infer that this is an allusion to the sacrificial death of Christ by which he atoned for the sins of the world. However, it is not certain that this is what the Baptist meant by it. The indications are that he expected the Messiah to carry out judgment against sinners, not to offer himself as a sacrifice for their sins (*cf*. Mt. 3:12: 'His winnowing fork is in his hand, and he will clear his threshing-floor, gathering his wheat into the barn and burning up the chaff with unquench-able fire'). John may have been identifying Jesus as the apocalyptic warrior lamb referred to in Jewish writings (*e.g. 1 Enoch* 90:9-12; *Testament of Joseph* 19:8-9) as did the author of the book of Revelation (Rev. 5:5-10; 17:14), though the latter fused the idea of the powerful lamb / lion of Judah with the sacrificial lamb. By the time the Fourth Gospel was written Jesus had been recognized as the one whose death had atoned for human sins, and the evangelist probably hoped his readers might appreciate its double meaning.

The reference to Jesus here as 'the Lamb of God' uses the word *amnos* for 'lamb'. It is one of only four references in the NT (Jn. 1:29, 36; Acts 8:32; 1 Pet. 1:19) that do so.[1] The word *amnos* is found 101 times in the LXX, of which 82 are references to sacrificial lambs. The two uses of *amnos* in the NT outside the Fourth Gospel are clear references to Jesus, who died as a sacrificial lamb: one speaks of Jesus as the servant of the Lord, who 'was led like a sheep to the slaughter, / and as a lamb before the shearer is silent' (Acts 8:32); the other refers to 'the precious blood of Christ, a lamb without blemish or defect' (1 Pet. 1:19). In the light of all this we are probably correct to say that the evangelist would be happy if his

---

[1] Another word, *arnion*, is used twenty-eight times in Revelation to denote Jesus as the Lamb.

readers took John's witness to Jesus as 'the lamb of God who takes away the sin of the world' to have a double meaning. He was both the apocalyptic lamb who judges unrepentant sinners, and the atoning sacrifice for the sins of those who believe. Perhaps the evangelist believed John spoke more than he knew, just as Caiaphas and Pilate were to do later on (11:50–52; 18:39; 19:14–15, 19, 21–22).

In 1:29 Jesus is the one who takes away the sin of 'the world'. There are a couple of other places in the Fourth Gospel where Jesus' significance for 'the world' is implied. In 3:16–17 God's love leads him to give his only Son for 'the world' so that those who believe might have eternal life, and in 4:42 the Samaritans come to recognize that Jesus really is 'the Saviour of the world', not just of the Jewish people.

30. Continuing his testimony about Jesus, John says, *This is the one I meant when I said, 'A man who comes after me has surpassed me because he was before me.'* Picking up something he said earlier (26–27), John explains that the one coming after me 'has surpassed me because he was before me'. Jesus came 'after' John in that his ministry for the most part followed John's. When John added that Jesus surpasses him because he was before him, it looks like an allusion to Jesus' pre-existence as the Word (1–4). However, it is unlikely that John was aware of this. He may simply have meant that Jesus had always been greater than him even though he was born six months later than him (for a more detailed discussion of this statement, see the commentary on 1:15). There may even be intentional ambiguity here, the evangelist suggesting that John spoke better than he knew.

31. John acknowledged that there was a time that he did not recognize Jesus: *I myself did not know him, but the reason I came baptizing with water was that he might be revealed to Israel.* John was related to Jesus and therefore knew him personally. What he did not know previously was that Jesus was the Messiah. Now he explained that the purpose of his baptizing ministry was that Jesus 'might be revealed to Israel'. John was aware that Jesus came to the Jewish people, 'to Israel', and the purpose of John's ministry was that Jesus should be revealed to Israel as her Messiah.

32. The evangelist begins to explain how John came to recognize who Jesus was: *Then John gave this testimony: 'I saw the Spirit come down from heaven as a dove and remain on him.'* This is a reference to Jesus' baptism by John and the descent of the Spirit upon Jesus at that time. The Fourth Gospel does not record this event, but the evangelist assumes his readers will know about it. The Synoptic Gospels all describe the descent of the Spirit upon Jesus at his baptism (Mt. 3:16; Mk. 1:10; Lk. 3:22), but only the Fourth Gospel adds that the Spirit came down from heaven 'and remained on him'. In OT times the Spirit came upon certain people at specific times for specific tasks. Isaiah 11:2 prophesies concerning the Messiah:

> The Spirit of the LORD will rest on him –
>> the Spirit of wisdom and of understanding,
>> the Spirit of counsel and of power,
>> the Spirit of knowledge and of the fear of the
>> LORD. (*Cf.* Is. 42:1; 61:1.)

The evangelist emphasizes the fact that the Spirit 'remained' upon Jesus. This is one of the ways in which the evangelist highlights the special relationship Jesus had with the Spirit (another is found in 3:34 where he says God gave the Spirit 'without limit' to Jesus).

All four Gospels speak of the descent of the Spirit 'as a dove' upon Jesus at his baptism. The symbolism of the dove in relation to the Spirit is difficult to determine, as the two are not connected anywhere else in either the OT or the NT. In Matthew 10:16 Jesus tells his disciples to 'be as shrewd as snakes and as innocent as doves'. The word translated 'innocent' (*akeraios*) can mean innocent, harmless or pure. If we allow this to guide us, then perhaps it is the purity and gentleness of the Spirit that is symbolized by the dove.

33. In this verse John says again, *I would not have known him, except that the one who sent me to baptize with water told me, 'The man on whom you see the Spirit come down and remain is he who will baptize with the Holy Spirit.'* It was the descent of the Spirit upon Jesus at his baptism that convinced John of the significance of Jesus. The one who sent John was God (6) and he told him that the one upon whom the Spirit descended and remained when he baptized him

81

was the one who would baptize with the Spirit. In contemporary Jewish belief the Messiah was to be the bearer of God's Spirit,[1] so John was being told how to identify the Messiah.

John distinguished his ministry from that of Jesus by saying he baptized with water, but Jesus would baptize with the Holy Spirit. During his earthly ministry Jesus did in fact baptize with water also, though he did not do so personally, but entrusted the actual baptizing to his disciples (3:22, 26; 4:1–2). However, it was Jesus' future baptizing with the Spirit that John emphasized. This would occur after Jesus' 'glorification' (*i.e.* after his death, resurrection and exaltation – 7:37–39). Jesus is the Spirit-baptizer, and he plunges all those who believe in him into the Spirit. Baptism is one of a number of expressions used in the Fourth Gospel to describe the bestowal of the Spirit upon all believers by the exalted Jesus – others include giving drink (7:37–39), breathing (20:22), and sending the Counsellor (14:15–17, 26; 15:26; 16:5–15). According to the Acts of the Apostles, the first believers were baptized in the Spirit by Jesus on the day of Pentecost (Acts 1:4–5; 2:1–4), and then as the gospel spread, each new believer received the same baptism in the Spirit (Acts 2:38–39).

34. John the Baptist concluded his testimony to Jesus with the words *I have seen and I testify that this is the Son of God*.[2] The title 'the Son of God', though not a common designation for the Messiah among first-century Jews, was nevertheless used in some texts in that way.[3] This is the first of many references in the Fourth Gospel which state either explicitly (34, 49; 5:25; 10:36; 11:4, 27; 19:7; 20:31) or implicitly (3:16, 17, 18, 35, 36; 5:19, 20, 21, 22, 23, 26; 6:40; 14:13; 17:1) that Jesus is the Son of God. The evangelist records the Baptist's testimony that Jesus is the Son of God in support of the overall purpose of his Gospel, which is 'that you may believe that Jesus is the Christ, the Son of God, and that by believing you may have life in his name' (20:31). It is significant that the titles 'the

---

[1]See *1 Enoch* 49:3; *Psalms of Solomon* 17:37; *Testament of Levi* 18:2–14; *Testament of Judah* 24:2–3.

[2]There is an important variant reading preserved in some ancient manuscripts that substitutes 'chosen one' (*eklektos*) for 'Son of God' (*huios tou theou*). Both 'the chosen one' and 'the Son of God' equally designate the Messiah.

[3]There are passages in the Dead Sea Scrolls that connect the Messiah with the title Son of God: 4QFlor 1:10–14; 1QSa 2:11–12; 4QpsDan A^a (4Q246) 2:1.

Christ (Messiah)' and 'the Son of God' stand in apposition as virtual synonyms in 20:31.

B. EARLY DISCIPLES FOLLOW JESUS (1:35-51)

1. John's disciples follow Jesus (1:35-39)

35-36. The evangelist begins to recount events that took place on the third day: *The next day John was there again with two of his disciples.* 'There' refers presumably to Bethany on the other side of the Jordan (28). One of two disciples was Andrew, the brother of Simon Peter (40), the identity of the other is not known. *When he saw Jesus passing by, he said, 'Look, the Lamb of God!'* John repeats his testimony of the previous day, though in shortened form (see commentary on 1:29).

37. John's testimony had a powerful impact upon these disciples: *When the two disciples heard him say this, they followed Jesus.* Not all of John's disciples followed Jesus (3:25-27; Acts 19:1-7), but these two did. Many people in John's situation would have been disappointed to see their followers going after someone else, but not John. When asked about it later, he said that a person can only receive what is given from heaven, and reminded his hearers that he had already testified that 'I am not the Christ but am sent ahead of him,' and explained that seeing people follow Jesus actually completed his own joy (3:28-30).

38-39. When these two disciples set out after Jesus, we are told that *Turning round, Jesus saw them following and asked, 'What do you want?* And because they wanted to become his disciples by accompanying him, *They said, 'Rabbi' (which means Teacher), 'where are you staying?'* Jesus is addressed several times as 'Rabbi' in this Gospel, always by those who are or are to be his disciples (38, 49; 3:2; 4:31; 9:2; 11:8). In NT times 'Rabbi' was the title used for authorized teachers of the law, but not restricted to them. Sometimes it was used as a title of honour or for respectful address, as in this verse.

Jesus responded to the two disciples' question by saying, *Come and you will see.* They wanted to become Jesus' disciples, so Jesus invited them to come with him. *So they went and saw where he was staying, and spent that day with him*. In this way they began their discipleship with Jesus. The evangelist notes that *It was about the tenth hour*, *i.e.* the tenth hour after sunrise, about 4.00 p.m. This meant the disciples spent the latter part of the day with Jesus, probably continuing their conversation until nightfall.

2. *Andrew brings Peter to Jesus (1:40–42)*

40. The evangelist identifies one of these disciples: *Andrew, Simon Peter's brother, was one of the two who heard what John had said and who had followed Jesus*. There has been speculation about the identity of the second disciple, some wanting to identify him with the beloved disciple, who is in turn identified with John the son of Zebedee (*cf.* 13:23; 19:26; 21:7, 20). This is attractive because John is not mentioned by name in the Fourth Gospel and neither is this second disciple who followed Jesus. While attractive, this suggestion can be neither proved nor disproved.

41–42. Andrew heard the Baptist testify that Jesus was the Lamb of God, the one who baptizes with the Holy Spirit (the Messiah). Having spent time with Jesus, Andrew himself came to believe Jesus was the Messiah. *The first thing Andrew did was to find his brother Simon and tell him, 'We have found the Messiah' (that is, the Christ)*. He did not to try to convince his brother that what he had said was true; instead, *he brought him to Jesus*. It was being with Jesus that had convinced Andrew that Jesus was the Messiah, and apparently he believed it would be the same for Simon. When he came, *Jesus looked at him and said, 'You are Simon son of John.'* Perhaps it was supernatural knowledge that enabled Jesus' instant recognition of Simon, as was to be the case later with Nathanael (47–49). Jesus continued, *'You will be called Cephas' (which, when translated, is Peter)*. Cephas is the transliteration of an Aramaic word (*kēpha*) meaning 'rock', and Peter is the English equivalent of the Greek word *Petros*, also meaning rock or stone. Hereafter the evangelist never refers to Simon as Cephas again.[1]

[1] The only other NT writer to use the name Cephas for Peter is the apostle Paul (1 Cor. 1:12; 3:22; 9:5; 15:5; Gal. 1:18; 2:9, 11, 14; though in the last five of these texts the NIV renders *Kēpha* wrongly as Peter).

He always refers to him as Simon or Simon Peter. Why Jesus should rename Simon as Cephas is not explained. In Matthew 16:18 Jesus says, 'And I tell you that you are Peter (*Petros*), and on this rock (*petra*) I will build my church.' Both *Petros* and *petra* are equivalents of the Aramaic *kēpha*, meaning rock. Perhaps it was because Peter was to be the primary preacher of the gospel after the resurrection that Jesus described him as the rock on which the church would be built.

3. Jesus calls Philip and Philip brings Nathanael to Jesus (1:43–51)

43–44. What has been described so far – John's testimony to Jesus, telling his disciples that he is the lamb of God and two of them then following Jesus – all appears to have taken place in Judea (see commentary on 1:28), because the evangelist continues his account by saying, *the next day Jesus decided to leave for Galilee.* The first two followers of Jesus came to him because of John's witness, and Peter was encouraged to follow Jesus by his brother Andrew, but now we see Jesus himself taking the initiative: *Finding Philip, he said to him, 'Follow me.'* Jesus both 'found' Philip and issued the invitation to him to become his disciple ('follow me'). The evangelist explains, *Philip, like Andrew and Peter, was from the town of Bethsaida*, a large fishing village on the northern shore of the Sea of Galilee, just to the east of the place where the Jordan River enters it.

45. Like Andrew, who sought out his brother, Simon, and told him about Jesus, *Philip found Nathanael and told him, 'We have found the one Moses wrote about in the Law, and about whom the prophets also wrote – Jesus of Nazareth, the son of Joseph.'* There is only one other reference to Nathanael in the NT (21:2), where he is described as 'Nathanael from Cana in Galilee' and listed as one of the disciples who were fishing when Jesus appeared to them after his resurrection.[1] Following his account of the call of Nathanael, 'a native of Cana', the evangelist immediately recounts Jesus' presence and miracle at the wedding feast in Cana (2:1–11).

---

[1] It has been suggested that Nathanael is to be identified with Bartholomew, seeing that his name is linked with that of Philip in three of the lists of the Twelve disciples (Mt. 10:3; Mk. 3:18; Lk. 6:14).

Philip's brief acquaintance with Jesus was enough to convince him that he was the one of whom Moses and the prophets spoke, and this is what he told Nathanael. His reference to 'the one Moses wrote about in the Law' is an allusion to Deuteronomy 18:18 where the Lord says to Moses, 'I will raise up for them a prophet like you from among their brothers; I will put my words in his mouth, and he will tell them everything I command him.' While there are few references to Deuteronomy 18:18 in rabbinic writings, evidence from the NT suggests that the coming of a prophet like Moses was included in first-century Jewish expectations for the end time. In the Fourth Gospel we are told the Jews who came to assess John the Baptist's ministry wanted to know if he claimed to be 'the prophet' (21, 25, 45). Other references to 'the prophet' are found in 6:14; 7:40 and Acts 3:22–23; 7:37.

It was normal to identify people in terms of the place they came from and who their parents were, so Philip described Jesus as 'Jesus of Nazareth, the son of Joseph'. Jesus was 'of Nazareth', for the holy family returned to Nazareth after his birth in Bethlehem and their sojourn in Egypt. Jesus grew to manhood in Nazareth, and so was known as a man of Nazareth. Nazareth was a small and insignificant village in Jesus' day, not the large bustling city it is today. Philip also described Jesus as 'the son of Joseph'. At this early stage it appears that Philip shared the inadequate Jewish understanding of Jesus' origins (cf. 6:42), something the evangelist makes no attempt to disguise. When Luke reports the beginning of Jesus' ministry, he describes him by saying, 'He was the son, so it was thought, of Joseph, the son of Heli' (Lk. 3:23). The fourth evangelist has already provided his readers with a clear presentation of the real origins of Jesus in the Prologue (1–18), so he does not need to comment on Philip's inadequate description.

46. When Nathanael heard that Jesus was from Nazareth, he expostulated, *Nazareth! Can anything good come from there?* Nazareth was such an insignificant place, and one that appears in none of the prophecies concerning the Messiah; so Nathanael was not willing to accept Philip's testimony. However, as Andrew said earlier to Simon Peter, Philip now said to Nathanael, *Come and see.*

47. *When Jesus saw Nathanael approaching, he said of him, 'Here is a true Israelite, in whom there is nothing false.'* The term 'Israelite', often used as a term of public address to Jewish people (Acts 2:22; 3:12; 5:35; 13:16; 21:28), was also used in connection with the special privileges of the chosen people,[1] and reflects Jewish pride of race (Rom. 11:1; 2 Cor. 11:22). Jesus described Nathanael as 'a true Israelite', defining this by adding that he was one 'in whom there is nothing false', literally 'in whom there is no guile' (*dolos*). In this respect Nathanael is different from the father of all Israelites, Jacob, who used guile (*dolos*) to take his brother's blessing (Gn. 27:35), and to whose experience at Bethel Jesus would shortly allude (51).

Jesus' knowledge of the true nature of Nathanael was supernatural. In 2:25 the evangelist says of Jesus, 'He did not need man's testimony about man, for he knew what was in a man.'

48–49. Nathanael was amazed that Jesus knew him and so asked, *How do you know me? Jesus answered, 'I saw you while you were still under the fig tree before Philip called you.'* To sit under one's own fig tree was a sign of prosperity. Jewish scholars sat under fig trees to study the Law. Whatever Nathanael's experience under the fig tree involved, it must have had significance for him, for when Jesus showed that he knew about it, Nathanael declared, *Rabbi, you are the Son of God; you are the King of Israel.* Nathanael addressed Jesus as 'Rabbi', showing respect, as John's disciples had done earlier (38). Nathanael also hailed Jesus as 'the Son of God'. This title is known to have had messianic overtones (see commentary on 1:34), and its being placed here in apposition to the messianic title 'King of Israel' confirms this. Later in this Gospel the crowds take branches and go out to meet Jesus as he approaches Jerusalem, and they shout, 'Hosanna! / Blessed is he who comes in the name of the Lord! / Blessed is the King of Israel!' (12:13), thus welcoming him as Messiah. For the evangelist, the title 'the Son of God' is very significant. For him it is more than a messianic title: it denotes Jesus' unique relationship with the Father.

---

[1] See Rom. 9:4–5, where Paul says of Israelites, 'Theirs is the adoption as sons; theirs the divine glory, the covenants, the receiving of the law, the temple worship and the promises. Theirs are the patriarchs, and from them is traced the human ancestry of Christ, who is God over all, forever praised! Amen.'

50–51. In response to Nathanael's confession, *Jesus said, 'You believe because I told you I saw you under the fig tree. You shall see greater things than that.'* Again Jesus referred to seeing Nathanael under the fig tree and then promised greater things. *He then added,* addressing not only Nathanael, but all those listening ('you' in this verse is plural – *hymin*), *'I tell you the truth, you shall see heaven open, and the angels of God ascending and descending on the Son of Man.'* Jesus introduced his explanation of the 'greater things' with the formula 'I tell you the truth' (*amēn amēn legō hymin*), found here for the first time in this Gospel. This formula is used twenty-five times in all,[1] and in each case it introduces an important statement by Jesus.

Jesus' promise that his disciples would see heaven open and the angels of God ascending and descending contains another allusion to the experience of Jacob (*cf.* 1:47). When fleeing from his brother, Esau, whose birthright he had taken by guile, Jacob stopped in a certain place, where he slept and dreamed of angels ascending and descending upon a ladder joining heaven and earth. Above the ladder stood the Lord, who made specific promises to Jacob, promises about the land, his descendants, the blessing that would come to the world through them, and finally about Jacob's return to the land from which he was fleeing. 'When Jacob awoke from his sleep, he thought, "Surely the LORD is in this place, and I was not aware of it." He was afraid and said, "How awesome is this place! This is none other than the house of God; this is the gate of heaven" . . . He called that place Bethel' (Gn. 28:16–19). For Jacob, then, Bethel was the place where he encountered God and where God revealed his plans for him. When Jesus, alluding to this incident, said to his disciples, 'you shall see heaven open, and the angels of God ascending and descending on the Son of Man', he was implying that the place where people encounter God was now in the person of his Son, Jesus, and that it was through him that God was now revealing his truth. The greater things people were to see, then, would be the revelation of God in the life, ministry, death, resurrection and exaltation of Jesus.

In this promise to his disciples Jesus referred to himself as 'the Son of Man'. This title has its background in Daniel 7 and carries

---

[1] 51; 3:3, 5, 11; 5:19, 24, 25; 6:26, 32, 47, 53; 8:34, 51, 58; 10:1, 7; 12:24; 13:16, 20, 21, 38; 14:12; 16:20, 23; 21:18.

overtones of authority, power and glory. But the title is used by Jesus in the Fourth Gospel also in connection with his suffering and death. It appears that Jesus complemented the notions of authority, power and glory (from Dn. 7) with the theme of suffering and death drawn from the suffering servant motifs of Isaiah 52:13 – 53:12 (see Additional Note: 'The Son of Man', below.)

Additional Note: 'The Son of Man'

The expression 'the Son of Man' is found twelve times in the Fourth Gospel (51; 3:13; 5:27; 6:27, 53, 62; 8:28; 9:35; 12:33–34 (2×); 13:31). In all cases except two it is used by Jesus in reference to himself. The two exceptions, where the expression is found on the lips of 'the crowd', nevertheless pick up on Jesus' use of the expression in reference to himself and question the idea that 'the Son of Man must be lifted up' (12:34a, b). Of the twelve uses, four relate to Jesus' suffering and death (8:28; 12:23, 34a; 13:31), two are found in the bread of life discourse, including references to eating his flesh and drinking his blood (6:27, 53), three relate to his authority or exaltation (3:13; 5:27; 6:62), and one each relate to his identity (12:34b), believing in him (9:35) and his being the 'place' of God's revelation (51).

The expression 'the Son of Man' is found sixty-six times in the Synoptic Gospels, and always on the lips of Jesus as a self-designation. Twenty-four of these relate to the 'coming' of the Son of Man, twenty-two relate to his suffering and death, eight to his authority, and two each to his humiliation, his behaviour, his resurrection, and speaking against him. There are single references to the Son of Man as the sower, his identity, his resurrection, the cost of discipleship, and to the Son of Man who comes to seek and save the lost.

There is only one other place in the NT where 'the Son of Man' is used as a title. This is in Acts 7:56 where Stephen at his trial before the Sanhedrin looks up to heaven and says, 'Look, I see heaven open and the Son of Man standing at the right hand of God.' Once again the reference is to Christ.[1]

[1] There are three references to 'a son of man' (without the definite article) meaning simply a human being in Heb. 2:6; Rev. 1:13; 14:14.

The background to the expression 'the Son of Man' is found in the OT. The singular form with the article (*ho huios tou anthrōpou*) is not found in the LXX, though the plural form with the article is found twenty-nine times, but always referring simply to human beings. The singular form without the article is found 111 times in the LXX, all but one of them referring simply to a human being. Ninety-four of these are used in direct address by God to his prophet in the book of Ezekiel. The one exception is Daniel 7:13–14:

> In my vision at night I looked, and there before me was one like a son of man, coming with the clouds of heaven. He approached the Ancient of Days and was led into his presence. He was given authority, glory and sovereign power; all peoples, nations and men of every language worshipped him. His dominion is an everlasting dominion that will not pass away, and his kingdom is one that will never be destroyed.

This passage is almost certainly the background to Jesus' use of 'the Son of Man' as his preferred self-designation, particularly those uses that relate to his authority, and coming with power and glory.

Extremely significant is Jesus' use of 'the Son of Man' in references to his humiliation, suffering and death. He appears to have taken the OT concept of the glorious Son of Man and added to it the notion of suffering and death, perhaps incorporating ideas from Isaiah 52:13 – 53:12. This is exactly what he did with the OT idea of the Messiah – the conquering Messiah is complemented with the notion of a suffering and dying Messiah.

There has been much debate about the authenticity and significance of Son of Man sayings attributed to Jesus in the Gospels,[1] but there are good reasons to believe that this expression was indeed Jesus' preferred self-designation, and that in many places he used it to present himself as a person of sovereign authority like the Son of Man in Daniel 7:13–14. The expression 'the Son of Man' in Daniel 7:13–14 was regarded as having messianic connotations in later Jewish writings – the actual expression is found in

---

[1] A debate described well by Marshall, 'Son of Man', pp. 775–781.

1 Enoch 46:1–6; 48:1–5 with messianic connotations. Though not actually using the expression, *4 Ezra 13* clearly speaks of the Messiah in terms dependent upon Daniel 7:13–14.

C. THE WEDDING FEAST AT CANA (2:1–12)

1–2. Following Jesus' encounter with Nathanael, *on the third day a wedding took place at Cana in Galilee*. Cana was situated about 8 miles north of Nazareth where Jesus was brought up, and about 17 miles south-west of Capernaum, the headquarters of his mission. The reference to 'the third day' is puzzling. While 1:19–51 is structured around four days (1:29, 35, 43), this does not correlate with 'the third day' of 2:1. Perhaps the evangelist is simply indicating that the wedding took place on the third day after Jesus' encounter with Nathanael. *Jesus' mother was there, and Jesus and his disciples had also been invited to the wedding*. We can assume that Jesus' family was known to the bridegroom. Jesus' presence at the wedding shows he was no ascetic (*cf.* Mt. 9:10–13; 11:19). We do not know why Jesus' disciples were included in the invitation or how many of them accompanied Jesus. Up until this point in the narrative only Andrew, Simon, Philip, Nathanael and one unnamed disciple have been mentioned. The first reference to 'the Twelve' comes later (6:67).

In the Fourth Gospel Jesus' mother is never called by her name, Mary; she is referred to only as Jesus' mother (2:1, 3, 5, 12; 6:42; 19:25, 26, 27). Ancient authors frequently used epithets like 'the mother of N' instead of the person's name, because the name was not known, was disputed or was very well known. Why the evangelist did so is not clear.

3. Wedding festivities often lasted a week, and each day new guests would appear. Much food and wine was consumed, involving considerable financial strain upon the bridegroom, whose responsibility it was to provide for his guests. Social catastrophe struck the bridegroom at this wedding in Cana. He was facing great embarrassment and loss of face because the wine had given out and guests were still present. *When the wine was gone, Jesus' mother said to him, 'They have no more wine.'* It has been suggested that Jesus' arrival with his disciples caused the embarrassing shortage of wine, but this cannot be proved. Why Jesus' mother approached Jesus with the problem is not explained. Perhaps she felt the relationship between her family and that of the bridegroom obliged her to take action to relieve their embarrassment. Perhaps she knew she could turn to her eldest son in time of need, and that there was an obligation resting upon him also to do something about it.

4. Jesus' response to the implied request in his mother's words was enigmatic: *'Dear woman, why do you involve me?' Jesus replied. 'My time has not yet come.'* The NIV's 'Dear woman, why do you involve me?' translates *ti emoi kai soi gynai*, which rendered literally would read, 'What [is it] to me and to you, woman?'[1] Jesus was perhaps questioning the need for either his mother or him to get involved. Maybe the kinship relationship between Jesus' family and the bridegroom's family was not close, so the responsibility rested with others. However, where this expression (*ti emoi kai soi*) is found elsewhere in the NT and in the LXX it always indicates some sort of confrontation or rebuke,[2] and it probably does so here also. Addressing his mother simply as 'woman', though abrupt to modern readers' ears, does not imply lack of affection. Jesus addressed his mother in this way from the cross when making loving provision for her care after his death (19:26).

The words 'my time (*hōra*) has not yet come' include the first of nine references to Jesus' 'hour/time' (4; 7:30; 8:20; 12:23, 27 [2×]; 13:1; 16:32; 17:1), a significant theme in this Gospel. The first three references indicate that Jesus' hour had not yet come; the last six indicate that it had come. The hour towards which everything moves is the hour of Jesus' glorification, which takes place through his death, resurrection and exaltation. Bearing this in mind, Jesus' response to his mother appears to have confronted her with the news that he was now acting only according to his Father's timetable, with his eyes fixed on the hour to come (even though he went on to fulfil her implied request).

---

[1] *Cf.* NRSV: 'What concern is that to you and to me?', RV: 'What have I do with thee?', RSV: 'What have you to do with me?'

[2] See Mk. 5:7/Lk. 8:28, where a demon (possessed person) confronts Jesus, Jdg. 11:12, where Jephthah confronts the Ammonites, 1 Ki. 17:18; 2 Ki. 3:13; 2 Ch. 35:21; and 1 Esdras 1:26, where kings and prophets confront one another.

5. Jesus' mother does not seem to have regarded her son's response as a refusal of her implied request: *His mother said to the servants, 'Do whatever he tells you.'* It has often been remarked that Jesus' mother only ever gave one instruction that has been preserved for us: people should do whatever Jesus told them to do. It seems that, as she knew she could turn to her Son in time of need, she also knew to leave things to him once she had made the need known.

6. Setting the scene for the miracle to follow, the evangelist says, *Nearby stood six stone water jars, the kind used by the Jews for ceremonial washing, each holding from twenty to thirty gallons.* Stone jars were used for holding water for ceremonial washing, because stone was believed not to contract ritual uncleanness. The reference to the jars being 'the kind used by the Jews for ceremonial washing' may simply be a factual detail, or suggestive of the symbolic significance of the miracle (see below). These were large jars, holding 20 to 30 gallons each, a detail included to enable the reader to appreciate the magnitude of the miracle soon to be performed.

7–8. The jars were not full, so *Jesus said to the servants, 'Fill the jars with water.'* Jesus' action confirms that his response to his mother was not a refusal to act. His mother had told the servants, 'Do whatever he tells you,' *so they filled them to the brim*. Their obedience is unquestioning. The evangelist draws attention to the fact that they filled the jars to the brim, emphasizing again the magnitude of the miracle to follow. Then Jesus told them, *Now draw some out and take it to the master of the banquet. They did so*. The servants did what Jesus told them without question. Their obedience showed implicit faith in Jesus' word, for the servants' embarrassment would be great if what they brought to the master of the banquet turned out to be just water!

9–10. The evangelist continues, *the master of the banquet tasted the water that had been turned into wine*. He does not tell us when the miracle occurred. Was it when the jars were filled? Was it when the servants drew from the jars they had filled? Was it as they carried what they had drawn to the master of the banquet? In any case, when the master of the banquet tasted what the servants

93

brought to him, it was wine. The evangelist adds, *He did not realize where it had come from, though the servants who had drawn the water knew.* By saying 'the servants who had drawn the water knew', the evangelist seems to suggest that what they drew from the stone jars was only water. If this was the case, the miracle occurred as they carried what they had drawn to the master of the banquet. The obedience of the servants and their faith in Jesus, then, played an important part in this miracle.

The master of the banquet was astonished by what he tasted. *Then he called the bridegroom aside and said, 'Everyone brings out the choice wine first and then the cheaper wine after the guests have had too much to drink; but you have saved the best till now.'* The custom of the day was to offer the best wine first, so that the guests would appreciate the host's provision, and then, when their palates had been dulled by too much drinking,[1] bring out wine of lesser quality. Jesus' provision of quality wine well into the celebration meant this custom was reversed.

By mentioning earlier that the six jars held 20 or 30 gallons each, the evangelist implies that the amount of wine Jesus would provide was substantial, even extravagant. The question arises, Why did Jesus make so much wine? Possibly he was fulfilling his obligations as a wedding guest. As invited guests Jesus and his disciples were expected to provide wedding gifts. On the other hand, it could have been a symbolic action. In the OT abundant wine (and oil or milk) are signs of the age of fulfilment:

> They will come and shout for joy on the heights of Zion;
>> they will rejoice in the bounty of the LORD –
> the grain, the new wine and the oil,
>> the young of the flocks and herds. (Je. 31:12)

> 'In that day the mountains will drip new wine,
>> and the hills will flow with milk;
>> all the ravines of Judah will run with water. (Joel 3:18)

> 'The days are coming,' declares the LORD,
>> 'when the reaper will be overtaken by the ploughman
>> and the planter by the one treading grapes.

[1]The NIV translation 'had too much to drink' softens the force of the verb used here, which actually means 'to be drunk' or 'intoxicated'.

New wine will drip from the mountains
    and flow from all the hills.
I will bring back my exiled people Israel;
    they will rebuild the ruined cities and live in them.
They will plant vineyards and drink their wine;
    they will make gardens and eat their fruit.' (Amos
    9:13-14)

Jesus' conversion of such a large quantity of water into wine
would indicate that the long-awaited kingdom of God had
arrived. God himself had drawn near in the person and ministry
of Jesus, and the fulfilment of the promise of abundant blessings
was beginning to be fulfilled.

11. *This, the first of his miraculous signs, Jesus performed at Cana in
Galilee.* This miracle is the first of seven signs the evangelist
records, by which he seeks to lead his readers to faith in Jesus (*cf.*
20:30-31). He enumerates the second sign (4:54) as he does this
first sign, but not subsequent ones. The evangelist concludes his
account of the miracle as he started it (1), by locating the event in
'Cana of Galilee', the home town of Nathanael.

Commenting on the significance of the miracle, the evangelist
makes two further points. First, he says, *he thus revealed his glory.*
The glory of Jesus was revealed both in his ability to change water
to wine, and also in his grace in providing an abundance of
quality wine to spare the bridegroom embarrassing loss of face.
Second, the evangelist says, *his disciples put their faith in him.* The
Prologue foreshadows two responses to the Word coming into the
world. Some reject him, but others accept him and believe in him.
In this story the disciples are examples of the latter group. As they
witnessed the sign performed in Cana, they put their faith in
Jesus.

12. *After this he went down to Capernaum with his mother and
brothers and his disciples. There they stayed for a few days.* Capernaum
was the place where Jesus lived when not travelling about (Mt.
4:13) and where people knew to look for him (Jn. 6:24). He
appears to have stayed in Peter's house in Capernaum (Mt. 8:14;
cf. Mt. 8:5). Jesus returned to Capernaum 'with his mother and

brothers'. It appears the brothers were pleased with Jesus' response to his mother's implied request, though later we learn they did not believe in him (7:5).

The evangelist's primary purpose in telling this story is to show how Jesus began to reveal his glory and how this led people to believe in him. He hoped his readers would be led to a similar faith, which is the purpose for which he wrote his Gospel (20:31). He may have had a secondary purpose also – to show how the ceremonial washings of the old covenant were replaced by the new wine of the kingdom. The water pots for ceremonial washing denote the provisions of the old covenant, while the provision of abundant wine denotes the blessings of the kingdom.

Additional Note: Signs

The presentation of signs in the Fourth Gospel differs from that in the Synoptic Gospels. In the latter, the word 'sign', meaning miracle, is used most often in contexts where 'the Jews' demand a sign from Jesus to prove his claims, and Jesus regards such demands as sinful and refuses to oblige (Mt. 12:38–39; 16:1–4/Mk. 8:11–12/Lk. 11:16, 29–30). There are also references to deceptive signs preformed by charlatans (Mt. 24:24/Mk. 13:22). On one occasion, without using the word 'sign', Jesus refers positively to his exorcisms as evidence that the kingdom of God is present (Mt. 12:28/Lk. 11:20), and the longer ending of Mark refers to signs to be performed by those who believe (Mk. 16:17, 20).

While the Fourth Gospel also mentions the Jewish demand for signs as proof of Jesus' authority and identity (2:18; 6:30), it does generally present signs in a more positive light. The evangelist deliberately recounts seven signs of Jesus in the first part of his Gospel[1] and says these are recorded so that people might believe Jesus is the Christ, and that believing they might have life in his name (20:30–31).

In the Fourth Gospel Jesus' signs evoke various responses. On occasions the signs caused the disciples (11) or the crowds (2:23)

---

[1]Changing water into wine (1–11), healing the nobleman's son (4:46–54), healing the man who had been crippled for 38 years (5:1–9), feeding the multitude (6:1–14), walking on the water and the miraculous landing (6:15–25), healing the man born blind (9:1–8), and raising Lazarus (11:1–46).

to put their faith in Jesus. On other occasions they caused people to conclude that Jesus had been sent by God (3:2), that he was the Prophet of whom Moses had spoken (6:14), or that he was the Messiah (7:31). When signs led to authentic faith, it was because the significance of the signs was perceived.

The Fourth Gospel notes that despite witnessing many signs some people still did not put their faith in Jesus (12:37). The Pharisees acknowledged Jesus performed signs, but were divided in their reading of their significance (9:16). Members of the Sanhedrin acknowledged that Jesus was performing remarkable signs. They feared that everyone would accept him as Messiah and thus attract unwanted attention from the Roman occupying forces, so they plotted to kill him (11:47–53).

When signs produced faith, it was not always authentic. In 2:23–24 people saw the miracles Jesus performed and 'believed' in him, but Jesus would not commit himself to them because 'he knew all men'. Presumably he knew their faith was not genuine. In 6:26 Jesus reproved those who followed him after the multiplication of the loaves and fishes because they were not interested in what this miracle signified, but only in filling their stomachs.

There is another line taken in regard to signs in the Fourth Gospel. People are rebuked for their inability to believe without the evidence of signs (4:48; 20:29). It is faith in the word of Jesus without the need for signs that is regarded as the ideal. Examples of such faith may be seen in Nathanael's belief on hearing Jesus say that he saw him under the fig tree (1:49–50), the attitude of Jesus' mother and the servants' unquestioning obedience to his word at the wedding feast in Cana (5–8), and the Samaritans' belief upon hearing the woman's testimony, and even more so upon hearing Jesus' word for themselves (4:42).

D. JESUS GOES UP TO JERUSALEM FOR PASSOVER (2:13–25)

1. Cleansing the temple (2:13–22)

13. Following the account of the miracle in Cana, the evangelist describes the cleansing of the temple that took place in Jerusalem. He begins the account, *When it was almost time for the*

Jewish Passover, Jesus went up to Jerusalem. This is the first of five festivals Jesus attended in Jerusalem that are mentioned in the Fourth Gospel (Passover, 2:13; 'a feast of the Jews', 5:1; the Feast of Tabernacles, 7:2, 10–11; the Feast of Dedication, 10:22; and a second Passover, 11:55; 12:20).

The evangelist places his account of the temple cleansing early in Jesus' ministry during this first Passover festival, not during the Passover in the last week of Jesus' ministry as the Synoptic Gospels do. There are a number of possible explanations for this. Because the Synoptic evangelists do not record Jesus' earlier visits to Jerusalem for the other four festivals, they could only include the temple cleansing in their account of the final Passover visit. Alternatively, the fourth evangelist may have brought forward his account of the temple cleansing for theological or literary reasons. In that case, the arrangement of his material was not meant to be chronological but thematic. A third possibility is that there were two temple cleansings, one at the beginning and another at the end of Jesus' ministry. While many scholars reject this alternative, it cannot be ruled out altogether.

The evangelist refers to Passover as 'the Jewish Passover' (lit. 'the Passover of the Jews') possibly because he had Gentile as well as Jewish readers in mind, or because Christians, even Jewish Christians, no longer celebrated Passover when he wrote.

14–16. Prior to the Passover Jesus came to the temple, and *in the temple courts he found men selling cattle, sheep and doves, and others sitting at tables exchanging money.* The provision of cattle, sheep and doves, and the exchange of money were all necessary for temple worship. Pilgrims who had travelled up from Galilee (a journey of about 90 miles), for example, could not bring animals for sacrifice with them. Pilgrims travelling from other countries would need to change their money into Tyrian coinage, the prescribed currency (Mishnah, *Bekorot* 8:7).

These necessary functions were being carried out in the temple court, in an area known as the Court of the Gentiles. This was barricaded off from the Court of Women and the Court of Israel, which were accessible only to Jews. The barricades carried warnings to Gentiles, two of which have been found, one containing the complete text, which reads, 'No foreigner is to enter within the forecourt and the balustrade around the sanctuary. Whoever is caught will have himself to blame for his subsequent death.' The only place, then, where Gentiles could come and pray in the temple was the court of the Gentiles, and this had been turned into a noisy market.

Jesus' response to what he found was dramatic: *So he made a whip out of cords, and drove all from the temple area, both sheep and cattle; he scattered the coins of the money-changers and overturned their tables. To those who sold doves he said, 'Get these out of here!'* Jesus drove out the sellers and their animals. Those selling doves were told to 'Get these out of here!' because the birds would have been in cages and could not be driven out. What motivated Jesus to take such drastic action is revealed in his next statement: *How dare you turn my Father's house into a market!* A number of things need comment. First, the temple, Jesus claimed, was his Father's house. God is his Father, and the temple authorities had allowed God's house to become a house of merchandise, thus dishonouring his Father. Second, his Father's house was intended to be a place of prayer, but the temple authorities, by allowing these activities to be carried out in the court of the Gentiles, had turned it into a marketplace. Jesus' objection was not to the buying and selling or the money changing themselves, but to the fact that these things were practised in the temple. In the parallel account in Mark 11:17, Jesus says:

> Is it not written:
> 'My house will be called
> a house of prayer for all nations'?
> But you have made it a den of robbers.

The quotation is from Isaiah 56:7, a prophecy in which the Lord's concern for the nations, as well as Israel, is emphasized. Jesus' anger, then, was aroused because the one place where people from other nations could pray had been turned into a noisy market. Third, the evangelist may have intended his readers to see in Jesus' action a fulfilment of OT prophecies. In Zechariah 14:21 the prophet speaks of a day when 'there will no longer be a Canaanite (RSV 'trader') in the house of the LORD Almighty'. Finally, the whole episode demonstrates that Jesus was concerned for the purity of temple worship, not its abolition at that time.

17. Jesus' disciples must have watched his actions with fear and amazement. Fear because the temple officials would not let this affront to their authority go unchallenged, and amazement because Jesus had acted so decisively and with no apparent concern for the consequences. The evangelist tells us, *His disciples remembered that it is written: 'Zeal for your house will consume me.'* It was probably much later, after the death and resurrection of Jesus, that the disciples made sense of what he had done by recalling the words of Psalm 69:9. Here the psalmist speaks of being consumed with zeal for God's house and how this brought down upon him the antagonism of his fellows. Jesus, like the psalmist, and like Phineas, Elijah and Mattathias before him (Nu. 25:6–13; 1 Ki. 19:10, 14; Sirach 48:1–4; 1 Maccabees 2:23–26), was consumed with zeal to preserve God's honour.

18. The response of the temple authorities was not long in coming: *Then the Jews demanded of him, 'What miraculous sign can you show us to prove your authority to do all this?'* Jesus' action was audacious and prophetic in character. The temple authorities challenged him to show them a sign to prove he had authority from God to do such things. They probably had in mind some impressive miracle. If he could not demonstrate his authority in this way, then he would presumably be arrested, tried and punished for disturbing the worship of the temple.

19–21. Jesus was not taken aback by this demand. He offered 'the Jews' a sign, but one they would not have expected, and which they misunderstood: *Jesus answered them, '[You] destroy this temple, and I will raise it again in three days.'* They thought he was challenging them to destroy the Jerusalem temple. *The Jews replied, 'It has taken forty-six years to build this temple, and you are going to raise it in three days?'* The reconstruction of the temple was begun by Herod the Great in 20 BC but ancient sources vary in their information about the date of completion. Josephus seems to imply the work on the temple continued until the outbreak of the Jewish–Roman war in AD 64 (*Antiquities* xx.219). In the question 'and you are going to raise it in three days?' the singular pronoun 'you' is emphatic, suggesting this response by the temple authorities was intended to mock Jesus. They both misunderstood and rejected his answer.

The evangelist explains what Jesus meant: *But the temple he had spoken of was his body.* Jesus was not saying to the authorities, 'You destroy the Jerusalem temple, and I will rebuild it in three days'; rather, he was offering them the sign of his death and resurrection as proof of his authority: 'You destroy/kill this body of mine and I will raise it up in three days.' The sign Jesus offered the temple authorities was in effect the same as that he offered the scribes and Pharisees in Matthew 12:39–40: 'A wicked and adulterous generation asks for a miraculous sign! But none will be given it except the sign of the prophet Jonah. For as Jonah was three days and three nights in the belly of a huge fish, so the Son of Man will be three days and three nights in the heart of the earth.' Jesus' answer, interpreted by the evangelist, constitutes the first clear reference to Jesus' death in the Fourth Gospel.

22. The evangelist explains that it was *after he was raised from the dead, his disciples recalled what he had said.* The disciples did not understand Jesus' predictions of his death and resurrection prior to the events any more than his opponents did. It was only in retrospect that they understood this, and it was *then they believed the Scripture and the words that Jesus had spoken.* The Scripture passage the evangelist refers to here may be Psalm 69:9, quoted in 2:17. If this is not the case, we can only surmise that he had in mind one or other of the scriptures mentioned elsewhere in connection with Jesus' death and resurrection. In the Acts of the Apostles, Peter cites Psalm 16:8–11 as the scripture fulfilled when Jesus was raised from the dead (Acts 2:24–28), Philip uses the passage about the death of the Servant of the Lord in Isaiah 53:7–8 (LXX) to proclaim Christ to the Ethiopian eunuch (Acts 8:30–35), and Paul cites Psalm 2:7 (Acts 13:33); Isaiah 55:3 LXX (Acts 13:34) and Psalm 16:10 LXX (Acts 13:35) as scriptures that foreshadow the resurrection of Jesus.

The evangelist's purpose in telling this story appears to be to present later reflections by the disciples upon the significance of the temple cleansing, and especially the sign Jesus offered in response to the temple authorities' demand. The evangelist shows how this led the disciples to believe 'the Scripture and the words that Jesus had spoken'. In this way the inclusion of this story contributes to the overall purpose of the Gospel, *i.e.* to lead readers to a similar faith in Jesus, so that they too might have eternal life. There may be a secondary purpose involved as well. As Jesus superseded Moses (1:17: 'the law was given through Moses; grace and truth came through Jesus Christ') and the blessings of the kingdom supersede the ceremonial washings of the old covenant (as exemplified in the miracle at Cana), so now the temple of Jerusalem as the dwelling place of God is superseded by Christ himself. His body is the new temple, the place where God was now making himself present. (Later the church as the body of Christ assumes this role.)

Additional Note: The different words used for 'temple' in 2:13–22

Different words are used to denote the temple in 2:13–22. The first, *hieron*, is used frequently in the Fourth Gospel to refer to the whole temple complex (14, 15; 5:14; 7:14, 28; 8:2, 20, 59; 10:23; 11:56; 18:20), whereas the second, *naos*, used only in this passage in the Fourth Gospel, can refer either to the whole complex or to the inner sanctuary.[1] Jesus uses *naos* when speaking metaphorically of his own body as a temple. The third expression used to denote the temple is *oikos tou patros mou* ('my Father's house'). Jesus used this expression when he accused people of turning his Father's house into a house of merchandise (16). It stresses that the temple belongs to God, and is to be used for his purposes.

2. Jesus and those who 'believed' (2:23–25)

23. A lot more than the temple cleansing took place during Jesus' visit to Jerusalem for this first Passover festival, much more than the evangelist records in detail, for he goes on to say, *Now while he was in Jerusalem at the Passover feast, many people saw the miraculous signs he was doing and believed in his name.* So far in the Gospel the evangelist has only recorded one sign performed by Jesus – turning water to wine in Cana of Galilee. He describes no signs performed by Jesus in Jerusalem up to this point, but he implies that Jesus 'was doing' signs there. The evangelist uses the

---

[1] 'Naos', BAGD, pp. 533–534.

imperfect tense ('was doing') to depict Jesus' performance of signs as an ongoing action. These signs had led 'many' to believe in Jesus, but as the next verse indicates, there was something defective about their belief.

24–25. Though many 'believed' in him, *Jesus would not entrust himself to them.* There is a play on words here. In 2:23 we are told 'many people . . . believed (*episteusan*) in his name', but in 2:24 the evangelist adds, 'Jesus would not entrust (*episteuen*) himself to them'. Their 'trust' in him was not of a sort to make Jesus 'entrust' himself to them. Evidently, the belief of these people, based upon witnessing the signs Jesus performed, was shallow and inauthentic. Perhaps it stopped at wonderment and did not progress to commitment. While Jesus would not entrust himself to those whose faith was not genuine, the opposite is also true: he will entrust himself to those whose faith is genuine. What it means for Jesus to entrust himself to people is probably best understood in the light of his word to his disciples at the Last Supper: 'You are my friends if you do what I command. I no longer call you servants, because a servant does not know his master's business. Instead, I have called you friends, for everything that I learned from my Father I have made known to you' (15:14–15).

The evangelist tells us that Jesus was able to recognize the shallowness of their belief *for he knew all men. He did not need man's testimony about man, for he knew what was in a man.* In this Gospel there are a number of places where Jesus' knowledge of people's thoughts is noted (1:47–48; 4:17–19, 29; 6:15, 64). These reflect his unique nature as the Son of God, and his exercise of divine powers (*cf.* Je. 17:10: 'I the LORD search the heart / and examine the mind, / to reward a man according to his conduct, / according to what his deeds deserve').

This passage forms the conclusion to the story of Jesus' actions in the temple, but it also acts as a bridging section to prepare the reader for another incident, which occurred during Jesus' first Passover visit to Jerusalem: the encounter with Nicodemus. In this case also we are shown how Jesus knew what was in a man, and dealt with him accordingly.

E. JESUS AND NICODEMUS (3:1–21)

It is difficult to determine where the evangelist's account of the exchange between Jesus and Nicodemus ends and his own comments begin. It would appear that the account runs from 3:1–15 and the evangelist's comments run from 3:16–21.[1]

1. Jesus' conversation with Nicodemus (3:1–15)

1. The evangelist introduces Nicodemus: *Now there was a man of the Pharisees named Nicodemus, a member of the Jewish ruling council.* As 'a man of the Pharisees', Nicodemus was a member of the most influential Jewish sect in Jesus' time. The Pharisees are mentioned twenty times in the Gospel of John, and are nearly always portrayed as antagonistic to Jesus. The only exceptions are here in 3:1, where Nicodemus the Pharisee comes to Jesus, and 9:16, where some of the Pharisees are bold enough to ask how Jesus could do miraculous signs if he were a sinner.

Nicodemus is also described as 'a member of the Jewish ruling council', or Sanhedrin. Members of the Sanhedrin are also generally presented as antagonistic towards Jesus in this Gospel. Apart from 3:1ff., the one exception is found in 12:42, where the evangelist says, 'Yet at the same time many even among the leaders (lit. 'rulers') believed in him. But because of the Pharisees they would not confess their faith for fear they would be put out of the synagogue'.

2. The evangelist says of Nicodemus, *He came to Jesus at night.* Rabbis did sometimes study the Law at night (Str-B 2, 419–420), but that does not seem very significant in this context. More significant is the fact that elsewhere in the Gospel the word 'night' appears to have negative connotations. In 9:4 Jesus urges people

---

[1]After introducing Nicodemus in 3:1, the evangelist's account of the exchange between Nicodemus and Jesus begins at 3:2. Throughout 3:2–12 he uses second-person forms, indicating direct speech. In 3:13 the use of the second-person forms gives way to third-person forms, which continue to be used throughout 3:13–21. On first reading this could be taken to indicate that the evangelist's comments begin at 3:13. However, wherever the evangelist presents Jesus' own statements which involve the use of the expression 'the Son of Man' (1:51; 3:13, 14; 6:27, 53, 62; 8:28; 9:35; 12:23; 13:31) these statements are always couched in third-person forms. This suggests that 3:13–15 continues the account of Jesus' conversation with Nicodemus, and that the evangelist's comments, then, begin at 3:16.

to work in the 'day', for the 'night' is coming when no-one can work. In 11:10 he says that those who walk in the 'night' stumble because they have no light. In 13:30, after receiving the bread from Jesus' hand, Judas went out into the 'night' to betray him. Bearing these things in mind, the statement in 3:2 that Nicodemus came 'by night' suggests he was in a state of spiritual darkness when he approached Jesus.

Nicodemus addressed Jesus as *Rabbi*, a teacher like himself (3:10; see also commentary on 1:38). Then, identifying himself with other (more reasonable) members of the Jewish leadership, he says, *we know you are a teacher who has come from God. For no-one could perform the miraculous signs you are doing if God were not with him*. On Jesus' first visit to Jerusalem many people 'believed' in him when they saw the signs he performed (2:23). Perhaps we are intended to conclude that Nicodemus and his associates were included among those who so 'believed' (but to whom Jesus was not yet prepared to entrust himself). Witnessing the 'signs', Nicodemus concluded that Jesus was 'a teacher who has come from God' and that he performed his miracles because God was with him. The theme of 'signs' is a pervasive one in this Gospel and is closely related to the whole purpose of the evangelist (see Additional Note: Signs, pp. 96–97).

3. While Nicodemus associated himself with others in his approach, Jesus' initial response was to Nicodemus alone. *In reply Jesus declared, 'I tell you (sing.) the truth, no-one can see the kingdom of God unless he is born again'*. The emphatic way in which Jesus' response is introduced, 'I tell you the truth' (*amēn amēn legō soi*), indicates the importance, both for Nicodemus and all later readers of this Gospel, of what Jesus said: 'no-one can see the kingdom of God unless he is born again'. To 'see' the kingdom is synonymous with entering the kingdom (*cf.* 3:5). Jesus' Pharisaic contemporaries believed all Jews would enter the kingdom of God through resurrection on the last day, the only exceptions being those who denied the faith and committed acts of apostasy (Mishnah, *Sanhedrin* 10:1–4). To be born a Jew was to be an inheritor of the kingdom of God. Nicodemus would have been astounded by Jesus' statement that he as a Jew would not see the kingdom of God unless he were' born again'.

The word translated 'again' here in 3:3 and also in 3:7 is *anōthen*, which when used elsewhere in the Fourth Gospel always carries the idea of 'from above', *i.e.* from heaven/from God (3:31; 19:11, 23). Elsewhere in the NT also mostly it means 'from above' (Mt. 27:51; Mk. 15:38; Jas. 1:17; 3:15, 17).[1] Jesus was saying what the Prologue foreshadows, that children of God (and therefore inheritors of the kingdom) are those who have been born of God, *i.e.* from above. However, Nicodemus took Jesus to mean he had to be born 'again' physically, as the next verse indicates.

4. Nicodemus responded, *'How can a man be born when he is old?' Nicodemus asked. 'Surely he cannot enter a second time into his mother's womb to be born!'* Nicodemus missed Jesus' reference to birth 'from above', interpreting what he said purely in a temporal fashion: 'a second time'. He thought Jesus meant that people would have to undergo a second physical birth in order to see the kingdom.

5. Continuing to address Nicodemus directly, *Jesus answered, 'I tell you* (sing.) *the truth, no-one can enter the kingdom of God unless he is born of water and the Spirit.'* Once again the gravity of what Jesus said is signalled by the words 'I tell you the truth' (*amēn amēn legō soi*). Jesus speaks here about 'entering' the kingdom, an expression synonymous with 'seeing' the kingdom (3). The condition for entry is again expressed in terms of another birth, this time described as being 'born of water and the Spirit'. This expression has been interpreted in various ways, but for reasons outlined below (see Additional Note: being born of water and the Spirit, below) it is probably best interpreted to mean the same as being born again / from above. Once again, then, Jesus was saying to Nicodemus that being born a Jew will not guarantee entrance to the kingdom; he must be born from above, born of water and the Spirit.

Additional Note: Being born of water and the Spirit

There have been four main ways in which this expression has been interpreted:

---

[1] There are only three exceptions: Lk. 1:3, 'from the beginning', Acts 26:5, 'for a long time', Gal. 4:9, 'again'.

1. Baptism in water by John the Baptist and baptism in the Spirit by Jesus. In support of this view is the fact that all previous references to 'water' in this Gospel relate to John's baptizing ministry (1:26, 31, 33), and in 1:33 his baptizing ministry with water is compared to Jesus' baptizing ministry with the Spirit. Accordingly, Jesus is saying that entrance to the kingdom involves submission to John's baptism with water for repentance and Jesus' baptism with the Spirit.

2. Christian water baptism and spiritual regeneration. In support of this view it can be said that the original readers of this Gospel would have seen in the reference to water an allusion to Christian baptism (rather than John's baptism), and so the reference to being born of water and the Spirit would denote submission to Christian baptism, which in the early church was connected with the reception of the Spirit (Acts 2:38).

3. Natural birth and spiritual regeneration. Being born of water is a metaphor for natural human birth, water being an allusion either to amniotic fluid or semen, so Jesus was saying that to enter the kingdom one must be born spiritually as well as physically; by the Spirit as well as by water. In support of this view is the fact that in 3:6 Jesus contrasts being born of the flesh (physical birth) with being born of the Spirit (spiritual regeneration).

4. Spiritual regeneration alone is depicted with a double metaphor. In support of this view is the fact that elsewhere in this Gospel water functions as a metaphor for the Spirit (4:10, 13–15; 7:38) as it also does in places in the OT (*e.g.* Ezk. 36:25–27). The expression 'water and the Spirit' is a hendiadys, a figure of speech using two different words to denote one thing, something suggested by the fact that both 'water' and 'Spirit' are anarthrous (without the article) and governed by the one preposition (lit. 'of water and spirit', *ex hydatos kai pneumatos*).[1] Jesus is saying that to enter the kingdom one must be born of water, *i.e.* of the Spirit. This view is also supported by the fact that in this passage Jesus uses a

[1]Cf. Tit. 3:5: 'he saved us, not because of righteous things we had done, but because of his mercy. He saved us through the washing of rebirth and renewal by the Holy Spirit', where 'the washing of rebirth and renewal by the Holy Spirit' is also a hendiadys.

number of parallel expressions that are all related to seeing and entering the kingdom: 3:3: 'born again / from above'; 3:5: 'born of water and the Spirit'; 3:7: 'born again / from above'; 3:8: 'born of the Spirit'. If all these expressions are in fact parallel and synonymous, then to be 'born again / from above' and to be 'born of water and the Spirit' mean the same as to be 'born of the Spirit'.

6. In this verse Jesus explains why it is necessary for people to be born again / from above to see/enter the kingdom, and why this has nothing to do with natural birth: *Flesh gives birth to flesh, but the Spirit gives birth to spirit*. The physical only gives birth to the physical. What is required is spiritual birth, effected by the Spirit. This is foreshadowed in the Prologue (1:13).

7-8. Nicodemus was surprised and puzzled by these words. Jesus, continuing to address him personally, but expanding the scope of what he said to include all those represented by Nicodemus, said, *You* (sing.) *should not be surprised at my saying, 'You* (pl.) *must be born again.'* Jesus then provided an analogy to help Nicodemus understand: *The wind blows wherever it pleases. You* (sing.) *hear its sound, but you* (sing.) *cannot tell where it comes from or where it is going. So it is with everyone born of the Spirit.* This statement involves a play on words. The Greek word *pneuma* can mean 'wind', 'breath' or 'spirit'.[1] This coincidence makes it easy to draw the comparison between the effects of the wind and the work of the Spirit. Just as people cannot see where the wind comes from or where it is going but can hear its sound, so too people cannot understand how they are born of the Spirit but nevertheless experience its reality in their lives.[2] This is a reminder for us not to tie the experience of being born of the Spirit to particular evangelistic formulae, but to recognize the ways of the Spirit with different people may be different, though always, as this Gospel makes abundantly clear, connected with faith in Jesus Christ.

---

[1] *Pneuma* is used in the LXX to translate *rûaḥ*, which likewise means 'wind', 'breath' or 'spirit'.

[2] Similar teaching is found in Eccl. 11:5: 'As you do not know the path of the wind,/or how the body is formed in a mother's womb,/so you cannot understand the work of God,/the Maker of all things.'

9–10. Jesus' explanation left Nicodemus deeply mystified: *'How can this be?' Nicodemus asked.* Jesus then chided Nicodemus for his inadequacies as a teacher: *'You* (sing.) *are Israel's teacher,' said Jesus, 'and do you* (sing.) *not understand these things?'* As a Pharisee, a member of the Sanhedrin (1), and a teacher of Israel, Nicodemus occupied a position of great responsibility. If anyone should have understood religious truth, it was Nicodemus, and yet he could not understand the most basic requirement for entry to the kingdom of God – what it means to be born of the Spirit. Regeneration by the Spirit is not an uncommon theme in the OT (see Is. 44:3; Is. 59:21; Ezk. 11:19, 20; 36:26–27; Joel 2:28–29; Ps. 51:10), and Jesus expected the revered teacher of Israel to understand these things. Nicodemus, of course, was not alone in this shortcoming. Jesus accused other Pharisees of being people who claimed to see but were in fact blind (9:39–41).

11. Using the solemn introductory formula again, Jesus addressed Nicodemus personally: *I tell you* (sing.) *the truth (amēn amēn legō soi)*, and then broadened his remarks (using first- and second-person plurals) to identify himself with his Father[1] in what he says and to direct his remarks both to Nicodemus and those whom he represented, the Jewish Sanhedrin: *we speak of what we know, and we testify to what we have seen, but still you people do not accept our testimony.* Jesus came into the world to make his Father known, to testify to the truth, and to offer eternal life. When Jesus spoke of these things, he was testifying to what he knew, to what he had seen. To this point in the story Nicodemus and those whom he represented had not accepted Jesus' testimony.

---

[1] Jesus speaks in the first-person plural four times elsewhere in this Gospel with three different meanings: (1) when telling the woman at the well that unlike the Samaritans 'we (Jews) worship what we do know, for salvation is from the Jews' (4:22); (2) when speaking to his disciples and reminding them that 'we must do the work of him who sent me' (9:4); and (3) when praying to his Father that his disciples may be one 'as we are one' (17:11, 22). In the context of 3:11 the first option is out of place, leaving as possibilities that Jesus' use of 'we' here could denote either Jesus and his disciples or Jesus and his Father. As there is no indication that the disciples are in view in Jesus' conversation with Nicodemus, it is best to take the 'we' to denote Jesus and his Father. This is in line with the fact that Jesus repeatedly says he speaks in the name of his Father and says what his Father commissions him to say (8:28; 12:49; 14:10; 15:15). It has also been suggested that Jesus' use of 'we' here is a parody of Nicodemus' use of 'we' in 3:2 when he said 'we know you are a teacher who has come from God', but this is too far back in the account to influence the thought in 3:11.

12. Continuing to address Nicodemus and those he represented, Jesus said, *I have spoken to you* (pl.) *of earthly things and you* (pl.) *do not believe; how then will you* (pl.) *believe if I speak of heavenly things?* He had already spoken of 'earthly things', the need to be born of the Spirit – something experienced in this world and the condition for entry to the kingdom. Nicodemus and his associates were not yet ready to accept these things. 'How then', Jesus asked, 'will you believe if I speak of heavenly things?' The 'heavenly things' are things that have to do with the heavenly world (as opposed to this world).[1]

13. Jesus explained his unique qualifications to speak of heavenly things: *No-one has ever gone into heaven except the one who came from heaven – the Son of Man.* Jesus identified himself as the heavenly figure of great sovereign authority, the Son of Man (see Additional Note: 'The Son of Man', pp. 89–91), who came down from heaven, and therefore was qualified to speak authoritatively of heavenly things. At the same time he rejected all Jewish speculations about other 'revealers' who were thought to have ascended to heaven (*e.g.* Abraham, Moses, Enoch and Isaiah) to return with revelations for those on earth (*cf.* Pr. 30:4).

14–15. Having come down from heaven, Jesus, the Son of Man, will be lifted up again, but in a paradoxical way: *Just as Moses lifted up the snake in the desert, so the Son of Man must be lifted up.* The allusion is to Numbers 21:4–9, which records an incident in the wilderness experience of Israel when the people turned against Moses and God. The Lord sent venomous snakes which bit the people so that many died. Those remaining alive confessed their sin to Moses and implored him to intercede for them. When Moses prayed, the Lord told him, 'Make a snake and put it up on a pole; anyone who is bitten can look at it and live' (Nu. 21:8).

As Moses lifted up the snake, so Jesus will be lifted up. The verb 'to lift up' (*hypsoō*) is used five times in the Fourth Gospel (3:14

---

[1] The word 'heavenly' (*epouranios*) is found only here in the Gospels, but occurs another eighteen times in the Pauline letters and Hebrews (1 Cor. 15:40 [2×], 48 [2×], 49; Eph. 1:3, 20; 2:6; 3:10; 6:12; Phil. 2:10; 2 Tim. 4:18; Heb. 3:1; 6:4; 8:5; 9:23; 11:16; 12:22), always in contexts where the heavenly realm is in view, and nearly always contrasting the heavenly world with this world.

[2×]; 8:28; 12:32, 34), and in every case it is used as an allusion to Jesus' crucifixion.[1] As the lifting up of the snake in the desert was God's provision for salvation from physical death for rebellious Israelites, so too the lifting up of the Son of Man (his crucifixion) will be God's provision for salvation from eternal death for people from all nations, so *that everyone who believes in him may have eternal life*. The Israelites bitten by venomous snakes had to believe in God's provision and look to the snake to live. Now God has provided salvation from the consequences of sin for all peoples by the death of his Son, and those who put their faith in Jesus will have eternal life. (See Additional Note: Eternal life, below.) In 3:14–15, then, Jesus answers Nicodemus' question 'How can a man be born when he is old?' The answer is, by believing in Jesus one is born again (*cf.* 1:13) and receives eternal life.

Jesus' conversation with Nicodemus ends at 3:15 (what follows is the evangelist's comment). Nicodemus appears twice more in this Gospel: in 7:45–52, where he raises a question in the Sanhedrin about the judicial processes that were being followed, or better, were not being followed, in deliberations about Jesus, and in 19:38–42, where, with Joseph of Arimathea, he prepares Jesus' body for burial and lays it in the tomb.

Additional Note: Eternal life

The expressions 'life' (*zōē*) and 'eternal life' (*zōē aiōnios*) are used extensively and interchangeably in the Fourth Gospel, being found a total of thirty-six times in thirty-two verses. Most of the occurrences are found in the first part of the Gospel, Jesus' work in the world / the Book of Signs, where the evangelist describes seven signs Jesus performed. These are recorded, he says later, so that 'you may believe that Jesus is the Christ, the Son of God, and that by believing you may have life in his name' (20:31). Thus the theme of eternal life is intimately related to the signs of Jesus, and so to the very purpose of the Gospel.

The nature of eternal life, as it is experienced by humans, is defined in 17:3: 'Now this is eternal life: that they may know you,

---

[1] The lifting up of Jesus on the cross denotes, paradoxically, not only his suffering but also the means of his departure from this world and his return to glory.

the only true God, and Jesus Christ, whom you have sent.' Eternal life is knowing God, but as in the OT this knowledge is not simply knowing information about God; it is having a relationship with him, involving response, obedience and fellowship.

In the Fourth Gospel Jesus employs three primary metaphors in relation to eternal life: (1) *birth*: one experiences eternal life by being born of the Spirit (3–8); (2) *water*: eternal life is likened to water, which quenches thirst (4:14; *cf.* 7:37); (3) *bread*: eternal life is likened to bread, which satisfies hunger (6:27, 35, 48, 51, 53–54).

Eschatologically speaking, 'eternal life' is life of the age (to come), which is the literal meaning of *zōē aiōnios*. Understood in the light of Christ this involves a changed perspective, for eternal life is now understood to be something that may be experienced in part in the present age: 'I tell you the truth, whoever hears my word and believes him who sent me has eternal life and will not be condemned; he has crossed over from death to life' (5:24). This is in line with the nature of primitive Christian eschatology: God's plans were inaugurated through the ministry, death and resurrection of Jesus, and will be consummated at his return as the Son of Man. In the Synoptics this is expressed in terms of the kingdom of God, which is already present but yet to come in its fullness. In Paul it is expressed in terms of salvation – believers are already saved, presently being saved, and yet to be fully saved. But in the Fourth Gospel this primitive Christian eschatology is expressed in terms of eternal life experienced now and consummated in the resurrection.

The source of eternal life is the Father, who has life in himself and has given the Son to have life in himself also (5:26). So the Logos/Jesus may be said to have life in himself (1:4), to be the resurrection and the life (11:25), the way the truth and the life (14:6). It was this life in him which was the light of all people (1:4) and those who follow him 'never walk in darkness, but have the light of life' (8:12).

The mission of Jesus can be stated in terms of eternal life: 'I have come that they may have life, and have it to the full' (10:10); 'For the bread of God is he who comes down from heaven and gives life to the world' (6:33). But this mission of providing eternal life necessitated Jesus laying down his own life for the beneficiaries: 'This bread is my flesh, which I will give for the life of the world' (6:51); 'I am the good shepherd. The good shepherd lays down his life for the sheep' (10:11); 'I lay down my life for the sheep' (10:15).

Eternal life, which Jesus came to provide, is mediated to people through his word: 'I tell you the truth, whoever hears my word and believes him who sent me has eternal life' (5:24); 'the words I have spoken to you are spirit and they are life' (6:63); 'Simon Peter answered him, "Lord, to whom shall we go? You have the words of eternal life"' (6:68). It is by belief in Jesus as he reveals himself through his words that, from the human perspective, people receive eternal life (15–16, 36; 6:40, 47; 20:31). From the divine perspective, people have eternal life because they have been 'born not of natural descent, nor of human decision or a husband's will, but born of God' (1:13).

2. *The evangelist's comments (3:16–21)*

16. Following his account of the conversation between Nicodemus and Jesus, the evangelist comments on its significance in 3:16–21. He begins his comments with the much loved words *For God so loved the world that he gave his one and only Son, that whoever believes in him shall not perish but have eternal life.* Traditionally, the first part of 3:16 has been interpreted to highlight the 'degree' of God's love for the world, *i.e.* 'how much' he loved the world: 'For God so loved the world that he gave his one and only Son'. While it may be said that the degree of God's love for the world is demonstrated in the giving of his Son, this may not be what the evangelist is saying here. The word translated 'so' (understood by most to mean 'so much') is *houtōs*, a word used frequently elsewhere in the Fourth Gospel, never to denote degree (how much) but always manner (in what way) (8, 14; 4:6; 5:21, 26; 7:46; 11:48; 12:50; 13:25; 14:31; 15:4; 18:22; 21:1).

Further, *houtōs*, indicating 'in what way', always refers back to something previously mentioned, not something about to be explained.[1] Allowing these things to guide us, we should translate the first part of 3:16 as follows: 'For in this way (referring to

---

[1]There is only one exception to this (21:1), but in this case the context makes it clear *houtōs* refers to what follows.

something already mentioned) God loved the world . . .' An understanding of the way God loved the world, then, is to be sought in the preceding verses, 3:14–15, where Jesus speaks of the Son of Man being 'lifted up' as the snake was lifted up on the pole by Moses. This means that the rest of 3:16 really belongs with what follows in 3:17. Thus the thought of 3:14–17 may be set out as follows, the two main clauses being in italics:

Just as Moses lifted up the snake in the desert,
in the same way the Son of Man must be lifted up,
   that everyone who believes in him may have eternal life,
      for in this way God loved the world;

And so [as a consequence of this love] he gave his one and only Son,
   that whoever believes in him shall not perish but have
      eternal life, for God did not send his Son into the world
         to condemn the world,
            but to save the world through him.

There are no great theological differences between this approach and the more traditional approach to these verses. However, it is closer to what the evangelist actually wrote in this passage.

When the evangelist says 'for God so loved the world', the word 'world' signifies humanity in general. It was God's love for all humanity that led him to give his 'one and only' (*ton mongenē*) Son. In some older translations *monogenēs* is translated as 'only begotten', but this is misleading, for the word *monogenēs* emphasizes uniqueness, not 'begottenness' (see Additional Note: *Monogenēs*, pp. 70–71). What the text is saying, therefore, is that God had only one Son, and because of his love for humanity he gave him to make eternal life available to the world.

The purpose for giving his only Son was so 'that whoever believes in him shall not perish but have eternal life'. To 'have eternal life' is to know God, *i.e.* be in relationship with him and experience all the blessings which flow from that, both in the present age and the age to come. In the Fourth Gospel these involve fellowship with God now and a share in the age to come (see Additional Note: Eternal life, pp. 111–113). 'To perish' means to miss out on these blessings, both now and in the age to come, because the wrath of God remains upon us (36).

On the human side, the key to experiencing eternal life is believing. The word 'to believe' (*pisteuō*) is used in a number of ways in the Fourth Gospel, but in 3:16 it denotes believing in the person of Jesus. However, this cannot be divorced from belief in his words, because knowledge of his person is mediated through his words.

17. To explain further the gracious act of God in giving his one and only Son, the evangelist adds, *For God did not send his Son into the world to condemn the world, but to save the world through him.* The idea of being sent is found in several places in the Fourth Gospel. However, it does not necessarily carry the idea of being sent into this world from outside. Speaking to his Father, and referring to his disciples, Jesus says, 'As you sent me into the world, I have sent them into the world' (17:18). In this context, to be 'sent into the world' means to be commissioned for a ministry to the people of the world; it does not mean entering the world from the outside. A couple of other texts are susceptible to the same interpretation (6:14; 11:27). However, there is one text which clearly implies that Jesus entered this world from the outside: 'I came from the Father and entered the world; now I am leaving the world and going back to the Father' (16:28). Finally, there are several other texts where the meaning of being sent into the world or coming into the world could be construed either way (1:9; 3:17, 19; 9:39; 10:36; 12:46; 18:37). The upshot of all this is that when in 3:17 the evangelist says 'God did not send his Son into the world to condemn the world' he could be alluding either to Jesus entering the world from the outside or his being commissioned to ministry on behalf of the people of the world (or both).

The evangelist says that 'God did not send his Son into the world to condemn the world'. There are three places in the Gospel where similar assertions are made (8:15, 26; 12:47), but there are also two places which imply that Jesus does pass judgment on people (5:22, 30). How shall we explain the apparent contradiction? The answer appears to be that in this world Jesus did not pass judgment upon people, because his purpose in coming into the world was to save, not condemn. However, having carried out that commission, the Father has now put into his hands the responsibility for the final judgment (5:22), and on the last day the very words Jesus spoke in this world will condemn those who rejected them (12:48). In a sense such people stand condemned already by their own refusal to believe in God's Son (18) (see Additional Note: Judgment, pp. 117–118). What that condemnation involves is not clearly spelt out but there are some statements that provide clues. Those who reject Christ and do evil are said (1) to forfeit life because God's wrath remains on them (36); (2) to die in their sins, *i.e.* to die unforgiven, and therefore to bear the consequences of their sins themselves (8:21, 24); and (3) to rise from the dead only to be condemned (5:29).

Jesus did not come into the world to condemn the world, but 'to save the world'. The word 'to save' (*sōzō*) is found only six times in the Fourth Gospel (17; 5:34; 10:9; 11:12; 12:27, 47), and of these only four relate directly to the salvation Jesus came to bring. Also of these, only three throw light on what it means to be saved. It is the opposite of being condemned (17; 12:47) and involves coming under the care of the good shepherd (10:9). The reason for the relative scarcity of salvation language in the Fourth Gospel is that the evangelist uses another set of concepts to express his understanding of salvation, *i.e.* eternal life consummated in resurrection, and these concepts pervade his Gospel (15, 16, 36; 4:14; 5:24, 29, 39, 40; 6:27, 33, 40, 47, 51, 54, 68; 10:10, 28; 11:25; 12:25, 50; 17:2, 3; 20:31).

God's purpose in sending the Son into the world was to save the world 'through him'. What 'through him' means has already been explained in 3:14–15, *i.e.* it was by allowing his Son to be 'lifted up' on the cross that salvation was made available 'through him'. By giving his one and only Son in this way God made provision for the forgiveness of sins so that people might experience eternal life now, culminating in resurrection life in the age to come.

18. In this verse the evangelist makes clear that, viewed from the human side, what distinguishes those who are condemned from those who are not is believing in Jesus: *Whoever believes in him is not condemned, but whoever does not believe stands condemned already*. He then explains why failure to believe is so serious an offence: *because he has not believed in the name of God's one and only Son*. God has given his one and only Son, allowing him to be 'lifted up' for our salvation. To refuse to believe in him, to accept his words and to live by them, is an affront to God himself; and those who affront God in this way, the evangelist says, 'are condemned already' (see commentary on 3:17 for explanation of what it means to be 'condemned').

19. The evangelist spells out the basis for the condemnation of those who do not believe: *This is the verdict: Light has come into the world, but men loved darkness instead of light because their deeds were evil.* Using the noun *krisis* (verdict), which is a cognate of the verb *krinō* (condemn) found in 3:17–18, the evangelist explains that the root cause of the condemnation of unbelievers is their rejection of the light because of their love for the darkness. The reason why people have not welcomed the light is that 'men loved darkness instead of light because their deeds were evil'.

Light and darkness are metaphors that have many and various meanings in the NT. Here the light refers to Jesus himself who came into the world and by his ministry brought the light of truth and righteousness to bear upon all whom he encountered. To be exposed to the light was not comfortable to those who wanted to persist in evil; they preferred not to be associated with Jesus, nor to accept his words – 'they loved darkness instead of light'.

20–21. Two different reactions to Jesus as the light are teased out in these verses: *Everyone who does evil hates the light, and will not come into the light for fear that his deeds will be exposed. But whoever lives by* (lit. 'does') *the truth comes into the light, so that it may be seen plainly that what he has done has been done through God.* People who want to persist in evildoing hate Jesus, for he exposes their wickedness (*cf.* 15:22). But those who want to 'live by the truth' delight in the presence of Jesus and welcome his teaching because it confirms for them that they do what they do through God('s grace). Instead of avoiding Jesus and his teaching like those who want to do evil, they seek him out ('come to the light') to make sure that what they are doing is pleasing to God.

Additional Note: Judgment

The teaching on judgment in the Fourth Gospel is quite complex. God is named as the judge (8:50) but he commits responsibility for judgment to the Son because he is the Son of Man (5:22, 27). However, the Son says that he has not come into the world to judge the world but to save it (17; 12:47) and that he judges no-one (8:15). Those who believe in him are not condemned; they have already passed over from death to life (18; 5:24), but those who do not believe are condemned already because they have rejected the revelation the Son brought into the world (18, 19). This rejection of the revelation reached its zenith in the crucifixion of Jesus, and in that hour the world and the prince of this world was truly judged (12:27-33; cf. 16:11). On the last day the Son will exercise judgment. The dead will hear his voice and rise, some for eternal life, others to be condemned. But even in carrying out this final judgment the Son will act in line with what he hears from the Father and his judgment will be just (5:27-30; cf. 8:16). On that day those who rejected Jesus' word will be judged by that word (12:48).

There is an apparent contradiction in what the Fourth Gospel says about Jesus and judgment. In one place we read that 'God did not send his Son into the world to condemn the world' (17), but other places imply Jesus does pass judgment on people (5:22, 30). The resolution to the apparent contradiction appears to be that in this world Jesus did not pass judgment upon people, because his purpose in coming was to save, not condemn. However, having carried out that commission, the Father has placed in his hands responsibility for the final judgment (5:22). On the last day the very words Jesus spoke in this world will condemn those who rejected him (12:48).

F. THE MINISTRIES OF JOHN THE BAPTIST AND JESUS (3:22-36)

After his comments following the account of the conversation between Jesus and Nicodemus, the evangelist reports the overlapping ministries of Jesus and John. This overlap gave rise to a debate between the disciples of John and a certain Jew concerning ceremonial washing. It also aroused concern on the part of John's disciples that his ministry was being eclipsed by Jesus' ministry, and this in turn prompted John's explanation of the relationship between himself and Jesus.

1. The overlapping ministries of Jesus and John (3:22–24)

22. The evangelist begins by saying, *After this, Jesus and his disciples went out into the Judean countryside, where he spent some time with them, and baptized.* The conversation with Nicodemus had taken place in Jerusalem during the Passover festival (2:13). Sometime after this Jesus left the city with his disciples and went into the Judean countryside, most likely near the Jordan River because there he could baptize. While the evangelist says Jesus baptized, elsewhere he explains that Jesus himself did not do the actual baptizing; it was carried out for him by his disciples (4:1–2). Only the Fourth Gospel mentions that Jesus baptized.

23. This verse explains the location of John's baptizing ministry (which was going on at the same time as Jesus' baptizing ministry) and something of its effects: *Now John also was baptizing at Aenon near Salim, because there was plenty of water, and people were constantly coming to be baptized.* There is uncertainty about the exact locations of Aenon and Salim, but one possible location for 'Aenon near Salim' is about 7 miles east-south-east of Jericho, near the Jordan River, and about 4 miles north of the place where the Jordan enters the Dead Sea. The name 'Aenon' is related to the Hebrew word *'ayin,* meaning 'spring', and this is consistent with the evangelist's comment that John baptized in this place 'because there was plenty of water'. The effectiveness of John's ministry is underlined by the statement 'people were constantly coming to be baptized'.

24. The evangelist explains parenthetically that *This was before John was put in prison.* This appears to be an unnecessary comment, because there is no mention of John being put in prison in the Fourth Gospel. However, Mark 1:14 (*cf.* Mt. 4:12) says, 'After John was put in prison, Jesus went into Galilee, proclaiming the good news of God.' This implies that Jesus began his ministry after John's imprisonment (from which he did not escape). It appears that the Fourth Evangelist was aware of what Mark had written and felt the need to explain to readers of Mark's Gospel that the parallel ministry of John and Jesus occurred prior to John's imprisonment. This reminds us of just how limited the records of

119

Jesus' ministry in the Synoptics (and the Gospel of John) are. There was much that occurred which is not recorded (*cf.* 21:25).

2. The debate between John's disciples and a Jew (3:25–30)

25. Following the parenthetical explanation in 3:24, the evangelist tells of a dispute that arose: *An argument developed between some of John's disciples and a certain Jew over the matter of ceremonial washing.* A more literal rendering of this text is, 'a debate occurred [was precipitated by, *ek*] John's disciples with a Jew concerning (ceremonial) washing'. It appears John's disciples started the argument, but the evangelist does not tell us why they were arguing about ceremonial washing. In the following verse John's disciples tell him that Jesus was baptizing more disciples than he was. Perhaps 'the Jew' had contrasted John's baptizing ministry unfavourably with that of Jesus and this prompted the disciples of John to take issue with him.

26. The evangelist relates their concern: *They came to John and said to him, 'Rabbi, that man who was with you on the other side of the Jordan – the one you testified about – well, he is baptizing, and everyone is going to him.'* This is the only place in the Fourth Gospel (and in any of the Gospels) where anyone other than Jesus is actually addressed as Rabbi. Here it functions as a title of respect for John. The reference to John's earlier testimony about Jesus harks back to 1:28–34, where the evangelist tells how Jesus came to John when he was baptizing at the Jordan. John's disciples were concerned because Jesus was now also baptizing, and 'everyone' was going after him. They were jealous for John's reputation and feared that his star was waning as Jesus' star rose. John's response, recorded in the following verses, is the most important part of the passage 3:22–30.

27. In response *John replied, 'A man can receive only what is given him from heaven.'* 'Given from heaven', of course, means 'given by God'. That all things derive ultimately from God is a principle found in the OT (Dn. 4:17, 25, 32) and reiterated in the NT (1 Cor. 4:7). Later in the Fourth Gospel Jesus says to Pilate, 'You would have no power over me if it were not given to you from above' (19:11).

John, recognizing that ultimately it is God who determines the role a person has, was content with the ministry God had given him and felt no need to promote himself or compete with Jesus.

28. After this general statement, John reminded his disciples of what he had said earlier (1:19–20) in response to questions from the priests and Levites: *You yourselves can testify that I said, 'I am not the Christ but am sent ahead of him.'* John knew that he had been sent ahead of the Christ as a witness to him, and therefore would not claim to be someone he was not.

29–30. John knew that he should point people to Christ and not to himself. To express this he used a marriage analogy: *The bride belongs to the bridegroom.* In the OT the metaphor of the bride/bridegroom is used of the relationship between Israel and God: 'As a bridegroom rejoices over his bride, so will your God rejoice over you' (Is. 62:5; *cf.* Ho. 1 – 2). John would certainly have been aware of the use of the metaphor in the OT, and saw his ministry as pointing Israel to the one to whom she belonged.

To explain his own relationship to Christ John extended his use of the marriage analogy: *The friend who attends the bridegroom waits and listens for him, and is full of joy when he hears the bridegroom's voice.* The background to this is found in Jewish marriage customs according to which the friend of the bridegroom/best man was responsible for leading the bridegroom to his bride and waiting outside the bridal chamber while the marriage was consummated. The reference to the bridegroom's voice refers to the shout of exultation by the bridegroom when he discovers he has married a virgin. The work of the friend of the bridegroom is then complete and he takes pleasure in the bridegroom's joy. Far from feeling jealous, then, as he witnessed the increasing success of Jesus' ministry and the waning of his own, John was able to rejoice that 'everyone is going to him' (26). It is a sign of true godliness and Christian maturity when we can rejoice in the achievements of others.

The exceptional nature of John's character and his understanding of his role is revealed in the fact that he could say, *That joy is mine, and it is now complete.* As he saw the growing popularity of Jesus, his joy, like the joy of a bridegroom's true friend, was now complete. John had fulfilled his purpose in life: to bear witness to

Christ and point people towards him. He summed up the whole matter in the famous words *He must become greater; I must become less*. He saw it as a divine necessity (expressed by the word 'must', *dei*) that Jesus should take precedence over him.

3. The evangelist's comments (3:31–36)

In this final section of chapter 3 the evangelist picks up themes Jesus mentioned in his conversation with Nicodemus, especially those in 3:11–13, and expands upon them.

31. In 3:13 Jesus referred to himself as the Son of Man who came down from heaven. Now the evangelist adds, *The one who comes from above is above all; the one who is from the earth belongs to the earth, and speaks as one from the earth*. The second part of the verse refers to John the Baptist, though it would be equally true as a general statement. It is not a denigration of John, but a way of highlighting the qualitative difference between John and Jesus. Though he was a prophet, John was only a human being, but Jesus was the Son of God come down from heaven. John was one who 'belongs to the earth', and therefore spoke 'as one from the earth'. Jesus said something similar about John when speaking to 'the Jews': 'You have sent to John and he has testified to the truth. Not that I accept human testimony: but I mention it that you may be saved' (5:33–34). John's testimony is 'human testimony': he 'speaks as one from the earth'.[1] The evangelist concludes this verse by reiterating how Jesus was different from John: *The one who comes from heaven is above all*.

32–33. Speaking again about Jesus, the evangelist says, *He testifies to what he has seen and heard, but no-one accepts his testimony*. He picks up something Jesus said in his conversation with Nicodemus: 'we testify to what we have seen, but still you people do not accept our testimony' (11). Jesus came into the world to make his Father known, to testify to the truth and to bring people the offer of eternal

---

[1]Some see this as further evidence that the evangelist was combating a Baptist cult by highlighting the fact that John the Baptist was merely a human being. However, the attitude of the evangelist towards John is elsewhere quite positive – he is one of the true witnesses to Jesus. See commentary on 1:8.

life, but, generally speaking, people did not accept his testimony. The evangelist adds, *The man who has accepted it has certified that God is truthful*. He uses a technical term, 'to certify' or 'to place a seal upon' (*sphragizō*). It is found in commercial documents among the papyri where it denotes the sealing of letters and sacks to guarantee that no-one tampers with the contents. In this verse it is used figuratively as a seal of approval, *i.e.* a person's confirmation of the truthfulness of God.[1] To accept Jesus' testimony is to certify that God is truthful, because Jesus, in his testimony to the world, passes on the message/words given him by God (*cf.* 7:15–18; 8:38, 46–47; 12:49; 14:10, 24; 17:8).

34. The evangelist explains why accepting the words of Jesus certifies that God is truthful: *For the one whom God has sent speaks the words of God*. Since Jesus' words are the words of God, to accept them is to accept that God is truthful. Behind this statement lies the idea of the Jewish 'envoy' of whom it is said, 'a man's envoy is like himself' (Mishnah, *Berakot* 5:5). The actions of a man's envoy were regarded as the action of the man himself.

The term used for 'words' in the expression 'the words of God' is *rhēma*, a term used repeatedly in the Fourth Gospel to denote Jesus' teaching both to believers and unbelievers (34; 5:47; 6:63, 68; 8:20, 47; 10:21; 12:47, 48; 14:10; 15:7; 17:8). Nowhere in this Gospel does it connote a specific word from God for one individual or group, as some claim.

Jesus, 'the one whom God has sent', faithfully speaks the words of God, *for God gives the Spirit without limit*. In context this can only mean that God gave his Spirit to the incarnate Jesus without limit or measure,[2] *i.e.* in a full and unrestricted way. In rabbinic literature is a statement that throws some light on this: 'R. Aha said: "Even the Holy spirit resting on the prophets does so by weight [or measure], one prophet speaking one book of prophecy and another speaking two books"' (*Leviticus Rabbah* 15:2), *i.e.* God

---

[1] Elsewhere in the NT *sphragizō* is used literally of sealing things so that they cannot be seen (Rev. 10:4), not sealing things so that they can be read (22:10), and sealing something up so that it cannot escape (20:3). It is used figuratively of marking people with a sign of identification or ownership (2 Cor. 1:22; Eph. 1:13; 4:30; Rev. 7:3, 4, 5, 8) or approval (Jn. 6:27).

[2] The word 'limit'/'measure' (*metron*) is found only here in the Fourth Gospel, but occurs another thirteen times in the rest of the NT, where it is used both literally (Rev. 21:15, 17) and metaphorically (Mt. 7:2; 23:32; Mk. 4:24; Lk. 6:38; Rom. 12:3; 2 Cor. 10:13; Eph. 4:7, 13, 16) as here.

gave his Spirit by measure to the prophets in accordance with the task he assigned them. If the evangelist is alluding to this sort of teaching, he is saying that God poured out his Spirit upon Jesus in much greater measure than he ever did on the prophets. Because God poured out his Spirit upon Jesus 'without limit', he can speak the words of God, and, when he does, those words are completely trustworthy.

35. The evangelist says, *The Father loves the Son and has placed everything in his hands.* The Father's love for the Son is a recurring theme in this Gospel. The Father gives glory to his Son because he loved him before the foundation of the world (17:24). The Father loves the Son because he lays down his life – to take it up again (10:17). The Father's love for the Son is the pattern for the Father's love for believers (17:26), and the pattern also for Jesus' love for believers (15:9).

In this verse the evangelist implies that the Father's love for the Son is the reason why the Father 'has placed everything in his hands'. As he gave Jesus the Spirit without measure, so he has placed everything else in his hands as well (13:3; 17:7). Elsewhere the evangelist mentions some of the things given by the Father to the Son: responsibility for the judgment (5:22, 27), to have life in himself (5:26), all believers as his possession (6:37, 39; 10:29; 17:6, 9), authority over all people (17:2), the 'name' (17:11, 12), and the glory (17:22, 24).

36. In the light of the Father's great love for the Son, and his having placed everything in his hands, two things follow. First, *whoever believes in the Son has eternal life.* Because the Father loves the Son, all who believe in his Son receive eternal life (see Additional Note: Eternal life, pp. 111–113). The greatest thing we can ever do for God is to believe in the Son whom he loves. Second, *whoever rejects the Son will not see life, for God's wrath remains on him.* The worst thing we can do against God is to reject the Son he loves and whom he gave for our salvation. Those who do this forfeit life, and are exposed instead to the wrath of God.

This is the only occurrence of the word 'wrath' (*orgē*) in the Fourth Gospel. It does occur four times in the Synoptic Gospels: twice where John the Baptist warns unrepentant people coming to him for baptism to flee from the coming wrath (Mt. 3:7; Lk. 3:7), once to describe Jesus' anger towards the stubbornness of Pharisees (Mk. 3:5), and once more when describing the great distress to befall the land of Judea when God's wrath is poured out upon it because its people rejected the Messiah (Lk. 21:23).

The evangelist does not explain here what it means for the wrath of God to remain upon people. Some clarifying comments may be ventured: (1) God's wrath is described as 'remaining' upon people, suggesting that it hangs over all and is only removed in the case of those who believe in his Son. (2) The passage 3:17–21 is probably the best place to seek further light on the wrath of God. While the word 'wrath' is not found in this passage, the words 'condemn'/'judge' and 'condemnation'/'judgment' are found there. Those who believe in Jesus are not condemned, but those who do not believe are condemned already because they have 'not believed in the name of God's one and only Son' (3:18). Those who are condemned are those whose deeds are evil, who hate the light Jesus brings, and refuse to come to the light, preferring the darkness where they hope their evil deeds will not be discovered (19–20). As in 3:36 it is the rejection of the one God loves, his one and only Son, and a refusal to come to him, that attracts condemnation.

G. JESUS AND THE WOMAN OF SAMARIA (4:1–42)

The events described in chapter 3 took place in Jerusalem and Judea. The events of chapter 4 took place in Samaria. This chapter consists of four sections.

1. The setting (4:1–6)

1–2. In 3:25–26 we read John's disciples were concerned because Jesus was also baptizing and everyone was going after him. In 4:1 we are told, *The Pharisees heard that Jesus was gaining and baptizing more disciples than John.*[1] Perhaps the unnamed Jew who

---

[1] The NIV transfers the opening words of 4:1, 'when Jesus / the Lord came to know that' [the Pharisees had heard . . .], to the beginning of 4:3 ('When the Lord learned of this [he left Judea . . .]').

was arguing with the disciples of John (3:25) relayed information about Jesus' baptizing ministry to the Pharisees. The evangelist explains that *in fact it was not Jesus who baptized, but his disciples*. Why he felt it necessary to add this explanation is not clear – perhaps it was to counter unhealthy pride on the part of his readers based on their association with those who had been baptized by Jesus himself. The matter of who was baptized by whom was one of the causes of unhealthy preferences for one leader instead of another in the Corinthian church (1 Cor. 1:11–16).

3. News that the Pharisees had heard this prompted action on Jesus' part: *When the Lord learned of this, he left Judea and went back once more to Galilee*. The evangelist does not explain why this news led Jesus to leave Judea. Perhaps he did not wish to be in competition with John, whose ministry he endorsed (5:32–35; *cf.* Mt. 11:7–15), or his increasingly high profile meant it was necessary for him to avoid premature confrontation with the Pharisees.

4. Describing Jesus' return to Galilee, the evangelist says, *Now he had to go through Samaria*. There were three routes between Jerusalem and Galilee – only one passed through Samaria; the others bypassed it.[1] The normal route taken by Jews travelling between Galilee and Jerusalem was through Samaria. Josephus comments, 'Samaria was now under Roman rule and, for rapid travel, it was essential to take that route, by which Jerusalem may be reached in three days from Galilee' (*Life* 269), and 'It was the custom at the time of a festival [for Galilean Jews] to pass through the Samaritan territory on their way to the Holy City' (*Antiquities* xx.118). Jesus, then, 'had to go through Samaria' because it was the shortest and normal way people travelled between Jerusalem and Galilee. However, in the light of the narrative that follows (the conversation with the Samaritan woman and the Samaritan townspeople coming to believe in him), Jesus' need to go through Samaria may have been determined by the divine will as well as geographical factors (34).

[1] One route was along the Jordan valley, bypassing Samaria to the east; the other involved cutting across to the Mediterranean sea coast and bypassing Samaria to the west. The route Jesus took was the central ridge road passing through the middle of the land, and thus through Samaria.

5. On Jesus' way to Galilee *he came to a town in Samaria called Sychar, near the plot of ground Jacob had given to his son Joseph.* Sychar, usually identified with present-day Askar, is located about a mile south-east of present-day Nablus, and very close to the site of ancient Shechem, which is located at the entrance to the valley separating the two mountains Gerizim and Ebal (Dt. 11:26–32; 27:13 – 28:68). Jacob bequeathed a piece of land near here to his son Joseph, and it was in this land that Joseph's bones were laid to rest when the Israelites came up out of Egypt (Gn. 33:19; Josh. 24:32).

6. The evangelist provides two final pieces of information to set the scene. First, he says *Jacob's well was there.* There is no mention in the OT of Jacob digging such a well, but it does indicate that he owned land in this area (Gn. 33:19). However, to this day there is a deep well at the place. Schnackenburg describes it as follows:

> The well of Jacob, which is still to be seen today in the same place where it was shown to earlier pilgrims, is undoubtedly genuine, though it is not mentioned in the O.T. It is a fine installation, with a cylindrical shaft seven feet in diameter and 106 feet deep driven into the rock and fresh subsoil water at the bottom (like Isaac's well in Gen. 26:19) ringed by a wall on top. There are two holes through which a bucket can be lowered (v. 11) and the water lies near the bottom of the shaft.[1]

Second, the evangelist adds, *Jesus, tired as he was from the journey, sat down by the well. It was about the sixth hour.* If Jesus had been baptizing in the same area as John (3:22, 26) and had left from there heading north-west to Sychar, he had covered a significant distance. As the crow flies, Sychar is about 30 miles from Aenon; but following the Roman roads it was about 40 miles. The journey would take a day and a half, so Jesus and his disciples would arrive in Sychar on the second day at about the sixth hour, *i.e.* about noon. Tired from this journey, Jesus sat down by the well and rested.

---

[1]Schnackenburg, vol. 1, p. 424.

2. Jesus' conversation with the Samaritan woman (4:7–30)

7–8. As Jesus sat by the well, *a Samaritan woman came to draw water*. It is strange that she came at about the sixth hour / noon, the hottest part of the day. Normally, women came to draw water in the morning or evening, the cooler parts of the day (Gn. 24:11; 29:7). It is also strange that she came alone. Both these things suggest the woman felt a sense of shame and was avoiding contact with other women.

Contact was initiated as *Jesus said to her, 'Will you give me a drink?'* In the culture of the day, it was strange for a man to initiate conversation with a woman in public, something noted by Jesus' disciples later (27). The evangelist, either to offer some explanation as to why he asked her for a drink, or simply to set the scene for the private exchange between Jesus and the woman, adds, *His disciples had gone into the town to buy food*. It is at first surprising that the disciples, being Jews, would go to buy food in a Samaritan town, especially in the light of the evangelist's comment in 4:9 ('Jews do not associate with Samaritans'). However, a distinction was made by even the strictest Jews between accepting food given by those considered unclean and buying it from them – the latter being considered appropriate (1QS 5:14–20). Nevertheless, it was a risky thing for the disciples to enter a Samaritan town, as Samaritans did not always welcome Jewish pilgrims travelling through their territory (Lk. 9:51–56).

9. Jesus' request, therefore, was highly unusual. *The Samaritan woman said to him, 'You are a Jew and I am a Samaritan woman. How can you ask me for a drink?'* The evangelist adds in parentheses, *For Jews do not associate with Samaritans*. There was a long and ongoing history of animosity between Jews and Samaritans (see Additional Note: Jews and Samaritans, p. 137), which meant that neither group welcomed contact with the other. Among Jews the name 'Samaritan' was used as a term of abuse for fellow Jews (8:48). The Samaritan woman was, therefore, amazed that Jesus asked her for a drink.

10. Jesus ignored the woman's comment about Jews and Samaritans and cut straight to the chase: *Jesus answered her, 'If you* *knew the gift of God and who it is that asks you for a drink, you would have asked him and he would have given you living water.'* Jesus drew the woman's attention to two important matters – who he was and the gift of God that he was able to give. These two things form the major themes of the conversation that ensues: in 4:10–15 'the gift of God', and in 4:16–26 'who it is that asks you for a drink'.

The gift of God that Jesus gives is living water, and this was the initial topic of their conversation. The word 'gift' (*dōrea*) is found only here in the Gospels, but it is used four times in Acts, always in reference to the gift of the Holy Spirit (Acts 2:38; 8:20; 10:45; 11:17).[1] In the OT God is described as the source of 'living water' (Je. 2:13; 17:13) and also of the Holy Spirit (Is. 44:3). The Samaritan woman would not have picked up these allusions even if she knew the Samaritan Bible, because it contained only the Pentateuch (Genesis–Deuteronomy), but Jesus' mind was soaked in the whole OT. The living water of which he spoke is the gift of the Holy Spirit. He spoke to Nicodemus about being born of the Spirit, to the woman of Samaria he spoke of drinking the living water of the Spirit, and during the Feast of Tabernacles he invited the crowds in Jerusalem to come to him and drink, referring again to the gift of the Spirit (7:37–39).

11–12. The woman's response revealed she did not understand what Jesus was offering her: *'Sir,' the woman said, 'you have nothing to draw with and the well is deep. Where can you get this living water?'* Perhaps she understood his reference to 'living water' to mean water from the underground spring that fed the well. She reminded him how deep the well was (about 100 feet) and pointed out that he had nothing to draw with, implying it was impossible for him to give her 'living water'. This led her to ask, *Are you greater than our father Jacob, who gave us the well and drank from it himself, as did also his sons and his flocks and herds?* The form of the question in the original language indicates a negative answer is expected ('You are not greater than our father Jacob, are you?'). She implied that Jesus thought too highly of himself, as if he were

[1]It is also found in Rom. 5:15, 17, where it refers to the gift of justification, in 2 Cor. 9:15, where it refers to what God has done for us in Christ, in Eph. 3:7; 4:7 and Heb. 6:4 the gift is related to the (work of) the Holy Spirit.

greater even than Jacob who gave them the well and drank from it himself together with his children and animals.

13–14. Jesus chose not to respond to the matters raised by the woman, including the apparent impossibility of his obtaining water for her. Instead, he brought her back to the central issue as far as he was concerned: *Jesus answered, 'Everyone who drinks this water will be thirsty again, but whoever drinks the water I give him will never thirst.'* Those who drink the water from Jacob's well will thirst again. Those who drink the living water Jesus gives, those who receive the gift of the Holy Spirit, will never thirst. Jesus explained why: *Indeed, the water I give him will become in him a spring of water welling up to eternal life.* The gift of the Spirit will be something experienced continually within the very being of those who receive it – like a spring of water welling up within them. The verb used for 'welling up' (*hallomai*) means literally 'to jump up', and in the only other places where it is found in the NT it has that literal meaning (Acts 3:8; 14:10). It is a vivid metaphor for the activity of the Holy Spirit within those who believe in Jesus, reminding us of the experiential as well as the cognitive side of the Christian faith. The fulfilment of this promise (with its future-tense verbs 'I will give', 'will never thirst'; 'I will give', 'will become') awaits the coming of the Spirit following Jesus' exaltation (7:37–39).

Jesus said this water wells up 'for eternal life' (*eis zōēn aiōnion*). Identical expressions are found in 4:36 in relation to those who harvest a crop 'for eternal life', in 6:27 in relation to the food that endures 'to eternal life', and in 12:25 in relation to those who hate their lives in this world but keep them 'for eternal life'. In each case the expression relates to life in the age to come, life in the kingdom of God. In the context of 4:14, then, the living water Jesus promised would well up continually within the believer until it reaches its culmination in the age to come.

In practice what does it mean to 'never thirst'? If the gift of living water refers to the gift of the Spirit, can we say that those who have received the Spirit never thirst? If by this we mean that they never feel any dissatisfaction and always feel content, this is patently untrue. In what way, then, does the Spirit satisfy human thirst in the present time? The answer is found in Jesus' teaching about the Spirit in chapters 14 – 16. There the role of the Spirit is to take Jesus' place in the disciples' lives after he returns to the Father. The Spirit mediates Christ's presence to the disciples, creating a sense of intimacy with the Father and the Son. It is this relationship that lasts 'to eternal life' and it is the human thirst for a relationship with God that the coming of the Spirit satisfies even in the here and now.

15. Responding to the promise of living water that quenches thirst for ever, *The woman said to him, 'Sir, give me this water so that I won't get thirsty and have to keep coming here to draw water.'* Her response indicates two things: first, she was now interested in Jesus' offer; and second, she still did not understand what he meant by 'living water'.

16–18. Jesus did not respond directly to her request. Instead, *He told her, 'Go, call your husband and come back.'* Jesus had touched upon a sore point, for the woman replied, *I have no husband*, to which Jesus responded, *You are right when you say you have no husband. The fact is, you have had five husbands, and the man you now have is not your husband. What you have just said is quite true.* This text has been interpreted in two ways. First, metaphorically so that the woman's past experience with five husbands symbolizes the Samaritan nation languishing under foreign gods. Those adopting this view point to 2 Kings 17:24–33, which tells how, following the deportation of many people from the northern kingdom of Israel, the Assyrians brought in people from five other nations who worshipped their own gods to repopulate the land. It was intermarriage between these people and those of the northern kingdom who were not deported that produced the Samaritan people. The Jews regarded them as a hybrid race and one whose relationship with Yahweh had been compromised. Their unfaithfulness was regarded as religious adultery (in the OT adultery was used as a symbol of Israel's unfaithfulness to Yahweh when she went after other gods). Interpreted along these lines, Jesus' words to the woman allude to the Samaritans' previous worship of the gods of the five nations. However, the evangelist did not intend Jesus' words to be understood in this way, for, as he unfolds the story, Jesus sends the woman away to get her husband

131

and then return – something that needs to be taken literally, not metaphorically. (It has also been noted that although people from five nations were brought in to repopulate the land, the gods they worshipped as listed in 2 Kings 17:30–31 were seven, not five.)

Second, the text has been interpreted literally, and this approach is the correct one. Nevertheless, it can still be understood in different ways. The word translated 'husband' (*anēr*) in the NIV can mean either 'husband' or 'man' (a male). If we take *anēr* to mean 'husband' she could have been married five times and each time her husband had died, or each time she had been divorced (in a society where divorce was almost entirely a male prerogative), and now she was living with a man who was not her husband (meaning someone else's husband). If *anēr* is taken to mean 'a man', it is possible that she had never been married, but had had a series of affairs with men, culminating in a final adulterous relationship. The text does not enable us to determine which of these interpretations is correct. Either way, it seems Jesus' intention in mentioning these things was not to create a sense of guilt, but to confront the pain in her relationships with men. This would accentuate her thirst for a meaningful relationship with God and make her receptive to the revelation he was offering her.

The striking thing about all this is not the number of husbands or lovers this woman had lived with, nor even that the man she now had was not her husband, but that Jesus had such knowledge about her personal life. This is another illustration of what the evangelist says in 2:24–25: 'Jesus . . . knew all men. He did not need man's testimony about man, for he knew what was in a man.' Jesus' supernatural knowledge, revealed in his understanding of Nathanael (1:48) and the Jews who 'believed' in him (2:24), is revealed again in the case of the woman of Samaria. This is what the evangelist focuses upon as he continues his narrative.

19. In response to Jesus' supernatural knowledge of her personal life, *'Sir,' the woman said, 'I can see that you are a prophet.'* She realized that Jesus was no ordinary Jew – only a prophet would have such supernatural knowledge. The Samaritans were looking for the coming of 'the Prophet' (Dt. 18:15), whom they identified as the Taheb, the Samaritan Messiah. Maybe the woman was wondering whether Jesus might be this prophet/ Messiah. Later she would say to her fellow townspeople, 'Come, see a man who told me everything I ever did. Could this be the Christ [Messiah]?' (29).

20. Regarding Jesus as a prophet, she said to him, *Our fathers worshipped on this mountain, but you Jews claim that the place where we must worship is in Jerusalem.* There was one great matter of disagreement between Jews and Samaritans, and it went back several centuries (see Additional Note: Jews and Samaritans, p. 137) and was related to the proper place to worship God. The woman speaks in this verse, not just for herself, but for the Samaritan people (using the first-person plural: 'our fathers') and puts their views over against those of the Jewish people (using the second-person plural: 'you [Jews]'). 'This mountain' refers to Mount Gerizim, which was in view as she spoke to Jesus at Sychar, and on which the Samaritan temple had been built (*c.* 388 BC) to rival the Jerusalem temple as a place of worship. Even to this day a small community of Samaritans worship God on Mount Gerizim near present-day Nablus. The Jews, on the other hand, insisted that only in Jerusalem should people worship God. This belief went back to the promise that God would choose a place to put his name, and there people should come to worship him; and this place was Jerusalem, Mount Zion (Dt. 12:4–7, 21; 14:22–26; 1 Ki. 14:21; 2 Ch. 12:13). The woman's statement contains an implied question – what do you think about the ancient disagreement between Samaritans and Jews?

21. Jesus did not answer the implied question immediately. First, he foreshadowed a new day: *Jesus declared, 'Believe me, woman, a time is coming when you will worship the Father neither on this mountain nor in Jerusalem.'* The question of the correct place to worship would soon be irrelevant, for the times were about to change. Worship would no longer be localized in a sacred place. This should caution us about thinking the worship of God is tied to sacred places today, whether that be in church buildings, holy cities (Jerusalem, Rome or Canterbury) or holy sites (the Church of the Nativity, the Church of the Holy Sepulchre *etc.*). It is good to visit these places to gain historic perspective and increase our sense of the reality of what we believe, but to think that one's worship of God is more acceptable in such places, or that we are somehow closer to God in these places, is to deny the truth of Jesus' teaching in this and the following verses.

22. Jesus now responded directly to the implied question in 4:20: *You Samaritans worship what you do not know; we worship what we do know, for salvation is from the Jews.* The plural forms used by Jesus ('you Samaritans' and 'we [Jews]') show that his remarks related to the Samaritan people and the Jewish people in the same way as the implied question of the woman did. Jesus insisted that Samaritan worship on Mount Gerizim was worship based upon ignorance. Jewish worship in Jerusalem was based on knowledge because it was in line with the revelation of God to his people. They worshipped at the place God himself had chosen. Jesus also insisted that God's purposes for salvation were being worked out through the Jewish people, not the Samaritans. No matter how much grace Jesus was to show to the Samaritan woman, it would not be at the expense of truth.

23. Having made plain that the Jews had the rights of the matter as far as worship was concerned, Jesus returned to the theme of 4:21 (a new day is coming) when he said, *Yet a time is coming and has now come when the true worshippers will worship the Father in spirit and truth, for they are the kind of worshippers the Father seeks.* The 'time' that was coming was the time when true worshippers would no longer need to go to Jerusalem, for Jesus' death, resurrection and sending of the Spirit would usher in the new way of worship. This time could be said loosely to have 'now come' because Jesus had already set in motion things that would bring in the new worship in spirit and truth.

Worship 'in spirit and truth' is easy to understand negatively: worship is no longer tied to sacred sites. It is harder to say what it means positively. Most likely it means worship through the Holy Spirit, whom Jesus would give to those who believed in him, and in accordance with the truth of God as it has been made known through the person and teaching of Jesus. The Father seeks people who will worship him in the Spirit and in accordance with the teaching of Jesus. This is a reminder that worship is not restricted to what we do when we come together in church, but about the way we relate to God through the Spirit and in accordance with the teaching of Jesus, and that touches the whole of life.

24. There is another reason why this new form of worship is necessary: *God is spirit, and his worshippers must worship in spirit and in truth.* The evangelist is not defining the essence of God, but rather showing that God is of a different order to human beings, and therefore worship must be 'in spirit and in truth'. To say this, reinforces Jesus' words to Nicodemus – that to see/enter the kingdom of God one must be born of the Spirit. That which is born of the flesh is flesh; that which is born of the Spirit is spirit. Only as people are born of the Spirit, only as they receive the gift of the Spirit, can they truly worship God who is spirit.

25–26. In response, *The woman said, 'I know that Messiah' (called Christ) 'is coming. When he comes, he will explain everything to us.'* It was all too difficult for her to understand. She would have to wait for the arrival of the Samaritan Messiah/Taheb to explain everything. *Then Jesus declared, 'I who speak to you am he.'* Literally Jesus said, 'I am (*egō eimi*), the one speaking to you.' Sometimes in the Fourth Gospel *egō eimi* stands for the divine name (8:58; 18:5–6), but in this context it simply means, 'I am he' (the Messiah) (see Additional Note: *Egō eimi*, p. 138). It is striking that Jesus revealed himself as Messiah to a Samaritan woman who had her own (Samaritan) beliefs about the Messiah. While Jesus believed the Samaritans were mistaken about a number of things and said that salvation 'was from the Jews' (22), he recognized the longings of the Samaritan people would be satisfied (they would only find 'living water') and they would be able to offer true worship only by putting their trust in him, the Jewish Messiah.

27. The conversation between Jesus and the Samaritan woman was interrupted: *Just then his disciples returned and were surprised to find him talking with a woman.* The disciples had been to one of the Samaritan towns to buy food (8) and when they returned were surprised to find Jesus talking with a woman. Such an attitude to women is reflected in the writings of the rabbis: 'One does not speak with a woman in the street, not even with his own wife, and certainly not with another woman, because of people's gossip'

(Str-B 2, 438). However, one should not assume that this statement from the learned writings of the rabbis necessarily reflects the attitude of people in their everyday relationships.[1]

Jesus' attitude to women was different from that of his disciples. He initiated a long and meaningful conversation with the Samaritan woman in public, unconcerned about other people's prejudices. Despite the disciples' surprise, *no-one asked, 'What do you want?' or 'Why are you talking with her?'* Out of deference to their master, the disciples did not question him about his conversation with the woman, but the evangelist makes it clear that in their own minds they wondered what (*ti*) he wanted and what (*ti* can mean 'what' as well as 'why') he was speaking to her about.

28–30. Sensing, perhaps, the negative attitudes of the disciples towards her, *leaving her water jar, the woman went back to the town.* She may have left her water pot so that Jesus could have the drink he requested or so that her return to the town might be carried out more quickly. It also suggests that she intended to return soon and was not completely put off by the disciples' negative attitudes. When she arrived in the town, she *said to the people, 'Come, see a man who told me everything I ever did. Could this be the Christ?'* What the woman did is strange in terms of the culture of the day. Women normally did not converse with men in public, only in the privacy of the home, and certainly they would not mention in public private marital experience or sexual affairs. It was Jesus' supernatural knowledge of her personal life that had impressed the woman, and this led her to conclude he was a prophet (16–19). Then Jesus had revealed himself to her as the Messiah (26). Deeply impressed by these things, she went back to the town and urged her fellow townspeople to come and see the man who was able to tell her everything she had ever done, asking whether this could really be the Christ. This question is tentative in form ('this man

[1] It is possible the disciples thought Jesus' contact with the Samaritan woman would render him 'unclean'. The Mishnah says, 'The daughters of the Samaritans are [deemed unclean as] menstruants from their cradle' (*Niddah* 4:1); but then it goes on to say, 'The daughters of the Sadducees, if they follow after the ways of their fathers, are deemed like to the women of the Samaritans; but if they have separated themselves and follow after the ways of the Israelites, they are deemed to be like to the women of the Israelites' (*Niddah* 4:2). All this suggests that the attitude of the rabbis towards Samaritan women and Sadducean women was rather extreme, and may not at all have been accepted by other people.

cannot be the Christ can he?'), but as the narrative unfolds it becomes clear that the woman was testifying to her belief that he was indeed the Christ (4:42). This section of the narrative concludes with a word about the townspeople's response to the woman's testimony: *They came out of the town and made their way towards him.* Before recounting what happened when they met Jesus, the evangelist tells about the return of the disciples (31–38).

Additional Note: Jews and Samaritans

The roots of the animosity between Samaritans and Jews go deep into history. In the eighth century BC when the northern kingdom of Israel fell to the Assyrians, the majority of the population was carried into exile. To repopulate the area the Assyrians brought in peoples from other parts of their empire, and these intermarried with those still left in the land, resulting in a mixed race of peoples later known as the Samaritans.

In the sixth century BC the southern kingdom of Judah was overrun by the Babylonians, and many of its people were taken into exile in Babylon. Later the Babylonian kingdom fell to the Persians, and Cyrus, king of Persia, allowed exiles from Judah to return to Jerusalem, where they began to rebuild the temple and later to repair the walls of Jerusalem. Those returning to rebuild were now called Jews; the Samaritans offered to assist them in rebuilding the temple but their offer was rejected. Having been rebuffed the Samaritans built their own rival temple on Mount Gerizim in Samaria. The Jews regarded the Samaritans as ethnically impure and repudiated them, and in the time of Ezra and Nehemiah marriages that had been contracted between Jews and Samaritans were broken up.

In the following centuries, down to and beyond the time of Jesus, there was much animosity between Jews and Samaritans. A number of incidents illustrate this. In 128 BC the Jewish king John Hyrcanus destroyed the Samaritans' temple. Between AD 6 to 9 Samaritans defiled the Jerusalem temple during Passover by scattering dead men's bones in it. In AD 52 pilgrims from Galilee travelling through Samaria *en route* to Jerusalem were massacred by Samaritans, and during the Jewish–Roman war of AD 66–70 Jewish rebels razed the city of Samaria to the ground.

Additional Note: *Egō eimi*

Jesus uses the *egō eimi* formula in three different ways in the Fourth Gospel: (1) With a *predicate*: 'I am the bread of life' (6:35, 41, 48, 51), 'I am the light of the world' (8:12), 'I am the gate for the sheep' (10:7, 9), 'I am the good shepherd' (10:11, 14), 'I am the resurrection and the life' (11:25), 'I am the way and the truth and the life' (14:6), and 'I am the true vine' (15:1, 5). (2) With an *implied predicate*: 'I am [he]', 'I am [the one]' indicating he is the Messiah (4:26; 8:24, 28; 13:19), and 'It is [I]' and 'I am [he]' simply to identify himself (6:20; 18:8, and possibly 18:5, 6, 8), as did the man born blind (9:9). (3) As an *absolute*, possibly in 8:24, 28; 18:5–6, and certainly in 8:58: 'before Abraham was born, I am!' The last of these uses needs further comment, for in this case *egō eimi* represents the divine name. In Exodus 3:14 God says to Moses, 'I AM WHO I AM. This is what you are to say to the Israelites: "I AM has sent me to you."' The 'I AM WHO I AM' is translated as *egō eimi ho ōn* in the LXX. In Isaiah 43:25; 51:12 *egō eimi* on its own functions as the divine name. Thus when Jesus said to 'the Jews', 'before Abraham was born, I am', he was identifying himself with God. He was not only pronouncing the name of God, which Jews normally did not dare to utter, but, even worse, he was claiming to be God.

3. *Jesus instructs his disciples (4:31–38)*

31–33. Picking up the story after the woman returned to the town, the evangelist says, *Meanwhile his disciples urged him, 'Rabbi, eat something.'* They had returned from one of the Samaritan towns with food they had bought (8) and they urged Jesus to eat some. *But he said to them, 'I have food to eat that you know nothing about.'* This bewildered them, so *then his disciples said to each other, 'Could someone have brought him food?'* Had he received food during their absence, maybe from a Samaritan, but surely not the Samaritan woman?

34. The disciples' consternation provided opportunity for Jesus to explain, *'My food,' said Jesus, 'is to do the will of him who sent me and to finish his work.'* The 'food' he had, which they knew nothing about, was doing his Father's will and completing the work he had given him to do. This was Jesus' whole purpose in coming into the world (6:38; 9:4; 17:4). Jesus was saying that the most satisfying thing for him, his 'food and drink' as it were, was doing his Father's will and completing his work. This statement throws light on the evangelist's words in 4:4 ('he had to go through Samaria'). Jesus had a divine appointment to keep with a needy woman and the Samaritan townspeople. They would accept the good news, which would bring them salvation. Satisfaction for us, as for Jesus, comes more from pursuing the will of God than from meeting our various physical needs (important as they are).

35. Continuing to instruct his disciples, Jesus said, *Do you not say, 'Four months more and then the harvest'?* From the time of autumn sowing to the beginning of the grain harvest was about six months, although the time between the last of the sowing and the beginning of harvest could be only four months. However, it was not Jesus' intention to discuss agricultural matters with his disciples.[1] He was speaking metaphorically, and wanted to draw his disciples' attention to the imminence of a gospel harvest among the Samaritans. So he said, *I tell you, open your eyes and look at the fields! They are ripe for harvest.* Jesus was probably referring to the Samaritan townspeople making their way towards him after hearing the woman's testimony, and was urging his disciples to open their eyes to the significance of what was happening. Harvest time had come!

36–37. Conscious of the approaching townspeople, Jesus said, *Even now the reaper draws his wages, even now he harvests the crop for eternal life, so that the sower and the reaper may be glad together.* Jesus, as the reaper, was already drawing 'his wages', in his case the joy of seeing the harvest being brought in. The idea of the sower and the reaper being glad together is reminiscent of Amos 9:13: ' "The

---

[1] Jesus' words here should not be used as a marker for establishing a chronology of his ministry. If it were, this Samaritan episode would have taken place four months before the beginning of the grain harvest in March–April, which would place it about December–January. However, other indications the evangelist provides in this section of his Gospel (2:1 – 4:54) seem to place the incident shortly after the conclusion of the Passover festival in March–April (see 2:13, 23; 3:22–26; 4:1–3, 40, 43, 45, 46–47, 54).

days are coming," declares the LORD, / "when the reaper will be overtaken by the ploughman / and the planter by the one treading grapes,"' a text that depicts the coming age as one of great fertility. With the coming of Jesus this new age was inaugurated, so that 'even now he harvests the crop for eternal life' among the Samaritans. His conversation with the woman and her testimony to the townspeople were leading even now to belief in him, and that would mean eternal life for them.

Jesus then said, *Thus the saying 'One sows and another reaps' is true.* If Jesus was the reaper, who was the sower? It was not his disciples – they had nothing to do with this work. Some suggest it was John the Baptist, but there is no evidence that he preached among Samaritans. Others suggest it is a reference to the work of OT prophets, but which of them laboured among the Samaritans? Another suggestion is that the Father was the sower and his Son the reaper. This would be consistent with the theme of the co-operation of the Son in the work of the Father in this Gospel. Alternatively, the saying could be regarded as a general statement meaning that those who labour in the initial proclamation of the kingdom will rejoice with those whose proclamation leads people ultimately to commitment. That it is a general statement is supported by the fact that in the next verse Jesus applies it to his disciples.

38. Addressing his disciples, Jesus said, *I sent you to reap what you have not worked for. Others have done the hard work, and you have reaped the benefits of their labour.* While the Fourth Gospel does not refer to the Galilean mission of the Twelve recorded in the Synoptic Gospels (Mt. 10:1–15; Mk. 6:7–13; Lk. 9:1–6), in 4:38 the evangelist seems to assume knowledge of their mission. If so, by alluding to that mission, Jesus was reminding his disciples of its purpose – to harvest a crop sown by others. There is evidence that the disciples' mission was successful (Lk. 10:17–20), but from whose prior labours did they benefit? John the Baptist had been commissioned to prepare the way for Jesus' mission (1:19–23), and when Jesus sent out the Twelve their mission was an extension of his. Those from whose labours the disciples benefited, then, could be John and his disciples (and we might add Jesus himself).

4. Jesus and the Samaritan townspeople (4:39–42)

39–41. The evangelist describes the effect of the Samaritan woman's witness: *Many of the Samaritans from that town believed in him because of the woman's testimony, 'He told me everything I ever did.'* She told her fellow townspeople about Jesus' supernatural knowledge about her past and suggested that he might be the Messiah. This led many to believe in Jesus. As a result they came out to meet Jesus for themselves. The evangelist continues, *So when the Samaritans came to him, they urged him to stay with them, and he stayed two days.* They were obviously impressed with him and prevailed upon him to stay in their town. That Samaritans should welcome Jesus in this way is remarkable when we remember the centuries of hostility between the two groups (see Additional Note: Jews and Samaritans, p. 137). It underlines the dramatic effect upon the townspeople of both the woman's testimony and their own encounter with Jesus. The evangelist indicates that the latter was more important than the former: *And because of his words many more became believers.*

42. The Samaritan townspeople stressed the importance of their own encounter with Jesus when *they said to the woman, 'We no longer believe just because of what you said; now we have heard for ourselves and we know that this man really is the Saviour of the world.'* It is noteworthy that the townspeople were willing to accept the testimony of a woman (contrast the attitude of the apostles to the reports of the women in Lk. 24:11 that Jesus had risen: 'they did not believe the women, because their words seemed to them like nonsense').

In accepting Jesus as Saviour the Samaritans had accepted the thrust of Jesus' earlier statement to the woman that 'salvation is from the Jews' (22). They were now convinced that he was 'the Saviour of the world', *i.e.* he came to bring the water of life to all people, Samaritans as well as Jews (see Additional Note: The Saviour of the world, p. 142). While the evangelist uses the word 'saviour' (*sōtēr*) only here in his Gospel, he speaks elsewhere of Jesus coming to save the world (3:17; 12:47). It is an important theme he wants his readers to understand and believe.

Additional Note: The Saviour of the world

The expression 'Saviour of the world' (*sōtēr tou kosmou*) is found only twice in the NT, here in 4:42 and in 1 John 4:14. In 4:42 the expression 'Saviour of the world' carries the sense that Jesus is the Saviour of all people, Samaritans as well as Jews. It is as Saviour *of the world* that he was recognized. This is in line with the purpose of the evangelist to acquaint his readers with the true identity of Jesus so that, believing in him, they might enjoy life in his name.

However, the concerns of 1 John are different from those of the Fourth Gospel. The background to 1 John was strife within the Johannine Christian community. The question of whether Jesus was the Saviour *of the world* was not the issue. The issue was whether Jesus should be recognized as *Saviour* at all. In particular, was belief in Jesus' death as an atoning sacrifice for sin necessary? Those who had seceded from the author's community denied they had sinned (see 1 Jn. 1:6 – 2:2) and argued that Jesus' atoning death was unnecessary and did not take place (see 1 Jn. 5:6–8). Those who with the author acknowledged their sins, confessed the importance of Jesus' atoning sacrifice, which provided cleansing from their sins. They confessed that the Father 'sent his Son to be the *Saviour* of the world'.

It is possible that the form of the Samaritans' confession that Jesus was 'the Saviour of the world' owes something to the way people thought of the Roman emperors. There is evidence that the emperors Julius Caesar, Augustus, Tiberius, Claudius, Nero, Titus, Vespasian, Trajan and Hadrian were all addressed in various ways as the 'saviour of the world'.[1] It may be that the Samaritans were recognizing that Jesus, not the emperor, was the true Saviour of the world. The evangelist does depict Jesus as the true king: Nathanael addressed him as the king of Israel (1:49), and before Pilate Jesus acknowledged that he was a king, although his kingship was not of this world (18:33–38).

[1]See Koester, p. 67.

H. THE HEALING OF THE ROYAL OFFICIAL'S SON (4:43–54)

43–44. Jesus stayed with the Samaritan townspeople for just a short while, then *after the two days he left for Galilee*. Next the evangelist foreshadows the reception Jesus will experience in Galilee with a parenthetical comment: *Now Jesus himself had pointed out that a prophet has no honour in his own country*. The evangelist is preparing his readers for the lack of faith Jesus will encounter in his homeland.

45. Rather surprisingly, then, the evangelist continues, *When he arrived in Galilee, the Galileans welcomed him. They had seen all that he had done in Jerusalem at the Passover Feast, for they also had been there.* Many Galileans had recently returned from the Passover Feast just as Jesus had done, and the miracles he did there (2:23; 3:2) were still fresh in their memories. But Jesus knew and so did the evangelist that this faith was not genuine (48).

46. Coming into Galilee, *Once more he visited Cana in Galilee, where he had turned the water into wine*. The evangelist reminds readers of Jesus' first miracle in Cana (2:11) before recounting the second (54). Setting the scene for this second miracle he says, *there was a certain royal official whose son lay sick at Capernaum*. The words 'royal official' translate *basilikos*, an adjective meaning 'royal' or 'belonging to the king'. Here it is used substantively and means a 'royal official'. During the period of Jesus' ministry, Herod Antipas was king of Galilee and Perea; presumably, therefore, this man was one of his officials. Being a person of significant status did not exempt him from the normal tragedies of life and he found his son sick and at the point of death (47). He lived in Capernaum, a town located on the north-western shore of the Sea of Galilee, about 17 miles from Cana as the crow flies. Capernaum was also the base for Jesus' mission (Lk. 4:23)

47. The evangelist continues, *When this man heard that Jesus had arrived in Galilee from Judea, he went to him and begged him to come and heal his son, who was close to death*. Whether he was a Jew or not we do not know. If he was, perhaps he had been to Jerusalem and seen the miracles Jesus had performed there (2:23; 3:2). In any case, he now found his son close to death. News reached Capernaum that Jesus had returned to Galilee and was in Cana. So the man made the journey from Capernaum to Cana to implore Jesus to come to Capernaum and heal his son.

48. Jesus' response was confronting: *'Unless you people see miraculous signs and wonders,' Jesus told him, 'you will never believe.'* Though he was speaking to the royal official ('Jesus told *him'*), Jesus' criticism was intended not only for him but for the Galileans in general ('unless *you people* see miraculous signs and wonders . . . you will never believe'). Jesus knew they would not believe in him, just as the evangelist foreshadowed (44).

49–50. The man was desperate and did not want to argue with Jesus: *The royal official said, 'Sir, come down before my child dies.'* Jesus persisted with his demand for true faith (that did not have to see miracles before believing), while at the same time responding to the man's desperation with compassion: *Jesus replied, 'You may go. Your son will live.'* By translating Jesus' reply as 'you may go' the NIV softens the original, which is a strong imperative, 'go' (*poreuou*). Attached to the command to go was the promise 'your son will live'. Jesus was both demanding unquestioning faith in his word and promising the healing for which the man asked. The royal official rose to the occasion: *The man took Jesus at his word and departed*. He believed without seeing a sign. This sort of faith is found in several places in the Gospel (1:47–49; 2:5–10; 4:39–42, 50; 9:35–38) and was explicitly praised by Jesus: 'blessed are those who have not seen and yet have believed' (20:29).

51–53. The royal official was making his way home, believing the word of Jesus, and *while he was still on the way, his servants met him with the news that his boy was living*. No doubt he was greatly relieved and overjoyed, but there was something else he wanted to know. *When he enquired as to the time when his son got better, they said to him, 'The fever left him yesterday at the seventh hour.'* This confirmed the faith he had placed in Jesus' word the day before, for *then the father realized that this was the exact time at which Jesus had said to him, 'Your son will live.'* The faith he had exercised without seeing a sign was now confirmed by hearing of the outcome. His son's life had been saved by the word of Jesus alone. But the story does not end there. The evangelist adds, *So he and all his household believed*. His faith in the promise of Jesus concerning his son's healing and seeing that faith rewarded led the man himself and his whole household to believe in Jesus. This man, and his household, were examples of those who exercised true faith in Jesus, examples the evangelist wants his readers to emulate.

54. The evangelist concludes his account with the words *This was the second miraculous sign that Jesus performed, having come from Judea to Galilee*. The first sign was turning water to wine at the wedding feast in Cana. The second was also performed in Cana when Jesus returned to Galilee from Judea after the Passover Feast in Jerusalem. The evangelist was, of course, aware that Jesus had already performed many more miracles than just these two which he chose to describe (see 2:23; 3:1–2; 4:45).

I. JESUS HEALS AN INVALID AT THE POOL OF BETHESDA (5:1–47)

In 5:1–18 the evangelist records a third miracle/sign of Jesus, the healing of an invalid at the Pool of Bethesda. It consists of six brief scenes.

1. The setting (5:1–3)

1. The evangelist begins his description of the setting: *Some time later, Jesus went up to Jerusalem for a feast of the Jews*. The time of this miracle is indefinite. It occurred on the second of Jesus' five visits to Jerusalem recorded in this Gospel. The reason for this visit was that he might attend 'a feast of the Jews'. We are not told which feast it was, and therefore the exact timing of the miracle is unknown. (That it is described as a feast 'of the Jews' suggests this Gospel was intended for Gentile readers also.)

2. The location of the miracle is described: *Now there is in Jerusalem near the Sheep Gate a pool, which in Aramaic is called Bethesda and which is surrounded by five covered colonnades*. The Sheep Gate was located near the north-east corner of the old city of Jerusalem. There are no other references to it in the NT, but it is mentioned in descriptions of the rebuilding of the walls of Jerusalem in Nehemiah 3:1, 32; 12:39.

The pool called Bethesda (house of mercy), is in other manuscripts called Bethzatha (house of olive oil) or Bethsaida (house of fishermen). It was a double pool, generally identified with the pools excavated near St Anne's Church just inside St Stephen's Gate of present-day Jerusalem. Each pool was trapezoidal in shape, and the overall length of the two pools (north to south) was about 318 feet. The smaller pool to the north was about 197 feet wide on its northern side and the larger southern pool was about 250 feet wide on its southern side. The five colonnades were located one on each of the four sides of the double pool and one across the centre dividing the two pools.

3. The evangelist completes his description of the setting: *Here a great number of disabled people used to lie – the blind, the lame, the paralysed*. Some manuscripts add as part of 5:3 the words 'and they waited for the moving of the waters'. Other manuscripts add also the words 'From time to time an angel of the Lord would come down and stir up the waters. The first one into the pool after each such disturbance would be cured of whatever disease he had' (4). These words are omitted by the best Greek manuscripts; however, some such belief is presupposed by 5:7 (see comments on that verse).

2. *Jesus heals the invalid (5:5–9a)*

5. The evangelist focuses upon one of the sufferers: *One who was there had been an invalid for thirty-eight years*. The nature of his complaint becomes clear in 5:7 where the man explains that unaided he is unable to get himself into the pool – he was lame and had been so for 38 years. The duration of his infirmity throws into bold relief the extraordinariness of the healing Jesus was to effect.

6–7. Unlike the two miracles recorded earlier in this Gospel, which Jesus performed in response to requests from others, this one takes place at Jesus' own initiative: *When Jesus saw him lying* *there and learned that he had been in this condition for a long time, he asked him, 'Do you want to get well?'* The word the NIV translates as 'learned' (*gnous*) is better translated 'knew' (so NRSV). Jesus had supernatural knowledge of the man's situation (*cf.* 2:25) as he did in the case of Nathanael (1:47–48) and the Samaritan woman (4:16–19). Seeing the lame man there and knowing how long he had suffered, Jesus asked him, 'Do you want to get well?' There is no point in psychologizing at this point, suggesting Jesus was referring to some reluctance on the man's part to see his situation changed, or that he was trying to elicit desire on the man's part to be healed. At a literary level, this question heightens the expectation of the readers of the Gospel that something miraculous is about to occur. *'Sir,' the invalid replied, 'I have no-one to help me into the pool when the water is stirred. While I am trying to get in, someone else goes down ahead of me.'* The belief was that only the first person into the waters after they were 'stirred' would be healed. Later tradition, reflected in the additions to the text in 5:3–4, attributed the stirring of the waters to an angel, but it is more likely to have been caused by the movement of subterranean water.

That so many people were at the pool waiting for the stirring of the waters suggests there were occasions when people had been healed at Bethesda. There were other healing shrines in the ancient world (*e.g.* the shrine of Asclepios in Corinth) and evidence exists that people did sometimes receive healing at these sites. From a Christian perspective such healings would be explained in terms of the 'lying wonders' of Satan (2 Thes. 2:9). In Matthew 24:24 / Mark 13:22 Jesus speaks of false Christs and false prophets who will perform great signs and wonders to deceive, if it were possible, even the elect.

The invalid addressed Jesus as 'Sir' (*kyrie*; lit. 'lord', but here used simply as respectful address) and explained his dilemma: he could never manage to be the first to get into the water after it was stirred. Perhaps he hoped Jesus would help him into the water. In any case, the man appears to be ignorant of the miracles Jesus had performed in Jerusalem (2:23; 3:1–2) and showed no sign of faith that Jesus could heal him.

8–9a. Ignoring the man's lack of faith, *Jesus said to him, 'Get up! Pick up your mat and walk.'* The very thing the man was unable to do, Jesus commanded him to do. With the command went forth the healing power: *At once the man was cured; he picked up his mat and walked.* Jesus' word of command to the invalid was like the creative word of God; the word was uttered and the deed was done. The man must have felt changes taking place in his body, and, feeling whole again, 'he picked up his mat and walked' – evidence of complete healing. This is one of those healing miracles that Jesus performed without any sign of faith on the part of the beneficiary (*cf.* Mk. 2:1–5; Lk. 22:49–51), a reminder to modern readers that healing does not always require faith on the part of the recipient.

3. 'The Jews' and the man who was healed (5:9b–13)

9b–10. With the description in 5:9a that the man was healed and then took up his mat and walked we might think the story had come to an end. But in 5:9b the story heads in a new direction. The evangelist informs his readers about something they do not yet know (though both Jesus and the man whom he had healed knew): *The day on which this took place was a Sabbath.* In obedience to Jesus' command the man was carrying his mat through the streets of Jerusalem on the sabbath, perhaps even through the temple precincts, *and so the Jews said to the man who had been healed, 'It is the Sabbath; the law forbids you to carry your mat.'* The OT forbad work (*i.e.* carrying out one's usual occupation) on the sabbath. This included bearing loads on the sabbath: 'This is what the LORD says: Be careful not to carry a load on the Sabbath day or bring it through the gates of Jerusalem. Do not bring a load out of your houses or do any work on the Sabbath, but keep the Sabbath day holy, as I commanded your forefathers' (Je. 17:21–22).

Jewish scholars, in their attempts to ensure the sabbath law was not broken, defined thirty-nine types of work forbidden on the sabbath, which are recorded in the Mishnah:

> The main classes of work are forty save one: sowing, ploughing, reaping, binding sheaves, threshing, winnowing, cleansing crops, grinding, sifting, kneading, baking, shearing wool, washing or beating or dyeing it, spinning, weaving, making two loops, weaving two threads, separating two threads, tying [a knot], loosening [a knot], sewing two stitches,

tearing in order to sew two stitches, hunting a gazelle, slaughtering or flaying or salting it or curing its skin, scraping it or cutting it up, writing two letters, erasing in order to write two letters, building, pulling down, putting out a fire, lighting a fire, striking with a hammer and taking out aught from one domain to another. These are the main classes of work: forty save one. (Šabbat 7:2)

What the man was accused of (carrying his mat on the sabbath) comes under the general restriction of taking something 'from one domain to another'. Carrying one's mat through the streets of Jerusalem, was certainly a culpable act according to rabbinic law.

11–13. To shift the blame away from himself, *he replied, 'The man who made me well said to me, 'Pick up your mat and walk.'* This immediately led 'the Jews' to ask, *'Who is this fellow who told you to pick it up and walk?'* They must have been frustrated because, the evangelist says, *The man who was healed had no idea who it was, for Jesus had slipped away into the crowd that was there.* Despite the fact that Jesus had performed many miracles in Jerusalem on his previous visit and many had believed in him, this man knew nothing about him; he did not even know his name. Here the story might have ended except for a further initiative by Jesus.

4. Jesus and the man whom he healed (5:14)

14. The evangelist tells us, *Later Jesus found him at the temple.* There would have been thousands of people in and around the temple for the festival, so Jesus finding him there might be another example of supernatural knowledge, which we meet again and again in the Fourth Gospel. Jesus said to the man, *See, you are well again.* The same word 'well' (*hygiēs*) was used in Jesus' question to the man 'do you want to get well'. Jesus then warned the man, *Stop sinning or something worse may happen to you.'* The NIV, in translating the negated present imperative (*mēketi hamartane*) as 'stop sinning', implies that the man was engaged in some sinful activity and Jesus was telling him to stop doing it. Jesus had already dealt with the man's physical infirmity; now he addressed his spiritual condition. Those who interpret Jesus' words as a command to 'stop sinning' suggest a couple of sins he may have been involved in: (1) he was flaunting his new-found freedom by carrying his mat around Jerusalem without any regard for the sabbath law (unsatisfactory because it was Jesus who told him to take up his mat and carry it in the first place); (2) he returned directly to 'the Jews' and told them who his benefactor was (this interprets in a very negative light the man's action in giving news about who healed him, which may be unjustified). However, neither of these explanations is necessary. The grammatical evidence for always rendering a negated present imperative as a command to stop doing something is far from conclusive. Jesus' words could be translated just as well as a general command not to do something, *i.e.* 'Do not sin or something worse may happen to you.' In the context of 5:14, where no particular sinful activity of the man is mentioned, Jesus' prohibition is best construed in this general way.

Warning the man that something worse may happen to him, Jesus might have meant he would suffer a worse physical affliction than the one from which he had just been delivered. If so, it raises the question of the link between sin and physical afflictions. In the case of the man born blind Jesus denied his affliction was due to his own sins or the sins of his parents (9:1–3). However, that does not necessarily exclude the possibility that Jesus was warning this man that if he sinned he might suffer physically. The apostle Paul connects sinning with physical illness and even death in 1 Corinthians 11:29–30.

Another interpretation of Jesus' warning is possible. If it was his spiritual condition Jesus was addressing he might have been telling this man that if he succumbed to sin he would come under condemnation and forfeit eternal life (*cf.* 3:18–21). His final condition, then, would certainly be worse than his former condition.

5. *The man who was healed and 'the Jews' (5:15)*

15. After hearing Jesus' warning, *The man went away and told the Jews that it was Jesus who had made him well*. He must have known 'the Jews' were antagonistic towards Jesus, and the reason they wanted to know his identity was so that they could accuse him of encouraging people to break the sabbath (10–11). Perhaps the man was intimidated by them. Or perhaps he saw himself bearing positive witness to Jesus – the evangelist does not say he informed 'the Jews' who it was who told him to 'pick up his mat and walk' (the terms in which their question was couched), but 'that it was Jesus who had made him well'. However, if we compare this man's attitude to 'the Jews' with that of the man born blind in chapter 9, his character appears less commendable.

6. Jesus and 'the Jews' (5:16–18)

16. Whatever the reason for the man's reporting to 'the Jews', they now knew who it was who had healed him and told him to take up his mat and walk. *So, because Jesus was doing these things on the Sabbath, the Jews persecuted him.* Unlike Nicodemus who said, 'Rabbi, we know you are a teacher who has come from God. For no-one could perform the miraculous signs you are doing if God were not with him' (3:2), these 'Jews' could focus only on what they regarded as a breach of the sabbath law – not that Jesus had breached their law, but he had told the man to do so.

17. In response *Jesus said to* (lit. 'answered') *them, 'My Father is always at his work to this very day, and I, too, am working.'* According to Genesis 2:1–2, God completed his work of creation and rested on the seventh day. Does he continue to observe the sabbath? Apparently not, for his providential care of the world, his administration of justice (when people die on the sabbath), and his creation of life (when children are born on the sabbath) all continue unabated. Jewish scholars acknowledged this and made efforts to show that while God worked on the sabbath he was not guilty of breaking the sabbath law. They argued that God was not guilty of carrying things from one domain to another, because the whole of creation is his house and so he never carries things 'outside'.

Jesus told his opponents that his Father continues to work 'to this very day' – even on the sabbath, something they would have to acknowledge. Jesus could then say that, just as the Father works on the sabbath in providential care of the universe as well as in other ways, so too he (Jesus) works on the sabbath to care for and redeem those affected by sin. More than that, the Father worked in and through what Jesus did (10:32, 37; 14:10).

18. 'The Jews' were quick to recognize the implications of Jesus' response to their criticism, and this made them even more angry with him: *For this reason the Jews tried all the harder to kill him; not only was he breaking the Sabbath, but he was even calling God his own Father, making himself equal with God.* In the OT God did sometimes allow human beings to stand in his place. So, for example, God said to Moses, 'See, I have made you like God to Pharaoh, and your brother Aaron will be your prophet' (Ex. 7:1). However, for human beings to make themselves equal with God was utterly reprehensible; but in Jesus' case this was not so, because he was God (1:1).

7. *The authority of the Son (5:19–30)*

19–20. The NIV translation begins this section with the words *Jesus gave them this answer*, omitting an inferential conjunction, 'therefore' (*oun*). The text should read, 'Jesus *therefore* answered and said to them.' Jesus' answer was a response to the anger of 'the Jews'. Jesus began his answer with the formula *I tell you the truth* (*amēn amēn legō hymin*), indicating the solemn nature of what he was to say: *the Son can do nothing by himself; he can do only what he sees his Father doing, because whatever the Father does the Son also does.* Jesus did not withdraw the claim that God is his Father; instead, he insisted that what the Father does he does. His claims to divine prerogatives did not mean he was independent of God or in competition with him.

Underlying these verses may be apprenticeship imagery. An apprentice copies the work of a qualified artisan. In the ancient word the artisan was often the father and the apprentice one of his sons. An artisan would show his son what to do, because he loved him. In the same way the Father shows Jesus what he is doing: *For the Father loves the Son and shows him all he does.* Continuing to address 'the Jews', Jesus said, *Yes, to your amazement he will show him even greater things than these.* Jesus had already performed numerous miracles in Jerusalem, culminating in the healing of the invalid at the pool of Bethesda (2:23; 5:1–9). He foreshadowed 'even greater things than these', which would amaze his adversaries. These are described in the next two verses.

21–23. The 'greater things' Jesus claimed his Father would 'show' him and that he would do are things that belong peculiarly to the divine prerogative. First he said, *just as the Father raises the dead and gives them life, even so the Son gives life to whom he is pleased to give it.* The 'just as . . . even so' (*hōsper . . . houtōs*) formula highlights the exact correspondence between what the Father and Son do. Raising the dead and giving them life is something only God can do (*cf.* 2 Ki. 5:7). Second, he said, *Moreover, the Father judges no-one, but has entrusted all judgment to the Son.* Judgment belongs to God (8:50), but he has entrusted this judgment to his Son, and on the last day Jesus will be the judge of all people. The reason the Father has entrusted judgment to the Son is *that all may honour the Son just as they honour the Father.* And because it is the will of the Father that all should honour his Son, *He who does not honour the Son does not honour the Father, who sent him.* This is what Jesus' opponents were guilty of doing.

24–25. While confronting his opponents with their refusal to honour the one whom God honours, Jesus still held out to them an offer of justification and life. The offer, introduced with the solemn formula *I tell you the truth* (*amēn amēn legō hymin*), was *whoever hears my word and believes him who sent me has eternal life and will not be condemned; he has crossed over from death to life.* Those who hear Jesus' word and believe the one who sent him will not be condemned on the day of judgment. In fact, they have already 'crossed over from death to life'. They have been transferred from the realm of sin and death into the realm of eternal life. Jesus reinforced this promise with yet another solemn announcement: *I tell you the truth* (amēn amēn legō hymin), *a time is coming and has now come when the dead will hear the voice of the Son of God and those who hear will live.* The 'time' coming when the dead would hear the voice of the Son of God and live is explained further in 5:28–29 where Jesus says those in their graves will hear his voice and rise from the dead. Jesus could say not only that this hour was coming but also that it had 'now come', because through his life (and imminent death and resurrection) he had set things in motion that would culminate in the resurrection of the dead.

26–27. Jesus explained why he is able to exercise these two divine prerogatives. In respect of giving life, he said, *For as the Father has life in himself, so he has granted the Son to have life in himself.* Of no others can it be said that God has granted them to have life in themselves. They may receive the gift of life through faith in Jesus' word, but they will never have life in themselves. Only God has life 'in himself', and saying that God has granted the Son to have life in himself is another way of saying he shared in divinity. This is why Jesus has power to call people to rise from their graves to eternal life.

In respect of judgment Jesus said, *And he has given him authority to judge because he is the Son of Man.* The title 'Son of Man' has its background in Daniel 7 and carries overtones of authority, power and glory (see Additional Note: 'The Son of Man', pp. 89–91). It is because Jesus is the Son of Man that the Father has given him the authority to judge.

28–29. In one sentence Jesus brings together the two divine prerogatives given him by God: *Do not be amazed at this, for a time is coming when all who are in their graves will hear his voice and come out* – this is giving life; then he added, *those who have done good will rise to live, and those who have done evil will rise to be condemned* – this is judgment.

Jesus' claim that on the last day he would call people from their graves is stupendous, and beyond all human experience. The evangelist will provide an indication of what this means in the raising of Lazarus. A man already dead and buried for four days will be called back to life, emerging from his grave at Jesus' command (11:38–44). The restoration to life of Lazarus, though not a resurrection in the full sense (Lazarus died again), foreshadows the time when 'all who are in their graves will hear his voice and come out'.

Jesus said, 'those who have done good will rise to live'. Though the evangelist alludes to the future dimension of eternal life several times (3:16; 6:40, 54; 12:25), he does not explain what it means. One hint may be found in 17:24, where Jesus prays, 'Father, I want those you have given me to be with me where I am, and to see my glory'. Jesus said also, 'those who have done evil will rise to be condemned'. Though the evangelist speaks of condemnation several times (3:17–18; 5:24, 29; 12:48), he does not spell out exactly what this involves.

The criterion for judgment leading either to life or condemnation in the age to come is doing 'good' or doing 'evil' in this age. Care must be taken not to import ideas about doing good and evil from elsewhere in the NT. In this Gospel doing good means believing in the one God sent into the world, while the ultimate evil is to reject this one, and refuse to believe in him.

30. Jesus continued, *By myself I can do nothing; I judge only as I hear, and my judgment is just, for I seek not to please myself but him who sent me.* Though he claimed to exercise divine prerogatives, Jesus rejected any suggestion that he acted independently of God, or that he saw himself as a rival to God, especially in the matter of exercising judgment. He will pronounce judgment in accordance with the judgment of God; and when he judges, therefore, it will be just because he seeks only to please God.

8. Witnesses to Jesus (5:31–47)

31–32. Jesus added, *If I testify about myself, my testimony is not valid.* According to the Mishnah, people's testimony to themselves was not valid in law; it had to be corroborated by other witnesses (*Ketubot* 2:9: 'But none may be believed [as a witness in a court of law] when he testifies of himself'). Jesus did not accept their rule (*cf.* 8:14), but acknowledging it for the sake of argument, he said, *There is another who testifies in my favour, and I know that his testimony about me is valid.* The Father himself is Jesus' other witness, his primary witness, but he had other corroborative witnesses. The primary meaning of the word translated 'valid' (*alēthēs*) is 'true', but in legal settings it may be translated 'valid'.

33–35. Jesus introduced his first corroborative witness: *You have sent to John and he has testified to the truth.* John the Baptist, someone well known to 'the Jews', had conducted a very public ministry, the focus of which, especially in this Gospel, was bearing testimony to Jesus (1:7–8, 15, 26–27, 29–30, 32–36; 3:26–30; 5:33, 36; 10:41). However, Jesus did not need even John's testimony to establish the truthfulness of his word: *Not that I accept human* *testimony; but I mention it that you may be saved.* Having the testimony of the Father, Jesus did not need that of John the Baptist. The reason he pointed to John as witness was for the sake of his hearers. If only they would accept John's testimony concerning him, they would be saved. Jesus was holding out to his opponents another opportunity to turn and be saved.

Describing the ministry of John the Baptist, Jesus said *John was a lamp that burned and gave light.* In the Fourth Gospel John is described as a 'lamp' (*lychnos*), not the 'light' (*phōs*), the latter being reserved for Jesus. A lamp must be lit from a source other than itself, and perhaps the evangelist's choice of the word 'lamp' to describe John was another way of saying 'he himself was not the light; he came only as a witness to the light' (1:8). The NIV describes John as a lamp that 'burned', but the word used (*kaiomenos*) is better translated 'was kindled', which indicates again that John's light was derivative. Jesus reminded 'the Jews', *you chose for a time to enjoy his light.* During John's early ministry 'people were constantly coming to be baptized' (3:23). Many of 'the Jews' were attracted to him, including both Pharisees and Sadducees (Mt. 3:5–7; Lk. 3:2–3). They were willing for a time 'to enjoy his light', *i.e.* the light of his preaching. By reminding 'the Jews' of their early acceptance of John, Jesus hoped, for their sakes, they might even now accept the one about whom John testified.

36. Jesus introduced the second corroborative witness: *I have testimony weightier than that of John. For the very work that the Father has given me to finish, and which I am doing, testifies that the Father has sent me.* Far more important than the testimony of John was the testimony of the works Jesus performed (not 'work' as in the NIV); works he had been commissioned to do by the Father. Jesus referred frequently to these works (9:3, 4; 10:37; 17:4) and their evidential value (10:25, 37), and he encouraged those who doubted his words to believe him when they contemplated his works (10:38; 14:11). Nicodemus believed Jesus' works were evidence that God was 'with him' (3:2). Jesus said they were evidence that the Father had 'sent him'.

Jesus spoke of 'finishing' the work the Father gave him to do. This is the second place in which he spoke of his mission in these terms (4:34; 5:36). On the eve of his betrayal, Jesus said to his Father, 'I have brought you glory on earth by completing the work you gave me to do' (17:4). Jesus' whole ministry was marked by a determination to 'finish' the work he had been commissioned to perform.

37-38. Next Jesus spoke of his primary witness: *And the Father who sent me has himself testified concerning me.* In the Synoptic Gospels the Father bears witness to Jesus in 'a voice from heaven' at his baptism (Mk. 1:11) and transfiguration (Mk. 9:7), but neither of these events is recorded in the Fourth Gospel. One way in which the Father may have borne witness to Jesus in the Fourth Gospel is by the bestowal of the Spirit and John's testimony concerning it: 'Then John gave this testimony: "I saw the Spirit come down from heaven as a dove and remain on him. I would not have known him, except that the one who sent me to baptize with water told me, 'The man on whom you see the Spirit come down and remain is he who will baptize with the Holy Spirit'"' (1:32-33). Alternatively, it has been suggested, that the whole of God's revelation from the beginning, in salvation history and through the prophets, pointed forward to the coming of his Son.

Despite the Father having testified to his Son, Jesus said to 'the Jews', *You have never heard his voice nor seen his form nor does his word dwell in you.* The Jews' have not 'heard his voice' because their spiritual ears were closed to his revelation, both in the past and now. It is a truism in both OT and NT, and certainly in the Fourth Gospel (1:18; 6:46), that no-one has ever seen God. While it is possible to interpret Jesus' statement about seeing his form along these lines, it is better to interpret it metaphorically. Their 'spiritual' eyes, like their spiritual ears, were closed. All this is evident, Jesus said, *for you do not believe the one he sent.* If they were listening to God, they would accept the message he was conveying to them through his Son.

39-40. Jesus introduced his third corroborative witness, one 'the Jews' knew well: *You diligently study the Scriptures because you think that by them you possess eternal life.* The Scriptures had a central role in Judaism as they did in the life and teaching of Jesus. Through the diligent study of Scriptures 'the Jews' believed they would find eternal life. The Mishnah says, 'the more study of the Law, the more life . . . If a man has gained a good name he has gained [somewhat] for himself; if he has gained for himself words of the Law he has gained for himself life in the world to come' (*'Abot* 2:7). The pursuit of eternal life through study of the Scriptures is valid, but in the case of 'the Jews', Jesus said, *These are the Scriptures that testify about me, yet you refuse to come to me to have life*. They studied the Scriptures but could not see that they bore witness to Jesus, and therefore refused to come to him and receive life. These verses stand as a warning to all who make the study of the Scriptures an end in itself and fail to relate to the one about whom the Scriptures testify.

41–42. Jesus pinpointed the basic flaw in his opponents that prevented them from hearing the witnesses: *I do not accept praise from men. But I know you. I know that you do not have the love of God in your hearts*. Earlier Jesus said he did not accept human testimony, not even the testimony of John the Baptist (34), and even less would he accept human praise, especially when it came at the expense of praise from God. But 'the Jews' were different. Their desire for praise from one another and the absence of real love for God, Jesus implied, prevented them from accepting the Scriptures as a valid witness to Jesus.

43. There was irony, Jesus said, in the unwillingness of 'the Jews' to accept him: *I have come in my Father's name, and you do not accept me; but if someone else comes in his own name, you will accept him*. They were ready enough to accept imposters but rejected their true Messiah. In OT times the people of Israel often embraced false prophets while persecuting the ones sent by God. In NT times Theudas and Judas the Galilean were accepted as Messiahs and led people in futile revolt against the Romans (Acts 5:36–37). Much later Rabbi Akiba hailed Simon bar Kosiba as Messiah and he led the tragic revolt of AD 132–135. 'The Jews' were taken in by false Messiahs, but rejected their true Messiah.

44. Jesus stated clearly what he implied in 5:41–42 when he asked 'the Jews', *How can you believe if you accept praise from one another, yet make no effort to obtain the praise that comes from the only*

God? If their controlling motive was to secure praise from one another, they would never obtain praise from God for accepting the one he had sent. This tension was real for those Jewish leaders who were disposed to accept Jesus but were not willing to forfeit the good opinion of their peers and the sanctions that would apply if they did (12:42).

It is worth noting that the evangelist here refers to 'the only God'. Despite insisting that Jesus and the Father are one, he did not see this as compromising monotheism in any way. A similar expression is found in 17:3, where eternal life is defined as knowing 'the only true God, and Jesus Christ, whom you have sent'.

45-47. In these verses Jesus introduced the final corroborative witness who was at the same time the accuser of 'the Jews'. *But do not think I will accuse you before the Father. Your accuser is Moses, on whom your hopes are set.* Jesus, who did not come into the world to condemn the world, informed 'the Jews' that they should not imagine that he would accuse them before the Father. Rather, it was Moses, in whom they trusted, who would be their accuser. Their trust in Moses is mentioned by the evangelist in a number of places (45; 9:28-29). What 'the Jews' did not realize was that Moses also was a witness to Jesus. Thus Jesus said, *If you believed Moses, you would believe me, for he wrote about me.* Philip knew this when he said to Nathanael, 'We have found the one Moses wrote about in the Law, and about whom the prophets also wrote – Jesus of Nazareth, the son of Joseph' (1:45). This is also something Jesus explained to his disciples after his resurrection: 'And beginning with Moses and all the Prophets, he explained to them what was said in all the Scriptures concerning himself' (Lk. 24:27). Jesus concluded by asking 'the Jews', *But since you do not believe what he wrote, how are you going to believe what I say?* If they could not understand and believe that Moses, the one in whom they trusted, wrote about Jesus, how then would they ever be able to believe what Jesus said, one in whom they certainly did not trust?

J. JESUS AND THE BREAD OF LIFE (6:1–71)

1. Jesus feeds the five thousand (6:1–15)

1. The evangelist begins his description of the setting for this miracle with the rather vague words *Some time after this*, which refer back apparently to the healing of the lame man in Jerusalem and the confrontation between Jesus and 'the Jews' that followed (5:1–47). The geographical note *Jesus crossed to the far shore of the Sea of Galilee (that is, the Sea of Tiberias)* is puzzling because nothing has been said about Jesus returning from Jerusalem to Galilee.[1] The evangelist provides two names of the Sea: the common NT name, the Sea of Galilee, and the name used later in the first century, the Sea of Tiberias. The latter is related to the major town, in fact, the capital of Herod Antipas' kingdom, situated on the western shore of the Sea. Reference to 'the far shore of the Sea of Galilee' refers to the eastern seaboard and places this miracle either in the Gentile area of the Decapolis on the eastern shore, or in the region of Philip the Tetrarch to the north-east.

2. Having located the miracle geographically, the evangelist introduces those who are to be the beneficiaries: *and a great crowd of people followed him because they saw the miraculous signs he had performed on the sick*. There are earlier references to miraculous signs Jesus had performed in Galilee (2:11; 4:46–54), and those performed in Jerusalem that had been witnessed by Galileans (4:45). Because they had witnessed these the crowd followed him.

3. Seeing the crowd, *Jesus went up on a mountainside and sat down with his disciples*, possibly in the area known today as the Golan Heights. Perhaps he was seeking some rest or wished to teach his disciples before the crowd arrived – it was Jesus' custom to sit to teach (8:2; Mt. 5:1ff.; 13:1ff.; 24:3ff.).

---

[1]This has lead some scholars to argue that chs. 5 and 6 have been displaced, and that ch. 5 should be placed between chs. 6 and 7. But there is no textual evidence to support such a re-arrangement, and it would not make for a smooth transition from the end of ch. 5 to the beginning of ch. 7, so not much is gained.

4. The evangelist provides his final piece of information to set the scene: *the Jewish Passover Feast was near*. This will be significant as the story unfolds, for Passover was a time when Jewish people recalled their deliverance from Egypt through Moses and were looking for the Prophet like him who was to come. They expected the Prophet to bring deliverance and provide 'manna' from heaven as Moses had done (*cf. 2 Baruch* 29:3 – 30:1). It was a time when nationalistic fervour was high.

5–7. The evangelist begins his account of the miracle, *When Jesus looked up and saw a great crowd coming towards him, he said to Philip, 'Where shall we buy bread for these people to eat?'* In the Synoptic accounts of the feeding of the five thousand we learn that when the crowd came to him Jesus taught them and healed their sick, and then because it was already late in the day he miraculously provided food for them (Mt. 14:13–21; Mk. 6:30–44; Lk. 9:10–17). These details are omitted in the Fourth Gospel, but knowledge of them allows readers to understand why Jesus felt a responsibility to provide food for them. If this episode took place on the north-eastern shore of the Sea of Galilee, it would be logical for Jesus to turn to Philip and ask, 'Where shall we buy bread for these people to eat?' because Philip was a native of Bethsaida, a town located in this part of the country. But Jesus' question to Philip had a different purpose: *He asked this only to test him, for he already had in mind what he was going to do*, i.e. he was going to multiply loaves and fish to feed the multitude.

Testing can be negative (*cf.* 8:6), or positive as it is here. Jesus' purpose was to test Philip's faith in him and confirm it with the miracle to follow. Not realizing what Jesus intended by his question, *Philip answered him, 'Eight months' wages would not buy enough bread for each one to have a bite!'* The NIV's 'eight months' wages' provides a helpful equivalent to the 'two hundred denarii' found in the original (a working man's wage for one day was one denarius), and highlights how much bread would be needed to feed such a large crowd. This alerts the reader to the extraordinary nature of the miracle soon to be performed.

8–9. The next vignette in the story concerns Jesus, Andrew and a small boy. As Jesus finished what he had to say to Philip, *another* *of his disciples, Andrew, Simon Peter's brother, spoke up, 'Here is a boy with five small barley loaves and two small fish.'* Andrew and his brother, Simon, like Philip, were from the town of Bethsaida (1:40–44). Andrew brought to Jesus a boy who had five little barley loaves (poor people's bread) and two small fish. It is hard to imagine that Andrew thought this would be of any help in the situation, and so it is likely he only brought the boy to Jesus because the boy himself had taken the initiative and wanted to offer what he had. Andrew voiced his own attitude to the offering: *but how far will they go among so many?* The whole incident is reminiscent of 2 Kings 4:42–44, which recounts how twenty loaves of barley bread where brought to Elisha, but were regarded by his servant as completely inadequate to feed one hundred men. 'But Elisha answered, "Give it to the people to eat. For this is what the LORD says: 'They will eat and have some left over'"' (2 Ki. 4:43).

10–11. The miracle itself is described in prosaic terms in just two verses. *Jesus said, 'Make the people sit down.'* The word 'people' translates *anthrōpous*, which is generic, as is its translation. Included among these people were men and women, boys and girls. We are then told, *There was plenty of grass in that place.* This would only occur during spring, which was also Passover time (4), and would make it suitable for the crowd to sit there. Mark's Gospel adds that the people sat down 'in groups on the green grass . . . in groups of hundreds and fifties' (Mk. 6:39–40). Two things should be noticed – the historical memory about the place (the grass there was 'green'), and that the disciples had obviously been involved in organizing the people to sit down 'in groups of hundreds and fifties'. The Fourth Gospel continues, *and the men sat down, about five thousand of them.* Here the evangelist does not use the generic term *anthrōpoi*, but the gender specific *andres*/ 'men'. Thus the crowd included five thousand men/males, but probably numbered more than twice that many. Matthew 14:21 makes it clear that many more than five thousand men were involved: 'The number of those who ate was about five thousand men, besides women and children.' *Jesus then took the loaves, gave thanks, and distributed to those who were seated as much as they wanted. He did the same with the fish.* Jesus probably used a traditional Jewish thanksgiving, which, when uttered over bread, ran like this: 'Blessed be thou, Yahweh our God, king of the world who causes bread to come forth from the earth.' Parallel accounts indicate that Jesus did not personally distribute the bread and fish, but that he delegated this task to his disciples (Mt. 14:19; Mk. 6:41; Lk. 9:16). The evangelist emphasizes the greatness of the miracle by adding that the food distributed to the people was 'as much as they wanted'.

12–13. The evangelist completes his account of the miracle, *When they had all had enough to eat, he said to his disciples, 'Gather the pieces that are left over. Let nothing be wasted.'* When God provided manna for Israel in the wilderness through Moses the people were not allowed to gather more than they needed nor to store it for future use. If they did, it went rotten (Ex. 16:16–20). When Jesus fed the five thousand (which is compared with the provision of manna in the wilderness later in the chapter (30–51) the opposite was the case. The disciples were told to collect what remained and keep it, presumably for future use. *So they gathered them and filled twelve baskets with the pieces of the five barley loaves left over by those who had eaten.* The twelve baskets may symbolize the twelve tribes of Israel, or perhaps twelve baskets were filled simply because there were twelve disciples doing the gathering.

14–15. The evangelist relates the immediate aftermath of the miracle: *After the people saw the miraculous sign that Jesus did, they began to say, 'Surely this is the Prophet who is to come into the world.'* Moses promised the Israelites, 'The LORD your God will raise up for you a prophet like me from among your own brothers. You must listen to him' (Dt. 18:15). Knowing this promise, and having seen Jesus provide food in the wilderness as Moses had done, the people concluded that Jesus was 'the Prophet who is to come into the world', the Prophet about whom Moses had spoken.

The evangelist adds, *Jesus, knowing that they intended to come and make him king by force, withdrew again to a mountain by himself.* Moses led Israel out of Egyptian captivity, and now this people wanted Jesus (whom they believed was the Prophet like Moses) to free them from Roman occupation. They wanted to 'make him king by force'.

The episode of the feeding of the five thousand began when Jesus went up on a mountain with his disciples (3). It ended when Jesus withdrew to a mountain by himself. He did this to escape the crowd who wanted to force him to be their king. The sort of kingship they had in mind was not what he had in mind. His kingship was 'not of this world' (18:36). Besides, later Jesus told the crowd that the only reason they followed him was 'because you ate the loaves and had your fill' (26)

Additional Note: Kingship

The matter of Jesus' kingship comes up repeatedly in the Fourth Gospel. Nathanael said to Jesus, 'Rabbi, you are the Son of God; you are the King of Israel' (1:49). During Jesus' triumphal entry to Jerusalem the crowd

> took palm branches and went out to meet him, shouting, 'Hosanna!'
> 'Blessed is he who comes in the name of the Lord!'
> 'Blessed is the King of Israel!' (12:13; cf. 12:15)

When Jesus was on trial before Pilate, he asked him, 'Are you the king of the Jews?' Jesus told him, 'You are right in saying I am a king' (18:33, 37). While Jesus was held in Roman custody the soldiers mocked him, saying, 'Hail, king of the Jews!' (19:3). In Pilate's exchanges with 'the Jews' he kept referring to Jesus as 'the king of the Jews', possibly sarcastically (18:39; 19:14–15), and when he had him crucified he insisted that the notice fastened to Jesus' cross read, 'JESUS OF NAZARETH, THE KING OF THE JEWS' (19:19). 'The Jews', of course, refused to accept Jesus as their king (19:15–21), but the evangelist wants his readers to recognize that Jesus is indeed the true king, even though his kingship was not of this world (18:36).

2. *Jesus walks on the Sea of Galilee (6:16–21)*

16–17a. After feeding the five thousand Jesus withdrew to the mountains alone, and *when evening came, his disciples went down to the lake, where they got into a boat and set off across the lake for*

Capernaum. Their journey to Capernaum was probably 4 or 5 miles (*cf.* 6:19–20) indicating a starting point to the south of Bethsaida, for Bethsaida was only about 3 miles from Capernaum.

17b–18. The setting for what was to follow is filled out: *By now it was dark, and Jesus had not yet joined them. A strong wind was blowing and the waters grew rough.* Though the Sea of Galilee was an inland sea, it was subject to strong winds that could make its waters treacherous. The fact that it was dark and the sea was rough probably did not concern the disciples over much. Some of them were professional fishermen used to being out on the lake at night (21:3; Lk. 5:5) and to strong winds and rough seas.

19–20. However, something occurred that did shake them: *When they had rowed about three or three and a half miles, they saw Jesus approaching the boat, walking on the water; and they were terrified.*[1] This is the fifth miraculous sign performed by Jesus and recorded in the Book of Signs. Jesus knew that his appearing and walking on the water was terrifying his disciples, so he said to them, *'It is I; don't be afraid.'* He identified himself with the words *egō eimi*, which in at least one other place in this Gospel carry connotations of divinity (see Additional Note: *Egō eimi*, p. 138), but here probably functioned simply as self-identification, as the NIV translation implies.

21. The disciples now realized it was Jesus; *then they were willing to take him into the boat, and immediately the boat reached the shore where they were heading.* It seems the evangelist wants us to see in this immediate arrival in Capernaum a further miracle.

3. *The crowd follow Jesus to Capernaum (6:22–24)*

22. In 6:22–24 the evangelist explains how the crowd came to be in Capernaum and to hear Jesus' bread of life discourse

---

[1] Some have suggested that the words *epi tēs thalassēs*, which the NIV translates as 'on the water', should be translated as 'by the side of the sea'. This is grammatically possible, but not appropriate in the context, for there is nothing terrifying about seeing a person walking 'by the side of the sea'.

(26–59). *The next day the crowd that had stayed on the opposite shore of the lake realized that only one boat had been there, and that Jesus had not entered it with his disciples, but that they had gone away alone.* They assumed Jesus was still there, but soon found they were wrong.

23–24. Next *some boats from Tiberias landed near the place where the people had eaten the bread after the Lord had given thanks.* Tiberias was on the opposite (western) shore of the lake, and boats from there landed on the eastern side where the feeding of the five thousand had taken place. *Once the crowd realized that neither Jesus nor his disciples were there, they got into the boats and went to Capernaum in search of Jesus.* Presumably, they thought Jesus would not be long separated from his disciples, and knowing they had headed for Capernaum (some of) the crowd went there looking for Jesus.

4. Jesus' bread of life discourse (6:25–59)

25. The crowd went in search of Jesus and *when they found him on the other side of the lake, they asked him, 'Rabbi, when did you get here?'* Their question, the first of five interjections from the crowd that punctuate this discourse (25, 30, 34, 42, 52), betrays no hint that they thought his crossing was miraculous. They just wanted to know 'when' he had reached Capernaum, presuming, perhaps, he had walked around the northern shore of the lake during the night.

26. Jesus' reply did not answer their question. Instead, he went straight to the heart of the matter, exposing the real reason the crowd had followed him: *Jesus answered, 'I tell you the truth, you are looking for me, not because you saw miraculous signs but because you ate the loaves and had your fill.'* The people had, of course, seen miraculous signs performed by Jesus earlier (2) and more recently the feeding of the five thousand. Jesus was saying they did not understand the significance of those signs. They did not recognize he was the Christ, the Son of God, in whom they should put their trust. They followed simply because they had eaten their fill of the loaves he had multiplied.

27. Seeking to redirect their efforts, Jesus continued, *Do not work for food that spoils, but for food that endures to eternal life, which the Son of Man will give you.* Jesus said, in effect, do not follow me in the hope of more food provided miraculously to meet your physical needs – 'food that spoils' – like the manna provided through Moses. Instead, work for the food that endures (does not spoil), food that brings eternal life, food that the Son of Man will give. The miraculous provision of food on the other side of the lake was meant to point to the 'food that endures to eternal life'. As Jesus distinguished between the water the Samaritan woman sought and the water he would give (4:13–14), so here he distinguishes between the food the crowd sought and the food the Son of Man will give. This food 'endures to eternal life', like the water 'welling up to eternal life' (4:14).

Jesus, of course, is the Son of Man who gives this food. 'Son of Man' was his preferred self-designation (see Additional Note: 'The Son of Man', pp. 89–91). As the Son of Man, he was able to give this 'food' *[for] on him God the Father has placed his seal of approval.* The evangelist uses for the second time (*cf.* 3:33) the technical term 'to place a seal upon' or 'to certify' (*sphragizō*). (See commentary on 3:33 for details of various uses of *sphragizō* in the NT.) Here in 6:27 it is used figuratively as a seal of approval, *i.e.* as God's imprimatur upon Jesus. The NIV omits the conjunction 'for' (*gar*) and so fails to make clear that it is *because* God has placed his seal of approval on him that Jesus can provide the food that endures to eternal life. It was, probably, by the bestowal of the Spirit at his baptism that the Father placed his seal of approval upon Jesus (1:33–34; see commentary on 5:37–38).

28–29. When Jesus told the crowd they should work for the food that endures to eternal life, *they asked him, 'What must we do to do the works God requires?'* They wanted to know what works (pl.) God required of them that they might qualify for the gift of the food that lasts forever. *Jesus answered, 'The work of God is this: to believe in the one he has sent.'* The work (sing.) that God requires of humanity is simply stated, 'to believe in the one he has sent'.[1]

---

[1] The author of 1 John sums up the whole obligation of the Christian person in words that include this same requirement: 'And this is his command: to believe in the name of his Son, Jesus Christ, and to love one another as he commanded us' (1 Jn. 3:23).

The evangelist's purpose for writing his Gospel was that people should 'believe that Jesus is the Christ, the Son of God' (20:31). As becomes clear later in the chapter, this is a 'work' the crowd was not ready to perform (41–42).

Jesus' status as the one whom 'he (God) sent (into the world)' is mentioned in many places in the Fourth Gospel (3:17, 34; 5:36, 38; 6:29, 57; 7:29; 8:42; 10:36; 11:42; 20:21) and especially in Jesus' great prayer (17:3, 8, 18, 21, 23, 25). Believing in the one whom God sent secures the gift of the food that endures to eternal life, because when people believe in him Jesus reveals himself to them, and his Father also reveals himself to them. It is in relationship with God through Jesus Christ that people experience eternal life (17:3) and human hunger is met.

30–31. The crowd's response is surprising: *So they asked him, 'What miraculous sign then will you give that we may see it and believe you? What will you do?'* It is surprising, because they followed him in the first place because they had seen the signs he had performed on the sick (2), and more recently they had witnessed his feeding of the five thousand (26). Why, then, ask for a further sign? Perhaps there is a clue in what they said next: *Our forefathers ate the manna in the desert; as it is written: 'He gave them bread from heaven to eat.'*[1] They were referring to the wilderness experience of Israel when God sent manna from heaven for the people to eat (Ex. 16:1–31). When the crowd saw Jesus provide food for them miraculously in the wilderness, they identified him as the Prophet like Moses (14), but it seems they were expecting something more spectacular than what they had already witnessed. Jewish people in the first century spoke of Moses as the one who gave the manna from heaven (in cooperation with God), and were looking for a second Moses/Redeemer who would do the same. Admittedly written later than the first century, but arguably representing first-century Jewish attitudes is *Qohelet Rabbah* 1:9.1, which reads, 'As the first redeemer was, so shall the latter Redeemer be . . . As the former redeemer caused manna to descend, as it is stated, *Behold, I will cause to rain bread from heaven for you* (Ex. xvi, 4), so

[1] There is no place in the OT/LXX where the exact words of the quotation can be found. Those that are close are Ex. 16:15; Ne. 9:15 and Ps. 78:24 (LXX Ps. 77:24), the last appearing to be the closest.

will the latter Redeemer cause manna to descend, as it is stated, *May he be as a rich cornfield in the land* (Ps. lxxii, 16).' The crowd wanted to see Jesus bring down from heaven a continual supply of bread (see commentary on 6:34), as Moses had supplied manna in the wilderness for forty years (Ex. 16:35; Jos. 5:12).

32–33. In reply, *Jesus said to them, 'I tell you the truth, it is not Moses who has given you the bread from heaven, but it is my Father who gives you the true bread from heaven.'* This is a solemn declaration introduced by the formula 'I tell you the truth' (*amēn amēn legō hymin*). In this declaration Jesus did three things: (1) He insisted it was not Moses (but God) who gave the manna. (2) He directed their attention away from that occasion altogether by saying that it was now the Father who was giving the true bread.[1] In the past God gave manna from heaven (through Moses), but now he was giving the true bread from heaven (through his Son). What the Jewish people were expecting at the end time – manna from heaven again – Jesus said was being given now. (3) He explains who the true bread is: *For the bread of God is he who comes down from heaven and gives life to the world.* In 6:27 Jesus said he would *give* people the bread of life. Here he implies, as he will shortly state explicitly (35), that *he* is the bread that comes down from heaven. Jesus said this bread would give life to 'the world', meaning probably all people who believe, irrespective of their ethnic background, *i.e.* Gentiles as well as Jews. In 4:42 the Samaritan townspeople said to woman, 'we know that this man really is the Saviour of the world'. By this they meant he was the Saviour, not only of Jews but Samaritans as well. In similar fashion here in 6:33 Jesus says the bread that comes down from heaven gives life to the world, meaning that all who believe in him, without distinction, will experience eternal life.

34. In response to Jesus' words about the true bread from heaven, the crowd said, *Sir, from now on give us this bread.* Literally translated, this verse reads, 'Sir, always (*pantote*) give us this bread', *i.e.* the crowd were looking for an ongoing provision for

---

[1] In 7:22 Jesus (or the evangelist) corrects a statement about Moses and circumcision in a similar way: 'Yet, because Moses gave you circumcision (though actually it did not come from Moses, but from the patriarchs), you circumcise a child on the Sabbath.'

their needs, as was the case with the provision of the manna in the wilderness. Just as the Samaritan woman asked for the water that wells up continuously so she would not have to come and draw water any more (4:15), so these people were asking for a continuous supply of bread so that they would not have to provide for themselves any more.

35. The crowd misunderstood the nature of the true bread of which Jesus spoke, so *then Jesus declared, 'I am the bread of life. He who comes to me will never go hungry, and he who believes in me will never be thirsty.'* Jesus explicitly identified himself as 'the bread of life'. This is the first of seven different 'I am' sayings with predicates in the Fourth Gospel (35, 48, 51; 8:12; 10:7, 9; 10:11, 14; 11:25; 14:6; 15:1, 5 – see Additional Note: *Egō eimi*, p. 138). Because Jesus was 'the bread of life' he could promise that those who came to him would never hunger, and, changing the metaphor, those who believed in him would never thirst (*cf.* 6:53–57). Hunger and thirst are metaphors for the human need to know God, and knowing God is the present experience of eternal life (17:3). Those who come to Jesus, *i.e.* those who believe in him, are brought into relationship with God and their hunger and thirst to know God are satisfied (see commentary on 4:13–14).[1]

36–37. However, Jesus knew that his invitation to come to him would meet varied responses. In respect of the majority of the crowd Jesus said, *But as I told you, you have seen me and still you do not believe.* They had seen him and some of the miracles he had performed (2), but still they did not believe (see commentary on 6:26). Lest it be thought he was surprised or disappointed by this response, Jesus added, *All that the Father gives me will come to me, and whoever comes to me I will never drive away.* The word translated 'all' (*pan*) is neuter singular, not masculine plural as might be expected, thus depicting those whom the Father gave Jesus as a collective entity. In several places in the Fourth Gospel Jesus speaks of believers as those whom the Father has given him (37, 39; 10:29; 17:2, 6, 9, 24). Viewed from the human side, those who

[1] Sirach 24:21, speaking of the Torah, says, 'Whoever feeds on me will be hungry for more, and whoever drinks from me will thirst for more.' While the terminology is similar, the difference between the statements in Sirach and the Gospel of John is obvious.

come to Jesus are those who believe in him; but viewed from the divine side, they are those whom the Father has given to Jesus. The Prologue says a similar thing in different words: 'Yet to all who received him, to those who believed in his name, he gave the right to become children of God – children born not of natural descent, nor of human decision or a husband's will, but born of God' (1:12–13).

Faced with lack of positive response Jesus affirmed that all the Father has given him will come and believe in him. The saying 'whoever comes to me I will never drive away' employs a strong double negative (*ou mē*) underlining the security of those who come to Jesus.

38–40. In these verses Jesus connects the eternal security of those who believe in him with his own mission: *For [because] I have come down from heaven not to do my will but to do the will of him who sent me.* The reason why none who come to him will be cast out is because Jesus came to do his Father's will, *and*, he said, *this is the will of him who sent me, that I shall lose none of all that he has given me, but raise them up at the last day.* The 'all' (*pan*) whom the Father has given are once again depicted as a collective entity (*cf.* 6:37). Their eternal security is tied to the Son's obedience to the Father, on the one hand, and to the will of the Father, on the other. For any of those whom the Father has given to his Son to be lost would mean that Jesus failed to carry out his Father's will, and that the will of the Father had been thwarted. Both of these things are unthinkable. *For my Father's will is that everyone who looks to the Son and believes in him shall have eternal life, and I will raise him up at the last day.* Those whom the Father has given him will receive eternal life in the here and now and be raised up on the last day. The 'last day' is the day of resurrection for those who believe in Jesus (5:28–29; 6:39, 40, 44, 54; 11:24), but a day of judgment for those who reject him (5:28–29; 12:48).

41–42. The evangelist explains the reaction of 'the Jews': *At this the Jews began to grumble about him because he said, 'I am the bread that came down from heaven.'* This is the first place in chapter 6 where those who listen and partake in a dialogue with Jesus are called 'the Jews'. Up until this point they have been described as 'the crowd' (2, 22, 24) or 'the people' (10, 14), or simply referred to as 'they' or 'them'. Only here and in 6:52 are they spoken of as 'the Jews'. In the Gospel of John this term very often refers to those who were opposed to Jesus (see pp. 49–50). Earlier (33–34) the crowd appeared to pass over Jesus' claim to have come down from heaven, because they were interested in the 'bread' he promised. But 'the Jews', now realizing the bread Jesus offered was not physical bread, took offence and grumbled, just as their Israelite forefathers grumbled in the wilderness (Ex. 16:2, 7, 12). *They said, 'Is this not Jesus, the son of Joseph, whose father and mother we know? How can he now say, "I came down from heaven"?'* This is the second of only two occasions in the Fourth Gospel when Jesus is referred to as 'the son of Joseph' (1:45; 6:42). There is irony here, for 'the Jews' were sure they knew Jesus' origins, but the readers of the Gospel know differently. The Prologue says that Jesus is the Logos become flesh, and readers aware of Synoptic traditions would know that though he was supposed to be the son of Joseph (Mt. 13:55; Lk. 4:22), this was a mistaken supposition (Lk. 3:23). Because of their mistaken view about his origins, 'the Jews' grumbled about Jesus' claim to have come down from heaven.

43–44. Jesus said to them, *Stop grumbling among yourselves*. Then, showing he was not surprised or downcast by their rejection, he said, *No-one can come to me unless the Father who sent me draws him*. In the OT God 'draws' people to himself with the bands of love (Je. 31:3; Ho. 11:4). Here, however, the Father draws people to his Son, and unless he does so no-one can come to him. Viewed from the human perspective, all may come to Jesus and believe in him, and in fact are required to do so (28–29). Viewed from the divine perspective, only those drawn by the Father can come and put their faith in Jesus, a perspective found also in other parts of the NT (Mt. 16:17; Acts 16:13–14). Concerning those whom the Father draws to him Jesus said, *I will raise him up at the last day*. In the Fourth Gospel Jesus speaks frequently of 'the last day'. For those who believe, their resurrection on 'the last day' is the consummation of the eternal life they experience now (39, 40, 44, 54; 11:24), but for those who do not accept his word it is a day of reckoning (12:48).

45. Expanding the idea of the Father drawing people to him, Jesus said, *It is written in the Prophets: 'They will all be taught by God.'* The quotation is from Isaiah 54:13 ('All your sons will be taught by the LORD, / and great will be your children's peace') and is part of a long passage that speaks of the blessings to be showered upon the Jews at the restoration following their Babylonian exile. Among these blessings is the fact that 'all your sons will be taught by the LORD'. Jesus took this text and applied it to his ministry: *Everyone who listens to the Father and learns from him comes to me.* People listen to and learn from the Father by listening to the teaching of his Son and learning from him. An example of this is found in the account of the confession of Peter at Caesarea Philippi. When he confessed Jesus as the Christ, Jesus said to him, 'Blessed are you, Simon son of Jonah, for this was not revealed to you by man, but by my Father in heaven' (Mt. 16:17).

46-47. Jesus explained why it was vital that people came to him: *No-one has seen the Father except the one who is from God; only he has seen the Father.* It is a fundamental teaching of the OT that no human being has seen God. The evangelist stresses this fact in the Prologue: 'No-one has ever seen God, but God the One and Only, who is at the Father's side, has made him known' (1:18). People need to come to Jesus for no-one else can reveal the Father to them. Perhaps it is significant that in a passage where Jesus denies contemporary beliefs that Moses was the one who provided the manna in the wilderness (32), he also implies that Moses never saw God.[1] Only the one who is from God has seen the Father. Although no-one can say they have seen God, Jesus said, *I tell you the truth, he who believes has everlasting life.* This statement is introduced by the solemn formula 'I tell you the truth' (*amēn amēn legō hymin*). While God cannot be seen in the present time, the gift of everlasting life, a relationship with the invisible God through faith in Christ (17:3), is available.

48-50. Picking up again the theme of 6:32-35, Jesus said, *I am the bread of life. Your forefathers ate the manna in the desert, yet they died.* The manna was not the true bread of life because all who

---

[1] In Ex. 33:20 the Lord told Moses, 'you cannot see my face, for no-one may see me and live'.

ate that still died. So Jesus said, *But here is the bread that comes down from heaven, which a man may eat and not die.* The one who 'eats' of the true bread from heaven will not die. To 'eat' the true bread is a metaphor for believing in Jesus (*cf.* 6:35), something that becomes abundantly clear when we compare the two statements that stand in parallel in this context: 6:47: 'he who believes has everlasting life', and 6:50: 'a man may eat and not die'.

51–52. Jesus reiterated, *I am the living bread that came down from heaven. If anyone eats of this bread, he will live for ever,* and then introduced a new and startling metaphor: *This bread is my flesh, which I will give for the life of the world.* In this verse it is no longer the Father who gives the living bread, but Jesus himself, and for good reason. The living bread was his flesh (not his 'body' as in Eucharistic texts), which he would give for the life of the world. This is an allusion to his death on the cross. Jesus, the Logos who became 'flesh' (1:14), became the bread of life for a sinful world only by laying down his life so that others might live. However, this allusion was not appreciated by his hearers: *Then the Jews began to argue sharply among themselves, 'How can this man give us his flesh to eat?'* Why 'the Jews' argued among themselves is not explained. Perhaps some were disposed to accept what Jesus said even though they could not understand it, while others who took his words literally found them repulsive.

53–55. Seeing them arguing, Jesus stated the same truth negatively, and *said to them, 'I tell you the truth, unless you eat the flesh of the Son of Man and drink his blood, you have no life in you.'* Once again he prefaced his words with the solemn introductory formula 'I tell you the truth' (*amēn amēn legō hymin*). He made no concessions to their misapprehension and even heightened the repulsive nature of his words. To the idea of eating his flesh he added that of drinking his blood. If 'the Jews' continued to take his words literally they would be disgusted and appalled. The drinking of any blood was forbidden (Lv. 17:10–14). He told them that unless they did this repulsive thing they would have no life in them – they would not experience eternal life that comes from a relationship with the Father. Having stated things negatively, Jesus then stated them positively: *Whoever eats*[1] *my flesh and drinks my blood has eternal life, and I will raise him up at the last day*. To understand properly what Jesus was saying in highly metaphorical language readers must remember that he said the same thing in more straightforward terms in 6:40: 'everyone who looks to the Son and believes in him shall have eternal life, and I will raise him up at the last day'. Placing these two verses side by side, it is clear that eating Jesus' flesh and drinking his blood is a metaphor for believing in him. Continuing the metaphor, Jesus said, *For my flesh is real food and my blood is real drink*. When this metaphor is unpacked, it means that Jesus is the source of true satisfaction; belief in him who gave his life for the world is the only way to satisfy human hunger and thirst for God.

56. Jesus took this thought one step further: *Whoever eats my flesh and drinks my blood remains in me, and I in him*. Eating his flesh and drinking his blood, as we have seen, is a metaphor for believing in him. Those who believe in him, Jesus said, would remain in him and he in them. The mutual indwelling of Jesus and his disciples is developed further in 15:4–7. Their remaining in Jesus involves loyalty and fellowship and it continues as his disciples obey his word. Jesus' remaining in his followers involves his continuing fellowship with them. However, there are indications elsewhere in the Gospel that more than loyalty and fellowship is involved in this mutual indwelling. In 17:20–21 this mutual indwelling of Jesus and his disciples is modelled upon the mutual indwelling of the Father and the Son, and is brought about through the Holy Spirit who comes to dwell within the disciples (*cf.* 14:15–20).

57. Jesus took things even deeper: *Just as the living Father sent me and I live because of the Father, so the one who feeds on me will live because of me*. Jesus lives because of the 'living Father', since it is in relationship with the Father that Jesus, the Son, has life. In a

---

[1]Here in 6:54 a different word for eating is introduced. Previously the word *esthiō* was used, but here, and also in 6:56, 57, 58, the word *trōgō* is used. Often it is said that *trōgō* carries the idea of chewing or gnawing on Jesus' flesh, which would make his statement even more repulsive. However, *trōgō* does appear to be used as a simple synonym for *esthiō* elsewhere (13:18; Mt. 24:38), as it is in 6:54, where both words are found.

similar way, Jesus said, 'the one who feeds on me will live because of me'. To feed on Jesus is to believe in him, and those who believe experience eternal life, which Jesus gives to them (*cf.* 3:15, 16, 36; 5:24; 6:40, 47). It is important to note that here Jesus speaks of feeding on 'him', rather than 'eating his flesh and drinking his blood', which supports the view that both these expressions are metaphors meaning 'believe in him'.

58. Jesus concluded his discourse with this summary: *This is the bread that came down from heaven. Your forefathers ate manna and died, but he who feeds on this bread will live for ever.* Now it is clear that Jesus himself was the true bread that came down from heaven. There was bread from heaven in Moses' time also, the manna the Jewish forefathers ate, but it did not prevent them from dying. Jesus promised that those who feed on him would live for ever. This does not mean they will not die as others die but that they will experience eternal life now in relationship with God, and this relationship will not be broken because of death, and Jesus will raise them up on the last day.

Some today interpret Jesus' words about eating his flesh and drinking his blood in 6:51–58 as a reference to the Lord's Supper /Eucharist. It is understandable how people might make this connection after the institution of the Lord's Supper, but Jesus' words here must be interpreted in their own context, which clearly indicates that eating his flesh and drinking his blood is a striking metaphor for believing in him. Those who believe in him benefit from his death on their behalf.

59. The evangelist closes his account of Jesus' discourse with the words *He said this while teaching in the synagogue in Capernaum.* It was to Capernaum that the crowd came searching for Jesus after the feeding of the five thousand (24–25), and it was in the synagogue at Capernaum that Jesus gave his teaching on the bread of life.

5. Many disciples stop following Jesus (6:60–71)

60. The reaction to Jesus' highly metaphorical discourse in 6:51–58 was not surprising: *On hearing it, many of his disciples said, 'This is a hard teaching. Who can accept it?'* While most references to 'disciples' in the Fourth Gospel relate to the Twelve, there are a number of places where 'disciples' refers to the wider group (4:1; 7:3; 8:31; 9:28; 19:38). It was 'many' of this wider group who found Jesus' teaching about eating his flesh and drinking his blood to be a 'hard teaching'. They found it so hard, so offensive, because they did not understand that it was couched in metaphorical language. This group did not include the Twelve, as 6:66–67 makes clear.

61–62. Jesus responded to their difficulties: *Aware that his disciples were grumbling about this, Jesus said to them, 'Does this offend you?'* He then asked, *What if you see the Son of Man ascend to where he was before!* There are two main ways of construing these words: (1) if they saw him ascend, they might be prepared to accept his hard saying; (2) if they saw him ascend, their difficulties would only increase. The second alternative is most likely the correct one. The ascension of Jesus, the Son of Man, in this Gospel is frequently linked with his being lifted up on the cross (prior to his resurrection and ascension). If the 'disciples' who grumbled about Jesus' hard saying about eating his flesh and drinking his blood should witness his ignominious death upon the cross they would be scandalized still further. How could one who claimed to come from God end his life in such a way?

63. Addressing again the disciples who stumbled over his words, Jesus said, *The Spirit gives life; the flesh counts for nothing.* The only other place in the Fourth Gospel where the Spirit and the flesh are placed in juxtaposition is 3:6, where Jesus tells Nicodemus that to see the kingdom of God he must be born again / from above because, 'Flesh gives birth to flesh, but the Spirit gives birth to spirit.' Here in 6:63 Jesus is saying to the disciples that in and of themselves, as people of the flesh, they can never experience eternal life. Only the Spirit (of God) can give life. He then indicated the way the Spirit normally mediates life to people: *The words I have spoken to you are spirit and they are life.* It is because Jesus had been endowed with the Spirit 'without limit' that he could speak the words of God (3:34), and these words mediated eternal life to those who believed (5:24). There is no-one else whose words have this power (68). It is worth noting that one cannot believe in Jesus without believing his words.

64. Jesus knew his words would mediate life to those who believed, yet sadly he had to say to the disciples, *there are some of you who do not believe.* For the benefit of the readers the evangelist adds, *For Jesus had known from the beginning which of them did not believe and who would betray him.* This is further testimony to the fact that Jesus 'knew what was in a man' (2:25). Perhaps this explains why he did not attempt to cajole people into belief nor worry when they rejected him. He knew 'from the beginning' those who would not believe. He even knew which of his inner circle of disciples would betray him.

65. After his explanatory addition, the evangelist returns to his account of Jesus' words to the disciples: *He went on to say, 'This is why I told you that no-one can come to me unless the Father has enabled him.'* The word translated 'enabled' (*dedomenon*) in the NIV would be better translated 'given'. The privilege of belief in Jesus is a gift bestowed by God. Unbelief was the obstacle to these disciples' acceptance of Jesus and his words, and he now made it plain that it was only by the gracious gift of the Father that this unbelief could be overcome. In 6:44 Jesus said a similar thing: 'No-one can come to me unless the Father who sent me draws him'.

66. The evangelist concludes his account of Jesus' address to the wider group of followers with the words *from this time many of his disciples turned back and no longer followed him.* The words translated 'from this time' (*ek toutou*) may also be rendered 'because of this' (*i.e.* because of Jesus' hard saying). Either way, many turned away at this time. These many 'disciples' who turned away from Jesus included those who followed him to Capernaum, not because they saw and understood the significance of the signs he performed, but because they had eaten the loaves and were filled (26).

67. After the departure of these people, only the Twelve were left, and Jesus addressed them next. *'You do not want to leave too, do you?' Jesus asked the Twelve.* Jesus' question (using *mē*) expects a negative answer. He was not encouraging the Twelve to leave with the other disciples but he was giving them opportunity to do so if they wished.

68–69. On behalf of the Twelve *Simon Peter answered him, 'Lord, to whom shall we go? You have the words of eternal life.'* If they were to leave Jesus there was no-one else to whom they could go who had the message of eternal life. He added, *We believe and know that you are the Holy One of God.* In the OT Yahweh is frequently referred as 'the Holy One' (Is. 40:25; 43:15; Hab. 1:12; 3:3) or 'the Holy One of Israel' (Ps. 71:22; Is. 12:6; 30:12, 15; 41:20; 43:3, 14; 45:11; 48:17; 49:7 [2×]). Most of these references are found in Isaiah and it may be that the prophet's vision of the Lord in the temple (Is. 6:1–4) lies behind his references to God as 'the Holy One' and 'the Holy One of Israel'. If so, these titles reflect the awesome majesty, glory and purity of the Lord.

Confessing Jesus as 'the Holy One of God', Peter used a title for Jesus found in this exact form elsewhere only in the Synoptic Gospels, where it is used by an evil spirit: 'What do you want with us, Jesus of Nazareth? Have you come to destroy us? I know who you are – the Holy One of God!' (Mk. 1:24/Lk. 4:34). In this context the title 'the Holy One of God' carries the idea that Jesus is the authoritative, powerful representative of God in whose hands the demon knew its fate rested. Here the title is associated with the role of judgment. However, when Peter confessed Jesus as 'the Holy One of God', it was a positive and willing recognition that Jesus, as the authoritative agent of God, had the authority and power to bestow eternal life on those who believed (no-one else, Peter said, has the words of eternal life).

Peter said, 'We *believe and know* that you are the Holy One of God.' The words 'believe' and 'know' here are virtual synonyms, and together they provide emphasis. These two verbs are brought together again in synonymous parallelism in 17:8, where Jesus, in his prayer to the Father, said of his disciples, 'They *knew* with certainty that I came from you, and they *believed* that you sent me.' In 6:69, then, the Twelve are making a strong confession of faith similar in its significance to the confessions of Martha (11:27) and Thomas (20:28), and as such it contributes to the overall purpose of the Fourth Gospel: to encourage readers also to believe Jesus is the Christ, the Son of God (20:31).

70–71. Following the confession of the Twelve, *Jesus replied, 'Have I not chosen you, the Twelve?'* He reminded them that while the confession they made was theirs, the relationship they enjoyed with him was based on his choice. Then he added, *Yet one of you is a devil!* Even among those he had chosen there was 'a devil'. Jesus may have referred to one of the Twelve as 'a devil' because he knew he was to yield to the devil's enticements and betray him (64). In the Synoptic Gospels Peter is called 'Satan' (Mt. 16:23/Mk. 8:33) because at one point he mouthed the sort of temptation that comes ultimately from Satan. It is a reminder that opposition to Jesus was satanic as well as human. The evangelist identifies the one Jesus referred to as 'a devil': *He meant Judas, the son of Simon Iscariot, who, though one of the Twelve, was later to betray him.* Twice in the Fourth Gospel it is stated explicitly that Jesus knew who was to betray him (64; 13:11), and, of course, his actions and words during the Last Supper also showed that he knew who it was (13:21-27). Beginning with 6:71, Judas is repeatedly and explicitly identified as the betrayer (71; 12:4; 13:2; 18:2, 5; 21:20).

K. JESUS GOES TO JERUSALEM FOR THE FEAST OF TABERNACLES (7:1-52)

The long section 7:1 – 10:21 describes things that happened when Jesus went up to Jerusalem for the Feast of Tabernacles. Chapter 7 falls into five sections, all relating to events that occurred just prior to and during the feast.

1. Prior to the feast: the unbelief of Jesus' brothers (7:1-9)

1. The evangelist begins by telling what happened after the feeding of the five thousand and the bread of life discourse: *After this, Jesus went around in Galilee, purposely staying away from Judea because the Jews there were waiting to take his life.* Jesus knew 'the Jews' there 'were waiting to take his life' (*cf.* 5:18). Nevertheless, he would soon go up to Jerusalem for the Feast of Tabernacles (10), and many more attempts would be made to seize him and put him to death (1, 11, 19, 20, 25, 30, 32, 44; 8:28, 37, 40, 59).

2. The feeding of the five thousand took place in March–April at Passover time (6:4). The events described in 7:1 – 10:21 occurred some six months later in September–October, *when the Jewish Feast of Tabernacles was near*. According to Leviticus 23:33–36, 39–43 the Feast of Tabernacles began with a solemn assembly on the first day and ended with another solemn assembly on the eighth day. The people were to live in booths for seven days, make daily offerings by fire, and rejoice before the Lord, waving bundles of palm fronds, leafy branches, poplars and fruit. The Feast of Tabernacles commemorated the time when Israel dwelt in temporary shelters in the wilderness (Lv. 23:42–43: 'All native-born Israelites are to live in booths so that your descendants will know that I made the Israelites live in booths when I brought them out of Egypt'). According to Deuteronomy 16:13–15 it took place after the gathering of produce from the threshing floor and the winepress. The people rejoiced in the promise that 'the LORD your God will bless you in all your harvest and in all the work of your hands, and your joy will be complete' (Dt. 16:15). The feast had a double purpose: to remember Israel's time in the wilderness when they lived in booths, and to rejoice before the Lord after harvest (in particular the grape, olive and fruit harvests). It also involved looking forward to a new exodus, the time when the kingdom of God would be brought in with all its attendant blessings. It was the most popular and joyful of the three pilgrim festivals (Passover, Pentecost and Tabernacles). In NT times it involved other practices: the water pouring and the great candle-lighting ceremonies, and these form the background to Jesus' actions and teaching at this festival. These ceremonies will be described at the appropriate places in the commentary below.

3–5. Aware that the Feast of Tabernacles was near, and that thousands of people would converge on Jerusalem, *Jesus' brothers said to him, 'You ought to leave here and go to Judea, so that your disciples may see the miracles you do.'* Jesus' 'brothers', his siblings, have already been mentioned along with his mother in connection with the first miracle in Cana (2:12). Now they appear again urging Jesus to 'go public' at the Festival and let his 'disciples' see his miracles. By 'disciples' here is not meant the Twelve, but those people who would be in Jerusalem for the Feast and who had been attracted to him (see 2:23; 4:45). His brothers shared with the Jewish crowds the belief that the Messiah would command belief by dramatic miracles. They said to him, *No-one who wants to become a public figure acts in secret. Since you are doing these things, show yourself to the world.* By saying 'since you are doing these things' his brothers showed they knew about his miracles, and now they urged him to show himself 'to the world', which in this context means the Jewish crowds in Jerusalem for the Festival. Perhaps his brothers had heard of the many 'disciples' who ceased following Jesus after the bread of life discourse, and so now urged him to do something to attract such people back. What better place to demonstrate who he was than in Jerusalem at the popular Feast of Tabernacles. The evangelist adds an explanatory comment: *For even his own brothers did not believe in him.* Why, if they did not believe in him, would they want him to do something in Jerusalem to attract his 'disciples' back? Perhaps the recent defection of many disciples had detracted from the family honour, and they wanted to see that restored.

6–7. In response *Jesus told them, 'The right time for me has not yet come; for you any time is right.'* The word used for 'time' in this verse (and in 7:8) is *kairos*, a word found in the Fourth Gospel only in these verses. Normally, another word, 'hour' (*hōra*), is used, a word that carries heavy theological meaning and relates primarily to the time of Jesus' crucifixion and exaltation (see commentary on 2:4). That the word *kairos* (instead of *hōra*) is used in 7:6, 8 suggests Jesus was simply saying that it was not yet the right time for him to go to this feast. Perhaps he knew that in the first few days 'the Jews' would be expecting him (11) and would seek to kill him (*cf.* 7:1). For his brothers there were no such concerns. For them 'any time is right'. This approach is confirmed by Jesus' next words: *The world cannot hate you, but it hates me.* Because 'the world' (here meaning 'the Jews' hostile to Jesus) had no reason to hate his brothers, they could go to the feast any time they liked. It was different for Jesus. He had to choose his time carefully because 'the world' hated him and planned to kill him. The reason it hated him, he said, was *because I testify that what it does is evil.* Jesus came as light into the world and in both his person and teaching he exposed its evil (see 3:19–21; 5:37–38, 41–45).

8–9. After telling his brothers that any time was right for them, he said, *You go to the Feast. I am not yet going up to this Feast.* Where the NIV has 'not yet' (*oupō*), as does the AV, other versions (*e.g.* RSV, NRSV, REB) have simply 'not' (*ouk*), reflecting variant readings in the Greek manuscripts. If we adopt the RSV, NRSV, REB reading, then Jesus told his brothers he was not going up to this feast, and this causes problems, because after his brothers departed Jesus did go up to the feast (10). Those who think the text should read 'not' (*ouk*) do so on the basis of the text-critical rule that the harder reading is more likely to be original because a scribe would change a reading to make it easier, not more difficult. A case can be made in favour of 'not yet' (*oupō*),[1] but even if 'not' (*ouk*) is the correct reading, the context indicates that Jesus was not saying he would not go to the feast at all, but he would not go when his brothers told him to do so, or for the purpose they said he should go. The reason, he said, was *because for me the right time has not yet come.* The time was not right, because he knew he would be expected to arrive at the beginning of the feast (11) and 'the Jews' would be waiting to kill him (1). *Having said this, he stayed in Galilee,* where he was in much less danger from his opponents.

2. During the feast: 'the Jews' look for Jesus (7:10–13)

10–11. The events described in 7:10–36 all took place during the Feast of Tabernacles. After telling his readers that Jesus remained in Galilee, the evangelist now says, *However, after his brothers had left for the Feast, he went also, not publicly, but in secret.* His brothers had urged him to show himself to the world (4), but Jesus rejected this advice, and chose to come to the feast, 'not publicly, but in secret', for good reason: *Now at the Feast the Jews were watching for him and asking, 'Where is that man?'* The Jewish leaders who were antagonistic towards Jesus were on the lookout for his arrival. Their antagonism is reflected in the question 'Where is that man?'

12–13. While Jesus' opponents were adamant in their opposition, the ordinary people were divided in their opinions: *Among*

---

[1] See Caragounis, pp. 177–187, which provides arguments in favour of 'not yet' (*oupō*).

the crowds there was widespread whispering about him. Some said, 'He is a good man.' Others replied, 'No, he deceives the people.' Those who had witnessed his miracles, especially his healing of the sick, would say 'he is a good man'. Others, probably influenced by their leaders, said 'he deceives the people', a very serious charge indeed (Dt. 13:1–5). *But no-one would say anything publicly about him for fear of the Jews.* Those disposed to speak well of Jesus would say nothing publicly, because they were afraid of 'the Jews'. They had good reason to be afraid, because 'the Jews' had decided to put anyone who acknowledged Jesus as Messiah out of the synagogue (9:22; 12:42; 16:2). The crowds who feared 'the Jews' were also Jews, another reminder that not all Jews were antagonistic towards Jesus.

3. During the feast: Jesus teaches in the temple (7:14–24)

14–15. After describing the division of opinion concerning Jesus, the evangelist picks up his account of Jesus' movements again: *Not until halfway through the Feast did Jesus go up to the temple courts and begin to teach.* He had gone up to Jerusalem in secret, and waited until the festival was halfway through before showing himself in the temple. Showing no fear of his opponents, he began to teach in the temple courts, the most public area in Jerusalem. As they listened, *The Jews were amazed and asked, 'How did this man get such learning without having studied?'* Jesus was not known to have been a disciple of any of the leading rabbis, yet his teaching reflected extraordinary learning and this made a huge impression upon the hearers (45–46). While the crowds were impressed by Jesus' teaching, religious leaders were not. If a person had not studied under a learned rabbi, his teaching was suspect; his teaching was just his own.

16–17. Knowing what they were saying, *Jesus answered, 'My teaching is not my own. It comes from him who sent me.'* To teach without reference to learned rabbis would betoken arrogance, as if teaching on one's own authority. Jesus claimed he was not teaching on his own authority. The teaching he gave came from the one who sent him, God the Father himself. To those who were inclined to question this claim, he said, *If anyone chooses to do God's* *will, he will find out whether my teaching comes from God or whether I speak on my own.* If they choose to do God's will, Jesus said, they will find out his teaching comes from God. This enunciates a very important fact: recognizing the truth of Jesus' teaching is not dependent upon intellectual ability or formal learning, nor is it a reward for the noble search for truth. It depends, rather, upon a person's willingness to do the will of God. The impediments to knowing the truth about God are more likely to be moral (lack of readiness to do God's will) than anything else. In the Gospel of John, God's will is that people believe in his Son (6:28–29, 40; *cf.* 1 Jn. 3:23). This means that only those who believe in Jesus will recognize the truth of his teaching. Believe, that you may know! This is not surprising, for why should God reveal truth to those who refuse to believe in his Son.

18. Continuing to respond to the criticism that he spoke on his own authority, Jesus said, *He who speaks on his own does so to gain honour for himself.* His opponents would have agreed with this statement. In their own teaching they cited the authority of others – rabbi so-and-so says this; rabbi so-and-so says that. Not to do so would be arrogant and evidence of seeking honour for oneself. Jesus did not appeal to the rabbis for his authority; nor was he arrogant. He said, *he who works for the honour of the one who sent him is a man of truth; there is nothing false about him.* Such a statement applies to a person's agent or representative. If the agent is 'a man of truth', he will act only for the honour of his principal, and in that case it may be said 'there is nothing false about him'. On the lips of Jesus, however, 'the one who sent him' refers to the Father. Jesus claimed he worked for the Father's honour alone, and therefore he was 'a man of truth' and there was 'nothing false about him'. Literally rendered, this last clause would read, 'there is no unrighteousness in him' – something implied by Jesus later when he challenged 'the Jews': 'Can any of you prove me guilty of sin?' (8:46).

19. Jesus' opponents prided themselves on knowing God's will already because they knew Moses' law (see 9:28–29; Rom. 2:17–20). Jesus asked them, *Has not Moses given you the law? Yet not one of you keeps the law. Why are you trying to kill me?* The evidence that they were not interested in doing God's will, not even as it was expressed in the law of Moses, was they wanted to kill Jesus contrary to the law of Moses. Jesus' references to Moses (19, 22, 23) were very appropriate at the Feast of Tabernacles, when the Jewish people remembered God's provision in the wilderness, given through Moses.

Jesus' opponents may have thought that by killing him they would be doing God's will and keeping the law of Moses. They may have concluded Jesus came under the strictures of Deuteronomy 13:1–5, where even a miracle worker was to be put to death if he led people away from the living God. They knew Jesus was a miracle worker and they believed he encouraged people to break the sabbath. Therefore, he led people away from God and should be put to death. More than that, they believed he was guilty of blasphemy because he claimed equality with God (5:18). The problem was, Jesus' opponents did not realize who he really was, and they were mistaken about the way the law of the sabbath should be applied. This latter matter Jesus addresses in 7:21–24.

20. What Jesus said to 'the Jews' was in the hearing of the crowd: *'You are demon-possessed,' the crowd answered. 'Who is trying to kill you?'* The crowd appear ignorant of their leaders' plans (5:18; 7:1). They took Jesus' statement about people wanting to kill him as evidence of the paranoia of a demon-possessed person.

21–22. Ignoring the insult, *Jesus said to them, 'I did one miracle, and you are all astonished.'* He was referring to the healing of the invalid at the Pool of Bethesda on the sabbath (5:1–18). He continued, *Yet, because Moses gave you circumcision (though actually it did not come from Moses, but from the patriarchs), you circumcise a child on the Sabbath.* The law of circumcision came from Moses in so far as it is found in the law of Moses (Lv. 12:3), but Jesus explained that the command to circumcise predated Moses, being first issued to Abraham (Gn. 17:10–13).[1] Jesus reminded his opponents that, in apparent violation of their understanding of the sabbath law, they circumcised children on the sabbath.

---

[1] In 6:32 Jesus corrects a loose statement that attributed the gift of manna to Moses, which strictly speaking should have been attributed to God. Here he does a similar thing, insisting that the rite of circumcision dates from the patriarchs, not the time of Moses.

23–24. Jesus drove home his point: *Now if a child can be circumcised on the Sabbath so that the law of Moses may not be broken, why are you angry with me for healing the whole man on the Sabbath?* Male Jews had to be circumcised on the eighth day after birth (Lv. 12:3). If the eighth day fell on a sabbath they were still circumcised in order to keep the law of Moses. This was in apparent violation of the sabbath law, but it was held not to be so because the law of circumcision overrode the sabbath law (Mishnah, *Nedarim* 3:11: 'Great is circumcision which overrides even the rigour of the Sabbath'). Jesus asked why, if they circumcised children on the sabbath, were they angry with him for healing a whole man on the sabbath (*cf.* 5:16–18)? Jewish scholars used a similar argument in defence of actions necessary to preserve the life of the whole person, which was more important than circumcision, which affects only one member.[1] Jesus applied their principle more widely – to healing people's whole bodies even when they were not in immediate danger of death.

Jesus told his opponents, *Stop judging by mere appearances, and make a right judgment.* Hearing that Jesus healed a man on the sabbath, they jumped to the conclusion Jesus was a sabbath breaker, but their judgment was wrong. Jesus was making a man perfect or whole, in the same way as circumcision made a man perfect. They needed to understand this so that they might learn to 'make a right judgment'.

4. During the feast: Jerusalemites ask, 'Is this the Christ?' (7:25–31)

25–26. Hearing Jesus teach, *some of the people of Jerusalem began to ask, 'Isn't this the man they are trying to kill?'* Some of the Jerusalemites knew their leaders were seeking ways to put him to death. So they were amazed and said, *Here he is, speaking publicly, and they are not saying a word to him.* The apparent inactivity of the authorities in the face of Jesus' public teaching led them to ask, *Have the authorities really concluded that he is the Christ?* They wondered, in the light of Jesus' recent activities, whether the authorities had changed their minds about him.

---

[1]'If circumcision, which affects one of man's two hundred and forty-eight members, supersedes the Sabbath, how much more must his whole body (if his life is in danger of death) supersede the Sabbath?' (*Yoma* 85b).

27. As they pondered this possibility, they faced another dilemma: *But we know where this man is from; when the Christ comes, no-one will know where he is from.* The Jerusalemites' statement needs to be explained carefully. On the surface they appear to be saying that the genealogy and birthplace of the Messiah were unknown. Clearly, this was not the case, for it was well known that the Messiah was to be of the lineage of David and that his birthplace was to be Bethlehem (42; Mi. 5:2/Mt. 2:4–6). The Jerusalemites thought they knew where Jesus came from, for he was commonly thought to be from Nazareth (1:45; 18:5, 7; 19:19), the village in which he grew up, but not where he was born.

The Jerusalemites did not have all their facts right. Because they thought they knew where Jesus came from, they believed he could not possibly be the Messiah. They believed the identity of the Messiah would not be known until he was revealed in glory. This belief is reflected in *4 Ezra* (= 2 Esdras) 13:52: 'He said to me, "Just as no-one can explore or know what is in the depths of the sea, so no-one on earth can see my Son or those who are with him, except in the time of his day"' (NRSV). It is also reflected in the dialogue between the Christian apologist Justin Martyr and Trypho, his Jewish opponent. Trypho said to Justin, 'But Messiah, if indeed He has ever been and now exists anywhere, is unknown, and does not even know Himself at all nor has any power, until Elijah shall have come and anointed Him, and shall have made Him manifest to all' (*Dialogue with Trypho* viii. 4).

28–29. Recognizing the Jerusalemites' quandary, *Jesus, still teaching in the temple courts, cried out, 'Yes, you know me, and you know where I am from.'* Because Jesus was making an important public declaration, the evangelist uses the verb 'to cry out' (*krazō*), as he does on three other occasions, all related to important public declarations (1:15; 7:37; 12:44). In this declaration Jesus acknowledged the people's problem when working from their assumptions, and said in effect, 'You think you know me; you think you know where I come from, and therefore you think I cannot be the Messiah.' They did not know Jesus had come from the Father. Jesus continued, *I am not here* (lit. 'I have not come') *on my own, but he who sent me is true.* The word 'true' (*alēthinos*) is used in two ways in the Fourth Gospel: (1) meaning true in the sense of correct or reliable (4:37; 8:16; 19:35); and (2) meaning genuine as in references to the true light (1:9), true worshippers (4:23), true bread (6:32), true vine (15:1) and the true God (17:3). It is in this second sense that Jesus says the one who sent him 'is true'. He had been sent by 'the true God', or as 17:3 has it, 'the only true God'. Jesus then said to the Jerusalemites, *You do not know him, but I know him because I am from him and he sent me.* They claimed to know God, but Jesus said they did not know him at all. Jesus substantiated his own claim to know God on the basis that he came from God and was sent by God.

30. Jesus' claim must have seemed like blasphemy to them, for the evangelist says, *At this they tried to seize him, but no-one laid a hand on him, because his time had not yet come.* This is the second in a series of references to the 'hour/time' of Jesus (*cf.* 2:4; 7:30; 8:20; 12:23, 27; 13:1; 16:32; 17:1). The 'hour' is an important concept in this Gospel. In the early part of the Gospel things move towards the 'hour', which is the hour of Jesus' passion, death and his subsequent exaltation (see commentary on 2:4). No machinations of Jesus' opponents could bring his ministry to a premature end; he would not surrender himself to their hands until his 'hour' had come. The sentiment of the psalmist's prayer was true in Jesus' case:

> My times are in your hands;
> deliver me from my enemies
> and from those who pursue me. (Ps. 31:15)

31. Despite the negative attitude of the Jerusalemites, *Still, many in the crowd put their faith in him.* These people, probably pilgrims who had come to Jerusalem for the festival, were prepared to ignore the common belief that 'when the Christ comes, no-one will know where he is from' (27). *They said, 'When the Christ comes, will he do more miraculous signs than this man?'* For these people the miracles they had witnessed outweighed the common belief. Such a response is exactly what the evangelist hoped for from those who read his Gospel (20:31), and clearly 7:25-31 contributes to his purpose.

5. During the feast: officers sent to arrest Jesus (7:32–36)

32. The willingness of many in the crowd to believe in Jesus did not go unnoticed. *The Pharisees heard the crowd whispering such things about him. Then the chief priests and the Pharisees sent temple guards to arrest him.* There had been earlier attempts to arrest Jesus and plans to kill him (5:18; 7:1, 19, 20, 25, 30), and now another attempt would be made to arrest him. The 'temple guards' sent to carry out this task would be Levites who functioned as temple police to ensure good order in the temple precincts, but under the command of the chief priests they could operate in a wider sphere as well (*cf.* 18:3, 12).

33–34. *[Therefore] Jesus said, 'I am with you for only a short time, and then I go to the one who sent me. You will look for me, but you will not find me; and where I am, you cannot come.'* The NIV omits the word 'therefore' (*oun*) with which this verse begins and which indicates that it was the coming of the temple guards that prompted Jesus to say these things. After the Feast of Tabernacles Jesus made only two more visits to Jerusalem, one for the Feast of Dedication (10:22), the other for his final Passover (11:55; 12:1, 12–13), when he would be handed over to be crucified. It would be through his death and subsequent exaltation that Jesus would return to the Father who sent him, and there would be no more opportunities for the crowd to see him. Where he was going, clearly they could not come.

35–36. Puzzled by what Jesus had said, *The Jews said to one another, 'Where does this man intend to go that we cannot find him? Will he go where our people live scattered among the Greeks, and teach the Greeks?'* The words 'where our people live scattered among the Greeks' translate *tēn diasporan tōn Hellēnōn*, which rendered literally would read 'the Diaspora[1] of the Greeks', *i.e.* Jewish people living among the Greeks. The crowd wondered if Jesus was going to leave Judea and Galilee, join the Diaspora and then teach the Greeks/Gentiles. If he did so he would be beyond the

---

[1] This is the only literal use of the word 'Diaspora' in the NT. There are two metaphorical uses that refer to Christians scattered in the world (Jas. 1:1; 1 Pet. 1:1).

reach of his Jerusalem opponents. This was not Jesus' intention, but readers of the Gospel would know that after his return to the Father Jesus would send his Spirit to the disciples and then indeed his message would be heard in the Diaspora and by the Greeks/Gentiles.

'The Jews' again (cf. 7:34) asked among themselves, *What did he mean when he said, 'You will look for me, but you will not find me,' and 'Where I am, you cannot come'?* Still they did not understand what he meant.

6. Last day of the feast: Jesus offers living water (7:37–39)

On the last day of the Feast of Tabernacles Jesus promised living water to those who believed in him (37). To appreciate the impact of Jesus' promise we need to understand the first-century water-pouring ritual during this feast. For the first six days of the feast they used to fill a golden flagon with water from the Pool of Siloam and carry it back to the temple. When they reached the Water Gate, three blasts on the shofar (ram's horn trumpet) were sounded. When they arrived at the temple, they processed around the altar and sang the Hallel (Pss. 113 – 118), the people shaking their lulabs (bundles of myrtle, palm and willow bound up with a citron), while the priests shook theirs (made from willow [-poplar] branches). The flagon was taken to the priest on duty at the altar who had two silver bowls, one for the water and the other for wine. These bowls were filled and then the contents poured over the altar. On the seventh day they processed around the altar seven times (*Sukkah* 3:9; 4:4–10; 5:1–4). People believed that when the Messiah came he would provide water (as he would provide manna) just as Moses had done:

> As the former redeemer made a well to rise, so will the latter Redeemer bring up water, as it is stated, *And a fountain shall come forth of the house of the Lord, and shall water the valley of Shittim* (Joel iii, 18). (*Qohelet Rabbah* 1:9.1)

In the light of this rabbinic text it is significant that, following chapter 6, where the evangelist records the feeding of the five thousand and the bread of life discourse, in chapter 7 he records Jesus' offer of living water.

37–38. The evangelist sets the context of Jesus' promise/proclamation: *On the last and greatest day of the Feast*. As noted above, the Feast of Tabernacles began with a solemn assembly on the first day, continuing for seven days, and was followed by another solemn assembly on the eighth day. When the evangelist refers to 'the last and greatest day of the Feast', it is difficult to know to which day he refers. If it was the eighth day, there would be no more water-pouring ceremonies, no more processions. These ceremonies had ceased. If it was the seventh day, when the priests and people processed around the altar seven times, singing the Hallel, shaking their lulabs, and rejoicing before the Lord while the water was poured over the altar, the symbolism in Jesus' proclamation would be striking. On the day when the last of the water-pouring ceremonies was performed amid much singing and rejoicing Jesus invited people to come to him, the one who provides the rivers of living water. It seems preferable to say that 'the last and greatest day' was, in fact, the seventh day, when the celebration of the Feast of Tabernacles reached its climax.

No matter whether the last and greatest day was the seventh or eighth day, on that day, *Jesus stood and said in a loud voice, 'If anyone is thirsty, let him come to me and drink. Whoever believes in me, as the Scripture has said, streams of living water will flow from within him.'* The evangelist uses here also the word *krazō*, 'to cry out', or 'to speak with a loud voice', as he does elsewhere when important public declarations are being made (1:15; 7:28; 12:44). In 4:10, 13–14 Jesus offered living water to a Samaritan woman; now here a similar offer is extended to his own people (see commentary on 4:10, 13–14 for a discussion of the meaning of 'living water').

There are two ways of punctuating and therefore interpreting Jesus' words. The first, represented by the NIV translation above, implies that the streams of living water flow from within those who come to Jesus and drink, *i.e.* from within those who believe in him. The alternate punctuation yields the following translation: 'If anyone is thirsty let him come to me and drink, whoever believes in me. As the Scripture has said, streams of living water will flow from within him.' Such a translation allows the first part of the text to be interpreted as Jesus' invitation to those who believe to come and drink, and the second part as a comment by the evangelist explaining that the Scriptures promised streams of water would flow from the Messiah.

In favour of the first alternative it may be noted that when Jesus offered the Samaritan woman living water, he said it would become in her 'a spring of water welling up to eternal life' (4:13–14), which is not that much different from saying 'streams of living water will flow from within him'. While the second alternative seems a little awkward on first reading, there are a couple of things that can be said in its favour. When Jesus offered living water to the Samaritan woman, he clearly was the source of that living water. In 7:39 the living water is said to symbolize the Holy Spirit, and Jesus and the Father are the sources of the Spirit in the Fourth Gospel. The believer is obviously never the source of the Spirit. In the end it does not really matter which alternative is chosen, because the living water, the Holy Spirit, is given by Jesus to his followers, and therefore he, not the believer, is ultimately its source. Once given, it may well up to eternal life within them or flow out of them like streams of living water, but always its source is Jesus.

The Scripture being cited here is difficult to identify as no passage in the OT reads just like this. One possibility is Isaiah 12:3:

> With joy you will draw water
> from the wells of salvation.

Although this text is not exactly like the quotation in 7:38, there is evidence that it was associated with the water-pouring ceremonies of the Feast of Tabernacles and the gift of the Holy Spirit. In the Talmud (*Sukkah* 5:1) Rabbi Joshua ben Levi cites Isaiah 12:3 when he says, 'Why is it called the place of drawing? For from there they draw the Holy Spirit, in line with the following verse of Scripture, "With joy you will draw water from the wells of salvation" (Is. 12:3).' It is also possible that the evangelist's allusion is to Ezekiel 47:1–11 or Zechariah 14:8.

39. In this verse the evangelist interprets Jesus's words about the streams of living water: *By this he meant the Spirit, whom those who believed in him were later to receive*. As Rabbi Joshua ben Levi connected the water-drawing ceremony at the Feast of Tabernacles with the Holy Spirit (see commentary on 7:37–38), so the evangelist connects Jesus' reference to rivers of living water with the promise of the Holy Spirit. An outpouring of the Spirit was expected at the dawning of the new age (Ezk. 11:19; 36:26–27; 39:29; Is. 44:3; Joel 2:28).

From the standpoint of those who heard Jesus speak on this occasion the reception of the Spirit was still in the future. Later in the Gospel Jesus explains to his disciples that when he returns to the Father following his death and resurrection, he will send the Holy Spirit to them in his place. The sending of the Spirit must await his return to the Father, something the evangelist goes on to explain in this verse: *Up to that time the Spirit had not been given, since Jesus had not yet been glorified.* The Fourth Gospel frequently speaks of Jesus being glorified, and it is nearly always in conjunction with his death, resurrection and return thereby to the Father (7:39; 12:16, 23, 28; 13:31, 32; 17:1, 5).

7. Last day of the feast: division among the people (7:40–44)

40. During the Feast of Tabernacles people remembered the wilderness experience of Israel, and Moses' miraculous provision of water from the rock. They knew that Moses had prophesied that the Lord would raise up for them a prophet like him (Dt. 18:15). Jesus' public declaration offering streams of living water to the thirsty on the last day of the feast was striking, and it is no wonder that *on hearing his words, some of the people said, 'Surely this man is the Prophet.'* They were identifying Jesus as the prophet like Moses.

41–42. This was not the only view being put forward. *Others said, 'He is the Christ.' Still others asked, 'How can the Christ come from Galilee?'* While some were prepared to acknowledge Jesus as the Messiah, the one anointed by God to bring in his kingdom, others were dissuaded from doing so because they believed he came from Galilee. They argued, *Does not the Scripture say that the Christ will come from David's family and from Bethlehem, the town where David lived?* That the Messiah would come from David's line is foreshadowed in 2 Samuel 7:12 and Psalm 98:3–4, and that he would come from Bethlehem is prophesied in Micah 5:2 (*cf.* Mt. 2:5–6). The irony was, of course, that Jesus was born in Bethlehem.

His origins were not in Galilee as these people supposed. More important than this, of course, is that Jesus' real origins were in heaven, from whence he had been sent by the Father.

43-44. The upshot was that *the people were divided because of Jesus*. Some were prepared to accept him as the Messiah, while *some wanted to seize him*, but once again *no-one laid a hand on him* (because his hour had still not yet come).

8. Last day of the feast: officers return empty handed (7:45-52)

When the Pharisees heard the crowds whispering about Jesus and realized that many of them believed that he was the Messiah, they and the chief priests sent temple guards to arrest him (31-32). This section tells of the return of the temple guards.

45-46. After observing events in the temple, *finally the temple guards went back to the chief priests and Pharisees, who asked them, 'Why didn't you bring him in?'* They had come back empty handed, and those who sent them wanted to know why. The temple guards, themselves Levites and religious men, had been deeply impressed by Jesus' teaching, and their answer to the Pharisees' and chief priests' question 'Why didn't you bring him in?' was, *No-one ever spoke the way this man does*. In the Synoptic Gospels the crowds were impressed with the way Jesus spoke: (he taught 'as one who had authority, and not as their teachers of the law' (Mt. 7:29; Mk. 1:22; Lk. 4:32) and the way his teaching was accompanied by deeds of power (Mk. 1:27; 2:10-12; Lk. 4:36). But it appears the evangelist wanted his readers to understand that the temple guards were impressed, not so much by Jesus' authoritative speech, but by his gracious offer of living water. In chapter 7 the only teaching of Jesus recorded after the dispatching of the temple guards and their return to those who sent them is Jesus' proclamation on the last day of the Feast offering living water to all who were thirsty.

47-49. The reaction of those who sent the temple guards was hostile: *'You mean he has deceived you also?' the Pharisees retorted*. As far as these Pharisees were concerned Jesus was a deceiver, and this assessment had rubbed off on some of the crowd (12; *cf.* Mt. 27:62–63). Appealing to their rank as religious leaders they asked the guards, *Has any of the rulers or of the Pharisees believed in him?* As the evangelist tells the story, there is irony involved here, for in 7:50–51 one of their own number will speak up in defence of Jesus. And there were other rulers who believed in him but were afraid to acknowledge it openly (12:42). Ignorant of these things, the Pharisees interrogating the temple guards answered their own question: *No! But this mob that knows nothing of the law – there is a curse on them.* They thought the temple guards had been influenced by the crowd, so they declared that the crowd was ignorant of the law and 'there is a curse on them'. Therefore the temple guards should give no credence to their opinions.

It is a sad fact that the Pharisees believed the common people were under God's curse because of their ignorance of, and therefore failure to carry out, the law. The technical term used by the Pharisees, which lies behind their reference to 'this mob', is 'the people of the land', a derogatory term for Jews who did not carefully observe the prescriptions of the law and the Pharisaic traditions. It was virtually impossible for the Pharisees to associate with the people of the land, because their 'uncleanness' was a threat to their ritual purity.

50–51. Despite earlier confident statements about no rulers or Pharisees believing in him, *Nicodemus, who had gone to Jesus earlier and who was one of their own number, asked, 'Does our law condemn a man without first hearing him to find out what he is doing?'* Nicodemus is described as the one 'who had gone to Jesus earlier' (3:1–2) and as 'one of their own number', for he was both a ruler and a Pharisee (3:1). At this point Nicodemus did not declare his belief in Jesus, but he did speak up on a point of legal procedure, and so questioned his colleagues' hasty judgments about Jesus. In Deuteronomy 1:16–17; 17:2–5; 19:15–19 judges in Israel are commanded to investigate charges thoroughly before reaching a judgment. Charges were to be entertained only if supported by two or three witnesses. In the Mishnah there are more detailed instructions about the way hearings should be conducted, including the statement 'Even if the accused said, "I have somewhat to argue in favour of my acquittal", they listen to him, provided that there is aught of substance in his words' (*Sanhedrin* 5:4). The irony of this whole affair was that the Pharisees and rulers who condemned the crowd because they did not know the law were themselves acting in contravention of the law and their own traditions in making such a hasty judgment about Jesus, as Nicodemus reminded them.

52. However, these people were in no mood to listen to Nicodemus' cautionary remarks. *They replied, 'Are you from Galilee, too? Look into it, and you will find that a prophet does not come out of Galilee.'* By questioning their hasty judgments, Nicodemus had associated himself with Jesus from Nazareth in Galilee. When his peers asked him, 'Are you from Galilee too?', it was an abusive question, for the Judeans looked down upon the Galileans. There is no reason to assume that Nicodemus was a Galilean. The claim of Nicodemus' fellow councillors that 'a prophet does not come out of Galilee' is problematic, for several of the OT prophets came from Galilee (Jonah, Hosea, Nahum, and perhaps Elijah, Elisha and Amos). One of the early papyri ($\mathfrak{p}^{66}$) has a variant for 7:52 that reads 'the prophet' instead of 'a prophet'. In this case they would not be saying that no prophets have arisen from Galilee, which is clearly mistaken, but that there is no evidence that 'the Prophet' (the one like Moses; see Dt. 18:15) would come from Galilee (nor is there any evidence that he would not). Already the evangelist has said that some of the crowd were saying that Jesus was truly 'the Prophet', while others were saying he was the Christ/Messiah (40–41). Perhaps, then, what Nicodemus' colleagues were saying to him was that there was no evidence that the Prophet or the Messiah would come from Galilee. If this were the case, then readers of the Gospel would sense the irony of the situation, knowing that Jesus was not born in Galilee, but in Bethlehem in Judea.

This passage includes the second of three appearances of Nicodemus in this Gospel. The first is in 3:1–15, where he approached Jesus by night saying, 'Rabbi, we know you are a teacher who has come from God. For no-one could perform the miraculous signs you are doing if God were not with him.' The final appearance is in 19:38–42, where he brought 75 pounds of spices and, with Joseph of Arimathea who had asked Pilate for the body of Jesus, prepared it for burial and laid it in the tomb.

L. JESUS FORGIVES A WOMAN TAKEN IN ADULTERY (7:53 – 8:11)

It is very unlikely that this attractive story was an original part of the Fourth Gospel. It is not found in the earliest and most reliable Greek manuscripts. Nevertheless, it has what Professor Metzger describes as 'all the earmarks of historical veracity'.[1]

7:53 – 8:2. The evangelist provides the setting for this story: *Then each went to his own home. But Jesus went to the Mount of Olives.* Because it is unlikely that this passage belongs here, we have no clear idea what the historical context was. On a later visit to Jerusalem Jesus stayed at the home of Mary, Martha and Lazarus in Bethany, which was just the other side of the Mount of Olives (12:1–11). *At dawn he appeared again in the temple courts, where all the people gathered round him, and he sat down to teach them.* It was the custom for teachers to sit while teaching. Jesus' teaching was open and public: 'all the people gathered round him'.

3–5. While Jesus was sitting and teaching, *the teachers of the law and the Pharisees brought in a woman caught in adultery.* This is the only place in the Fourth Gospel where 'teachers of the law' (*grammateis*; often translated, 'scribes') are mentioned. It is appropriate that they are here associated with the Pharisees in their encounter with Jesus, for it was to involve a question about the application of the law of Moses. Together the Pharisees and the teachers of the law confronted Jesus with 'a woman caught in adultery', and *they made her stand before the group.* As far as the teachers of the law were concerned, the woman simply provided the occasion for the encounter. Her humiliation would have been acute, as she was made to 'stand before the group' (lit. 'in the midst') surrounded by her accusers, and 'all the people' who were listening to Jesus' teaching.

The teachers of the law said to Jesus, *Teacher, this woman was caught in the act of adultery.* They addressed Jesus as 'Teacher', which suggests this story is all about an encounter between rival teachers. That the woman was 'caught in the act of adultery' means there were eyewitnesses. The woman's accusers continued, *In the*

---

[1]Metzger, p. 188.

Law Moses commanded us to stone such women. Now what do you say?
They limited the application of the law by saying it applies to 'such
women', when in fact the law applies to both the adulterers and
adulteresses: 'If a man commits adultery with another man's wife
– with the wife of his neighbour – both the adulterer and the adulteress must be put to death' (Lv. 20:10); 'If a man is found sleeping
with another man's wife, both the man who slept with her and the
woman must die' (Dt. 22:22). If the law demanded the death of
both the adulterer and the adulteress, and if the woman was
'caught in the act of adultery', one wonders about the discrimin-
atory action of those who seized only the woman.

According to the law (Dt. 17:7) witnesses were required to cast
the first stone. That the teachers of the law say 'in the Law Moses
commanded *us* to stone such a woman' could reflect the fact that
they were witnesses. On the other hand, the 'us' may be inclusive,
meaning 'us Jews', and that would include Jesus as well. In any
case, they wanted to know whether Jesus agreed with the law of
Moses or not.

6a. The evangelist explains that *they were using this question as a
trap, in order to have a basis for accusing him.* These words are located
in different places in a few of the manuscripts (D, M, 1071, it^d).
This has led some scholars to suggest that these words were not
part of the original story. Were this to be true, it could cast a different light on the motives of the teachers of the law. Perhaps they
were not trying to trap Jesus, but were seeking his help to get them
out of a dilemma. How could they be faithful to the law without
putting this woman to death? This puts their motives in the best
possible light, but it is building a rather large edifice upon a small
foundation. It is better to read the passage and the motives of the
teachers of the law in the light of these words in 8:6a. The rest of
the story makes better sense if we do, and there is evidence elsewhere to show that the Pharisees and teachers of the law did seek
to trap Jesus with questions (Mt. 12:10/Mk. 3:2/Lk. 6:7). They
knew he showed compassion towards sinners, and hoped his
compassion might lead him to make a statement contrary to the
law. There would be dangers also if he supported the law, because
he would be advocating capital punishment, which was for the
most part forbidden to the Jews by the Romans.

6b–8. When he heard what the teachers of the law said, *Jesus bent down and started to write on the ground with his finger*. Being seated as he was to teach, Jesus stooped down to write on the ground. This action has been variously interpreted. Some say Jesus was embarrassed to be confronted by a promiscuous woman (unlikely); others, that it was a ploy to gain time to think how best to answer. Again others have suggested it was a prophetic action modelled after Jeremiah 17:13 ('O LORD, the hope of Israel, / all who forsake you will be put to shame. / Those who turn away from you will be written in the dust / because they have forsaken the LORD, / the spring of living water'), but the connection between Jesus' action and this text is slight. A better suggestion is that Jesus' action was a sign of his refusal to debate the issue on the terms dictated by the teachers of the law. This would account for their persistent questioning. *When they kept on questioning him, he straightened up and said to them, 'If any one of you is without sin, let him be the first to throw a stone at her.'* According to the law, witnesses to a capital offence had to cast the first stone when the accused was condemned to death (Dt. 17:7). Jesus regarded the teachers of the law as witnesses to the offence. Therefore, they should begin the execution if it were to go ahead. But Jesus' words challenged the accusers, implying that none of them was without sin and therefore they were in no position to condemn this woman. What sin Jesus was implying they were guilty of is not clear. Perhaps they too were guilty of adultery. Perhaps they were malicious witnesses in terms of Deuteronomy 19:15–21, because they were not interested in seeing justice done, but only in trapping Jesus. However, this is unlikely, because in Deuteronomy 19:15–21 the malicious witness is a false witness; the question of motive is not mentioned. Having said this, *Again he stooped down and wrote on the ground*. This is probably best understood as an indication that Jesus was refusing further debate. We are not told what Jesus actually wrote, so it is pointless to speculate. What he wrote plays no part in the story, because the teachers of the law, the crowd and the woman all responded to what Jesus said, not what he wrote. Therefore it did not need to be recorded.

9. Jesus' actions and words struck home: *At this, those who heard began to go away one at a time, the older ones first, until only Jesus was* *left, with the woman still standing there.* This remarkable response was perhaps silent acknowledgment that in many ways they were no better than her. In the end everyone had departed: the crowd, the teachers of the law and the Pharisees. Now 'only Jesus was left, with the woman still standing there' where she had been placed by her accusers.

10–11. After writing on the ground a second time, *Jesus straightened up and asked her, 'Woman, where are they? Has no-one condemned you?'* This was the first time in the whole episode that anyone addressed the woman. Jesus spoke, not about her sin, but asked, 'Has no one accused you?' She replied, *No-one, sir.* All her accusers had disappeared. Hearing her say this, Jesus declared, *Then neither do I condemn you. Go now and leave your life of sin.* Such a response reflects Jesus' compassion for sinners, and reinforces the teaching of the evangelist in the Fourth Gospel: 'For God did not send his Son into the world to condemn the world, but to save the world through him' (3:17); 'For the law was given through Moses; grace and truth came through Jesus Christ' (1:17). It should be noted that while Jesus refused to condemn the woman, he did not condone her sin. He told her, 'Go now and leave your life of sin.' He said something similar to the invalid he healed at the Pool of Bethesda: 'See, you are well again. Stop sinning or something worse may happen to you' (5:14).

M. JESUS IN CONFLICT WITH 'THE JEWS' OF JERUSALEM (8:12–59)

1. *Jesus, the light of the world (8:12–20)*

If, as most scholars think, 7:53 – 8:11 was not originally part of the Fourth Gospel, what we read in 8:12–20 would follow on from Jesus' invitation to the crowds to come to him and drink (7:37–39). (What intervenes in 7:40–52 simply recounts the reactions of the crowd and the authorities to Jesus' teaching in the temple.)

12. The evangelist continues, *When Jesus spoke again to the people, he said, 'I am the light of the world.'* This is the second of seven different 'I am' sayings with predicates in the Fourth Gospel (6:35,

48, 51; 8:12; 10:7, 9; 10:11, 14; 11:25; 14:6; 15:1, 5). Jesus' claim to be 'the light of the world' was made against the background of another Jewish practice at the Feast of Tabernacles, the great candle-lighting ceremonies that took place each night except on an intervening sabbath. A passage from the Mishnah (*Sukkah* 5:2–3) describes these ceremonies:

> At the close of the first Festival-day of the Feast they went down to the Court of the Women where they had made a great amendment. There were golden candlesticks there with four golden bowls on the top of them and four ladders to each candlestick, and four youths of the priestly stock and in their hands jars of oil holding a hundred and twenty *logs* which they poured into all the bowls. They made wicks from the worn out drawers and girdles of the priests and with them they set the candlesticks alight, and there was not a courtyard in Jerusalem that did not reflect the light of the Beth ha-She'ubah.

Jesus presented himself as the light of the world at the Feast of Tabernacles; a festival during which great candles lit up the courtyards of Jerusalem every night. However, Jesus' claim to be the light of the world contained more than allusions to the great illuminations of the Feast of Tabernacles. It had its roots in OT prophecies, especially Isaiah 42:6; 49:6 and 51:4, which speak of the Servant of the Lord, and indeed the Lord himself, as the light to the nations (world).

Jesus promised, *Whoever follows me will never walk in darkness, but will have the light of life*. Those who followed him by accepting his teaching would no longer walk in the darkness of ignorance under the power of the evil one (*cf.* 1 Jn. 5:19). As the apostle Paul said, 'he has rescued us from the dominion of darkness and brought us into the kingdom of the Son he loves' (Col. 1:13). As life in the darkness culminates in death, life in the light of Christ culminates in eternal life; it is 'the light of *life*'. In the Prologue the evangelist said of the Logos, 'In him was life, and that life was the light of men' (1:4). To come to Christ means coming to the one in whom is found the life of God, and that life is the light of men, the light of life.

13. Not all were willing to accept Jesus' claim to be the light of the world. *The Pharisees challenged him, 'Here you are, appearing as your own witness; your testimony is not valid.'* According to rabbinic teaching, testimony to oneself was not valid in law; only testimony by another could be accepted. In the Mishnah, for example, we read, 'So, too, if there were two men and one said, "I am a priest", and the other said, "I am a priest", they may not be believed; but when they testify thus of each other they may be believed' (*Ketubot* 2:7). The Pharisees accused Jesus of bearing testimony to himself.

14. In response, *Jesus answered, 'Even if I testify on my own behalf, my testimony is valid, for I know where I came from and where I am going.'* As the one who has come from God and is going to God (*cf.* 13:3), he is not subject to rabbinic rules concerning valid testimony. Even though he might accommodate himself to their rules (5:31–46; 8:17–18) he did not need to do so. What rendered Jesus' testimony valid was something of which his opponents were completely ignorant: *But you have no idea where I come from or where I am going.* They did not understand that he had been sent by God into the world and that he would shortly return to God. The testimony of God's emissary did not need human validation.

15–16. Confronting his opponents, Jesus said, *You judge by human standards.* Because they rejected the light of the world, the Pharisees were shut up to fallible human wisdom when they made judgments, and in respect of Jesus' teaching they were sadly mistaken. While his opponents judged him by human standards, Jesus said, *I pass judgment on no-one. But if I do judge, my decisions are right, because I am not alone. I stand with the Father, who sent me.* Jesus did not come to judge or condemn the world, but to save it, so he reserved judgment. However, he insisted that if he were to judge, his decisions would be correct, because, unlike the Pharisees, he stood with the Father, and his judgments would be in accordance with his Father's will.

17–18. Alluding to Deuteronomy 17:6; 19:15, Jesus said, *In your own Law it is written that the testimony of two men is valid.* The testimony of one person is no basis for convicting anyone of a crime;

there must be two or three witnesses. When Jesus spoke of 'your own law' he was not distancing himself from the law of the Pharisees, for it was his law also. In the OT Moses and Joshua spoke to the Israelites of 'your God', and of 'the land that the LORD, the God of your fathers has given you', without distancing themselves from either God or the land (Dt. 1:10, 21; Jos. 18:3). Jesus was reminding the Pharisees of the provisions of the law, which both he and they accepted.

The law says the testimony of two witnesses is valid, and Jesus insisted that he was not a lone witness: *I am one who testifies for myself; my other witness is the Father, who sent me.* Readers know that there could be no more valid witnesses than God the Father and his unique and only Son. Jesus had other witnesses as well (John the Baptist, the works Jesus performed, the Scriptures, and Moses; 5:31–47) but they were not of the same order as Jesus himself and the Father.

19. The Pharisees thought Jesus was appealing to a human father as his second witness: *they asked him, 'Where is your father?'* Jesus' response related, not to the question 'Where is your father', but to the fact that they did not know his Father: *You do not know me or my Father. If you knew me, you would know my Father also.* If they realized he was speaking of God, this would have been exceedingly confronting to the Pharisees, who were proud of their knowledge of God (see Dt. 4:7; Rom. 2:17). The evidence that they did not 'know' the Father was that they did not know Jesus. They did not realize that those who see Jesus see the Father also, something Jesus would explain to his disciples during the Last Supper (14:8–10).

20. The evangelist concludes this part of his account by describing the place where Jesus' exchange with the Pharisees took place: *He spoke these words while teaching in the temple area near the place where the offerings were put.* The words translated 'the place where the offerings were put' (*tō gazophylakiō*) literally rendered would be 'the treasury'. Josephus uses *gazophylakion* for the treasury chambers, where vast sums of money were stored (*Jewish War* v.200; vi.282). Jesus would neither have had access to nor have taught in these rooms. The same word is used in Mark

12:41, 43 and Luke 21:1 for the boxes into which people placed their offerings. The NIV rendering assumes Jesus was teaching near these boxes. It was a public place, probably in the Court of Women (see Mk. 12:41–44), the place where the great candelabra were lit at night during the Feast of Tabernacles – an appropriate place for Jesus' proclamation that he was 'the light of the world'.

Despite the fact that the Pharisees rejected his teaching and thought it was dangerous, *Yet no-one seized him, because his time had not yet come.* This is the third of nine references to Jesus' 'hour/time' (2:4; 7:30; 8:20; 12:23, 27 [2×]; 13:1; 16:32; 17:1), a significant theme in this Gospel. The first three references all say that Jesus' hour had not yet come, the last six indicate that it had come. The hour towards which everything moves is the hour of Jesus' glorification, which took place through his death, resurrection and exaltation. This 'hour' was determined by God, not Jesus' opponents. Once again, therefore, the evangelist says 'no-one seized him, because his time had not yet come'.

2. *Where I am going you cannot come (8:21–29)*

In the previous passage, 8:12–20, the Pharisees challenged the validity of Jesus' testimony. In 8:21–29 Jesus warns his opponents that unless they change their attitude and believe in him they will die in their sin.

21. The evangelist begins, *Once more Jesus said to them, 'I am going away.'* This was the third time during the Feast of Tabernacles Jesus said he was going away (7:33; 8:14, 21), but on this occasion it carried an ominous warning: *and you will look for me, and you will die in your sin.* At the beginning of the Feast his opponents had been looking for him with evil intent (7:11; *cf.* 7:1). Jesus now told them that after he had gone they would look for him again, but they would not find him, because, he said, *Where I go, you cannot come.* When Jesus went away he would return to the Father, and because they did not believe in him they could not follow him there, and they would die unforgiven in unbelief. This warning is repeated and expanded in 8:24 (see commentary on that verse). His opponents would not be looking for Jesus himself – glad perhaps that he had departed the scene – but they would

be looking for the Messiah, and they would not find him, because
Jesus was their Messiah. They would die in their sin while looking
for another.

22. What Jesus said caused bewilderment: *This made the Jews
ask, 'Will he kill himself? Is that why he says, "Where I go, you cannot
come"?'* They wondered if he would commit suicide (a grievous
sin in Jewish eyes, though in times of defeat in battle it could be
regarded as more noble than submitting to capture and slavery).
There is perhaps some irony here. 'The Jews' asked if he would
commit suicide, but already they themselves were planning to kill
him (7:1).

23–24. While Jesus' opponents wondered what he meant, *he
continued, 'You are from below; I am from above. You are of this world;
I am not of this world.'* His opponents, like the rest of humankind,
were from below (this world), but he was not from this world; he
was from above (heaven) (3:13, 31; 6:38–51). When he returned to
heaven they would not be able to follow him or find him.
Repeating the ominous warning of 8:21, Jesus said, *I told you that
you would die in your sins; if you do not believe that I am [the one I claim
to be], you will indeed die in your sins.* Jesus came into the world so
that those who believe in him might not perish but have eternal
life (3:16). But the sins of those who would not believe remained
unforgiven and their guilt remained (9:41). To die in their sins
meant they themselves would bear the consequences of their sins
(3:36). The only escape was to believe in Jesus, and even at this
stage he held out this possibility to his opponents: the warning 'if
you do not believe' implies that an opportunity to believe still
remained.

The NIV has added what is in square brackets in the statement
'if you do not believe that I am [the one I claim to be]'. The words
'I am' translate *egō eimi*, which carries various meanings when
used by Jesus in this Gospel. In this context they are ambiguous.
They could mean, as the NIV addition suggests, that Jesus was
simply saying that he was the one he claimed to be, the Messiah,
sent from God. However, it is possible that, in these words, Jesus
was applying the self-description of Yahweh to himself, as he did
later (58). See Additional Note: *Egō eimi*, p. 138.

25. Jesus' opponents challenged him, *'Who are you?' they asked.* The 'you' (*sy*) is emphatic, so the question functions as a challenge, 'Who do you think you are?' His opponents knew people were saying he was 'the Prophet' or the Messiah (7:31, 40–41), but they rejected those ideas (7:47–48). As translated in the NIV, Jesus' response to this challenge was, *Just what I have been claiming all along.* The wording of Jesus' response is notoriously difficult to translate.[1] The NRSV translates it as, 'Why do I speak to you at all?' (similarly NEB). If we adopt this translation, then Jesus refused to answer their question, asking why he should bother speaking to them at all. Such a response seems appropriate, given the offensive way in which his opponents addressed him ('Who do you think you are?'). This interpretation makes 8:25b a suitable transition to 8:26 with its warnings about judgment. However, there is a difficulty with this approach, because Jesus did speak to them further. It is better, then, to adopt a modified version of the NIV translation, so Jesus' response becomes something like 'What I told you at the beginning.' He had publicly declared who he was: the Son of Man (5:27), the one sent by God (5:23–30, 36–38; 7:16, 28–29, 33), and the Son of God (5:25–26), but his opponents rejected these claims.

26. Jesus continued, *I have much to say in judgment of you.* The theme of judgment in the Fourth Gospel is complex (see Additional Note: Judgment, pp. 117–118). Jesus introduces it here in response to the unbelief of 'the Jews'. He still had much to say in judgment of his opponents, and it would be in accord with the Father's will: *But he who sent me is reliable, and what I have heard from him I tell the world.* Jesus was sent into the world to declare what he had heard from the Father – to expose sin, yes, but to offer salvation and eternal life also. The Father who sent him is reliable and it was his message that Jesus proclaimed.

27–28. When Jesus spoke of the one who sent him, his opponents *did not understand that he was telling them about his Father.*

---

[1] The difficulty arises in large part because of the obscurity of the original, *tēn archēn ho ti lalō hymin*, in which *tēn archēn* could be construed either as an accusative noun (the beginning) or as an adverbial phrase (at all). The difficulty increases when it is realized that *ho ti* (what) could also be read as *hoti* (why).

Knowing this, *Jesus said, 'When you have lifted up the Son of Man, then you will know that I am [the one I claim to be] and that I do nothing on my own but speak just what the Father has taught me.'* There are two other occasions in the Fourth Gospel when Jesus speaks about being 'lifted up', and on both these occasions being 'lifted up' refers to his death on the cross (3:14; 12:32), and this is its meaning here also. In the other two references the passive voice is used ('the Son of Man must be lifted up'; 'when I am lifted up') and those who would do the lifting up are not identified. Here Jesus told his opponents they were the ones who would 'lift him up'; they would be responsible for his crucifixion. When they lifted him up, Jesus said, 'you will know that I am' [the one I claim to be]'.

Once again the NIV has added the interpretive addition in brackets in the statement 'you will know that I am [the one I claim to be]'. With this addition Jesus would be saying to 'the Jews' that when they 'lift him up' they will realize that he is the Messiah as he has claimed. Without the addition, Jesus could be applying Yahweh's self-designation to himself (see comments on 8:24). It is difficult to decide in this case what the evangelist's intention is.

It is not clear whether the discovery by 'the Jews' of who Jesus was would be one of joy leading to salvation or one of despair, leading to destruction. In the context of rejection and challenge on the part of 'the Jews' and of strong rejoinder on the part of Jesus, the discovery is more likely to be one of despair, leading to destruction. When they have 'lifted him up', and when they see the exalted one coming with the clouds of heaven, they will realize who he is, and that he said and did nothing on his own, and that all he said was what the Father taught him, but then it will be too late.

29. Jesus concluded this exchange with 'the Jews' with the words *The one who sent me is with me; he has not left me alone, for I always do what pleases him*. Because Jesus always did what pleased the Father, the Father never abandoned him. He protected him throughout his ministry, and no attempts to bring it to a premature end succeeded (see 7:30; 8:20).

3. The truth will make you free (8:30–38)

30–32. Referring to Jesus' teaching in the previous section, the evangelist says, *Even as he spoke, many put their faith in him.* Then he adds, *To the Jews who had believed him, Jesus said, 'If you hold to my teaching, you are really my disciples.'* To be true disciples they must hold to his teaching (lit. 'remain in my word'). The hallmark of the true disciple is remaining in Jesus' word, *i.e.* obedience to his teaching (see 14:15, 21, 23, 24; 15:10; 17:6). Perhaps the 'believers' needed this exhortation to continue in his word because there were many present who rejected it, and would urge them to reject it also. If they did 'remain in his word', Jesus promised, *Then you will know the truth, and the truth will set you free.* Jesus spoke of freedom from sin (as the next verse makes plain), and all it involves: freedom from condemnation (5:24), darkness (12) the power of the evil one (17:15; *cf.* 1 Jn. 5:18) and death (5:24; 8:51).

33. These people who 'put their faith in him' were not true disciples, for straightaway they rejected what Jesus said: *They answered him, 'We are Abraham's descendants and have never been slaves of anyone.'* This is the first of eleven references to Abraham in the Fourth Gospel, all of which are found here in the latter part of chapter 8 (vv. 33, 37, 39 [3×], 40, 52, 53, 56, 57, 58). They all relate to a claim by the 'believers' that they were Abraham's children and their rejection of Jesus' teaching. Reference to Abraham in the context of the Feast of Tabernacles is not surprising, because of the Jewish tradition that Abraham himself celebrated this feast and was the first to do so (*Jubilees* 16:20–31).

Jewish people rightly thought of themselves as Abraham's children, and Jesus himself used the expression for them (Lk. 13:16; 19:9). But in some cases this led to presumption. They believed that because they were Abraham's descendants they would automatically inherit the kingdom of God. John the Baptist warned them not to presume upon this (Mt. 3:9/Lk. 3:8). Jesus warned that not all Jews would inherit the kingdom (Mt. 8:11–12).[1]

---

[1] The Christian apologist Justin Martyr made the same point in his dialogue with Trypho the Jew: 'And you utterly deceive yourselves, in supposing that because you are Abraham's seed according to the flesh you will certainly inherit the good things which God has announced that He will give to men through Christ' (*Dialogue with Trypho* xliv.1)

By presuming they would inherit the kingdom on the basis of physical descent from Abraham alone, Jewish people were on shaky ground.

The 'believers', who prided themselves on being Abraham's descendants, were incensed by Jesus saying that if they held to his teaching they would be truly free, for it implied that they were presently enslaved. So they replied, *How can you say that we shall be set free?* Once again the 'you' (*sy*) is emphatic (*cf.* 8:25), indicating that their words are intended as a challenge to Jesus: 'How can *you* say that we shall be set free?' Although the Jewish people were in bondage, languishing under Roman occupation, the Pharisees believed they were spiritually free despite the occupation,[1] and these 'believers' thought the same.

34. Responding to their challenge, *Jesus replied, 'I tell you the truth, everyone who sins is a slave to sin.'* The 'believers' boasted of their spiritual freedom as children of Abraham, but Jesus warned them they were still in bondage because of their sins. This bondage was not something they could break free from themselves. Later, the rabbis used various metaphors to describe the insidious enslavement of sin: 'At the beginning it is like a spider's thread, but finally it will be like a ship's rope' (R. Akiba, c. AD 135), 'at the beginning it is like a guest, later it will become the ruler of the household' (R. Jicchaq, c. AD 300), and 'at the beginning it is weak like a woman, afterwards it will be strong like a man' (R. Sch^emuël, c. AD 325).[2]

35–36. Jesus used a household metaphor to drive home his point: *Now a slave has no permanent place in the family, but a son belongs to it for ever.* Literally translated this verse would read, 'the slave does not remain in the house(hold) (*oikia*) for ever; the son remains [in it] for ever'. In this statement Jesus is 'the son'[3] who remains for ever in God's house(hold). As the Son he was able to make those who were slaves free, and Jesus said, *if the Son sets you*

---

[1]This did not satisfy all Jews. The Zealots would acknowledge no Lord but Yahweh and were involved in a violent struggle for independence.

[2]See Str-B 2, 523.

[3]In the Fourth Gospel the word 'son' (*huios*) is reserved for Jesus; believers are referred to as 'children of God' (*ta tekna tou theou*).

free, you will be free indeed. Those whom he released from slavery to sin enjoyed freedom from judgment (3:18; 5:24) and the power of death (5:24; 8:51), and an end to alienation from God, as they were adopted into God's family (1:12).

37. Because of their misplaced pride in being children of Abraham, the 'believers' could not accept Jesus' teaching about freedom. So he said to them, *I know you are Abraham's descendants. Yet you are ready to kill me, because you have no room for my word.* The word 'descendants' translates *sperma* (lit. 'seed'), used also by the 'believers' of themselves in 8:33. Jesus agreed that they were physical descendants (*sperma*) of Abraham, though later he would deny they were true children (*tekna*) of Abraham.

The NIV's translation 'because you have no room for my word' is not as good as the RSV's 'because my word finds no place in you', seeing that in this sentence the subject is 'my word', not 'you' (*hoti ho logos ho emos ou chōrei en hymin*). Jesus was saying his word did not find a place in the 'believers' because of their prejudices. It was like the seed sown on the path in the parable of the sower.

It is surprising that Jesus accused 'believers' of being ready to kill him. It would seem that Jesus, who knew what was in people, knew how shallow their belief was and how quickly they would turn against him and join their leaders in being ready to kill him. This was so, he said, because 'my word finds no place in you'.

38. To those who rejected his words, Jesus said, *I am telling you what I have seen in the Father's presence, and you do what you have heard from your father.* His teaching was based on what he had seen in the Father's presence. What they were rejecting was a revelation of God. In rejecting it and being ready to kill him, they were doing what they had heard from their father, not Abraham, as they claimed, but the devil, as 8:39–44 makes clear.

4. *Your father the devil (8:39–47)*

39–41. In response to Jesus' statement that they were doing what they had heard from their 'father', the 'believers' answered, *Abraham is our father.* Falling back on their claim to be descendants of Abraham, they rejected the implication in Jesus' words that they were children of someone else. Jesus responded, *If you were Abraham's children, then you would do the things Abraham did.* Jesus acknowledged they were Abraham's seed (*sperma*) (37), *i.e.* Abraham's physical descendants, but he denied they were Abraham's children (*tekna*). Jesus told them true children of Abraham would behave as Abraham did. (Paul makes a similar point in Rom. 4:12.) This was not the case with the 'believers', as Jesus pointed out: *As it is, you are determined to kill me, a man who has told you the truth that I heard from God.* Once more Jesus accused them of wanting to kill him (*cf.* 8:37) – something they wished to do because they could not accept the truth he had told them, truth he had heard from God. Jesus said, *Abraham did not do such things* – he was renowned for his humble acceptance of the word of God, even when he did not understand it (Gn. 12:1–4; 22:1–14). Having said they were not acting as Abraham had done, Jesus added, *You are doing the things your own father does.* The 'believers' were incensed once more and declared, *We are not illegitimate children,* perhaps implying that Jesus was. In Hosea 2:4 God, speaking through the prophet, called Israel 'children of adultery' because they had forsaken him and gone after other gods. The 'believers', sensing that Jesus was accusing them of being spiritual illegitimates, asserted, *The only Father we have is God himself.* They claimed not only that they were Abraham's children but children of God also. There is scriptural warrant for such a claim, for Israel was regarded as God's son (Ex. 4:22) and God was regarded as Israel's father (Je. 31:9).

42. Without denying the truth of the Scriptures, Jesus pointed out that it did not apply in their case: *If God were your Father, you would love me, for I came from God and now am here.* Jesus denied the claim of the 'believers' that God was their Father. The evidence for this was that they did not love him, the one who came from the Father and was present among them. Jesus added, *I have not come on my own; but he sent me.* If they rejected the one whom God sent, they could not claim God as their Father. As Jesus said to 'the Jews' in 5:23, 'He who does not honour the Son does not honour the Father, who sent him.'

43. Jesus explained the fundamental problem with the 'believers': *Why is my language not clear to you? Because you are unable to hear what I say*. His 'language' (lit. 'speech' or what he said) was not clear to them because they were unable/unwilling to hear his message. The verb 'to hear' (*akouō*) means not only to hear, but also to heed or obey what is said. Obedience is the key to understanding (7:17: 'If anyone chooses to do God's will, he will find out whether my teaching comes from God'). These people were not willing to obey Jesus' message; no wonder it was not clear to them.

44–45. Having rejected the claim of the 'believers' that God was their Father, Jesus told them who their father was: *You belong to your father, the devil, and you want to carry out your father's desire*. The devil is mentioned three times in the Fourth Gospel, always in relation to people who did the devil's work. Judas Iscariot is twice said either to be a devil (6:70) or to be motivated by the devil (13:2) because he planned to betray Jesus. In 8:44 the 'believers' are said to belong to their father, the devil, because they are intent upon carrying out the devil's desire by killing Jesus (*cf.* 8:37, 40). They were acting not like Abraham (39), but like the devil, because *he was a murderer from the beginning, not holding to the truth, for there is no truth in him*. The 'believers' rejected Jesus' call to hold to the truth and enjoy true freedom (31–33), and became like the devil who did not hold to the truth and was a murderer from the beginning. This is probably an allusion to Genesis 3, where the devil tempted the first couple to disobey God and so caused them to lose eternal life. Then their sin spread to Cain, who murdered his brother Abel (1 Jn. 3:8 also refers to the devil sinning 'from the beginning'). Jesus then described something of the nature of the devil: *When he lies, he speaks his native language, for he is a liar and the father of lies*. The words the NIV translates 'he speaks his native language' rendered literally would read 'he speaks from his own self'. By nature, in his own self, the devil 'is a liar, and the father of lies'. This is an allusion to Genesis 3, where the devil, through his lie, introduced sin into the world; and in that sense the devil is the 'father of lies'.

When Jesus told the 'believers' they were of their father the devil, he was speaking ethically, and as a Jew to Jews. The statement is not anti-Semitic, nor is the Fourth Gospel as a whole anti-Semitic. Its purpose is to show the love of God for all peoples and to encourage Jews and Gentiles to put their faith in Christ and so experience eternal life.

The 'believers', Jesus said, were prepared to do the work of the devil, the father of lies, *Yet because I tell the truth, you do not believe me!* Here is irony. They were prepared to do the will of the father of lies, but they would not believe the one who told them the truth! It was because the truth cut across their misplaced pride in being the descendants of Abraham.

46. Jesus then asked, *Can any of you prove me guilty of sin?* The verb translated 'prove guilty of sin' is *elenchō*, a verb used in only two other places in the Fourth Gospel: in 3:20, where it is translated 'expose' ('everyone who does evil hates the light, and will not come into the light for fear that his deeds will be exposed'), and in 16:8, where it is translated 'convict' ('when he [the Holy Spirit] comes, he will convict the world of guilt in regard to sin and righteousness and judgment'). In 8:46 Jesus challenged the 'believers' to expose the sin in him that prevented them from believing in him. Knowing they could not do this, he asked the question that logically followed: *If I am telling the truth, why don't you believe me?* Jesus was pressing the point. If they could not prove him guilty of sin, they must face the possibility that he was telling the truth; and if he was telling the truth they would have to show why they did not believe him.

47. Jesus explained the underlying causes for belief and unbelief. First he stated the matter positively: *He who belongs to God hears what God says.* Then he stated it negatively in relation to those who rejected his word: *The reason you do not hear is that you do not belong to God.* Jesus had already told them they were children of their Father, the devil – they listened to him and did his will. It was because they belonged to the devil and not to God that they would not heed the word of Jesus.

5. Before Abraham was I am (8:48–59)

48. The evangelist now introduces other opponents. In 8:31–47 Jesus addressed the 'believers' who by their response to his teaching showed they did not truly believe. In 8:48–59 it is 'the Jews' who attack Jesus: *The Jews answered him, 'Aren't we right in saying that you are a Samaritan and demon-possessed?'* 'The Jews' had already made up their minds Jesus ought to die (5:18; 7:1, 19, 20). They heaped abuse upon him, declaring him to be 'a Samaritan and demon-possessed'. There were Samaritan prophets who made great claims (see Acts 8:9–11) whom Jews regarded as demon-possessed. It was in this vein that 'the Jews' called Jesus 'a Samaritan and demon-possessed'. This was not the first nor last time Jesus was branded as demon-possessed in the Fourth Gospel (*cf.* 7:20; 8:48, 52; 10:20). In the Synoptic Gospels the teachers of the law, to explain Jesus' miraculous powers without recognizing that God was with him, said, 'He is possessed by Beelzebub! By the prince of demons he is driving out demons' (Mk. 3:22/Mt. 9:34; 12:24).

49–50. In response to this abuse Jesus said, *I am not possessed by a demon, but I honour my Father and you dishonour me.* Jesus rejected their defamatory statement, asserting rather that he was intent upon honouring God, his Father, and that 'the Jews' were guilty of dishonouring the one who was honouring God. Jesus insisted, *I am not seeking glory for myself.* As one who was honouring his Father, Jesus did not seek glory for himself. He added, *there is one who seeks it, and he is the judge.* God the Father is judge of all and he seeks glory for the Son. In the OT the righteous committed their case to the Lord, the righteous judge who vindicated them. Jesus did not have to defend himself or seek his own glory. The Father would vindicate him and glorify him as well (*cf.* 17:4–5).

51. In what looks like another attempt to offer eternal life to his opponents, Jesus said, *I tell you the truth, if anyone keeps my word, he will never see death.* This statement was introduced with the solemn formula 'I tell you the truth' (*amēn, amēn legō hymin*), underlining the importance of what he was saying to his opponents. If any of them would change their minds and give heed to Jesus' word, they could still receive the gift of eternal life, and 'never see death'. From earlier statements of Jesus it is clear that this did not mean those who believed would not experience physical death, for obviously all but the last generation would do so.

Rather, it meant that eternal life, which people experience now through belief in Jesus, will not be interrupted by physical death: 'He who believes in me will live, even though he dies; and whoever lives and believes in me will never die' (11:25–26).

52–53. The evangelist tells how Jesus' gracious words were misunderstood and rejected: *At this the Jews exclaimed, 'Now we know that you are demon-possessed!'* They felt confirmed in their opinion that Jesus was demon-possessed, and explained why: *Abraham died and so did the prophets, yet you say that if anyone keeps your word, he will never taste death.* Taking Jesus to mean that none who keep his word would experience physical death, they pointed out that even Abraham and the prophets had died, and mockingly they asked him, *Are you greater than our father Abraham? He died, and so did the prophets.* 'The Jews' question 'Are you greater than our father Abraham?' recalls the question of the Samaritan woman 'Are you greater than our father Jacob?' (4:12). In both cases the evangelist hopes his readers will see the irony involved, for Jesus was indeed greater than both these patriarchs. 'The Jews' concluded by challenging Jesus with the words *Who do you think you are?* (lit. 'Who are you making yourself?'). They were convinced Jesus had an inflated opinion of his own importance, because he claimed the divine prerogative of preserving people from death. They believed he was glorifying himself.

54–55. Contrary to what 'the Jews' thought, *Jesus replied, 'If I glorify myself, my glory means nothing.'* Self-glorification is meaningless, and Jesus was not interested in it. However, he told 'the Jews', *My Father, whom you claim as your God, is the one who glorifies me.'* Jesus did not need to glorify himself, because the Father did that for him (see 12:28; 13:31–32; 17:1, 5). And his Father is the one his opponents claimed as their God, but Jesus was aware they did not even know God and said, *though you do not know him, I know him.* This was something Jesus could not deny: *If I said I did not, I would be a liar like you, but I do know him and keep his word.* They were liars because they claimed to know God when they did not. Jesus would be a liar if he denied he knew God when he did. He did know him and kept his commands.

56. Acknowledging only for the sake of argument the claim of 'the Jews' that Abraham was their father, Jesus said, *Your father Abraham rejoiced at the thought of seeing my day; he saw it and was glad.* There are two ways of interpreting this statement. Some appeal to Genesis 17:17, which records Abraham's laughing reaction to the promise that he and Sarah would have a child in their old age, viewing this not only as his joy at the promise of Isaac, but also his joyful hope for the day of the Messiah (see *Jubilees* 15:17; 16:19–20). Others appeal to *Genesis Rabbah* 44:22, which describes a disagreement between two rabbis concerning what God revealed to Abraham: 'R. Johanan b. Zakkai and R. Akiba disagree. One maintains: This world He revealed to him, but not the next. The other maintains that He revealed to him both this world and the next. R. Berekiah said: R. Leasar and R. Jose b. R. Hanina disagreed. One maintained: He revealed to him [the future] *until* that day; while the other said: He revealed to him the future *from* that day.' Despite the disagreements of the rabbis concerning the exact nature of what God revealed to Abraham, they all assumed that something of the future was revealed to him. Two of them spoke about 'that day', the day of the Messiah, being revealed to him. Thus, it is claimed, Jesus was alluding to the Jews' own belief that Abraham saw 'my day', the day of the Messiah.

57. While we might have difficulty explaining exactly what Jesus meant, the response of his opponents shows they took him literally: *'You are not yet fifty years old,' the Jews said to him, 'and you have seen Abraham!'* The mention of Jesus being 'not yet fifty years old' is puzzling in the light of Luke 3:23 which says he was 'about thirty years old when he began his ministry'. There is some evidence that Jewish people spoke of people achieving a jubilee of years (50 years of age) or even two jubilees (100 years of age). To say that a person was not yet 50 years old was equivalent to saying he had not yet even achieved his first jubilee. Such a comment was not intended to reflect accurately a person's age. There is therefore no real conflict with Luke 3:23. There is a stipulation in the Dead Sea Scrolls (CD 14:7–10; *cf.* 1Qsa 1:13–18) that candidates for some offices in the Qumran community must not be younger than 30 nor older than 50 years of age. Neither Luke nor the fourth evangelist was trying to provide precise information about Jesus' age.

Both reflect a knowledge of the traditions concerning age require-
ments for public office.

Jesus, of course, did not say he had seen Abraham, but that
Abraham had seen his day.[1] Based on their own misunderstanding, and recognizing that Jesus was clearly not 50 years of age,
they thought what Jesus said was ludicrous, and said so.

58. Responding to 'the Jews' in terms of their misunderstanding, Jesus made a solemn pronouncement. Beginning with the
formula *I tell you the truth* (amēn amēn legō hymin), *Jesus answered,*
'before Abraham was born, I am!' Jesus' opponents ridiculed the idea
that he could have seen Abraham (their statement not his), but in
response Jesus gave them something far more astounding to think
about. He claimed to have existed prior to Abraham's birth (just
as God existed prior to the creation of the world: Ps. 90:2). This
comes as no surprise to readers of the Fourth Gospel, because in
the Prologue they are informed that the Word who became flesh
in the person of Jesus was with God in the beginning. But there is
more involved in Jesus' statement 'before Abraham was born, I
am'. The words 'I am' (*egō eimi*) are used in a number of different
ways on the lips of Jesus in the Fourth Gospel (see Additional
Note: *egō eimi*, p. 138). Here they are clearly used in an absolute
sense representing the divine name. Thus when Jesus said to 'the
Jews', 'before Abraham was born, I am', he was identifying
himself with God. Perhaps Jesus was also implying that Abraham,
great though he was, had lived and died, but that he, Jesus,
because he is one with God, remains forever as the 'I am'.

59. Jesus' opponents understood the implications of what he
said, and because they did not believe in him it appeared to them
as blasphemy of the worst sort. The evangelist says, *At this, they*
picked up stones to stone him. Stoning was the penalty for blasphemy
prescribed in the OT (Lv. 24:14–16, 23; *cf.* 1 Ki. 21:13–14). In terms of
the law they would have been right to stone him, *i.e.* unless Jesus
was who he claimed to be. Later on 'the Jews' made another
attempt to stone Jesus, this time stating explicitly that they were

[1]There is a minority variant reading that has 'Abraham has seen you' instead of 'you have
seen Abraham', which, if adopted would remove this problem.

doing so because they were convinced he was a blasphemer (10:31–33). But both then and now their attempts were unsuccessful. On this occasion *Jesus hid himself, slipping away from the temple grounds.*[1] All indications are that Jesus hid himself, not because he was afraid, but because his 'hour had not yet come'. Jesus would return quite openly to the temple again (10:22–23; 12:20–22).

It is ironic that at the Feast of Tabernacles 'the Jews' rejected Jesus and, as it were, turned their backs on him. The Mishnah describes one of the daily rituals of this Feast: 'When they [two priests] reached the gate that leads out to the east, they turned their faces to the west and said, "Our fathers when they were in this place turned with their backs toward the Temple of the Lord and their faces toward the east, and they worshipped the sun toward the east; but as for us, our eyes are turned toward the Lord"' (*Sukkah* 5:4). While their priests were dissociating themselves from their forefathers who turned their backs on the temple of the Lord and worshipped the sun, 'the Jews' were turning their backs on the Lord himself as he visited them in the person of his Son.

N. JESUS HEALS A MAN BORN BLIND (9:1–41)

The story of the healing of the man born blind is set in Jerusalem and took place as Jesus left the temple at the conclusion of the Feast of Tabernacles (8:59 – 9:1). It is a brilliant and dramatic presentation comprising eight scenes.

1. *Jesus' disciples ask about the man born blind (9:1–5)*

1–2. Jesus left the temple (8:59) and *as he went along, he saw a man blind from birth.* The evangelist's reference to the man's congenital blindness prepares his readers for the extraordinary miracle that is to follow. Seeing him, the disciples asked Jesus, *'Rabbi, who sinned, this man or his parents, that he was born blind?'* This question reflects a view that all suffering was punishment for

---

[1]It has been asked where 'the Jews' would have obtained stones to throw at Jesus in the temple grounds. One possibility is that there were stones lying about in the temple grounds because the process of building the temple initiated by Herod the Great had not yet been completed.

sin of one kind or another. There is a general connection between sin and suffering due to the fall. There is sometimes a direct connection between a particular sin of an individual and suffering (see 5:14), but not always (see Lk. 13:2–5). Congenital afflictions raise the problem of sin and suffering in a particularly sharp fashion. The disciples' question implied that congenital afflictions were punishments (1) for sins of unborn children committed either in their mothers' wombs or by their pre-existent souls; (2) visited upon children for the sins of their parents.

3. Jesus rejected both these explanations for the man's affliction: *'Neither this man nor his parents sinned,' said Jesus, 'but this happened so that the work of God might be displayed in his life.'* However, he did not himself offer a third explanation. Instead, he spoke of the opportunity it provided for a display of God's power in the extraordinary healing he was about to perform. The 'work of God' is, as it nearly always is in the Fourth Gospel, the work that God does through Jesus (see 5:36; 14:10–11; 17:4).

4. Before healing the man, Jesus made a general statement about the importance of carrying out the works of God while it was still possible to do so: *As long as it is day, we must do the work of him who sent me. Night is coming, when no-one can work.* Jesus' was sent into the world to do the work given him by the Father to do (4:34; 5:36; 17:4). He associated his disciples with him in doing this work (*'we* must do the work of him who sent me'). Jesus' work was to reveal the Father through his teaching and actions/miracles (1:18). For Jesus, night would fall and the opportunity for work in the world would cease when he was betrayed by Judas, arrested, tried and crucified. Before 'nightfall' he was determined to continue his work, unhindered by the machinations of his enemies (*cf.* 11:7–11).

Verses 3 and 4, punctuated as they are in the NIV (and most other English versions and modern Greek texts), present an unattractive theodicy. They imply that God allowed the man to be born blind so that many years later God's power could be shown in the restoration of his sight. However, it is not necessary to read the text in this way. Two things need to be noted. First, the words 'this happened' have been added by the NIV translators and there are no corresponding words in the Greek text. Second, early Greek manuscripts of the NT were not punctuated; later editors added the punctuation. Rendered literally and without punctuation 9:3-4 would read, 'Jesus replied neither this man sinned nor his parents but so that the works of God may be revealed in him it is necessary for us to work the works of him who sent me while it is day night is coming when no-one is able to work.' It is possible to punctuate this so as to provide the following translation: 'Jesus replied, "Neither this man sinned nor his parents. But so that the works of God may be revealed in him it is necessary for us to work the works of him who sent me while it is day; night is coming when no-one is able to work."' Punctuated in this way, the text implies not that the man was born blind so that the works of God may be revealed in him, but that Jesus had to carry out the work of God while it was day so that God's work might be revealed in the life of the man born blind.

5. Concluding the discussion with his disciples, Jesus said, *While I am in the world, I am the light of the world*. The Logos incarnate in Jesus Christ was the true light coming into the world (1:4, 5, 7). He brought the light of truth into the world – truth about God (1:18) and the human condition (3:19-21). For unbelievers this light would shine only as long as Jesus was in the world. As he told them in 12:35, 'You are going to have the light just a little while longer. Walk while you have the light, before darkness overtakes you.' For those who believed, however, the light would continue to shine even after Jesus' departure, so that they would never walk in darkness (8:12).

2. *Jesus heals the man born blind (9:6-7)*

6. The evangelist continues, *Having said this, he spat on the ground, made some mud with the saliva, and put it on the man's eyes*. On two other occasions Jesus used saliva in acts of healing (Mk. 7:33; 8:23). Here he used saliva to make mud, mixing it with dirt. This becomes significant later in the story when we are told he performed the healing on a sabbath, because the act of kneading (which is involved in making mud from saliva and dirt) was regarded as one of the thirty-nine forms of work that violated the

221

sabbath (see commentary on 5:9b-10). The verb translated 'put on' is *epichriō*, which means 'to anoint'. It is found only here and in 9:11 in the NT. According to the Mishnah, normal anointing such as one might do on weekdays was allowable on the sabbath, but anointing with special substances not normally used was forbidden because that constituted a healing activity that was not allowed (*Šabbat* 14:4).

7. After Jesus made mud and anointed the blind man's eyes, *'Go,' he told him, 'wash in the Pool of Siloam' (this word means Sent). So the man went and washed, and came home seeing.* Unlike Naaman who objected when Elisha sent him to wash in the Jordan (2 Ki. 5:10–14), the man born blind responded with unquestioning obedience when Jesus sent him to wash in the Pool of Siloam (an example of true faith). After he washed he came home seeing.

Water for the Pool of Siloam was channelled through Hezekiah's tunnel from the Gihon spring. The Pool of Siloam was the source of the water used in the water-pouring ceremonies during the Feast of Tabernacles (see commentary on 7:37–39). The evangelist explains that Siloam means 'Sent'. The consonants of the Hebrew verb 'to send' (*šālaḥ*) are the same as those of the Hebrew for Siloam (*šilôaḥ*), which allowed popular etymology to make the link. Perhaps the evangelist added this explanation to connect the name of the Pool with the fact that Jesus sent the man there to wash, so as to make clear that the miracle occurred because Jesus sent him, not because of any healing qualities in the water itself.

3. The man is questioned by his neighbours (9:8–12)

8–9. Jesus' healing of the man born blind produced an immediate transformation: he no longer sat and begged. Confronted with this reality, *His neighbours and those who had formerly seen him begging asked, 'Isn't this the same man who used to sit and beg?'* The answers were various: *Some claimed that he was. Others said, 'No, he only looks like him.'* The latter thought it was impossible for a man born blind to be healed, and so distrusted their eyes – the man before them must be someone else. No-one bothered to ask the man whether he was the one who used to sit and beg, *But he* *himself insisted, 'I am the man.'* In responding he used the formula *egō eimi* (lit. 'I am'; here correctly rendered 'I am the man'), often used by Jesus himself, sometimes with the same basic meaning 'I am he', but sometimes with much greater theological significance (see Additional Note: *Egō eimi*, p. 138)

10–12. Confronted with the man's insistence that he was the one born blind, his neighbours asked, *How then were your eyes opened? He replied, 'The man they call Jesus made some mud and put it on my eyes. He told me to go to Siloam and wash. So I went and washed, and then I could see.'* The man knew Jesus' name ('the one they call Jesus'), but as yet he had not seen him – he was still blind when he left Jesus and went to the pool to wash. So when his neighbours asked him, *Where is this man?*, he could only respond, *I don't know.* He would not have known Jesus if he saw him!

4. *The man is questioned by the Pharisees (9:13–17)*

13–14. What follows is puzzling: the neighbours *brought to the Pharisees the man who had been blind.* This action might have arisen from a desire on their part to bring to the Pharisees' attention evidence of the great miracle Jesus had performed. However, the next words foreshadow difficulties their action would create: *Now the day on which Jesus had made the mud and opened the man's eyes was a Sabbath.* Mixing saliva and dirt was regarded as kneading, and applying an unusual salve was regarded as healing. Both these actions were prohibited on the sabbath according to Pharisaic tradition (see commentary on 9:6). Whether intended or not, the neighbours' action provided the Pharisees with evidence against Jesus, and threw the man born blind to the wolves.

15. Hearing the miracle was performed on the sabbath, *Therefore the Pharisees also asked him how he had received his sight.* They were not interested in the miracle that had occurred, nor the benefits it procured for the man. They wanted only to know 'how' it was done, because they wanted evidence to use against Jesus. The man responded more cautiously to the Pharisees than he had to his neighbours: *'He put mud on my eyes,' the man replied, 'and I washed, and now I see.'* He made no reference to Jesus' 'kneading'

223

saliva and dirt to make mud; only that he put mud on his eyes. He did not say Jesus sent him to the Pool of Siloam to wash; only that he washed, with the result 'now I see'.

16. Confronted with the man's simple testimony, the Pharisees were divided in their opinions: *Some of the Pharisees said, 'This man is not from God, for he does not keep the Sabbath.'* For them the overriding concern was sabbath observance. No matter what miraculous signs Jesus performed he could not possibly be 'from God', because he violated God's law. Such reasoning, though based on a false interpretation of the sabbath law, followed warnings found in Deuteronomy 13:1–5. There the people of Israel are warned about those who perform miraculous signs and at the same time lead people away from God. Such people were to be put to death because they preached rebellion against the Lord. Some of the Pharisees appear to have interpreted Jesus' action this way. He had performed a miracle, but he also broke the sabbath law. He must be a sinner and therefore could not be from God. *But others asked, 'How can a sinner do such miraculous signs?'* For this second group the nature of Jesus' signs, especially the healing of a man born blind, forced them to ask whether one who did such things could be described as a 'sinner', *i.e.* a violator of the law. Their reasoning was defective (false prophets sometimes produce miracles, as Dt. 13:1–5 attests) though their conclusion was correct. Because of differing opinions, *they were divided*.

17. Being divided in their opinions, *finally they turned again to the blind man, 'What have you to say about him? It was your eyes he opened.'* Why, when they could not agree among themselves about Jesus, they should ask the man for his opinion is not clear. At first it seems they asked him because, as the one who benefited from Jesus' healing, he ought to know about his benefactor. But as the story unfolds it becomes clear they were in no mood to receive the man's testimony (24). The man gave his opinion without hesitation: *He is a prophet*. In the OT and Jewish tradition prophets were known to be miracle workers, and it seemed to the man that his benefactor must fall into this category.

5. Parents of the man are questioned by 'the Jews' (9:18–23)

18–19. As the evangelist continues his account, he speaks of the reaction of 'the Jews', not 'the Pharisees'. This is probably a stylistic variation, though possibly 'the Jews' denotes the Jewish Sanhedrin, which included some Pharisees (3:1; 7:32, 45, 47–48; 11:47; 18:3). It appears earlier questions about how the man born blind had been healed were asked with mental reservations, just going along with the report about a miracle for the time being. In fact, the evangelist says, *The Jews still did not believe that he had been blind and had received his sight until they sent for the man's parents.* Being unwilling to accept the testimony either of the man's neighbours or the man himself, they summoned his parents, from whom they demanded answers to three questions: *'Is this your son?' they asked. 'Is this the one you say was born blind? How is it that now he can see?'*

20–21. The man's parents answered the first two questions in the affirmative: *'We know he is our son,' the parents answered, 'and we know he was born blind.'* But the third question involved hidden dangers for them and they responded cautiously: *But how he can see now, or who opened his eyes, we don't know. Ask him. He is of age; he will speak for himself.* A Jewish boy comes of age at 13 years and one day and is then able to give legally viable testimony – his vows are valid.[1] The parents pointed out that he had come of age and therefore could answer for himself. They must have heard from their neighbours, if not their son, how his sight had been restored, but they were afraid to say so in front of 'the Jews'.

22–23. The evangelist explains why they were so cautious: *His parents said this because they were afraid of the Jews, for already the Jews had decided that anyone who acknowledged that Jesus was the Christ would be put out of the synagogue.* This is the first of three occasions in the Fourth Gospel where belief in Jesus as the Christ is linked with the threat of expulsion from the synagogue (22; 12:42; 16:2). The word used in each case is *aposynagōgos*, a word found in the

---

[1] *Cf.* Mishnah, *Niddah* 5:6, which also says a girl comes of age at 12 years and a day, and then her vows are valid.

NT only in the Fourth Gospel, which means 'put out of the synagogue' or 'excommunicated'. Excommunication could take two forms: *temporary* for remedial purposes (Heb. *niddâ)* and *permanent* (Heb. *ḥērem*), although it is not clear whether this distinction existed among the Jews in NT times. That some form of excommunication was practised is evident, not only from the three texts in the Fourth Gospel, but also from the beatitude in Luke 6:22 ('Blessed are you when men hate you, / when they exclude you and insult you / and reject your name as evil, / because of the Son of Man'). Paul called for remedial excommunication for the incestuous person in 1 Corinthians 5:4–5, 6–7, 13, and permanent expulsion may be implied by references to cursing or anathematizing people, found in Mark 14:71; Acts 23:12, 14, 21; Romans 9:3; 1 Corinthians 12:3; 16:22 and Galatians 1:8–9. The evangelist reiterates, *That was why his parents said, 'He is of age; ask him'*; they were afraid of excommunication.

The evangelist's three references to expulsion from the synagogue of Jews who believed in Jesus suggests that when he wrote, those who contemplated such a step still faced this threat. While this does not mean what the evangelist says about the threat of excommunication in Jesus' day is anachronistic, it does suggest that he wrote at a time when there was tension between the Jewish synagogue and the Christian community. Jews would know they could not confess Christ and continue as members of the synagogue, something that was possible in the early years of the Christian movement.

6. The man is questioned by 'the Jews' again (9:24–34)

24. Following the interrogation of the man's parents, 'the Jews' could no longer deny a miracle had been performed, so *a second time they summoned the man who had been blind. 'Give glory to God,' they said. 'We know this man is a sinner.'* 'The Jews' were convinced Jesus was a 'sinner', because he violated their sabbath rules. By demanding the man born blind 'give glory to God' they were demanding he tell the truth about Jesus, because they suspected he was hiding something. In similar fashion Joshua exhorted Achan to 'give glory to God' by acknowledging the truth he was hiding when his sin was discovered (Jos. 7:19–20). The Achan passage is cited in the Mishnah, where a person condemned to death by stoning is urged to make a final confession, 'giving glory to God' by acknowledging his sin (*Sanhedrin* 6:2).

25. The man was not intimidated by these demands: *He replied, 'Whether he is a sinner or not, I don't know. One thing I do know. I was blind but now I see!'* He did not wish to engage in debate about the character of Jesus; he simply reiterated the one undeniable fact: 'I was blind but now I see.'

26. Realizing they were making no progress by trying to get the man to testify against Jesus, 'the Jews' took another tack: *Then they asked him, 'What did he do to you? How did he open your eyes?'* They reverted to their previous question about what Jesus actually did to give the man his sight (15a), hoping perhaps the man might contradict himself under interrogation or say something that would show that Jesus was a sabbath breaker and therefore a sinner.

27. The man's response reflects growing boldness. *He answered, 'I have told you already and you did not listen. Why do you want to hear it again? Do you want to become his disciples, too?'* He had already answered this question (15b) and they did not believe his response then. What had changed? Cheekily he suggested their repetition of the same question indicated they also wanted to become Jesus' disciples.

28–29. 'The Jews' responded indignantly to the man's cheeky suggestion. *Then they hurled insults at him and said, 'You are this fellow's disciple!'* They interpreted the man's question whether they 'also' wanted to become disciples of Jesus as an admission that he was his disciple. They claimed for themselves what they believed was a higher loyalty: *We are disciples of Moses!* This is one of several places in the Fourth Gospel where Jewish allegiance to Moses is set over against the claims of Jesus (5:45–46; 6:32; 7:19–23; [8:5]; 9:28–29). There is evidence that the claim to be 'disciples of Moses' was made by the Pharisees to the exclusion of the Sadducees (Str-B 2, 535), but in the present context the claim is made by 'the Jews', probably meaning the members of the Sanhedrin (which included both Sadducees and Pharisees).

In support of Moses' credentials, and to disparage those of Jesus, 'the Jews' added, *We know that God spoke to Moses, but as for this fellow, we don't even know where he comes from.* Moses' credentials were established by the fact that God spoke to him, sending him to lead the Israelites out of Egypt and giving him the law for Israel. As for Jesus, 'the Jews' believed he was without credentials. His family and place of origin (important for establishing identity in the ancient world) were unknown to these 'Jews', and therefore they regarded Jesus as a nobody.

30–33. In the face of the insults heaped upon him, the man's boldness only increased: *The man answered, 'Now that is remarkable! You don't know where he comes from, yet he opened my eyes.'* The unbelief of 'the Jews' was remarkable in the light of what Jesus had done. Their ignorance of Jesus' origins did not detract from Jesus' worth, but reflected an appalling lack of knowledge on their part. Here was one who could cure congenital blindness and they knew nothing about him! The man then proceeded to give 'the Jews' a lesson in theology: *We know that God does not listen to sinners. He listens to the godly man who does his will.* 'The Jews' had rightly insisted that God *spoke to* Moses; the man born blind pointed out that God *listens to* Jesus! That God listened to Jesus was evident from the fact that he granted him the power to give sight to one who was congenitally blind. That God listened to Jesus indicated 'the Jews' were mistaken when they said Jesus was a sinner (24). The statement of the man born blind includes an implicit definition of a 'godly man': one who does God's will. The man drove his point home: *Nobody has ever heard of opening the eyes of a man born blind. If this man were not from God, he could do nothing.* This is the first and only instance in the entire biblical record of one born blind receiving sight. Jesus had performed an astounding miracle. This added to the man's conviction that Jesus was from God, otherwise 'he could do nothing'. Applied to Jesus, the blind man's argument was correct, but applied generally to all miracle workers it could be misleading. False prophets can perform miracles as well (see Mt. 24:24; Mk. 13:22), although there is no evidence of their having healed the congenitally blind.

34. This lesson in theology from an unlearned man was more than 'the Jews' could abide, even though restoration of sight to the blind was known to be one of the blessings of the messianic age (Is. 29:18; 35:5; 42:7). *To this they replied, 'You were steeped in sin at birth; how dare you lecture us!'* They resented his presumption in pointing out their ignorance, but they had no answer to his straightforward theology. Therefore they resorted to abuse. Their insulting assertion that he was 'steeped in sin at birth' may reflect the view that his blindness was due to sin (2). The reaction of 'the Jews' showed they rejected the testimony of the man, the significance of the miracle, and the claims of the one who performed it. They were people who rejected the light, preferring the darkness, because their deeds were evil (1:5, 9–11; 3:19–21).

The evangelist's final words in this section, *And they threw him out*, could mean they thrust him from their presence in anger, or they excommunicated him because he supported Jesus (22).

7. Jesus reveals himself to the man (9:35–39)

35. The evangelist continues, *Jesus heard that they had thrown him out, and when he found him, he said, 'Do you believe in the Son of Man?'* Since receiving his sight, the man born blind had been taken to the Pharisees by his neighbours (13), left to answer for himself by his parents (23), interrogated, insulted and thrown out by 'the Jews' (24–34). Through it all, his appreciation of Jesus grew. At first he referred to him as 'the man called Jesus' (11); then he said he was 'a prophet' (17); and most recently he argued that he must be a godly person who did God's will (31). After all, the man was 'found' by Jesus.

Jesus caught up with him in a public place, probably the temple precincts (40). He asked him, 'Do you believe in the Son of Man?' The evangelist has already presented Jesus as the Son of Man: the one in whom God reveals himself (1:51), who has come down from heaven (3:13), the one upon whom God has set his seal of approval (6:27), who will ascend again to heaven from whence he came (6:62), and later in the Gospel he speaks of the Son of Man as the one who will return to his place of glory via death and resurrection (12:23; 13:31). See Additional Note: 'The Son of Man', pp. 89–91.

36–37. The man's response to Jesus' question was typically straightforward: *'Who is he, sir?' the man asked.* He knew about the Son of Man; all he needed to know was in whom this glorious figure was to be revealed. So he said, *'Tell me so that I may believe in him.'* In response *Jesus said, 'You have now seen him; in fact, he is the one speaking with you.'* With his new-found sight, the man had already seen the Son of Man, but had not yet recognized him. In fact, Jesus himself, his benefactor, the one now speaking to him, was the Son of Man.

38. Without hesitation, *the man said, 'Lord, I believe,' and he worshipped him.* He was making his final step to faith in Jesus. That he 'worshipped' him shows he identified Jesus as the glorious Son of Man of Daniel 7:13–14. The man born blind had been blessed with spiritual as well as physical sight. The story of his journey to faith in Jesus is a powerful example for the readers of the Fourth Gospel, intended to lead them to similar faith, which is the purpose of the Gospel (20:31).

39. Thinking of the immediate response of faith on the part of the man born blind, on the one hand, and the obstinate refusal of 'the Jews' to believe, on the other, *Jesus said, 'For judgment I have come into this world, so that the blind will see and those who see will become blind.'* Jesus' purpose in coming into the world was not to judge the world (3:17; 8:15), but there was a sense in which judgment occurred because of his very presence in the world (3:18). This is illustrated by the reaction of the man born blind and 'the Jews' respectively. The man born blind knew very little. He did not know whether Jesus was a sinner or not (25), he did not know who the Son of Man was (36), all he knew was that once he had been blind but now he saw (25). To this 'blind' person Jesus revealed himself as the Son of Man, and the blind man 'saw'! 'The Jews' claimed to know. They 'knew' Jesus was not from God (16), that he was a sinner (24) and therefore not the Christ. 'The Jews', who were sure they could 'see' were confirmed in their blindness. Judgment had occurred with Jesus' coming into the world. It functioned like the ministry of the messengers of the gospel, which Paul described as 'the aroma of Christ among those who are being saved and those who are perishing. To the one we are the smell of death; to the other, the fragrance of life' (2 Cor. 2:15–16).

8. Jesus accuses the Pharisees of 'blindness' (9:40–41)

40. Jesus and the man born blind were not alone when Jesus told him he was the Son of Man, nor when he said he had come into the world to make the blind 'see' and to render 'blind' those who thought they saw. Hence *some Pharisees who were with him heard him say this and asked, 'What? Are we blind too?'* The form of their question in the original language is better translated, 'We are not blind too, are we?' They expected a negative answer.

41. Jesus' response was not what they expected. *Jesus said, 'If you were blind, you would not be guilty of sin; but now that you claim you can see, your guilt remains.'* If they, like the man born blind, had been prepared to acknowledge ignorance, they, like him, would not be guilty of sin. Because they claimed to know and were unwilling to learn, their guilt remained. Their presumption of knowledge kept them from seeing the truth. They were like the one described in Proverbs 26:12:

> Do you see a man wise in his own eyes?
> There is more hope for a fool than for him.

The Pharisees here function as a negative example, something to be avoided by those who read this Gospel. They were guilty of unbelief, the cardinal sin in the Fourth Gospel.

O. JESUS, THE GOOD SHEPHERD (10:1–21)

Chapter 10 falls into three sections. The first, 10:1–21, continues the account of Jesus' ministry at the Feast of Tabernacles, and has connections with the account of the healing of the man born blind. It includes the parable of the sheepfold (1–6) and Jesus' presentation of himself as the good shepherd (7–21). The connection between 10:1–21 and the previous chapter is established by the reference back to the healing of the man born blind (21).

1. The parable of the sheepfold (10:1–6)

To appreciate this parable it is important to understand its setting in a small Jewish village. Most village families owned a few sheep. The houses of the villagers had small walled courtyards where the sheep were kept. Because each family had only a few sheep, a shepherd for each household was not justified, so several households would have one shepherd to look after their sheep. Often the shepherding was done by a son (or two daughters) from one of these families. If such a person was not available a stranger/hireling was employed. Early each morning the sheep would be taken out to graze in the open country. The shepherd moved from house to house, and because he was known to the doorkeepers they opened their courtyard doors to allow him to call out the sheep. The sheep knew his voice and eagerly followed him into the open country to feed. The walls of the courtyards could be up to six and a half feet high. One who was not the shepherd, who had ulterior motives, would have to climb over the walls because the doorkeeper would not admit him, and, of course, the sheep would not recognize his call and would flee from him.[1]

1. The parable of the sheepfold in 10:1–6, like the whole of 10:1–21, has links with the story of the healing of the man born blind in chapter 9. Jesus begins the parable, *I tell you the truth, the man who does not enter the sheep pen by the gate, but climbs in by some other way, is a thief and a robber*. The NIV translation is unfortunate in that it refers to the 'gate' and the 'sheep pen', giving the impression that the setting of the parable is the open country instead of the village. The word translated 'gate' is *thyra*, which means 'door', and the word translated 'sheep pen' is *aulē*, which means 'court' or 'courtyard'. When translated correctly it is clear that the parable is set in the village, not the open country. Only thieves and robbers sought to enter the courtyard by a way other than the door, for they knew the doorkeeper of the house would not admit them.

2–4. In contrast, *The man who enters by the gate is the shepherd of his sheep*. The one appointed as shepherd enters by the door into

[1]For fuller details and documentation see Bailey, pp. 2–7.

the courtyard. *The watchman opens the gate for him*. Once again the NIV translation is unfortunate. The word translated 'watchman', *thyrōros*, is a cognate of *thyra*, 'door', and should be translated 'doorkeeper' or 'porter', not 'watchman'. The word translated 'gate' should be rendered 'door'. A watchman might be appropriate in the open country, but a doorkeeper guards the entry to courtyards in the village. When the doorkeeper opens the door for the shepherd, *the sheep listen to his voice. He calls his own sheep by name and leads them out*. There is some evidence that ancient Middle Eastern shepherds did know their sheep by name. In the parable the shepherd called the sheep by name and led them out of the courtyards into the narrow streets of the village. *When he has brought out all his own, he goes on ahead of them, and his sheep follow him because they know his voice*. Having called out all his sheep, the shepherd leads (not drives) them, going on ahead. This part of the parable is reminiscent of Moses' prayer for a successor in Numbers 27:16–17: 'May the LORD, the God of the spirits of all mankind, appoint a man over this community to go out and come in before them, one who will lead them out and bring them in, so the LORD's people will not be like sheep without a shepherd.'

5. The opposite would be true if a stranger tried to bring out the sheep: *But they will never follow a stranger; in fact, they will run away from him because they do not recognize a stranger's voice*. In fact, when a sheep is bought from one owner and placed with different sheep in its new owner's courtyard, it experiences great trauma for the first few days. It hears the voice of a shepherd calling out the sheep in the mornings, but it is not the voice to which it is accustomed, and it runs from him, even though it is desperate to get out to the countryside to graze.

6. The evangelist comments, *Jesus used this figure of speech but they did not understand what he was telling them*. The word translated 'figure of speech' (*paroimia*) is equivalent to the Hebrew word *māšal*, and is used with a wide range of meanings, including parable, riddle, fable, allegory, proverb *etc.*, all of which involve something enigmatic. Jesus' 'figure of speech' was also enigmatic, for 'they' did not understand what he was telling 'them'. Those referred to as 'they'/'them' here are the Pharisees and 'the Jews' introduced in chapter 9; those who insulted and threw out the man born blind because he supported Jesus. These are the 'thieves and robbers' of 10:1. Jesus is the 'shepherd' whose voice the sheep recognize and follow, just as the man born blind gave his allegiance to Jesus as soon as he realized who he was (9:35–38).

2. Jesus, the good shepherd (10:7–21)

The setting of this passage is different from that of 10:1–6. There it was the village setting; the courtyards and narrow streets on to which they opened. Here the setting is the open country into which the shepherd led the sheep for grazing, and where in the summer months shepherd and sheep might spend the night. Overnight the sheep were placed in roughly constructed round stone-walled enclosures. The top of the dry-stone wall was covered with thorns to keep out wild animals. Inside the enclosure the sheep were safe so long as the entrance was secured by the shepherd. He slept across the entrance as there was no door and no doorkeeper.

7. Because they did not understand, *Therefore Jesus said again, 'I tell you the truth, I am the gate for the sheep.'* This is the third of seven 'I am' sayings with predicates in the Fourth Gospel (6:35, 48, 51; 8:12; 10:7, 9; 10:11, 14; 11:25; 14:6; 15:1, 5). It is introduced with the solemn formula 'I tell you the truth' (*amēn amēn legō hymin*) to emphasize the importance of what is said. The word translated 'gate' is again *thyra*, meaning 'door'. Jesus portrayed himself as the shepherd who makes himself the 'door' to the enclosure to protect the sheep.

8. Jesus continued, *All who ever came before me were thieves and robbers*. There may be an allusion here to OT passages like Jeremiah 23:1–8 and Ezekiel 34, in which the prophets pronounced judgment upon the shepherds of Israel for their failure to care for the people. Jesus may have had in mind messianic pretenders (*cf.* Mt. 24:24; Mk. 13:22), or more likely 'the Jews', who treated the man born blind so badly. Of such leaders, Jesus says, *the sheep did not listen to them*. The man born blind certainly did not listen to them. Those who belong to Jesus, the true shepherd, do not resonate with voices such as theirs.

9. Alluding again to the enclosures built for the sheep, Jesus said, *I am the gate; whoever enters through me will be saved. He will come in and go out, and find pasture.* As the sheep entering the stone enclosure of which the shepherd himself was the door were safe, so too people who believe in Jesus are eternally secure (27–30). As the shepherd led his sheep out to pasture during the day and brought them in at night, so too Jesus provides for those who believe in him.

10. Jesus added, *The thief comes only to steal and kill and destroy.* He depicted 'the Jews' as sheep stealers who had no thought for the well-being of the people – they came only 'to kill and destroy'. They were like the wicked shepherds of Israel denounced by Jeremiah and Ezekiel (see commentary on 10:8). Contrasting his own ministry with theirs, Jesus said, *I have come that they may have life, and have it to the full.* The imagery is of a shepherd ensuring that his sheep are well cared for and contented. Jesus, the good shepherd, came into the world so that people might have (eternal) life, and have it to the full. To have eternal life is to know God through Jesus Christ (17:3). To have it to the full could refer either to enjoying the richness of life in relationship with God in the here and now or to resurrection to eternal life at the end of the age (5:24–29), or both.

11. For Jesus to bring life to the full to his followers, there was a cost, as he explained: *I am the good shepherd. The good shepherd lays down his life for the sheep.* This is the fourth of seven 'I am' sayings with predicates in the Fourth Gospel (6:35, 48, 51; 8:12; 10:7, 9; 10:11, 14; 11:25; 14:6; 15:1, 5). The background imagery is still shepherding in the open country. There the shepherd has to lay his own life on the line to protect his sheep from wild animals. Jesus presented himself as a good shepherd who was prepared to do likewise. A shepherd would rarely, if ever, actually die in protection of his sheep (to do so would leave the sheep defenceless). Jesus was extending the imagery beyond its normal limits and pointing forward to the time when he would, in fact, lay down his life for the sake of his people.

12–13. There was a big difference between a shepherd from one of the families who owned the sheep and someone outside the family who was just paid to do a job. This is the background to Jesus' next statement: *The hired hand is not the shepherd who owns the sheep. So when he sees the wolf coming, he abandons the sheep and runs away.* The primary motivation of the hired hand is depicted as self-preservation. He flees in the face of danger and deserts his duty to the sheep, with dire results: *Then the wolf attacks the flock and scatters it.* The sheep are left defenceless before the attack and are scattered. Jesus saw the common people of his day as 'sheep without a shepherd' (Mt. 9:36/Mk. 6:34).

The reason why the hired hand flees in the face of danger is further explained, *The man runs away because he is a hired hand and cares nothing for the sheep.* Because the sheep do not belong to the hired hand or his family, he does not care for them in the same way as a family member would, and that is why he will desert the sheep and flee. Jesus was referring to the Jewish leaders who were not carrying out their responsibility of care for the people.

14–15. Contrasting himself with Jewish leaders who were like hired hands, Jesus said, *I am the good shepherd; I know my sheep and my sheep know me – just as the Father knows me and I know the Father.* Unlike the Jewish leaders who did not 'know' the people, Jesus knew his people and they knew him. When Jesus spoke about the Father 'knowing' him, he did not mean that he knew about him, or was acquainted with him, but that he enjoyed an intimate personal relationship with him. It is amazing that Jesus said his knowledge of his disciples and their knowledge of him involved a similar intimate personal relationship.

Jesus reiterated what he had said earlier (11) by saying, *I lay down my life for the sheep.* The imagery is the same: those who shepherd in the open country must be prepared to lay their lives on the line for the sheep. Jesus said he would actually lay down his life for the sake of his sheep (the disciples). It was his love that led him to do this for them (*cf.* 15:13: 'Greater love has no-one than this, that he lay down his life for his friends'), and his love made him the 'good shepherd'.

References to Jesus as 'the good shepherd' recall Jeremiah 23:2–4, where God himself promises to gather the scattered people Israel, and Ezekiel 34:11–16, where God promises to look after his sheep, providing them with good pasture, caring for the injured and weak, and shepherding the flock with justice. There are also possibly allusions to Psalm 23, in which God is again depicted as the good shepherd. So Jesus' claim to be 'the good shepherd' was more than a claim to do what the national leaders of his day failed to do. It was also a claim to be one with God the Father, who is 'the good shepherd' of his people.

16. In the OT God is depicted as the true shepherd of Israel, and Jesus' own ministry was predominantly to Israel also (see Mt. 15:24; *cf.* Mt. 10:5–6). However, Jesus widened the role of the good shepherd when he said, *I have other sheep that are not of this sheep pen. I must bring them also.* The word translated 'sheep pen' is again *aulē*, which means 'courtyard'. The imagery is of a shepherd who has called sheep from one courtyard to lead them out to pasture, and then says there are sheep from another courtyard for which he has responsibility also. The allusion is to Gentile people, those who are not part of Israel. They too must hear the message of the gospel. Of these Jesus said, *They too will listen to my voice, and there shall be* (lit. 'they shall become') *one flock and one shepherd.* Jesus was foreshadowing apostolic times, when his gospel would be taken to non-Jews, to Samaritans and Gentiles, something that would take place through the preaching of his disciples. Then all peoples would hear his voice, believe in him and be incorporated into the body of his disciples. Believers from different races would become 'one flock' (a church made up of Jews, Samaritans and Gentiles) led by 'one shepherd' (Jesus himself).

17–18. In 10:11, 15 Jesus said he would lay down his life for the sheep. In those texts laying down his life was motivated by love for the sheep. In 10:17–18 another aspect of Jesus' motivation is implied: *The reason my Father loves me is that I lay down my life – only to take it up again.* Here is implied what will be stated explicitly very shortly, that Jesus laid down his life in obedience to his Father, an obedience that drew out again the Father's love for his Son. In the plan of salvation it was required that the Son lay down his life for his people, but that was not the end of it: he laid down his life 'only to take it up again' (lit. 'in order to take it up again') – he would rise from the dead. This is one of the few places in the NT where the resurrection of Jesus is attributed to the action of

Jesus himself. In most other places it is God who raises Jesus from the dead.

While Jesus' life, humanly speaking, was taken from him by the actions of evil men, it was not outside his control. He said, *No-one takes it from me, but I lay it down of my own accord. I have authority to lay it down and authority to take it up again. This command I received from my Father*. In his account of the passion the fourth evangelist portrays Jesus, not as a victim of circumstance, but as one who was in control of his destiny. In two places this is particularly clear: (1) in the betrayal and arrest scene, when Jesus identified himself to those who came to seize him and they fell backwards to the ground; (2) during the Roman trial, when Pilate said to him, 'Don't you realize I have power either to free you or to crucify you?' (19:10). To this Jesus replied, 'You would have no power over me if it were not given to you from above' (19:11). These incidents show that Jesus was in control of his own destiny. He had the authority to lay down his life and to take it up again, because it was what he had been commanded to do by his Father.

19–21. When Jesus concluded the parable of the sheepfold in 10:1–6, 'the Jews' did not understand what he was saying to them. When he finished his teaching about the good shepherd in 10:7–18, they were divided in their opinions: *At these words the Jews were again divided. Many of them said, 'He is demon-possessed and raving mad. Why listen to him?'* On previous occasions people who did not like what Jesus said accused him of being demon-possessed (7:20; 8:48, 52). *But others said, 'These are not the sayings of a man possessed by a demon.'* It was clear to this latter group, as it would be to any fair-minded person, that Jesus' sayings were not the ravings of a demon-possessed man. And remembering how Jesus had given sight to the man born blind, they asked, *Can a demon open the eyes of the blind?* It was not only the words of Jesus that bore testimony to who he was, but also his works (25). Verse 21 brings to an end the section 10:1–21, and also indicates its connection with the story of the healing of the man born blind in chapter 9. These verses also bring to a conclusion the longer section 7:1 – 10:21, which records Jesus' ministry in Jerusalem during the Feast of Tabernacles. At this time there were many who believed in him (7:31, 40–41; 8:30), but the hard-core leadership rejected him and his message (7:32; 10:20).

1. Conflict with 'the Jews' (10:22–39)

The setting for 10:22–39 is the Feast of Dedication, or Hanukkah (celebrated in November–December), and thus differs from that of the preceding section, whose setting was the Feast of Tabernacles (celebrated in September–October). The Feast of Dedication is not one of the feasts prescribed by the Mosaic law. It celebrates an event that took place in intertestamental times. Following the victories of Alexander the Great in the fourth century BC, Greek culture and language were introduced to the subjugated nations, including Judea. After the death of Alexander this policy was continued by the rulers who held sway over Judea, first the Ptolemies of Egypt, up till about 200 BC, and thereafter the Seleucids of Syria. Hellenization, as the spread of Greek culture and language is called, flourished as many in the subjugated nations, including many Jews, were attracted to it. However, when Antiochus IV became ruler of the Seleucid Empire he tried to force Greek culture upon the peoples he ruled. For the Jews this meant that practices such as sabbath observance and circumcision were prohibited, and the books of the Law were burnt. In 167 BC the temple in Jerusalem was desecrated by offering swine's flesh on the altar, and Jewish people were required to offer sacrifice to pagan deities. This led pious Jews to revolt against Antiochus IV, a revolt led by Mattathias and his sons. They fled to the mountains, from whence they conducted guerilla warfare against the Seleucid armies. Their campaign was crowned with success, and in 164 BC the temple was rededicated to the worship of Yahweh. The rededication of the temple and the institution of the annual remembrance in the Feast of Dedication is described in 2 Maccabees 10:1–8 (RSV):

> Now Maccabaeus and his followers, the Lord leading them on, recovered the temple and the city; they tore down the

altars that had been built in the public square by the foreigners, and also destroyed the sacred precincts. They purified the sanctuary, and made another altar of sacrifice; then, striking fire out of flint, they offered sacrifices, after a lapse of two years, and they offered incense and lighted lamps and set out the bread of the Presence. When they had done this, they fell prostrate and implored the Lord that they might never again fall into such misfortunes, but that, if they should ever sin, they might be disciplined by him with forbearance and not be handed over to blasphemous and barbarous nations. It happened that on the same day on which the sanctuary had been profaned by the foreigners, the purification of the sanctuary took place, that is, on the twenty-fifth day of the same month, which was Chislev. They celebrated it for eight days with rejoicing, in the manner of the festival of booths, remembering how not long before, during the festival of booths, they had been wandering in the mountains and caves like wild animals. Therefore, carrying ivy-wreathed wands and beautiful branches and also fronds of palm, they offered hymns of thanksgiving to him who had given success to the purifying of his own holy place. They decreed by public edict, ratified by vote, that the whole nation of the Jews should observe these days every year.

From this passage it is clear that the Feast of Dedication was modelled on the Feast of Tabernacles (for details of this feast see commentary on 7:2). It lasted for eight days, involved the carrying of palm fronds and beautiful branches, and eventually included singing of the Hallel (Pss. 113 – 118). According to the Talmud, lamps were lit in the people's homes as well as in the temple (*Šabbat* 21b).

22–23. The evangelist begins his account, *Then came the Feast of Dedication at Jerusalem. It was winter, and Jesus was in the temple area walking in Solomon's Colonnade*. The Feast of Dedication, celebrated in November–December, took place in winter. Solomon's Colonnade was located on the eastern side of the temple precincts, overlooking the Kidron valley. It was a covered area with a cedar-panelled ceiling spanning 49 feet supported by white marble columns 38 feet tall. It offered protection from cold winds and was used as a meeting place where people discussed Scripture after ceremonies in the temple. In Acts 5:12 we learn that early Christians used to meet in Solomon's Colonnade.

24. As Jesus was walking in Solomon's Colonnade *the Jews gathered round him, saying, 'How long will you keep us in suspense? If you are the Christ, tell us plainly.'* Their request did not arise from a genuine desire to know if Jesus was the Messiah, and whether they should believe in him (as Jesus' response to them in 10:25 indicates). Rather, it was another attempt to get Jesus to say something that would incriminate him.

25-26. 'The Jews' did not achieve their aim, for *Jesus answered, 'I did tell you, but you do not believe.'* While Jesus never claimed publicly among 'the Jews' that he was the Messiah, in various ways his words had indicated to them who he was. He told Nicodemus, a Pharisee and a ruler of the Jews, that he was the Son of Man who came down from heaven (3:13-14). Following the healing of the lame man at the Pool of Bethesda Jesus told 'the Jews' the works he did were the works of his Father, and they sought to kill him because, by so saying, he was making himself equal with God (5:16-18). Jesus told them God had entrusted all judgment to him and granted him to have life in himself so that he could raise the dead, both of which are divine prerogatives (5:22, 24-26). During the Feast of Tabernacles he told 'the Jews' that he knew God and had been sent by God (7:28-29). He also publicly invited those who were thirsty to come to him and drink, promising to give them the streams of living water of which the Scriptures spoke (7:37-38). He told 'the Jews' that 'before Abraham was born I am' (8:58), appropriating for himself the divine name. He presented himself as the good shepherd (11, 14), identifying himself with God who, in the OT, is the shepherd of Israel. Despite all these things, Jesus said, 'you do not believe'.

It was not only what Jesus said that revealed who he was; it was also the things he did: *The miracles I do in my Father's name speak for me, but you do not believe because you are not my sheep.* He performed many miracles in Jerusalem (2:23; 3:2; 7:21, 31; 9:16), but still 'the Jews' refused to believe. They refused to believe, Jesus said, because they were not his sheep. This indicates that even in the matter of those who do not believe, God's sovereignty and election operate. This does not remove people's responsibility for their unbelief, nor does it compromise the reality of the invitation to believe (cf. 10:37-38).

27-28. The response of Jesus' disciples' was the opposite: *My sheep listen to my voice; I know them, and they follow me.* Concerning them, Jesus said, *I give them eternal life, and they shall never perish; no-one can snatch them out of my hand.* The gift of eternal life is depicted in several ways in this Gospel. It is (1) like water for the thirsty (4:14; 7:37-38); (2) something experienced now, culminating in the resurrection on the last day (5:24-26); (3) like bread for the hungry (6:27); and (4) a relationship with the living God (17:3). Those to whom Jesus gives eternal life 'shall never perish'; they are safe in his hands.

29-30. Underlining the eternal security of those who follow him, Jesus said, *My Father, who has given them to me, is greater than all; no-one can snatch them out of my Father's hand.* Jesus referred to his disciples repeatedly as those the Father had given him (6:37, 39; 17:2, 6, 9, 24; 18:9). Because the Father is greater than all, the security of believers is guaranteed – no-one can snatch them out of his hand. Jesus implied that just as his disciples are in his hand (28), so too they are in the Father's hand, because, as he said, *I and the Father are one* (cf. 14:8-11). This is the first explicit statement of Jesus' oneness with the Father. Describing this oneness, the evangelist does not use the masculine form of the adjective 'one' (*heis*), which would suggest that Father and Son are one person. Instead, he uses the neuter form (*hen*), suggesting that the oneness of Father and Son here is oneness in mission and purpose. Father and Son are at one in their commitment to prevent anyone from snatching believers out of their hands. Here the nature of oneness is functional; later in the Gospel it involves unity of being (17:21-23).

31-33. Jesus' claim to be one with the Father provoked an angry response: *Again the Jews picked up stones to stone him, but Jesus said to them, 'I have shown you many great miracles from the Father. For which of these do you stone me?'* Miracles of Jesus in Jerusalem already described include the healing of the lame man (5:1–9), and giving sight to the man born blind (9:1–7). But he had performed many more than these, as general references to his miracles in Jerusalem indicate (2:23; 3:2; 7:31; 9:16; 10:25, 32–33). Perhaps Jesus drew their attention to these miracles in the hope that 'the Jews' might yet recognize their significance as far as his true identity was concerned. Perhaps he was confronting them with the injustice of their intended action. Anyway, they brushed aside his reference to his miracles and focused upon his claim to be one with the Father: *We are not stoning you for any of these,' replied the Jews, 'but for blasphemy'*. In the Mishnah (*Sanhedrin* 7:5) blasphemy involves the pronunciation of the divine name itself (the Tetragrammaton, YHWH), which does not coincide with what Jesus said. Why 'the Jews' thought Jesus was guilty of blasphemy is clear enough: *you, a mere man, claim to be God*. What Jesus said would have been blasphemous if he and the Father were not one.

34–36. In response, *Jesus answered them, 'Is it not written in your Law, "I have said you are gods"'?* The expression 'Law' here is used in its widest sense, meaning the entire OT, including the Psalms from which the quotation comes. Referring to 'your Law', Jesus was not denigrating or distancing himself from the law, but reminding his opponents that his appeal was to what they too held as sacrosanct. Jesus' argument based on the quotation from Psalm 82:6 ran, *If he called them 'gods,' to whom the word of God came – and the Scripture cannot be broken – what about the one whom the Father set apart as his very own and sent into the world? Why then do you accuse me of blasphemy because I said, 'I am God's Son'?* To understand these verses one needs some knowledge of events surrounding the giving of the law at Sinai, and rabbinic exegesis of Psalm 82:6–7 in relation to the Sinai events. The full text of Psalm 82:6–7 reads:

> I said, 'You are "gods";
> you are all sons of the Most High.'
> But you will die like mere men;
> you will fall like every other ruler.

The statement 'You are gods' was understood in later rabbinic exegesis to be God's word to the Israelites at Sinai when they received the law. God said to them, 'You are gods,' because in receiving the law and living by it they would be holy and live like gods. But because they departed from the law and worshipped the golden calf while still at Sinai, he said to them, 'you will die like mere men'. The opening words of Jesus' argument, 'If he called them "gods", to whom the word of God came', suggest that he interpreted the quotation from the psalm in relation to the Sinai events as did later rabbinic scholars. Jesus reminded 'the Jews' that 'the Scripture cannot be broken'. Both Jesus (7:38; 10:35; 13:18; 17:12) and 'the Jews', especially the Pharisees (5:39; 7:42), regarded the Scriptures as authoritative, as did the evangelist (2:22; 19:24, 36, 37; 20:9). To be a follower of Jesus involves a commitment to the authority of the OT Scriptures, as well as to the gospel message.

Jesus' question, based on his reading of Psalm 82:6, was that if God named those to whom he gave his law 'gods', why should he be charged with blasphemy if he, as the one whom God himself 'set apart as his very own and sent into the world', said, 'I am God's Son.' It is an argument from the lesser to the greater: if those to whom the law was given can be called 'gods', then surely the one whom God has commissioned and sent into the world can call himself 'the Son of God' without being guilty of blasphemy. Jesus used the exegetical methods of his opponents to show they had no grounds for accusing him of blasphemy. It did not mean Jesus endorsed this approach. It did, however, buy him time.

There is a possible irony in Jesus' reference to his being 'set apart . . . and sent into the world': while 'the Jews' celebrated the rededication of the temple, they rejected the one 'dedicated' (*i.e.* set apart) by God and sent into the world.

37-38. Jesus said to 'the Jews', *Do not believe me unless I do what my Father does.* Several times Jesus claimed that he did the works of his Father (5:36; 10:25, 37-38; 14:10; 17:4). He now invited 'the Jews' *not* to believe him if he did not do what God does. However, there is a corollary: *But if I do it, even though you do not believe me, believe the miracles.* The miracles of Jesus were the works of God, and Jesus invited his opponents to believe in him on account of the miracles, even if they could not believe what he said. This he said was so *that you may know and understand that the Father is in* *me, and I in the Father.* Though belief based on miracles is not ideal (4:48), many did believe because of his miracles (7:31). Sadly, there were many who saw the miracles and still refused to believe (12:37). Nevertheless, the evangelist records Jesus' miracles to engender belief in his readers (20:31).

39. Jesus' opponents could not counter his arguments, so *they tried to seize him, but he escaped their grasp.* Several attempts had already been made to arrest or kill Jesus, but they had all failed (7:30, 32, 44; 8:20). Jesus did not allow fear of such attempts to deter him from his mission (see 11:7–10). The reason was, his hour had not yet come (7:30; 8:20). His times were in God's hands, and all attempts to bring his ministry to a premature end failed for that reason.

2. *Jesus departs from Jerusalem (10:40–42)*

40–42. After yet another failed attempt on the part of 'the Jews' to arrest him, the evangelist says, *Then Jesus went back across the Jordan to the place where John had been baptizing in the early days.* Jesus left Jerusalem, thus concluding his stay there for the Feast of Dedication (22–39), and made his way to the place where John had baptized (see 1:28). *Here he stayed and many people came to him.* As many people had come out to see John, now they came out to see Jesus at the same place. *They said, 'Though John never performed a miraculous sign, all that John said about this man was true.'* In the Synoptic Gospels John is presented as a preacher of repentance in the light of the imminent coming of the kingdom of God, but in the Fourth Gospel he is presented primarily as a witness to Jesus (1:6–8, 15, 19, 32–34; 3:26, 28; 5:33). The people who came to see Jesus testified to John's faithfulness: he never performed a miracle, but all he said about Jesus was true – the ultimate endorsement of a witness. As the people remembered the witness of John, and then encountered the one of whom he spoke, *in that place many believed in Jesus.* Thus John's witness bore its intended fruit.

Q. JESUS RESTORES LAZARUS TO LIFE AND ITS AFTERMATH
(11:1–54)

The account of Jesus raising Lazarus occupies a pivotal place in the Fourth Gospel. It is the last and greatest of the miracles/signs of Jesus the evangelist records, and as such constitutes the high point of Jesus' work in the world (1:19 – 12:50). However, Lazarus' death and restoration to life also foreshadow the death and resurrection of Jesus, which is the focus of the second part of the Gospel: Jesus' return to the Father (13:1 – 20:31). It not only foreshadows these events; it is also the main factor, humanly speaking, that precipitated them. News of Lazarus' restoration to life spread like wildfire among the people, and the Jewish leadership decided they needed to eliminate Jesus to deal with the threat his popularity was to their position (45–53, 57; *cf.* 12:10–11). The evangelist's account of the raising of Lazarus comprises six scenes.

1. *Jesus receives news of Lazarus' illness (11:1–6)*

1–3. The evangelist begins, *Now a man named Lazarus was sick. He was from Bethany, the village of Mary and her sister Martha.* This is the first reference to Lazarus, and the evangelist does not expect his readers to know who he is; so he explains that he is from Bethany, the village of Mary and Martha, adding later that he is the brother of these two sisters (2–3). The evangelist presumes his readers will know who Mary and Martha are, perhaps from a reading of Luke's Gospel (Lk. 10:38–42). However, he provides a further description of Mary: *This Mary, whose brother Lazarus now lay sick, was the same one who poured perfume on the Lord and wiped his feet with her hair.* In the Fourth Gospel, the story of Mary anointing Jesus' feet comes in the next chapter (12:1–8). So people reading the Gospel for the first time would not have encountered it yet. The evangelist, therefore, assumes his readers already knew about the anointing, perhaps from oral tradition, or from parallel accounts in Matthew 26:1–13 and Mark 14:3–9.[1]

---

[1] The parallel accounts are similar to that in the Fourth Gospel, but there are some differences: the woman is not named; she anoints Jesus' head, not his feet; and the action takes place in the house of one Simon the leper. Luke has an account of an anointing, but in this case it is

Having explained Lazarus' relationship to Mary and Martha, the evangelist continues, *So the sisters sent word to Jesus, 'Lord, the one you love is sick.'* Implied in this message was a request that Jesus come and heal Lazarus (*cf.* 11:21–22, 32). The basis of this request was Jesus' love for Lazarus (*cf.* 5).

4. Jesus' response to the message was enigmatic: *When he heard this, Jesus said, 'This sickness will not end in death. No, it is for God's glory so that God's Son may be glorified through it.'* The way this is recounted suggests that when Jesus received the news, Lazarus had not yet died ('this *sickness* will not end in death'). If one had not read the story before, one would assume that Lazarus' sickness would not be fatal, though that interpretation is ruled out as the story unfolds (11–14). Lazarus was to die, but by restoring him to life, Jesus would be glorified, and this in turn would redound to God's glory. Glory would be brought to God through Jesus' actions, for in them God's power and love would be manifested for all to see (40).

5–6. Jesus' next words have puzzled many: *Jesus loved Martha and her sister and Lazarus. Yet when he heard that Lazarus was sick, he stayed where he was two more days.* The sisters' implied request to Jesus to come and heal their brother was based upon his love for Lazarus (3). In 11:5 the evangelist reiterates Jesus' love for Lazarus and his sisters. This shows that Jesus' failure to respond in the normal way, staying where he was for two more days, was not due to any lack of love for either Lazarus, who was on the verge of death, or his sisters, who had sent the urgent request for help. The NIV translation 'yet when he heard', which implies that Jesus' delay was somehow at odds with his love for them, is misleading. The original (*hōs oun ēkousen*) should be rendered 'so when he heard' (as in the RSV), which shows that Jesus' delay was not at odds with his love, but motivated by it. How could this be? When Jesus arrived, Lazarus had been dead for four days. Had he left immediately, Lazarus would still have been dead for two days.

Jesus' feet that have perfume poured over them, and his feet are wiped by the woman with her hair. In this case the woman is one 'who had lived a sinful life in that town', and the anointing took place in the house of Simon the Pharisee (Lk. 7:36–50).

So nothing would have been gained by an immediate departure. However, there was something to be gained by waiting two days before setting out. The spirit of the departed was thought to hover around the body for three days in the hope of a resuscitation. The raising of Lazarus after four days, then, would be clearly seen as a manifestation of the glory of God (4), which would strengthen the two sisters' faith.

2. Jesus decides to return to Judea (11:7–16)

7–8. Having delayed for two days, *Then he said to his disciples, 'Let us go back to Judea.'* Jesus was outside Judea when he received the message, perhaps still at the place where John used to baptize (10:40). His disciples were reluctant to return to Judea: *'But Rabbi,'* they said, *'a short while ago the Jews tried to stone you, and yet you are going back there?'* They reminded him of attempts made by 'the Jews' during the Feast of Dedication to stone him (10:31, 33), implying it would be dangerous for him to return there.

9–10. However, he would not let fear of his opponents determine his course of action: *Jesus answered, 'Are there not twelve hours of daylight? A man who walks by day will not stumble, for he sees by this world's light. It is when he walks by night that he stumbles, for he has no light.'* The Jewish day was reckoned from sunrise to sunset, and night from sunset to sunrise. The 24-hour period was divided roughly into 12 hours of daylight and 12 hours of darkness. One who goes about in the day does not stumble, because he has light. The one who walks about in the night stumbles, because 'he has no light'. Jesus regarded the period of his ministry as the 'day' (9:4), and during the day he would accomplish his Father's purpose without stumbling, *i.e.* without being deflected by reminders of previous attempts by 'the Jews' to stone him, or because of the possibility that they would try to do so again if he returned to Judea. Despite his disciples' fears, then, Jesus was determined to go into Judea, in his own time, to respond to the request of Mary and Martha.

11–13. The evangelist continues, *After he had said this, he went on to tell them, 'Our friend Lazarus has fallen asleep; but I am going there* *to wake him up.'* While Jesus described Lazarus as *'our* friend', it was Jesus alone who could 'wake him up'. Jesus was speaking metaphorically, but failing to understand this, *His disciples replied, 'Lord, if he sleeps, he will get better.'* There would be no need for Jesus to risk his life in Judea if Lazarus were merely asleep; he would wake up in due course. The evangelist explains the meaning of Jesus' metaphorical statement and the nature of the disciples' misunderstanding: *Jesus had been speaking of his death, but his disciples thought he meant natural sleep.* Sleep was a common metaphor for death (see *e.g.* 1 Ki. 2:10; 2 Ki. 8:24; 2 Ch. 9:31 NRSV).

14–15. To make things clear for his disciples, *he told them plainly, 'Lazarus is dead,'* adding, *'and for your sake I am glad I was not there, so that you may believe.'* Jesus was not saying that he was glad that Lazarus was dead (which would be callous indeed), but that for his disciples' sake he was glad he was not there to prevent it, because he knew he was going to raise Lazarus from death, and when his disciples saw that happen it would be a tremendous boost to their faith. By saying, *But let us go to him,* Jesus invited his disciples to come and see the manifestation of God's glory (*cf.* 11:4).

16. Seeing Jesus was determined to return to Judea despite the danger, *Thomas (called Didymus) said to the rest of the disciples* (lit. 'the [his] fellow-disciples'), *'Let us also go, that we may die with him.'* In the Synoptic Gospels Thomas appears only in lists of Jesus' disciples. We learn much more about him in the Fourth Gospel, where he features in four separate places: here in 11:16, urging his fellow disciples to follow Jesus into Judea, even if it means death; in 14:5, where he speaks on behalf of the other disciples, telling Jesus they do not know where he is going; in 20:24–29, where he expresses his unwillingness to believe Jesus has risen from the dead unless he sees him for himself; and in 21:2–3, where he is numbered among those disciples who go fishing with Peter, and to whom Jesus appears again following his resurrection.

Thomas distinguished himself from those disciples who tried to dissuade Jesus from returning to Judea (8) by his exhortation to them to follow him and die with him. At one level, Thomas missed what Jesus had in mind – they were not being invited to accompany Jesus on a suicide mission, but to see a manifestation of the glory of God and believe (4, 15). At another level, however, Thomas' words were true; Jesus was on his last trip to Judea and there he would die. Despite his professed willingness to die with Jesus, when the crunch came Thomas was among those who forsook him and fled (16:32; *cf.* Mt. 26:56; Mk. 14:50). In the end, only the 'disciple whom Jesus loved' and the women stood by him at the cross (19:25-27). In any case, Jesus' death was unique, and no-one could 'die with him'.

3. *Jesus meets Martha (11:17-27)*

17. After telling his disciples Lazarus was dead, Jesus made his way back to Judea. *On his arrival, Jesus found that Lazarus had already been in the tomb for four days*. Lazarus was still alive when news reached Jesus of his sickness (4), though he must have died very shortly afterwards. Jesus waited two days before heading back to Judea, a journey of two days, arriving when 'Lazarus had already been in the tomb for four days'.

18-19. The evangelist explains, *Bethany was less than two miles from Jerusalem, and many Jews had come to Martha and Mary to comfort them in the loss of their brother*. Bethany lay to the east of Jerusalem on the other side of the Mount of Olives, less than 2 miles (lit. 15 stadia) away.

In the Mishnah we read, 'Even the poorest in Israel should hire not less than two flutes and one wailing woman' (*Ketubot* 4:4). Martha and Mary must have been well off and well known for 'many Jews' to come from Jerusalem to comfort them. It is important to note that here 'the Jews' are presented in a positive light, coming to comfort those who were followers of Jesus in their loss. It is a reminder that the Fourth Gospel is not anti-Semitic, as is sometimes suggested, and that its presentation of 'the Jews' is not monochrome.

20-22. News that Jesus was coming reached Bethany before he did. *When Martha heard that Jesus was coming, she went out to meet him, but Mary stayed at home*. Why the sisters' response to the news of Jesus' approach was so varied is not explained. '*Lord,*' *Martha*

said to Jesus, 'if you had been here, my brother would not have died.'
Martha's words carried some reproach: Jesus had failed to appear
before her brother died. Despite her disappointment, Martha continued, *But I know that even now God will give you whatever you ask.*
Whatever Martha's expression of faith in Jesus meant, she was not
expecting him to restore her brother to life straightaway, as her
subsequent response to Jesus makes clear (24). She seems to have
been expressing a general belief in Jesus' relationship to God and
that God listens to his prayers.

23–24. In response *Jesus said to her, 'Your brother will rise again.'*
These words could be taken to mean either 'your brother will rise
again in the general resurrection on the last day' or 'your brother
will be restored to life immediately'. Martha did not realize that
Jesus was speaking of an immediate restoration to life, so *Martha
answered, 'I know he will rise again in the resurrection at the last day.'*
This was orthodox Pharisaic (but not Sadducean) belief (Mt.
22:23/Mk. 12:18/Lk. 20:27; Acts 23:8), a belief shared by Jesus
(5:21, 29; Lk. 14:14; 20:35–36). For Martha to make this statement
showed no understanding of what Jesus meant. He was about to
restore her brother to life, a symbol of the resurrection on the last
day.

25–26. To move her beyond the orthodoxy of the Pharisees,
Jesus said to her, 'I am the resurrection and the life.[1] *He who believes in
me will live, even though he dies; and whoever lives and believes in me
will never die.'* This statement contains the fifth of seven different
'I am' sayings with predicates in the Fourth Gospel (6:35, 48, 51;
8:12; 10:7, 9; 10:11, 14; 11:25; 14:6; 15:1, 5). It involves three claims:
(1) Jesus himself is the resurrection and the life, *i.e.* the Father has
given him to have life in himself and to bestow resurrection life
upon whomever he will (5:21, 26). (2) People who believe in him,
even if they die (as Lazarus had done) will live – Jesus will raise
them from death on the last day. What he would soon do for
Lazarus would foreshadow the resurrection of the last day. (3)
People who live and believe in him will never die. This will be

[1]A few ancient manuscripts omit the words 'and the life', though many more include them.
The important place the idea of life plays in the whole passage supports their inclusion.

literally true of the last generation of believers. Of other believers it is true in the sense that not even death can break their relationship with God. With these claims Jesus made himself central to the Jewish hope of the resurrection and eternal life, and by asking Martha, *Do you believe this?*, he encouraged her to recognize this.

27. Martha's response took the form of a confession: *'Yes, Lord,'* *she told him, 'I believe that you are the Christ, the Son of God, who was to come into the world.'* She had moved beyond her previous beliefs (22: 'I know that even now God will give you whatever you ask') and Pharisaic beliefs (24: 'I know he will rise again in the resurrection at the last day'). She was affirming Jesus' central role in bringing about the resurrection on the last day, adding that she believed he was the Christ, the Son of God, the one whom the Father had sent into the world. The title 'the Son of God' is now known to have been used as a messianic title among first-century Jews (see commentary on 1:34). Martha's confession echoes Nathanael's confession (1:49), and is an example of the faith the evangelist hopes will be evoked by his Gospel in the hearts and minds of his readers (20:31).

4. Jesus meets Mary (11:28–37)

28. Following her confession, Martha was given a message to convey: *And after she had said this, she went back and called her sister Mary aside. 'The Teacher is here,' she said, 'and is asking for you.'* She had to tell Mary that Jesus was asking (lit. 'calling') for her. The reason Martha called her sister 'aside' (lit. 'secretly') to convey this message was probably so Mary could slip away, unnoticed by those who had come to offer comfort, and so make her way to Jesus privately. This proved to be impossible (31). Despite Martha's recent confession of Jesus as 'the Christ, the Son of God', when she spoke to Mary she referred to him simply as 'the Teacher'. This was probably the way they spoke of him among themselves, and should not be interpreted as evidence that Martha was already drawing back from her confession or that it had been insincere.

29–31. Mary's response was instantaneous: *When Mary heard this, she got up quickly and went to him.* The evangelist continues,

Now Jesus had not yet entered the village, but was still at the place where Martha had met him. This meant that Mary had to leave the house and the village to meet Jesus. Martha's efforts to enable Mary to meet Jesus privately failed: *When the Jews who had been with Mary in the house, comforting her, noticed how quickly she got up and went out, they followed her, supposing she was going to the tomb to mourn there.* 'The Jews', thinking she was going to the tomb, would feel obliged to accompany Mary and share in the mourning there.

32. Mary, of course, was not going to the tomb, but to meet Jesus, who had called for her. *When Mary reached the place where Jesus was and saw him, she fell at his feet and said, 'Lord, if you had been here, my brother would not have died.'* Mary did two things. First, 'she fell at his feet'. Perhaps the evangelist wants us to see in Mary's prostration an act of worship. Second, and seemingly in tension with her worship, she reproached him as Martha had done (21) for not coming in time to prevent her brother's death. Perhaps these two things can coexist, reflecting her faith in Jesus and her despair at the same time.

33. The evangelist continues, *When Jesus saw her weeping, and the Jews who had come along with her also weeping, he was deeply moved in spirit and troubled.* The word translated 'deeply moved' is *embrimaomai*. It is a rare word, found only here and in 11:38 in the Fourth Gospel, and elsewhere in the NT only in Matthew 9:30 and Mark 1:43; 14:5. In Matthew and Mark its meaning is 'to rebuke' or 'to give a stern warning'. Two interpretations of *embrimaomai* in 11:33 have been suggested. First, Jesus was 'deeply moved' with compassion for Mary when he saw her weeping, and second, that he was 'deeply moved' with anger. In the latter case there have been a number of suggestions why he was angry: (1) he was angry because of the faithless weeping and wailing of Mary and 'the Jews' – they were grieving, as St Paul said, 'like the rest of men, who have no hope' (1 Thes. 4:13); (2) he was angry with death itself, the consequence of sin, which caused such pain; (3) he was angry with himself for not coming sooner to heal Lazarus and so prevent his death and the grief it caused Mary and Martha. This last suggestion is unlikely because Jesus knew he was going to raise Lazarus from death. The first suggestion has most to commend it, because the text says it was when Jesus saw Mary weeping like the rest that he became angry – she had joined them in faithless grief.

34-35. Jesus asked Mary and 'the Jews' who were with her, *Where have you laid him?* to which they replied, *Come and see, Lord.* The evangelist then simply tells us, *Jesus wept.* How Jesus' weeping is interpreted depends on how his being 'deeply moved in spirit' (33, 38) is understood. If he was moved with compassion, his weeping would have been a sign of his sorrow at the death of Lazarus and the pain it caused his friends. This is hard to reconcile with the fact that he knew he would shortly raise Lazarus from death. If he was moved with anger, his weeping might have reflected deep disappointment with the faithless weeping and wailing of Mary and 'the Jews'.

The weeping of Mary and 'the Jews' is denoted by the Greek word *klaiō*, found forty times in the NT and eight times in the Fourth Gospel, and very often in the context of weeping and wailing. There is only one other place in the Gospels where it is recorded that Jesus wept: when he wept over Jerusalem and its impending judgment (Lk. 19:41). On this occasion the common Greek word *klaiō* is used of Jesus' weeping. It may be significant that the evangelist uses a different and rare word, *dakryō*, for Jesus' weeping in 11:35, the only place it is found in the NT. Perhaps he is showing by his choice of this word that Jesus' weeping was of a different order from that of Mary and 'the Jews'. He was not joining with them in their weeping and wailing, but expressing his sorrow at the faithlessness he found all around him.

36-37. Seeing Jesus weep, *the Jews said, 'See how he loved him!'* They interpreted Jesus' weeping as a sign of his love for Lazarus, and grief at his death. But did the evangelist agree with them? Has he included their comment because it correctly interprets the reason for Jesus' weeping, or simply because that is what 'the Jews' thought (mistakenly) without endorsing it? Did 'the Jews' fail to realize he was weeping because of their faithlessness, not the death of Lazarus? Seeing Jesus weeping, *some of them said, 'Could not he who opened the eyes of the blind man have kept this man from dying?'* Jesus' healing of the man born blind during the Feast of Tabernacles was well known among 'the Jews', and some of them asked the question that was also in the minds of Mary and Martha (21, 32): Had he come earlier could he not have kept Lazarus from dying?

5. Lazarus restored to life (11:38–44)

38. In 11:34 Jesus asked, 'Where have you laid him?' and they replied, 'Come and see, Lord.' The evangelist continues, *Jesus, once more deeply moved, came to the tomb. It was a cave with a stone laid across the entrance.* Jesus was still in a state of some agitation when he came to the tomb. Again the word used for 'deeply moved' is *embrimaomai*, signalling perhaps his anger in the face of the faithless weeping and wailing still all about him.

The tomb is described as a cave (*spēlaion*), suggesting a natural cave, rather than a man-made rock tomb (in Heb. 11:38; Rev. 6:15 *spēlaion* is used in reference to naturally occurring caves). When the body of the deceased, Lazarus, was put into it, a large stone was placed across the entrance, as was later to be the case when Jesus was buried (20:1).

39. Standing before the tomb, Jesus said, *Take away the stone.* This instruction created problems: *'But, Lord,' said Martha, the sister of the dead man, 'by this time there is a bad odour, for he has been there four days.'* Despite her earlier confession (23–27) Martha was not expecting a miracle. She was concerned that the corpse by the fourth day would be starting to decompose and be giving off a bad odour. The fourth day has another significance in Jewish belief. As already mentioned, the soul of the departed was believed to stay near the body of the dead person for three days in the hope it might resuscitate. When it saw the change in the colour of the face that takes place by the third day it departed permanently. The person was then well and truly dead. That Lazarus had been in the tomb four days indicated there was no hope of resuscitation, thus highlighting the greatness of the miracle Jesus was about to perform.

40. Unperturbed by Martha's objection, Jesus reminded her of what he had said earlier (something not recorded by the evangelist): *Did I not tell you that if you believed, you would see the glory of God?*

Addressing Martha individually (using the second-person singular) and recalling what he had said before, he urged her to focus, not upon the apparently hopeless situation of her dead brother, but upon the revelation of the glory of God about to occur.

41–42. Jesus' reply was enough to satisfy Martha's objections, *So they took away the stone*. All was now ready. But before Jesus acted he prayed: *Then Jesus looked up and said, 'Father, I thank you that you have heard me. I knew that you always hear me, but I said this for the benefit of the people standing here, that they may believe that you sent me.'* On this occasion Jesus' prayer was not for his own benefit, but for the benefit of those standing around him. His public prayer was to make it clear that what he was about to do was connected with his commission from God. All this was to make it easier for the people, his disciples, Mary, Martha and 'the Jews', to believe that he had been sent by God.

43–44. The miracle itself followed: *When he had said this, Jesus called in a loud voice, 'Lazarus, come out!'* In 5:28–29 Jesus said, 'Do not be amazed at this, for a time is coming when all who are in their graves will hear his voice and come out'. He was speaking of the command that would bring about the general resurrection on the last day. His word of command to Lazarus foreshadowed the command he would give on the last day, and its effect upon Lazarus foreshadowed what would take place then: *The dead man came out!*

The evangelist describes the condition of Lazarus when he emerged from his tomb: *his hands and feet wrapped with strips of linen, and a cloth around his face.* In the Mishnah reference is made to both burial 'clothes' (*Sanhedrin* 6:5) and 'wrappings' for corpses (*Kil'ayim* 9:4; *Šabbat* 23:4; *Ma'aśer Šeni* 5:12). It is the latter that were used for Lazarus' hands and feet. The word used for the 'cloth' (*keiria*) around his face is the same as that used for the grave cloth on Jesus' face (20:7). Some say that Lazarus emerging from the grave with his hands and feet still bound in grave clothes is 'a miracle within a miracle'. This is not necessary, as we can think of him only loosely wrapped in the strips of linen.

When Lazarus emerged from the tomb, shuffling in his grave clothes, *Jesus said to them, 'Take off the grave clothes and let him go.'*

His concern was not to bathe in the glory of what he had done, but to care for the one who had been restored to life. Such also was the case following the raising of Jairus' daughter described in Luke 8:51–55. When Jesus restored her to life he said to those standing by 'give her something to eat' (8:55).

6. The decision to kill Jesus (11:45–54)

This passage describes two flow-on effects of the raising of Lazarus: belief on the part of many of 'the Jews' (45) and the plot to kill Jesus (46–53).

45. This verse describes the first flow-on effect: *Therefore many of the Jews who had come to visit Mary, and had seen what Jesus did, put their faith in him*. The great miracle Jesus performed led them to believe. In earlier parts of the Gospel belief based upon miracles proved to be superficial (2:23–25; 6:14, 66; 8:31–38), but the evangelist gives no hint of that being the case on this occasion. On the contrary, these Jews function as an example of those who see the signs and believe (20:31). Their belief is another reminder that 'the Jews' in the Fourth Gospel are not always opponents of Jesus.

46. In this verse the evangelist begins to describe the second flow-on effect of the raising of Lazarus. While many of 'the Jews' who came to comfort Mary and Martha believed when they saw Jesus raise Lazarus, *some of them went to the Pharisees and told them what Jesus had done*. Like the lame man healed by Jesus at the Pool of Bethesda who informed 'the Jews' it was Jesus who healed him (5:15), so these people ran off to inform the Pharisees about the raising of Lazarus. They must have known these Pharisees were the enemies of Jesus.

47–48. Hearing the report, *the chief priests and the Pharisees called a meeting of the Sanhedrin*. This is the only explicit reference to the Sanhedrin in the Fourth Gospel, though there are repeated references to meetings of the 'chief priests and the Pharisees' (7:32, 45; 11:57; 18:3). The Sanhedrin consisted of seventy men, presided over by the high priest, and was modelled after Moses and the seventy elders. It was the highest ruling body of the

Jews, with responsibility for local rule over Jews in the Roman province of Judea. Included in its responsibilities were the investigation of charges related to the violations of the Mosaic law and the assessment of claims made by people to be prophets or the Messiah. Politically, the Sanhedrin walked a tightrope, answering to the Roman governor while at the same time trying to stay in favour with the majority of the people.

There was an urgent matter to be discussed at this meeting of the Sanhedrin: *'What are we accomplishing?' they asked. 'Here is this man performing many miraculous signs. If we let him go on like this, everyone will believe in him, and then the Romans will come and take away both our place and our nation.'* The members of the Sanhedrin faced a dilemma. The many miraculous signs Jesus performed in and around Jerusalem (2:23; 3:2; 7:31; 9:16; 11:47; 12:18, 37) led large numbers of the Jewish people to believe in him as the Messiah. If this continued, and the majority of the people gave their allegiance to him, it would certainly come to the notice of the Roman governor and be seen as a threat to imperial rule in Judea. This would invite a Roman crackdown involving, the Sanhedrin thought, the taking away from us 'our place' (the temple) and nation (the people). If they stood by while the populace acknowledged Jesus as Messiah, the Romans would remove them from office and they would lose their privileged position in regard to the temple and the people. However, it was increasingly hard for the Sanhedrin to move against Jesus, because of growing popular support for him.

49–50. A drastic resolution to their problems was proposed by their president: *Then one of them, named Caiaphas, who was high priest that year, spoke up, 'You know nothing at all! You do not realize that it is better for you that one man die for the people than that the whole nation perish.'* Caiaphas was high priest in the year that Jesus came to Jerusalem for the last time – in fact, he was high priest from AD 18 to 36. Seeing the members of the Sanhedrin caught on the horns of a dilemma, he suggested a radical solution: do away with Jesus! His argument was that it was better for one man, Jesus, to be put to death, than that the whole nation of the Jews should perish because of a Roman crackdown. Caiaphas' solution was rational and ruthless.

51–52. The evangelist comments on Caiaphas' 'final solution', *He did not say this on his own, but as high priest that year he prophesied that Jesus would die for the Jewish nation.* There is evidence in the writings of Josephus that a high priest might function as a prophet and that it was thought that a 'true priest' was necessarily a prophet.[1] There is also evidence in rabbinic writings that it was thought people might prophesy without knowing that they were doing so (Str-B 2, 546). In any case, the evangelist explains that Caiaphas was not speaking 'on his own' when he said Jesus would die for the nation. The evangelist explains further that Jesus would die, *not only for that nation but also for the scattered children of God, to bring them together and make them one.* Some suggest this means Jesus' death would benefit not only Jews of the Holy Land, but also Jews of the Diaspora, those scattered throughout the world. Alternatively, and perhaps closer to the mark, is the suggestion that this text refers not only to Jews, but also to Gentiles. Such a gathering of disparate peoples is foreshadowed in 10:16, where Jesus, as the good shepherd, says, 'I have other sheep that are not of this sheep pen. I must bring them also. They too will listen to my voice, and there shall be one flock and one shepherd.' The prophet Isaiah also spoke of a day when God would gather the Gentiles into his people (Is. 56: 6–8).

53. Caiaphas' words were taken at face value as counsel to do away with Jesus, *So from that day on they plotted to take his life.* The verb translated 'plotted' (*ebouleusanto*) is better translated 'resolved', as it was an official decision of the Sanhedrin. The decision of the Sanhedrin contrasted markedly from what Jesus himself resolved to do. The Sanhedrin decided to sacrifice an innocent man to retain their place in the nation. Jesus was ready to sacrifice himself to gather the scattered children of God.

54. While Jesus did not allow fear of the authorities to determine his activities (7–10), he took appropriate action to preserve his life (*cf.* 7:1), and did so again in the light of the moves made

---

[1]John Hyrcanus is described as having three great roles: 'the supreme control of the nation, the high priesthood and the gift of prophecy' (Josephus, *Jewish War,* i.68; *Antiquities* xiii.299). Philo says that 'the true priest is necessarily a prophet . . . and to a prophet nothing is unknown' (*On the Special Laws* iv.192).

by the Sanhedrin: *Therefore Jesus no longer moved about publicly among the Jews. Instead he withdrew to a region near the desert, to a village called Ephraim, where he stayed with his disciples*. There is no other mention of a village called Ephraim in either the OT or the NT. In the OT Ephraim is one of the sons of Joseph, and there are many references to the tribe of Ephraim and the hill country of Ephraim, but no village or town of Ephraim. However, in Josephus' account of the conquest of Judea by Vespasian there is such a reference: 'he captured the small towns of Bethala and Ephraim' (*Jewish War* iv.551). This Ephraim has been identified with the modern Et-Taiyibeh, 4 miles north-east of Bethel. Perhaps Jesus withdrew to this village because someone there offered him lodgings. It was far enough away from Jerusalem to avoid 'the Jews' of that city, yet close enough to be able to return for Passover (55; 12:1).

R. JESUS' HOUR HAS COME (11:55 – 12:50)

1. 'The Jews' look for Jesus in Jerusalem at Passover (11:55–57)

55. This verse provides the setting for the final stage of Jesus' life and ministry – the Passover Festival during which his betrayal, crucifixion and death took place: *When it was almost time for the Jewish Passover, many went up from the country to Jerusalem for their ceremonial cleansing before the Passover*. This was the third (2:13, 23; 6:4; 11:55) or possibly the fourth (5:1) Passover Festival that occurred during Jesus' ministry, the second or third that he attended. The ceremonial cleansing for which many came early to Jerusalem was carried out in Mikvah baths located near the entrance staircases on the southern side of the temple precincts.[1] Levitical purity was required of lay people at Passover because the men had to enter the court of the priests to bring their lambs to be sacrificed. Those requiring ritual cleansing needed to undergo this seven days before Passover (see 12:1).

[1]References to ceremonial cleansing in preparation for the Passover are found in Nu. 9:6–13; 2 Ch. 30:15–19; Josephus (*Jewish War* i.229; vi.290) and the Mishnah (*Pesaḥim* 9.1). References to Paul's cleansing himself are found in Acts 21:24, 26; 24:18.

56. The evangelist says that when the pilgrims came up to Jerusalem *they kept looking for Jesus, and as they stood in the temple area they asked one another, 'What do you think? Isn't he coming to the Feast at all?'* The form of the question in the original language (introduced with *ou mē*) indicates that a positive answer is expected: 'He is coming to the feast, isn't he?' On a recent visit to Bethany, just 2 miles from Jerusalem, Jesus raised Lazarus from the dead, and Jerusalem was buzzing with news of this event (45–48). So, as people gathered in the temple precincts they awaited Jesus' appearance with great anticipation.

57. Not everyone awaited his arrival with positive anticipation: *But the chief priests and Pharisees had given orders that if anyone found out where Jesus was, he should report it so that they might arrest him.* In 11:47–53 the evangelist tells of a meeting of the Sanhedrin called to deal with the 'threat' Jesus posed, at which the decision to kill him was taken. To facilitate the implementation of this decision the chief priests and the Pharisees ordered the people to notify them of Jesus' location once it was known. This was the dangerous situation into which Jesus came to celebrate his last Passover.

2. Mary anoints Jesus' feet at Bethany (12:1–8)

If Jesus was 'deeply moved' because Mary had joined in the faithless weeping and wailing of her 'comforters' when he met her after the death of Lazarus (11:33), then 12:1–8 shows that she redeemed herself with an extravagant act of devotion: anointing Jesus' feet with costly perfume.

1–2. The setting for the anointing is provided first: *Six days before the Passover, Jesus arrived at Bethany*. Like many others (11:55), Jesus was making his way to Jerusalem for Passover. *En route* he came to Bethany, now described as the place *where Lazarus lived, whom Jesus had raised from the dead*, reminding us of the fame now attaching both to Lazarus and Bethany because of what had happened there. Not surprisingly, *Here a dinner was given in Jesus' honour* (lit. 'for him'). *Martha served, while Lazarus was among those reclining at the table with him*. It is not specified in whose house this was held. The natural assumption is that it was held in the house of Mary, Martha and Lazarus, though if harmonization with the Matthean/Marcan accounts is sought, this dinner would have to be placed in the house of Simon the leper, also in Bethany (Mt. 26:6–13; Mk. 14:3–9). Both Lazarus and Jesus would then have been Simon's guests, and Martha would have been enlisted to help serve. The guests are described as 'reclining at table'. They would have been reclining, leaning on their left elbows with their heads towards the low U-shaped table (triclinium) and their feet away from the table.

3. It was the arrangement of guests around the triclinium that made possible what occurred next: *Mary took about a pint of pure nard, an expensive perfume; she poured it on Jesus' feet and wiped his feet with her hair*. Guests were served from the inside of the triclinium, but Mary came around the outside and therefore could pour her perfume over Jesus' feet. She anointed his feet with 'about a pint of pure nard'. The NIV is very free in its rendering of this phrase, which should read 'a pound of pure nard' (*i.e.* indicating weight not volume). The word for 'pound', *litra*, denotes a Roman pound weighing 11.5 ounces or 326 grams. That much perfume was a very large amount indeed. Nard is an extract from an aromatic Nepalese plant, *Nardostachys jatamansi*. The perfume was expensive because it was imported from a great distance, as well as having to be extracted from plant material. The process of extraction usually involved large amounts of plant material yielding only a little aromatic oil. Just how expensive this perfume was is revealed in 12:5. Anointing Jesus' feet with so much expensive perfume was an act of great devotion.

Mary's wiping Jesus' feet with her hair also expresses great devotion. A woman's long hair was regarded as her glory (1 Cor. 11:15; *cf.* 1 Pet. 3:3). Each time Mary's anointing is mentioned reference is made to her wiping Jesus' feet with her hair (11:2; 12:3). In Luke 7:44 Jesus contrasts the lack of love in the welcome accorded him by Simon the Pharisee with the love shown by a sinful woman: 'Do you see this woman? I came into your house. You did not give me any water for my feet, but she wet my feet with her tears and wiped them with her hair.'[1] Whatever else it

---

[1]There are so many differences between the Matthean/Marcan/Johannine passages and the Lucan passage (Lk. 7:36–50) that the Lucan passage appears to relate something that happened on a different occasion.

signified, wiping Jesus' feet with her hair revealed the depth of Mary's devotion to him.

One effect of Mary's act of devotion was that *the house was filled with the fragrance of the perfume*. The fragrant power of perfume was measured by the extent of its permeation. This is reflected in the Midrash on Ecclesiastes 7:1: '[the scent of] good oil is diffused from the bed-chamber to the dining-hall while a good name is diffused from one end of the world to the other'. The scent of Mary's perfume filled the house.

4–6. Not everyone was impressed with Mary's gesture of devotion. *One of his disciples, Judas Iscariot, who was later to betray him, objected, 'Why wasn't this perfume sold and the money given to the poor? It was worth a year's wages.'* Taken at face value, and adopting a utilitarian approach to things, Judas' objection would be justified. The perfume was very valuable – 'worth a year's wages' (lit. 300 denarii, one denarius being a working man's wage for one day). One has only to calculate what this means in today's currencies to realize just how much money would be involved. Great good could have been done for the poor with such a large sum of money. However, the evangelist is quick to explain, *He did not say this because he cared about the poor but because he was a thief; as keeper of the money bag, he used to help himself to what was put into it.* Judas' disapproval of Mary's action related not to loss of opportunity to do more for the poor but to his own loss of opportunity to steal from the common purse. He was the 'treasurer' of the little band of disciples (13:29) and used that position to help himself to the funds entrusted to him.

7–8. However, Jesus' approach was not just utilitarian, and he spoke up in defence of Mary to Judas. *'Leave her alone,' Jesus replied.* Jesus' words are addressed to Judas (the command 'leave her alone' is in the second-person singular form). After rebuking Judas, he explains Mary's motive: *[It was intended] that she should save this perfume for the day of my burial.* The word translated 'burial' (*entaphiasmos*) really means 'laying out for burial'. As the NIV construes these words, Jesus is saying that Mary originally purchased this expensive perfume to be used in laying out his body for burial, but now instead she was using it to express her devotion to him while he was still alive. In the parallel accounts Jesus tells his disciples that the woman who anointed him did so to prepare him for burial (Mt. 26:12/Mk. 14:8). He saw it as a symbolic embalming of his body for burial.

There is another way of construing these words of Jesus, which rendered literally read, 'Leave her alone so that she may keep it for the day of my [preparation for] burial.' For Jesus to say that she should be able to keep the perfume for the day of his burial makes no sense, but if he meant that she should keep it (her action) in her memory until the day of his burial it would. So when Nicodemus and Joseph of Arimathea actually anointed Jesus' body for burial after the crucifixion (19:38–42) she would know her act of devotion had preceded and foreshadowed theirs.

In response to Judas' utilitarianism, Jesus said, *You will always have the poor among you, but you will not always have me.* Jesus was then addressing not just Judas, but all his disciples (the 'you' here is plural). There was no need to reproach Mary for the extravagance of her devotion. There would be no shortage of opportunities for them to do good to the poor. Acts of devotion and acts of compassion for the poor are not mutually exclusive. He also reminded them the time for expressions of devotion was growing short: they would not always 'have' him in the way they had him at that time.

3. *The plot to kill Lazarus (12:9–11)*

9. Many of 'the Jews' who had come up to Jerusalem for the Passover Festival were asking whether Jesus would also come (11:55–56). It did not take long for news that he was in Bethany to reach them: *Meanwhile a large crowd of Jews found out that Jesus was there and came, not only because of him but also to see Lazarus, whom he had raised from the dead.* Their natural curiosity made them want to see not only Jesus but also Lazarus. Like many they were attracted by sensations.

10–11. The effect of Lazarus' restoration to life had a powerful impact upon the crowd, which made things even more difficult for Jesus' opponents: *so the chief priests made plans to kill Lazarus as well, for on account of him many of the Jews were going over to Jesus and* *putting their faith in him.* The chief priests (mostly of the Sadducean party) had most to lose. They cooperated with the Romans in the administration of the province of Judea, and Jesus' rapidly increasing fame was a growing threat to their position. Earlier the Sanhedrin, of which the chief priests were a most influential part, decided to kill Jesus to remove the threat. Now Lazarus too was adding to that threat, so the simple solution was to kill him as well.

4. Jesus' triumphal entry into Jerusalem (12:12–19)

The triumphal entry is one of the few events in Jesus' ministry that is recorded in all four Gospels (Mt. 21:1–11/Mk. 11:1–11/Lk. 19:28–40/Jn. 12:12–19). It was a crucial event in which Jesus, by a dramatic act, presented himself to Jerusalem as her king, in accordance with prophecy.

12–13. The evangelist begins his account, *The next day the great crowd that had come for the Feast heard that Jesus was on his way to Jerusalem.* It was the day after the anointing at Bethany that the pilgrims in Jerusalem for Passover heard that Jesus was approaching. The population of Jerusalem swelled enormously at Passover time. Josephus, a first-century Jewish writer, says that when a count was taken on one occasion the numbers present for Passover reached 2,700,000, a figure hard to believe, given the size of first-century Jerusalem.[1] Certainly, vast numbers of people came to Jerusalem for this festival. No doubt influenced by Jesus' growing fame, *they took palm branches and went out to meet him.* Palm fronds were used by pilgrims at the Feast of Tabernacles and the Feast of Dedication as part of the worship (see commentary on 7:2 and 10:22–39). Palm branches were also used as

[1]Josephus, *Jewish War* vi.422–425: 'That the city could contain so many is clear from the count taken under Cestius. For he, being anxious to convince Nero, who held the nation in contempt, of the city's strength, instructed the chief priests, if by any means possible, to take a census of the population. Accordingly, on the occasion of the feast called Passover, at which they sacrifice from the ninth to the eleventh hour, and a little fraternity, as it were, gathers round each sacrifice, of not fewer than ten persons (feasting alone not being permitted), while the companies often included as many as twenty, the victims were counted and amounted to two hundred and fifty-five thousand six hundred; allowing an average of ten diners to each victim, we obtain a total of two million seven hundred thousand, all pure and holy.'

symbols of victory and kingship. By meeting Jesus with palm branches the crowd showed they were welcoming him as king. Earlier in his ministry he eluded the crowds who wanted to make him king (6:15), but now he accepted their gesture and its significance.

As well as waving palm branches, the crowd was *shouting, 'Hosanna!' / 'Blessed is he who comes in the name of the Lord!'* This acclamation is based on Psalm 118:25–26. The literal meaning of 'Hosanna' is 'save now'. By the first century the word may have lost its literal sense and was used, as it is today, simply as a shout of praise. The words 'Blessed is he who comes in the name of the Lord' in their original context are addressed to pilgrims coming to the temple:

> Blessed is he who comes in the name of the LORD.
>   From the house of the LORD we bless *you*.
> The LORD is God,
>   and he has made his light shine upon us.
> With boughs in hand, join in the festal procession
>   up to the horns of the altar. (Ps. 118:26–27)

The 'you' in these verses is plural, and the picture is of those already at the temple blessing God for the arrival of other pilgrims. There would be nothing surprising, then, about the crowds welcoming Jesus in this way. However, in Jesus' case more was involved, because they greeted him with palm branches (symbols of victory and kingship), and the acclamation *Blessed is the King of Israel!* The NIV translation here represents a modification of the original. Literally translated it would read 'even the King of Israel'. Jesus accepted their acclamation of the pilgrims, unlike his reaction to earlier attempts by the crowd to make him king (*cf.* 6:15).

14–15. To make his final approach to Jerusalem *Jesus found a young donkey and sat upon it*. He did not need to ride the last couple of miles – he was used to walking long distances, and would have been physically fit. Also, pilgrims usually approached the holy city on foot. Jesus' action made a statement. The evangelist makes this plain by his OT quotation:

> *as it is written,*
> *Do not be afraid, O Daughter of Zion;*
> *see, your king is coming,*
> *seated on a donkey's colt.*

The quotation is from Zechariah 9:9, where the Lord is portrayed not in a militaristic fashion mounted on a war-horse but as a king of peace sitting on a donkey.[1] In fact, the following verse, Zechariah 9:10, says he will take away chariots and war-horses from Ephraim and Jerusalem, and proclaim peace to the nations. In conscious fulfilment of this prophecy Jesus entered Jerusalem on a donkey to show he was the king of the Jews, not the militaristic Messiah of popular expectation but the universal prince of peace.

16. The evangelist says, *At first his disciples did not understand all this. Only after Jesus was glorified did they realize that these things had been written about him and that they had done these things to him*. In this matter, as in others, Jesus' disciples only realized the significance of things after Jesus' death and resurrection (2:22; 13:7, 12, 28). Jesus promised that the Holy Spirit, when he came, would make these things clear to them (14:26; 16:12–15).

17–18. *Now the crowd that was with him when he called Lazarus from the tomb and raised him from the dead continued to spread the word*. Among those accompanying Jesus on his ride into Jerusalem were many who had witnessed the raising of Lazarus at Bethany, and they were spreading the word to other pilgrims. The result was, *Many people, because they had heard that he had given this miraculous sign, went out to meet him*. Thus the numbers of those who went out to meet him continued to swell. The evangelist refers to the raising of Lazarus as 'this miraculous sign'. It is the last and greatest of the signs recorded in the Book of Signs (1:19 – 12:50), the record of Jesus' work in the world.

19. The escalating popularity of Jesus caused consternation among his opponents: *So the Pharisees said to one another, 'See, this is getting us nowhere.'* 'This' may refer to the order they gave that anyone

---

[1]The evangelist's quotation of Ze. 9:9 corresponds exactly with no known version of this text. It is possible he was quoting from memory, or using a version of the LXX no longer extant.

who knew Jesus' whereabouts should make it known to them so they might arrest him (11:57). However, events had moved on quickly. Jesus was now appearing openly and in public places. Even though the Pharisees knew where he was, they could not arrest him because he was held in such esteem by the populace – as the Pharisees said to one another, *Look how the whole world has gone after him!*

5. Greek pilgrims seek Jesus (12:20–26)

20. People of many ethnic backgrounds were attracted to the monotheism and ethical purity of Judaism and many came to Jerusalem for the pilgrim festivals (see Acts 2:5–11). Thus it is no surprise when the evangelist says, *Now there were some Greeks among those who went up to worship at the Feast.* These Greeks 'went up to worship', indicating they were not pagan Gentiles but proselytes or God-fearers. The coming of the Greeks underlined what the Pharisees said: 'the *whole world* has gone after him' (19).

21–22. The Greeks would have heard reports of Jesus raising Lazarus, and therefore, like many of the Jews, they wanted to meet Jesus. *They came to Philip, who was from Bethsaida in Galilee, with a request. 'Sir,' they said, 'we would like to see Jesus.'* Bethsaida in Galilee[1] had a significant number of non-Jews and bordered on pagan territory. Possibly the Greeks approached Philip because he had a Greek name (though Philip himself was a Jew) and came from Bethsaida, thinking therefore he would be more open towards them. *Philip went to tell Andrew; Andrew and Philip in turn told Jesus.* Perhaps it is significant that Philip went first to Andrew with the request, because he was the one other member of the Twelve who bore a Greek name. Together they conveyed the Greeks' request to Jesus. We can only guess why Philip needed Andrew's moral support. Perhaps it reflects their doubts about Jesus' willingness to deal with Gentiles (Mt. 10:5–6; 15:22–24).

23–24. We are not told whether Jesus met with the Greeks, but hearing of their desire to meet him proved to be a significant

---

[1]Strictly speaking, Bethsaida was not in Galilee, ruled by Herod Antipas, but in the Tetrachy of Philip, in Gaulanitis. Bethsaida was, however, close to the border with Galilee.

moment. He replied, *The hour has come for the Son of Man to be glorified*. These words contain the fourth of nine references to Jesus' 'hour/time' (2:4; 7:30; 8:20; 12:23, 27 [2×]; 13:1; 16:32; 17:1), a significant theme in this Gospel. The first three references all say that Jesus' hour had not yet come; this fourth reference is the first of the remaining references, all of which indicate that his hour had come. The trigger for this change was the coming of the Greeks. Jesus' next words, though heavily metaphorical, indicated what the hour of his glorification was: *I tell you the truth, unless a kernel of wheat falls to the ground and dies, it remains only a single seed. But if it dies, it produces many seeds*. The primary reference was to Jesus' own death. Just as a kernel of wheat 'dies' when it is planted but then produces many seeds as it sprouts and the plant grows to maturity, so too Jesus would die, but the effects of his death would be a vast harvest of people who through faith in him would find eternal life. The coming of the Greeks made Jesus think of the great harvest (not only among Jews but also among Gentiles) that would occur following his death. The hour towards which everything was moving, then, was the hour of his death, followed by his resurrection and exaltation. This was when the Son of Man would be glorified.

25. Jesus' giving of his life provided a pattern for his disciples: *The man who loves his life will lose it, while the man who hates his life in this world will keep it for eternal life*. Those who 'love' their lives, giving priority to the retention of life and all that makes it up in this world, will lose it for eternal life. In parallel passages in the Synoptic Gospels Jesus mentioned certain important aspects of life in this world, which nevertheless must not be given priority over following him. These include love of father and mother, brothers and sisters, wives, sons and daughters, and even life itself. None of these may be given priority in the lives of Jesus' disciples (Mt. 10:37–39; Lk. 14:25–27; 17:33).

26. Jesus made explicit what was implicit in the preceding verses – his life was the pattern for all who would be his servants: *Whoever serves me must follow me*, *i.e.* as he denied himself for their sakes, they must deny themselves for his sake. Two promises attach to such a way of life: (1) *Where I am, my servant also will be.*

Those who follow Jesus in the path of self-denial in this world will have a place with him in his future glory (14:2–3; 17:24). (2) *My Father will honour the one who serves me.* In this life Jesus' disciples may experience disdain from the 'world' as he did, but on the last day they will receive honour from the only one who counts ultimately, God himself. When Samuel pronounced judgment upon the house of Saul, he said, in the name of God, 'Those who honour me I will honour, but those who despise me will be disdained' (1 Sa. 2:30). Jesus promised honour from God to all who serve him.

6. Jesus faces the prospect of the cross (12:27–36)

There is no account of Jesus' Gethsemane prayer in John's Gospel. Perhaps this passage functions as its counterpart. It reveals Jesus facing up to the hour of his death and resolutely choosing to go forward to glorify the Father. As in Gethsemane, so here Jesus was deeply troubled. He contemplated praying to be saved from the hour of death, but determined to carry out his Father's will at any cost. There was also a response from heaven to Jesus' prayer: in Gethsemane angels were sent to strengthen him; here a voice from heaven declared his prayer that God would glorify his name had already been answered and would be answered again. In this passage the evangelist also reveals the way Jesus would die, and the great benefits that would flow from his death.

27–28a. The arrival of the Greeks seeking for Jesus led him to speak of his death in terms of a grain of wheat falling into the ground and dying (24), and this led in turn to a sense of foreboding, expressed in the words *Now my heart is troubled.* On two other occasions Jesus is described as troubled: when he saw Mary and 'the Jews' weeping and wailing faithlessly following Lazarus' death (11:33, 38), and when he contemplated his betrayal by Judas (13:21). Matthew portrays similar deep emotions on Jesus' part in Gethsemane: 'My soul is overwhelmed with sorrow to the point of death' (Mt. 26:38). In his troubled state, Jesus asked, *what shall I say? 'Father, save me from this hour'?* This is the fifth reference to Jesus' 'hour/time' in John's Gospel and the second that speaks of the hour having now come. Clearly, the 'hour' is the hour of his death. Being truly human, Jesus wanted to be delivered from this dreadful hour, something he prayed for three times in Gethsemane (Mt. 26:39, 42, 44). But he wanted something else even more, and that led him to answer his own question: *No, it was for this very reason I came to this hour. Father, glorify your name!* To glorify his Father's name meant more to Jesus than life itself. To glorify the Father's name means simply to glorify the Father, for the name stands for the person. God was glorified in the hour of Jesus' death because then the grace of God was most clearly seen. The glory of God is his character, and he is glorified when his character is revealed (see Ex. 34:5–8).

28b–30. There was an immediate response to Jesus' prayer: *Then a voice came from heaven, 'I have glorified it, and will glorify it again.'* It was the Father's voice, declaring he had already glorified his name in Jesus' ministry (through Jesus' words and works; see 7:18; 11:4, 40; 17:4) and he would glorify it again through his death. *The crowd that was there and heard it said it had thundered; others said an angel had spoken to him.* The voice from heaven must have been a booming sound, for some of the bystanders thought it was thunder. Others thought it was a loud voice, and said 'an angel had spoken to him'. Neither opinion was correct. Though the crowd may not have understood what the voice said, nevertheless its very occurrence indicated that God had responded to Jesus' prayer. Jesus' only comment to the crowd was *This voice was for your benefit, not mine.* He needed no confirmation that his prayer would be answered, for this was guaranteed by his relationship to the Father. As Jesus' prayer before raising Lazarus was for the benefit of the onlookers (11:41–42), so this voice from heaven was for the crowd's benefit, not his, showing them God listened to Jesus' prayer.

31. Continuing to address the crowd, Jesus said, *Now is the time for judgment on this world.* The words 'the time for' have no counterparts in the original language, being added by the editors of the NIV, but they do bring out the meaning well. The judgment of the world was 'now' because the hour of Jesus' death had come (27–28). In the Fourth Gospel 'the world' often stands for those members of the Jewish leadership who were antagonistic towards Jesus. When they brought Jesus before Pilate and succeeded in getting a decision to have him crucified, they felt they had secured judgment against him. Ironically, their very rejection of Jesus and having him crucified sealed God's judgment upon them.

The 'hour' of Jesus' death meant more than judgment for the world, as he went on to say, *now the prince of this world will be driven out.* This is the first of three references to 'the prince of this world' in the Fourth Gospel (31; 14:30; 16:11), referred to elsewhere as 'the devil' (8:44; 13:2), 'Satan' (13:27) and 'the evil one' (17:15). He is described as 'the prince of this world' because human beings, since they fell into sin, have been under his power. As 1 John 5:19 says, 'the whole world is under the control of the evil one'. Through the death of Jesus the power of the prince of this world has been destroyed, and he has been driven out of office, as it were. The writer to the Hebrews expresses it this way: 'Since the children have flesh and blood, he [Jesus] too shared in their humanity so that by his death he might destroy him who holds the power of death – that is, the devil – and free those who all their lives were held in slavery by their fear of death' (Heb. 2:14–15). The prince of this world has power over human beings because he can accuse them before God and demand judgment upon their sins (Job 1:9–11; 2:3–5). In Revelation 12:10 he is called 'the accuser' (*katēgōr*). By his death Jesus dealt with the problem of human sins, and removed the ground of accusation. In this way the power of the prince of this world was broken, and he was driven out.

32–33. There was another very positive effect of Jesus' death: *But I, when I am lifted up from the earth, will draw all men to myself.* The evangelist adds a comment to explain what being lifted up from the earth meant: *He said this to show the kind of death he was going to die, i.e.* he would be lifted up on a cross (*cf.* 3:14). Jesus said, when this happened he would 'draw all men to myself'. The word 'to draw' (*elkyō*) is used five times in John's Gospel (6:44; 12:32; 18:10; 21:6, 11) and only once elsewhere in the NT (Acts 16:19). It is used literally in 18:10; 21:6, 11 of drawing a sword or drawing in a fishing net. It is used metaphorically in 6:44 and 12:32 of people being 'drawn' to Jesus, *i.e.* drawn to put their faith in him. Jesus' death on the cross would result in 'all' people being drawn to him. This does not mean that all people without exception would put their faith in him, for clearly some did not. It means people of all ethnic backgrounds would put their faith in him, one example of this being the Greeks seeking Jesus (20–22). A similar point is made in 10:16, where Jesus says, 'I have other sheep that are not of this sheep pen. I must bring them also. They too will listen to my voice, and there shall be one flock and one shepherd.'

34. The crowds who had just welcomed Jesus as their king (12–13) were perplexed by him saying he would 'lifted up', so *the crowd spoke up, 'We have heard from the Law that the Christ will remain for ever.* There is no passage in the OT which says exactly that 'the Christ will remain for ever'. There is one place where the Messiah's priestly role is said to be eternal (Ps. 110:4), and there are other places where his throne/reign is said to endure for ever (Ps. 89:3–4, 20–37; Is. 9:7). There are also passages in the Pseudepigrapha which speak of the eternal reign of the Messiah (*e.g. 1 Enoch* 49:1–2; 62:14; *Sibylline Oracles* 3:49–50). In the light of these beliefs the crowd asked, *how can you say, 'The Son of Man must be lifted up'?* In the immediate context Jesus did not actually say 'the Son of Man must be lifted up', but 'if I am lifted up' (32). In any case, the crowd, rightly assuming that implicit in Jesus' teaching was a claim to be the Christ, and that the titles 'Christ' and 'Son of Man' denoted the same divinely appointed person, asked how Jesus could say 'the Son of Man must be lifted up'. To them the idea of a suffering and dying Son of Man/Messiah/ Christ was nonsense. They asked, *Who is this 'Son of Man'? i.e.* what sort of a Son of Man are you talking about? – he is certainly not the one for whom we are looking. The same sort of incredulity is found in the statement of Trypho the Jew to the Christian apologist Justin: 'According to scripture the Son of man is to be full of honour and glory and establish the eternal kingdom (Dn. 7:13–14), but your so-called Christ was without honour or glory and was struck by the worst curse in the law of God by being crucified' (*Dialogue with Trypho* xxxii.1).

35–36. Instead of answering their question, *Jesus told them, 'You are going to have the light just a little while longer.'* Jesus was the light of the world (8:12), and they would have access to it only a 'little

273

while longer'. Soon he would be betrayed, condemned to death and crucified, and as far as the crowd was concerned the light would be gone. Jesus would rise from the dead, but in his resurrected form he would appear only to his disciples (14:22–24). Therefore Jesus said to the crowd, *Walk while you have the light, before darkness overtakes you*. Darkness would 'overtake' the unbelieving world when Jesus' physical presence was removed, and then it would be a case of *The man who walks in the dark does not know where he is going*. Without access to his light they would wander around like people in the dark. Therefore, Jesus urged the crowd, *Put your trust in the light while you have it, so that you may become sons of light*. He called upon them to trust him rather than challenge what he said, even if it ran counter to their notions of Messiahship. If they accepted the light he brought, they would become children of the light. Then they would never walk in the darkness, but have the light of life (8:12). *When he had finished speaking, Jesus left and hid himself from them*. Jesus' action suggests the crowd did not accept what he said (something confirmed by the evangelist in the next verse). By hiding himself from them he cut even shorter the time when they would have the light living among them.

7. *The evangelist explains the unbelief of the crowd (12:37–43)*

37–38. Referring to Jesus' activities in Jerusalem, the evangelist says, *Even after Jesus had done all these miraculous signs in their presence, they still would not believe in him*. Jesus performed numerous miracles in Jerusalem (2:23; 3:2; 7:31; 9:16; 11:47; 12:18, 37), but to no avail, for 'they' persisted in unbelief. 'They' refers to the crowd and the Jewish leaders, or some of them, who despite the signs they had witnessed rejected Jesus. *This was to fulfil the word of Isaiah the prophet:*

> *'Lord, who has believed our message*
> *and to whom has the arm of the Lord been revealed?'*

The evangelist cites exactly the LXX version of Isaiah 53:1 to show that Isaiah's experience was similar to that of Jesus. Isaiah preached the message given him by God, but few believed, just as Jesus performed many miracles and still people would not believe.

39–40. The evangelist not only found a paradigm of Jesus' experience in that of Isaiah; he found a reason for it also in his prophecy: *For this reason they could not believe, because, as Isaiah says elsewhere:*

> 'He has blinded their eyes
>   and deadened their hearts,
> so they can neither see with their eyes,
>   nor understand with their hearts,
>   nor turn – and I would heal them.'

There are significant differences between the citation of Isaiah 6:10 here in John's Gospel and the corresponding LXX and Hebrew texts. The evangelist, largely following the Hebrew text, presents the ultimate reason for people's rejection of God's messengers as God's own actions of blinding their spiritual eyes and hardening their hearts. It is important that this truth is balanced by the fact that people so blinded and hardened had also made their own choice to reject the message, and for their own reasons (*cf.* 11:47–50).

41. Referring to the prophecy, the evangelist says, *Isaiah said this because he saw Jesus' glory and spoke about him*. The allusion is to Isaiah's vision of God in the temple and his commission to be his messenger to Israel (Is. 6:1–13). The evangelist implies that what Isaiah saw in the temple was in fact 'Jesus' glory', *i.e.* the glory of the pre-existent Christ. There are other NT and early Christian writings which imply the pre-incarnate Christ appeared in OT times. Paul speaks of the rock in the wilderness from which the water gushed as Christ (1 Cor. 10:4). Justin Martyr says, when Moses 'was tending the flocks of his maternal uncle in the land of Arabia, our Christ conversed with him under the appearance of fire from a bush' (*I Apology* lxii.3–4; *cf. Dialogue with Trypho* 128).

42–43. Lest his readers should think all Jewish leaders were antagonistic towards Jesus, the evangelist says, *Yet at the same time many even among the leaders believed in him*. One example of the leaders who believed is Nicodemus, 'a man of the Pharisees' and 'a member of the Jewish ruling council' (3:1–15; 7:45–52; 19:38–42).

Having made this positive statement about many of the Jewish leaders who believed, sadly, the evangelist had to qualify it: *But because of the Pharisees they would not confess their faith for fear they would be put out of the synagogue*. The fear of the Pharisees on the part of those who believed in Jesus was connected with the decision already taken by 'the Jews' to put out of the synagogue any who acknowledged that Jesus was the Christ (9:22). The Pharisees are frequently linked with the chief priests in actions against Jesus and his followers (7:32, 45; 11:47, 57; 18:3). There are indications, as here, that the Pharisees took a leading role in these actions (7:47-48; 8:3, 13; 9:13, 15, 16, 40; 12:19, 42).

This is the second of three occasions in the Fourth Gospel where belief in Jesus as the Christ is linked with the threat of expulsion from the synagogue (9:22; 12:42; 16:2). Expulsion from the synagogue was a terrible thing in a society where one's identity was tied up with one's place in the family and community. The fear of the leaders who believed in Jesus was very real. Nevertheless, Jesus did expect his followers to confess him openly, and refusal to do so would show *they loved praise from men more than praise from God*. In 5:44 Jesus asked 'the Jews', 'How can you believe if you accept praise from one another, yet make no effort to obtain the praise that comes from the only God?' Wanting praise from their peers meant they could not acknowledge Jesus openly, and this meant forfeiting the praise that comes from God. While the opinion of others is important to well-being, if it is a choice between the good opinion of others and the good opinion of God, the disciple's choice is clear.

8. *Jesus' final word to 'the Jews' (12:44–50)*

This is the final section of the Book of Signs (1:19 – 12:50) in which the evangelist recounts Jesus' work in the world. What follows is the Book of Glory (13 – 20), which is dominated by the theme of Jesus' return to the Father. This final section contains Jesus' last words to 'the Jews' during his public ministry.

44–45. The evangelist introduces these last words by saying, *Jesus cried out*. The evangelist uses the verb 'to cry out' (*krazō*) on four occasions, all related to public declarations (1:15; 7:28, 37;

12:44). Jesus addressed all who were in earshot, but what he had to say would be of particular relevance to those who believed in him but were afraid to confess it openly (42). Jesus declared, *When a man believes in me, he does not believe in me only, but in the one who sent me.* Jesus insisted repeatedly that his words and works were those of the one who sent him (7:16; 10:37–38; 14:10–11, 24). It was a reminder to all that to believe in him was to believe in God. It was a challenge to those who claimed to believe in God but rejected Jesus, for in refusing to believe in him they were refusing to believe in God also. Jesus reinforced this declaration by saying, *When he looks at me, he sees the one who sent me.* Jesus revealed God not only by his words and works but also in his person. To see Jesus was to see God. Later, Philip will ask to see the Father, and Jesus will say to him, 'Don't you know me, Philip . . . Anyone who has seen me has seen the Father' (14:9).

46. Jesus continued, *I have come into the world as a light, so that no-one who believes in me should stay in darkness.* Jesus was holding out to his hearers for the last time an opportunity to escape from the 'darkness' by believing in him. The images of light and darkness are used metaphorically with many different meanings in the NT. Here the light is the revelation of the Father, which Jesus brought into the world, and the darkness is the ignorance about God in which people languish, and which leaves them prey to the evil one (1 Jn. 5:19).

47. Included in Jesus' final words to the Jews was a reminder that he was not passing judgment even upon those who did not obey his teaching: *As for the person who hears my words but does not keep them, I do not judge him. For I did not come to judge the world, but to save it.* Jesus was repeating here what he had said on previous occasions (3:17; 8:15). While he says here that he did not come to judge the world, there are other places in this Gospel which imply that Jesus will pass judgment on people (5:22, 30). The explanation for the apparent contradiction is that as long as Jesus was in this world he did not pass judgment, because his purpose in coming into the world was to save, not to condemn. On the last day he will exercise judgment (see Additional Note: Judgment, pp. 117–118)

48–50. Jesus went on to say, *There is a judge for the one who rejects me and does not accept my words; that very word which I spoke will condemn him at the last day*. Jesus spoke of 'the last day' several times. Mostly he referred to it as the time when he would raise up those who had believed in him (6:39, 40, 44, 54), but on this occasion he spoke of it as a day of judgment. He warned those who rejected his words that those same words would condemn them on the last day. Jesus then explained the reason why his word would be so determinative: *For I did not speak of my own accord, but the Father who sent me commanded me what to say and how to say it*. The word of Jesus was the word the Father gave him to speak. Therefore, to reject Jesus' word was to reject God's word, and no-one can reject God's word with impunity. Tragically, the word of God that people rejected was a word offering eternal life; thus Jesus concluded, *I know that his command leads to eternal life, so whatever I say is just what the Father has told me to say*. Jesus spoke as the Father commanded him, offering eternal life to those who accept his words, which only underlines again how important, for both time and eternity, it is that people accept his word.

III. JESUS' RETURN TO THE FATHER (13:1 – 20:31)

Chapter 13 is the beginning of the second major section of this Gospel, Jesus' return to the Father / the Book of Glory (13:1 – 20:31). It begins with the account of the Last Supper (13:1–30).

A. THE LAST SUPPER (13:1–30)

Jesus' teaching to prepare his disciples for his departure was given, or at least begun, during the Last Supper. He had come to Bethany (located about 2 miles east of Jerusalem) six days before Passover (1). There he was anointed by Mary 'for the day of his burial' (2–8). The following day he made his way into Jerusalem and was greeted by the crowds with palm branches and shouts of 'Hosanna!' (12–15). Then, on the eve of his betrayal and crucifixion, Jesus presided at a Passover meal, his last supper with the disciples.

1. Jesus washes his disciples' feet (13:1–11)

1. At the beginning of the Last Supper Jesus washed his disciples' feet. Setting the scene for the footwashing, the evangelist says, *It was just before the Passover Feast.* The footwashing took place as the Passover meal was being served (2). To bring out the significance of this moment he adds, *Jesus knew that the time had come for him to leave this world and go to the Father.* The theme of Jesus' hour/time has been to the fore throughout the Gospel. In the earlier part we are told that things did not happen 'because his hour had not yet come' (2:4; 7:30; 8:20). In 12:23 and thereafter (12:27; 13:1; 16:32; 17:1) we learn that 'the hour has come'. The hour was the hour of Jesus' departure from this world to return to the Father through his death, resurrection and exaltation. In full awareness of these things, Jesus carried out the footwashing.

There was more on Jesus' mind than this when he washed his disciples' feet: *Having loved his own who were in the world, he now showed them the full extent of his love* (lit. 'he loved them to the end'). Jesus' love was expressed not only in performing the menial service of footwashing but also in what this act symbolized: his humiliating death upon the cross by which spiritual cleansing was made possible (this becomes clear as the story unfolds). Referring to Jesus' disciples as 'his own' the evangelist picks up Jesus' references to his 'own' sheep who hear his voice (10:3, 4). The disciples are described as 'in the world' even though they are not 'of the world' (17:11, 14).

The evangelist's statement that Jesus loved them 'to the end' can be construed in two ways: (1) *adverbially*, meaning to the uttermost, or as the NIV has it, 'he showed them the full extent of his love'; (2) *temporally*, meaning to the end of his life, *i.e.* Jesus' love for his disciples did not fail; it persisted to the last moments of his life. Perhaps there is intended ambiguity here, for Jesus did indeed show the full extent of his love, and he did so until the end of his life.

2–3. The evangelist further explains the context of Jesus' gracious act. *The evening meal was being served, and the devil had already prompted Judas Iscariot, son of Simon, to betray Jesus.* Jesus knew well beforehand who was to betray him (6:70–71). Shortly, recognizing that Satan had taken hold of Judas, Jesus would send him on his way to do what he had planned (27). Being fully aware of these things, Jesus washed his disciples' feet, including the feet of the betrayer. There is yet something else we need to understand: *Jesus knew that the Father had put all things under his power, and that he had come from God and was returning to God.* It was knowing God had given him power over all things, and that he had come from God and was returning to God, that Jesus performed the footwashing. Knowing this did not make him think he was above carrying out menial service. Knowing full well who he was, Jesus washed his disciples' feet.

4–5. The evangelist now describes the footwashing: *so he got up from the meal, took off his outer clothing, and wrapped a towel round his waist. After that, he poured water into a basin and began to wash his disciples' feet, drying them with the towel that was wrapped round him.* Jesus' action was unprecedented. A wife might wash her husband's feet, children might wash their father's feet, and disciples might wash their master's feet, but in every case it would be an act of extreme devotion. Footwashing was normally carried out by a servant, not by those participating in the meal, and certainly not by the one presiding at the meal. According to later Jewish tradition, a Jewish slave would not be asked to wash people's feet. That task was assigned to a Gentile slave. Presumably, there was no servant at the venue where Jesus ate the Passover with his disciples. There must have been a period of embarrassment as the disciples realized there was no-one available to do the footwashing, and none of them was prepared to carry out this menial service for the others. The consternation of the disciples would have been palpable as they realized Jesus was preparing himself to carry out this lowly service. But still none of them moved. They just sat there, probably in stony silence, as Jesus washed and dried one disciple's feet after another. The silence was broken when he came to Peter.

6–7. Peter expressed what must have been in the minds of all: *He came to Simon Peter, who said to him, 'Lord, are you going to wash my feet?'* What Peter emphasized in his question was the inappropriateness of Jesus' action: 'Are *you* going to wash *my* feet?' Jesus

was not only the one presiding at the meal; he was also their disciple-master. Disciples were expected to serve their masters, not
the other way around. *Jesus replied, 'You do not realize now what I am
doing, but later you will understand.'* Peter realized only too well
what Jesus was doing at one level, but he did not understand what
Jesus' humble action in washing their feet symbolized. Jesus told
him that, while at that moment he could not understand, later (lit.
'after these things') he would.

8. Peter was still thinking only of the inappropriateness of
Jesus' action. *'No,' said Peter, 'you shall never wash my feet.'* Peter,
like the rest of the disciples, was not prepared to carry out this
menial service for the others himself, but he was appalled to think
that Jesus would do it. He virtually forbad his master to wash his
feet. But *Jesus answered, 'Unless I wash you, you have no part with me.'*
Such a response by Jesus makes no sense if all that was involved
was footwashing. In fact, Peter's refusal was commendable. At
least he recognized the inappropriateness of a disciple allowing
his master to wash his feet. The meaning of Jesus' response, therefore, must be sought at a deeper level. Jesus' self-humiliation in
washing his disciples' feet symbolized his self-humiliation in
accepting death upon the cross to bring about their cleansing from
sin. In this respect, Peter and the rest of the disciples must accept
what Jesus did for them, for if they did not, clearly they could
have no part with him. 'To have a part with Jesus' means literally
'to share things with Jesus', or, less literally, to have fellowship
with him. Jesus was saying to Peter that unless he was prepared
to accept what he would do for him on the cross, there could be
no relationship between them.

9. Peter did not understand the symbolic significance of what
Jesus was doing, but he did know what Jesus meant when he said,
'Unless I wash you, you have no part with me': *'Then, Lord,' Simon
Peter replied, 'not just my feet but my hands and my head as well!'* Peter
so wanted to have a part with Jesus that he said to him, in effect,
'If I must be washed so that I can have a part with you, then wash
me all over!' Peter thought Jesus was making the washing itself
the condition of their relationship, but this was not the case. It was
what the footwashing symbolized that was important.

10–11. Responding to Peter's enthusiastic but ignorant response, *Jesus answered, 'A person who has had a bath needs only to wash his feet; his whole body is clean.'* There are two ways of explaining this: (1) Jesus was drawing out a lesson from the custom of the day. Footwashing was offered to people who came together for a meal because, although they had bathed before they set out from home, walking to the appointed place along dusty roads meant that their feet were dirty. There was no need for them to bathe again; all they needed was to have their feet washed to refresh them before the meal. (2) The implied prior washing was the ceremonial bathing in Jerusalem required before the celebration of the Passover (11:55). In this case Jesus was saying to Peter there was no need for him to wash his hands and head as well as his feet. Peter had already undergone the ritual bathing. He needed only to have his feet washed. In both cases Jesus' metaphor implied that Peter, having once been cleansed by accepting the word of Jesus (*cf.* 15:3), and because of what he was to do for him upon the cross, needed no further cleansing.

Some have interpreted 13:8 ('Unless I wash you, you have no part with me') and 13:10 ('A person who has had a bath needs only to wash his feet; his whole body is clean') in terms of the need for Christian baptism and the question of sin after baptism. It is understandable how people might make these connections, but this was not Jesus' intention in saying these things to Peter, and there is little to suggest the evangelist wanted his readers to see such an allusion here either.

Jesus went on to say, *And you are clean*. The cleanliness Jesus was speaking about was forgiveness of sins, which makes people fit to have fellowship with him, fit to enter the presence of God. The disciples were already clean in this sense because they had accepted Jesus' word. Accepting Jesus' word is the means by which people are made clean, because it is the means by which they receive the benefits of Jesus' death. Later, Jesus would say to his disciples, 'You are already clean because of the word I have spoken to you' (15:3). While Jesus could say of most of his disciples 'you are clean', this was not true of all of them, so he added, *though not every one of you*. The evangelist explains this by adding, *For he knew who was going to betray him, and that was why he said not every one was clean*. Judas Iscariot was present. His feet were also washed by

Jesus, he too would eat the Passover, but then he would leave the meal and betray Jesus to the Jewish authorities who wanted to destroy him.

2. A lesson for the disciples (13:12–17)

12–15. Jesus' action in washing his disciples' feet contained a symbolic message about the need to receive the cleansing made possible by his self-humiliation on the cross. However, Jesus had more to teach them, and this involved something quite practical. The evangelist continues, *When he had finished washing their feet, he put on his clothes and returned to his place.* Apart from Peter's attempt to prevent Jesus washing his feet, the footwashing was carried out, as far as we know, in embarrassed silence. Then Jesus put on his outer garments again and resumed his place as president of the meal. Then he began to teach his disciples another lesson: *'Do you understand what I have done for you?' he asked them.* This was apparently a rhetorical question, for there was no response to it, and Jesus continued, *You call me 'Teacher' and 'Lord', and rightly so, for that is what I am.* It was because Peter recognized Jesus as teacher and Lord that he was at first unwilling to allow Jesus to wash his feet. Jesus said the disciples were right to regard him as their teacher and Lord, and his humble act had not changed that. That he had adopted a servant role did not change the fact that he was their teacher; he was just a different sort of teacher. That he had humbled himself and washed their feet did not change the fact that he was their Lord; he was just a different sort of Lord than the one they had hitherto understood him to be.

In the Fourth Gospel the titles 'teacher' (*didaskalos*) or 'Rabbi' (= teacher) are used frequently of Jesus. He was addressed as 'Rabbi' by the disciples of John the Baptist (1:38) and Nicodemus (3:2), and as 'teacher' by the Pharisees and teachers of the law (8:4). Martha referred to him as 'the Teacher' (11:28), and Mary Magdalene addressed him as 'Rabbi' (20:16). That Jesus' disciples regarded Jesus as their teacher (13, 14) indicates they had come to recognize him as at least equivalent in status to the other teachers in Israel.

Jesus is also addressed or spoken of as 'Lord' (*kyrios*) many times in the Fourth Gospel. Sometimes *kyrios* is translated correctly as 'Sir', a term of respectful address, when used by people who did not realize, or had not yet realized, who he was, such as the Samaritan woman (4:11, 15, 19), the royal official (4:49), the invalid at the Pool of Bethesda (5:7), the crowds (6:34), the woman taken in adultery (8:11), the blind man (9:36) and Mary Magdalene (20:15). In other places *kyrios* is translated correctly as 'Lord', when something more than respectful address was intended by those using it, such as the evangelist himself (6:23; 11:2; 20:20; 21:12), Peter (6, 9, 36, 37; 21:15, 16, 17, 21), the man born blind (9:38), Mary and/or Martha (11:3, 21, 27, 32 34, 39), the disciples as a group (11:12; 20:25), the beloved disciple (25; 21:7, 20), Thomas (14:5; 20:28), Philip (14:8), Judas, not Iscariot (14:22) and Mary Magdalene (20:2, 13, 18). When Jesus said to his disciples that they rightly regarded him as their 'Lord' he implied they were beginning to realize that he was much more than a person deserving respect; he deserved their obedience as well. On that basis he proceeded, *Now that I, your Lord and Teacher, have washed your feet, you also should wash one another's feet*. The lesson was a simple one. If, as their Lord and Teacher, it was not beneath his dignity to wash their feet, then it was not below their dignity to do the same for one another. The 'greatest' of Jesus' disciples needs to be ready to render humble service to the 'least' of the disciples when necessary. In cultures different from the one in which Jesus' and his disciples lived, that will not take the form of footwashing, but there will always be ample opportunity for humble service in other ways. To drive home this lesson, Jesus said, *I have set you an example that you should do as I have done for you*.[1]

16–17. Jesus reinforced this teaching by saying to his disciples, *I tell you the truth, no servant is greater than his master, nor is a messenger greater than the one who sent him*. The terms 'master' and

[1] The word 'example' (*hypodeigma*) used here is used often in the LXX of an exemplary death (see *e.g.* 2 Maccabees 6:28, 31; 4 Maccabees 17:22–23). Perhaps, then, there may not be such a big break between 13:1–11 and 13:12–17. The idea of Jesus' death may continue into the latter passage. It may not just be humble service Jesus was speaking about as an example for his disciples to follow, but his death which the footwashing foreshadowed. And if this was the case it adds another dimension to Jesus' teaching. It was not just that people should be ready for humble service, but that they should be ready to sacrifice themselves for their fellow believers. This is something the writer of 1 Jn. 3:16 understood: 'This is how we know what love is: Jesus Christ laid down his life for us. And we ought to lay down our lives for our brothers.'

284

'servant' used in this maxim need no explanation, but references to 'the messenger' (*apostolos*) and 'the one who sent him' call for extra comment. *Apostolos* is the Greek translation of the Hebrew word *šālîaḥ* (envoy). According to rabbinic teaching 'the one sent (*šālîaḥ*) by a man is as the man himself' (Mishnah, *Berakot* 5:5). This means, the treatment accorded messengers is regarded as done to those who sent them. Messengers (*apostoloi/šĕlûḥîm*) have great dignity, but are never above those who send them.

Jesus used the same maxim when he warned the disciples of the opposition they would face: 'Remember the words I spoke to you: "No servant is greater than his master." If they persecuted me, they will persecute you also' (15:20; *cf.* Mt. 10:24–25). He used it also to assure the disciples that although they, as students, were certainly not greater than their teacher, they could look forward to being like their teacher when their training was complete (Lk. 6:40). However, in this context, the maxim reinforces the lesson that the disciples should not hesitate to follow the example of Jesus. As his servants and messengers they were not greater than him, their master and the one who sent them, so there was no reason for them to think they were above carrying out menial service for one another, as he did for them.

Jesus concluded his instruction on this matter with the words *Now that you know these things, you will be blessed if you do them*. In the matter of rendering service to others, as in all matters related to Christian living, it is one thing to know what we should do; it is another thing to do it. The blessing comes, not with the knowing, but with the doing. Jesus' teaching at the end of the 'Sermon on the Mount' concludes in similar vein with the parable of the two builders. One built on sand; the other built on rock. The destruction of the house built upon the sand symbolizes the fate of those who hear the teaching of Jesus but do not carry it out; whereas the survival of the house built upon the rock symbolizes the blessing experienced by those who obey Jesus' word (Mt. 7:24–27; Lk. 6:47–49).

3. *Jesus' knowledge of what was to happen (13:18–20)*

18. Jesus concluded the exhortation to his disciples with the words 'Now that you know these things, you will be blessed if you do them,' indicating that blessing was in store for his obedient disciples. But sadly this was not true of them all. So he added, *I am not referring to all of you; I know those I have chosen*. He knew that one of them, Judas Iscariot, would betray him (*cf.* 6:70–71; 12:4; 13:2, 21–27) and saw it as a fulfilment of the Scriptures: *But this is to fulfil the scripture: 'He who shares my bread has lifted up his heel against me.'* [1] The quotation is from Psalm 41:9, where the psalmist calls upon God to have mercy upon him in his sickness because his enemies are gloating over his misfortune, and even his close friend whom he trusted and with whom he shared bread has turned against him. In Middle Eastern culture it is particularly reprehensible for those who accept hospitality and the intimacy of a shared meal to then turn against their hosts. As Jesus faced imminent death, he felt like the psalmist, because a close friend, one of the Twelve, was going to turn against him and betray him. But while this was deeply disappointing for Jesus, it came as no surprise: it was 'to fulfil the scripture'.

19. By telling his disciples he was soon to be betrayed, Jesus was not sharing his distress with them, understandable though that would be. He was showing concern for them: *I am telling you now before it happens, so that when it does happen you will believe that I am He*. Being forewarned of these events, he hoped their faith might not fail when they occurred. The forewarning did not prevent them falling into despair, though ultimately their faith did not fail. The mood of Jesus' disciples is reflected in Luke 24:19–21. The two disciples on the Emmaus road said in response to a question from and about Jesus: 'He was a prophet, powerful in word and deed before God and all the people. The chief priests and our rulers handed him over to be sentenced to death, and they crucified him; but we had hoped that he was the one who was going to redeem Israel.' Clearly, their belief that Jesus was the Christ had been shaken. Later, Jesus opened the disciples' eyes to understand all that was written about him in the Scriptures, and then their faith was restored (Lk. 24:45–47).

[1] The wording of this quotation differs significantly from the LXX (from which John's quotations normally come), but neither is it a literal rendering of the Hebrew text. It appears the evangelist made his own translation from the Hebrew text, rather than using the LXX.

20. The connection between the words of this verse *I tell you the truth, whoever accepts anyone I send accepts me; and whoever accepts me accepts the one who sent me* and what precedes is not easy to determine. In the Synoptic Gospels Jesus used words similar to these on a number of occasions and for different purposes (Mt. 10:40; 18:5; Mk. 9:37; Lk. 9:48). But what connection does the fourth evangelist intend for us to see between Jesus' use of them in this verse and what precedes? Perhaps the connection is that the disciples, once their faith that Jesus is the Christ was restored after the resurrection, when they realized that all that had happened to him was in fulfilment of Scripture, would then take up their mission as Jesus' sent ones in the world. Then if people accepted them and their witness, they would be accepting Jesus also; and those who accepted Jesus in that way would be accepting the one who sent him, God the Father.

4. Jesus predicts his betrayal by Judas Iscariot (13:21–30)

21. Referring back to Jesus' statements in the previous section, the evangelist says, *After he had said this, Jesus was troubled in spirit.* This is the third occasion on which Jesus was 'troubled'. The first occasion was when he met Mary following the death of Lazarus and saw her caught up in faithless weeping (11:33, 38), and the second was when, being aware the time of his crucifixion was drawing near, he shank from the prospect of the cross (12:27). On this third occasion Jesus was 'troubled in spirit' as he faced betrayal by one of his own disciples, and he *testified, 'I tell you the truth, one of you is going to betray me.'* This declaration (introduced with the solemn formula 'I tell you the truth', *amēn amēn legō hymin*) shows that the prospect of betrayal, though exceedingly disturbing, did not take Jesus by surprise. He announced it beforehand.

22–25. Jesus' announcement caused consternation: *His disciples stared at one another, at a loss to know which of them he meant.* They understood clearly *what* he meant, but consternation set in as they wondered *which of them* he meant. The evangelist then tells us that *one of them, the disciple whom Jesus loved, was reclining next to him.* When people reclined on cushions around a triclinium

287

(see commentary on 12:2), leaning on their left elbows, the head of the person on the right would be close to the other person's chest. This verse contains the first of four references (23; 19:26; 21:7; 21:20) to 'the disciple whom Jesus loved', and it is his witness that is recorded in this Gospel (21:20–24). While many are reluctant to identify this person as the apostle John, it does, nevertheless, seem to be the fairest way to read the evidence (see pp. 24–30). *Simon Peter motioned to this disciple and said, 'Ask him which one he means.'* So then, *Leaning back against Jesus, he asked him, 'Lord, who is it?'* It was easy for the disciple whom Jesus loved to make use of his close proximity to Jesus to ask the question quietly.

26–27. The Lord's response is then recorded: *Jesus answered, 'It is the one to whom I will give this piece of bread when I have dipped it in the dish.' Then, dipping the piece of bread, he gave it to Judas Iscariot, son of Simon.* In this verse the NIV translates the Greek word *psōmion* as 'a piece of bread'. Actually, the word itself means only a 'piece' or a 'morsel', without indicating a piece or morsel of what. To this would have to be added *artou* ('of bread') to make it unambiguously mean 'a piece of bread'. So it is not clear whether Jesus offered Judas a piece of bread or a piece of something else. A possible alternative would be a portion of bitter herbs which, at a Passover meal, was dipped in the sauce and eaten. If, however, a piece of bread is intended, then Jesus' action would certainly have reinforced what he said earlier: 'He who shares my *bread* has lifted up his heel against me' (18). Either way, Jesus' action in giving the morsel functioned as a silent answer to the beloved disciple's question. Reading Jesus' action in the light of the scriptural citation in 13:18, it would seem that this act was a last token of Jesus' love to Judas, as well as a silent answer to the beloved disciple's question. It is difficult to understand why the beloved disciple, receiving this information, took no action to prevent the betrayal. Perhaps it was because Jesus himself did nothing to prevent it, but instead told Judas to get on with it (27).

The evangelist has already mentioned Judas Iscariot by name three times as the one who was to betray Jesus (6:71; 12:4; 13:2). Now he says, *As soon as Judas took the bread* (lit. 'after the morsel'), *Satan entered into him.* He received the morsel, but not the love with which it was offered, and then 'Satan entered into him'.

Earlier in this chapter the evangelist says that 'the devil had already *prompted* Judas . . . to betray Jesus' (2), and now that Satan *entered* him, making clear that Judas was not acting on his own. In 6:70 Jesus referred to the betrayer as a devil ('Have I not chosen you, the Twelve? Yet one of you is a devil!'). In 8:44 Jesus said to 'the Jews' who wanted to kill him, 'You belong to your father, the devil, and you want to carry out your father's desire.' In the same way, when Judas betrayed Jesus, he carried out the devil's desire.

It seems that early Christian writers believed the devil did not know what the outcome of Jesus' death would be. In 1 John 3:8 we read, 'The reason the Son of God appeared was to destroy the devil's work,' and in Hebrews 2:14–15 we read, 'Since the children have flesh and blood, he [Jesus] too shared in their humanity so that by his death he might destroy him who holds the power of death – that is, the devil – and free those who all their lives were held in slavery by their fear of death.' If the devil had known his power would be 'destroyed' by the death of Christ, he might not have been 'prompting' Judas to betray him or be 'entering' him to bring about the betrayal. Recognizing what was happening with Judas and that he was now determined to betray him, Jesus told him to get on with his wicked work: *What you are about to do, do quickly*.

28–29. Apparently, Jesus' words to the beloved disciple indicating who the betrayer was were heard only by the beloved disciple, but when he told Judas to do what he was going to do quickly, all the disciples heard. The evangelist adds, *but no-one at the meal understood why Jesus said this to him*. The evangelist explains what they thought Jesus was telling Judas to do: *Since Judas had charge of the money, some thought Jesus was telling him to buy what was needed for the Feast, or to give something to the poor*. The evangelist notes that 'Judas had charge of the money'. Earlier in the Gospel (12:2–8) we are told of Mary anointing Jesus' feet with expensive perfume and of Judas Iscariot's objection to this 'waste' of money that could have been given to the poor. But there the evangelist explains, 'He did not say this because he cared about the poor but because he was a thief; as keeper of the money bag, he used to help himself to what was put into it' (12:6). Judas was the treasurer of the disciple band, and before he hardened in his intention to betray Jesus he was already guilty of embezzlement. Seeing Judas leave the room, the disciples, who had not heard Jesus' words to the beloved disciple identifying him as the betrayer, thought Judas was being sent out as treasurer either to buy something for the feast or to give something to the poor.

Some have argued that the fact that the disciples thought Judas was being sent out to buy something for the feast proves Jesus' last meal with the disciples was not a Passover meal, the disciples thinking Judas would be buying provisions for Passover the following night. However, this makes no sense, as there would have been opportunity to buy provisions the next day in that case, and there would have been no urgency. Possibly the disciples thought Judas was being sent to buy provisions, not for the Passover meal itself, but for the feast of unleavened bread which began at midnight. The Mishnah allows purchase of food on Passover night as long as no cash changes hands; something could be left in trust instead and payment made after the feast (Šabbat 23:1).

The other reason the disciples thought Jesus was sending Judas out was to give something to the poor. It was customary to make donations to the poor during Passover. That Jesus and his disciples used to give to the poor is implied in 12:6, where Judas objected to Mary's extravagant devotion, saying the perfume she used could have been sold and the proceeds given to the poor.

30. Jesus offered Judas the morsel, and *as soon as Judas had taken the bread, he went out*. If there had been in Jesus' offer one last token of love, it was rejected. Judas' mind was made up. He straightaway rose from the table and went out to betray Jesus. The evangelist adds the poignant words *And it was night*. The reference to 'the night' appears to carry both a natural meaning (it was night) and a symbolic meaning (Judas, leaving Jesus, was going out into spiritual darkness to betray him). This is supported by the fact that the other references to the 'night' in the Gospel of John appear to have negative connotations. Two of these relate to Nicodemus' coming to Jesus 'by night' (3:2; 19:39), where the night allows Nicodemus to approach Jesus without being seen, and possibly symbolizes the spiritual darkness he lived in before his encounter with Jesus. A third reference (9:4) includes Jesus' words about doing the works of God while it is day, because the night is coming in which no-one can work. Here the night has negative spiritual connotations. In the fourth reference (11:10) Jesus speaks about those walking 'by night' without the 'light' he brings, who stumble because they cannot see where they are going. Here also the night symbolizes spiritual darkness. The fifth reference (21:3) may also carry some symbolic meaning when the evangelist describes the disciples' unsuccessful fishing expedition before Jesus appeared on the shore and gave them directions ('that night they caught nothing').

B. THE FIRST PART OF THE FAREWELL DISCOURSE (13:31 – 14:31)

After the departure of Judas recorded in 13:30, Jesus began preparing the remaining disciples for events shortly to follow: his betrayal, arrest, trials and crucifixion, to be followed by his resurrection and ascension. Through these events Jesus would return to the Father. The long passage 13:31 – 16:33 constitutes Jesus' farewell discourse in which he prepared his disciples for life without him.[1] The first part of the discourse is found in 13:31 – 14:31, and comprises the following sections.

1. Jesus to be glorified and the love command (13:31–35)

31. Judas' departure signalled the time for further explanations: *When he was gone, Jesus said, 'Now is the Son of Man glorified and God is glorified in him.'* Jesus' use of 'the Son of Man' as a self-designation picks up the concept of the glorious Son of Man from Daniel 7:13–14. To this one is given 'authority, glory and sovereign power' and his 'dominion is an everlasting dominion that will not pass away'. In the Fourth Gospel the glorifying of the Son of Man involves suffering and death as well as sovereign power – Jesus

---

[1]There are certain formal parallels between Jesus' farewell discourse and Jewish farewell speeches, most notably the *Testaments of the Twelve Patriarchs*, which appear to have been written in the second century BC. These speeches purport to be the final words of the twelve sons of Jacob just prior to their deaths. In each case the patriarch reflects on his past life, mentioning both his failures and virtues, and uses these as a basis for exhortations to his children. But there are obvious differences. While Jesus does remind his disciples about his teaching and presents his actions as an example for them to follow, he does not speak of his failures and urge his disciples to avoid these.

enters his glory via the cross (see Additional Note: 'The Son of Man', pp. 89–91). That is why Judas' departure to betray Jesus elicited the statement 'Now is the Son of Man glorified'. However, the death of Jesus was not just his passage to glory. In death itself Jesus was glorified. In giving his life for sinful humans the glory of his gracious character was most clearly seen. And it did not stop there, for Jesus said that when the Son of Man was glorified, God also would be glorified in him. In Jesus' self-sacrificing love for human beings the glory of God was revealed, for the Father loves the world, and this led him to give his one and only Son so that those who believe might have eternal life (3:16). In the giving of his Son, the glory of God's own self-giving love was revealed.

32. Because Jesus was to glorify God in his death, he added, *If God is glorified in him, God will glorify the Son in himself, and will glorify him at once*. Because Jesus glorified his Father through his death, he knew God would in turn glorify him without delay. Jesus was referring to his resurrection and ascension. St Paul expressed the same thing in Philippians 2:8–11:

> And being found in appearance as a man,
> he humbled himself
> and became obedient to death – even death on a cross!
> Therefore God exalted him to the highest place
> and gave him the name that is above every name,
> that at the name of Jesus every knee should bow,
> in heaven and on earth and under the earth,
> and every tongue confess that Jesus Christ is Lord,
> to the glory of God the Father.

33. Referring again to his imminent departure, Jesus said to his disciples, *My children, I will be with you only a little longer*. The time was short. Judas had gone out to betray Jesus and events were moving quickly, and would soon culminate in his arrest, crucifixion, resurrection and ascension. Then Jesus added, *You will look for me, and just as I told the Jews, so I tell you now: Where I am going, you cannot come*. Earlier, Jesus had told 'the Jews', 'I am with you for only a short time, and then I go to the one who sent me. You will look for me, but you will not find me; and where I am, you cannot come' (7:33–34; *cf.* 8:21). They could not follow Jesus into the Father's presence, because they did not believe in him. Jesus' message for his disciples was similar, but with one significant difference. While the disciples could not follow Jesus now, they would do so later (36), but 'the Jews' who rejected Jesus could not do so at all, and they would die in their sins (8:21, 24).

34. Jesus said to his disciples, *A new command I give you: Love one another*. This is the first of two instances (13:34; 15:12) in which Jesus commanded his disciples to love one another, but only on this occasion did he refer to it as a 'new' command. In the OT the Israelites were commanded to love their neighbour as they loved themselves (Lv. 19:18), but Jesus said to his disciples, *As I have loved you, so you must love one another*. This raised the ante considerably. The measure of love for their neighbour was no longer their love for themselves, but Jesus' love for them. The Fourth Gospel speaks of Jesus' love for the disciples in three places (1; 15:9, 13), a love that led him to lay down his life for them. Now he said they should love one another in the same way (*cf.* 1 Jn. 3:16). Jesus' love command was 'new' because it demanded a new kind of love, a love like his own.

35. Jesus highlighted the importance of the disciples' love for one another by adding to his command the explanation *By this all men will know that you are my disciples, if you love one another*. This was not the reason they should love one another, but was rather the outcome of their love. People would be able to recognize them as Jesus' disciples by their mutual love. Knowing the truth about Jesus is vital, but so also is believers' love for one another. This love is not sentimental, but real self-sacrificing love by which they place other believers' needs above their own. Lovelessness among believers nullifies their witness to the world, and reveals them as hypocrites.

2. Peter's denial predicted (13:36–38)

Sombre notes have already been sounded in chapter 13: Judas' departure to betray Jesus (21–30) and Jesus' enigmatic words about the Son of Man being 'glorified' (31–33). The evangelist adds to these by recounting Jesus' prediction that Peter would deny his master (36–38).

36. Jesus' warning about Peter's denial was prompted by a question from him relating to something Jesus had said earlier (33b): *Simon Peter asked him, 'Lord, where are you going?' Jesus replied, 'Where I am going, you cannot follow now, but you will follow later.'* Jesus did not answer Peter's question about 'where' he was going, but told him that he could not follow him there now, but would do so later. It was not yet time for Peter to follow Jesus into the Father's presence. Also, the rigours of suffering and death through which Jesus would make his way to the Father were not something Peter was yet able to bear, but later he would do so (21:18–19).

37. In response, *Peter asked, 'Lord, why can't I follow you now? I will lay down my life for you.'* Peter thought Jesus was saying to him that he did not have the commitment necessary to follow him as he faced what lay ahead. Peter, however, felt he was ready to lay down his life for Jesus (*cf.* Mt. 26:35; Mk. 14:31; Lk. 22:33), but clearly he did not understand what that would mean. He was certainly ready to take up arms to defend his master, as he would do in the olive grove, wielding his sword against the servant of the high priest (18:10–11). But to follow Jesus in the way of suffering without resistance proved to be more than he could then bear.

38. Knowing that Peter would not be able live up to his profession at this stage, *Jesus answered, 'Will you really lay down your life for me?'* These must have been hard words for Peter to hear, but worse was to follow: *'I tell you the truth, before the cock crows, you will disown me three times!'* It was already night when Judas went out to betray Jesus, and now Peter was told before that night had run its course ('before the cock crows') he would disown Jesus three times (these denials are recorded in 18:17, 25, 26–27).[1]

[1]John follows Matthew and Luke in saying that Peter will deny Jesus three times before the cock crows (Mt. 26:34; Lk. 22:34), but Mark says that Peter will deny Jesus three times 'before the cock crows twice' (Mk. 14:30). This has led some to suggest Peter denied Jesus six times, an expedient to overcome what might otherwise be thought to be an 'error' in the Gospel accounts. This is surely an unnecessary expedient, as Matthew's, Luke's and John's references to the cock crowing surely do not mean it would crow only once; hence there is no real conflict between the accounts.

3. The way to the Father (14:1–11)

After Jesus washed his disciples' feet, he spoke of deeply troubling matters: one of them would betray him, he was going to leave them, and Peter would disown him. Shortly the disciples would see their master led away for trial; then be condemned to death on a cross. Their faith would be sorely tested. It was to fortify them in these circumstances that Jesus' teaching, beginning in 14:1–11, was given.

1. Though deeply troubled by the prospect of his own betrayal and crucifixion, Jesus concerned himself with his disciples' distress. He said to them, *Do not let your hearts be troubled. Trust in God; trust also in me.*[1] Their faith in God, and in particular their faith in Jesus, would enable them to calm their hearts as they faced what lay ahead.

2. Having urged his disciples to maintain their trust in him even though he was soon to leave them, Jesus gave them further grounds for doing so: *In my Father's house are many rooms; if it were not so, I would have told you. I am going there to prepare a place for you.*[2] God's eternal dwelling place is portrayed as his 'house' (*oikia*) with many 'rooms' (*monai*), sufficient to provide a 'place' (*topos*) for all Jesus' disciples. Jesus' going was to prepare 'a place' for them in God's 'house', and he assured them that if this were not the case he would have told them so.

The word translated 'rooms' (*monai*) is rare. It is not found in the LXX, and occurs only twice in the NT, both in the Fourth Gospel

[1] This is only one of four possible translations of Jesus' words. The two words translated 'trust' (*pisteuete*) could be construed either as indicatives or imperatives, yielding one of the following four translations: (1) 'trust in God; trust also in me'; (2) 'you trust in God; trust also in me'; (3) 'you trust in God; you also trust in me'; (4) 'trust in God; you also trust in me'. While the third and fourth translations do not make good sense in the context, either the first or second translations make quite good sense. In a context where Jesus was urging his disciples not to let their hearts be troubled, it is one of the translations which urges them to maintain their trust in him that is most appropriate. It does not matter much whether that is prefaced with an exhortation to trust God or with a reminder that they did trust God.

[2] The NIV text 'if it were not so, I would have told you. I am going there to prepare a place for you' represents one textual variant according to which Jesus is making a statement. Another variant in which the word 'that' (*hoti*) is added would translate as a question, 'If it were not so, would I have told you that I am going to prepare a place for you?' There is no real difference in meaning between the two.

(1, 23). In 14:23 Jesus says, 'If anyone loves me, he will obey my teaching. My Father will love him, and we will come to him and make our home (*monēn*) with him.' The text speaks of the Father and the Son making their 'home' with believers, *i.e.* making themselves present with them. When we unpack the metaphor of 14:2, then, we should think not so much of 'rooms' in God's house (much less 'mansions' as the AV has) but of the privilege of abiding in God's presence.

When Jesus said, 'I am going to prepare a place for you,' we should not think of him returning to heaven, and having arrived there, setting about the construction of 'rooms' for his disciples to occupy – a task he has now been occupied with for some two thousand years! Rather, we should recognize that it was by his very going, by his betrayal, crucifixion and exaltation, that he made it possible for us to dwell in the presence of God. The imminent departure of Jesus, which so troubled the hearts of his disciples, was in fact for their benefit.

3. Jesus added, *And if I go and prepare a place for you, I will come back and take you to be with me that you also may be where I am.* Jesus' coming back has been variously interpreted: (1) his coming to the disciples following his resurrection (*cf.* 20:19–29); (2) his coming in the person of the Holy Spirit (*cf.* 14:15–21); (3) his second coming at the end of this age (*cf.* 14:28; 21:22–23); and (4) his 'coming' to take his disciples to be with him when they die. The third alternative is the correct one: Jesus' going in this context is his return to the Father's presence in heaven (via his crucifixion, resurrection and ascension), and it is to heaven he will take his disciples when he returns for them. This did not occur when he came to them following the resurrection, nor with the coming of the Holy Spirit, but will occur at his second coming. (The fourth suggestion, comforting though it is to think of Christ 'coming' for us when we die, is not something that receives any support in this passage.) Jesus' return at the end of the age is not a major theme in the Fourth Gospel; nevertheless, it is implied in a couple of other places (28; 21:22–23). These are sufficient to show that, while the Fourth Gospel emphasizes the present experience of eternal life and the presence of Jesus with his disciples through the Holy Spirit, the hope of his return and of their being with him in the Father's presence still remains the ultimate goal.

Jesus' promise to come back and take his disciples to be 'with me' is expressed by the words *pros hemauton*, which is idiomatic for 'to my home' (*cf.* Lk. 24:12 NRSV). Thus Jesus sought to fortify his disciples by telling them that by his departure he would prepare places for them in his Father's house, and that he would return to take them to his home there.

4-5. Having told his disciples the purpose of his departure, Jesus said, *You know the way to the place where I am going*. He had spoken about the place he was going – to the Father – and the way he was to get there – by way of the cross and resurrection – and he expected his disciples to understand this. But they did not, and speaking for them all, *Thomas said to him, 'Lord, we don't know where you are going, so how can we know the way?'* They wanted to follow Jesus, but said they did not know where he was going, and therefore they could not know the way he was taking.

6. In response to Thomas' implied question about the way to the Father, *Jesus answered, 'I am the way and the truth and the life.'* This statement contains the sixth of seven 'I am' sayings with predicates in the Fourth Gospel (6:35, 48, 51; 8:12; 10:7, 9; 10:11, 14; 11:25; 14:6; 15:1, 5). Fundamental to Jesus' response to Thomas' question was that Jesus himself is the way – that he is the truth and the life[1] are supporting statements. Jesus is the way to the Father primarily because his death made access to the Father's presence possible for sinful human beings. He is also the way to God because he is the truth: he brought the truth of God into the world (1:14, 17; 8:32, 40, 45–46; 14:6; 18:37), proclaiming it and embodying it. Therefore, when people come to Jesus, they come to the one in whom the truth about the Father is found.

Jesus is also the way to the Father because he is the life. In various ways the Fourth Gospel speaks of Jesus as 'the life'. In 1:4 we are told, 'In him was life, and that life was the light of men,' and in 5:26 Jesus says, 'as the Father has life in himself, so he has granted the Son to have life in himself'. In 6:33, 35, 48, 51 Jesus speaks of himself as the 'bread of life', and in 11:25 he says, 'I am

---

[1]Some suggest that this should be construed as 'I am the true and living way', but the fact that each of these three elements (the way, the truth and the life) is preceded by the definite article militates against this.

the resurrection and the life.' All these texts reflect the fact that the life of God was found in Jesus. Therefore, when people come to Jesus they come to the one in whom the life of the Father is found, and in this sense also Jesus is the way to the Father.

In this text Jesus not only said that he was 'the way the truth and the life'; he also added, *No one comes to the Father except through me*. No-one else can bring people to God, for no-one else has seen God or made him known (1:18; 3:13), no-one else speaks and embodies the truth about God as he does, no-one else shares the very life of God, and no-one else has dealt with the problem of human sin so as to bring people back to a holy God. This means that no-one can claim to know God while rejecting Jesus his Son (5:23; 8:42).

7–8. Because Jesus was one with the Father and embodied the truth and the life of the Father, he could say to his disciples, *If you really knew me, you would know my Father as well.* The word 'really' has no counterpart in the original language, but has been added by the NIV translators to bring out the sense of Jesus' statement. He implied that his disciples did not yet really understand who he was. If they did, they would realize they knew the Father as well. Jesus explained, *From now on, you do know him and have seen him.* They did know the Father and had seen him because they knew and had seen Jesus who was one with the Father and embodied the true revelation of the Father. Responding on behalf of all the disciples, *Philip said, 'Lord, show us the Father and that will be enough for us.'* His response indicated that they did not yet realize who Jesus really was. It also reflected a fundamental human longing – to see God.

9–10. Disappointed with the response of the disciples voiced by Philip, *Jesus answered: 'Don't you know me, Philip, even after I have been among you* (pl.) *such a long time?'* Despite the fact that Jesus had lived among his disciples for a long time, they still did not know who he really was. So he explained further, *Anyone who has seen me has seen the Father.* Because Jesus and the Father are one, anyone who sees Jesus sees the Father also. Jesus asked, *How can you* (sing.) *say, 'Show us the Father'? Don't you* (sing.) *believe that I am in the Father, and that the Father is in me?* Even though the disciples had come to acknowledge Jesus as the Holy One of God who had the words of eternal life (6:66–69), and as their teacher and Lord (13:13–14), still they did not comprehend his unique union with the Father. So Jesus explained, *The words I say to you* (pl.) *are not just my own. Rather, it is the Father, living in me, who is doing his work.* Even the words he spoke were not merely his own words, for as he spoke, the Father living in him was 'doing his work'.

11. What Jesus expected of his disciples is expressed in the words *Believe me when I say that I am in the Father and the Father is in me.* He wanted them to understand he was not just a prophet, not just a teacher, not just their disciple-master, not only the Messiah; he was the Word made flesh, God incarnate. To be in his presence was to be in the presence of the Father. Recognizing that it was stretching the faith of the disciples to accept this teaching, Jesus added, *or at least believe on the evidence of the miracles themselves.* The word translated 'miracles' (*erga*) means, in fact, 'works'. On several occasions Jesus urged 'the Jews' to view his works as evidence that the Father had sent him (5:36), that he was the Christ (10:25), and that the Father was in him and he in the Father (10:37–38). Now he urged his disciples also to believe on the basis of his works if they could not believe his word.

4. Greater works and prayer (14:12–14)

12. Having urged his disciples to believe in him on the basis of his works (*erga*), Jesus made a remarkable statement: *I tell you the truth, anyone who has faith in me will do what* (lit. 'the works', *erga*) *I have been doing. He will do even greater things than these, because I am going to the Father.* To know what this means we need first to understand what is meant by 'the works' of Jesus. This expression is used repeatedly in connection with Jesus' ministry, and denotes (1) evangelizing the Samaritan woman (4:34); (2) healing the lame man at the Pool of Bethesda (5:20; 7:21); (3) healing the man born blind (9:3, 4); (4) Jesus' miracles generally (7:3; 10:25, 32, 33, 37, 38; 14:11, 12; 15:24); (5) Jesus' teaching (10); and (6) Jesus' entire ministry generally (5:36; 17:4). Second, we need to recognize that the disciples would do greater works than Jesus did because he was 'going to the Father' (*cf.* 13:1). He promised that when he returned to the Father he would send the Counsellor, the Holy Spirit, to them (16:7). In the power of the Spirit they would do 'greater things/works'.

If the works of Jesus are his miracles, his teaching, his entire ministry, how can it be said that the works of his disciples will be greater than his? One suggestion is that after Jesus' return to the Father, and the coming of the Spirit, the works the disciples would perform in the expanding mission of the church would be quantitatively greater than his – more works performed by many disciples in many different places. However, the word translated 'greater' (*meizona*) does not mean greater in number, but greater in quality, more important or more impressive, and it is used in this way throughout the Fourth Gospel (1:50; 4:12; 5:20, 36; 8:53; 10:29; 13:16; 14:12, 28; 15:13, 20; 19:11). Did Jesus mean, then, that the disciples' works would be qualitatively greater than those he had performed? This is highly unlikely. The disciples did later heal and exorcise in Jesus' name, Peter did pray and Dorcas was restored to life (Acts 9:36–42), and through Paul's ministry Eutychus was restored to life (Acts 20:7–12). But they did not miraculously feed multitudes, calm storms, restore sight to those who had been born blind, or call people out of their graves when they had already been dead for four days. The disciples' works did not reveal the Father in the same way as Jesus did in his ministry and teaching. From apostolic times until now, as far as we know, Jesus' followers have never performed works that were qualitatively the same, let alone greater, than those of Jesus.

If the 'greater works' of the disciples cannot be understood as quantitatively or qualitatively greater, what did Jesus mean by saying their works would be greater than his? One suggestion is that the greater works of the disciples are the results of their missionary endeavours, bringing many converts into the church. It has also been suggested that what Jesus said about John the Baptist provides a clue: 'I tell you the truth: Among those born of women there has not risen anyone greater than John the Baptist; yet he who is least in the kingdom of heaven is greater than he' (Mt. 11:11). John was the herald of the kingdom that Jesus brought in, but John himself lived, worked and died before people entered it. In terms of privileges, then, the least in the kingdom were greater than John. If we apply this to the differences between

Jesus' works and those of his disciples, we might say that the disciples' works were greater than his because they had the privilege of testifying by word and deed to the finished work of Christ, and the fuller coming of the kingdom that it ushered in, whereas Jesus' ministry prior to his death and resurrection only foreshadowed these things.

13. Linked to the statement that his disciples will do greater works than he did, is Jesus' promise *And I will do whatever you ask in my name, so that the Son may bring glory to the Father*. The success of the disciples' mission was to be intimately connected with prayer in Jesus' name. This is the first of four places in the farewell discourses where Jesus' promises concerning prayer are found (13–14; 15:7, 16; 16:23–26). In all cases except one, prayer was to be 'in his name'. The only exception is 15:7, where the condition attached to answered prayer is that the disciples 'remain' in him and his words 'remain' in them.

A couple of things in this verse call for comment. First, what does it mean to ask 'in Jesus' name'? It cannot mean to use Jesus' name to gain access to the Father, for, as the next verse (14) makes clear, prayer in Jesus' name is addressed not to the Father but to Jesus himself. To ask something of Jesus in Jesus' name is best understood to mean to ask something for Jesus' sake (see Additional Note: 'In my name / in his name', pp. 302–303). What is for Jesus' sake in this context is made clear in the reason he gave for making this promise: 'so that the Son may bring glory to the Father'. Asking for Jesus' sake is asking for things that will enable him to bring glory to the Father.

Second, how is glory brought to God? In this Gospel the things that bring glory to God include (1) the raising of Lazarus (11:4); (2) Jesus' obedience in going to the cross (12:28; 13:31–32); (3) fruit-bearing in the life of Jesus' disciples (15:8); (4) Jesus' completing the work the Father gave him to do on earth (17:4); and (5) Peter's martyrdom (21:19). All this suggests that what brings glory to the Father is our obedience in carrying out the Father's will, *i.e.* playing the part assigned to us in God's redemptive plan. If this is the case, we can understand better the sort of prayer for which answers are guaranteed. It is certainly not wrong to pray for other things (*e.g.* our own needs), but the promise of answered prayer attaches primarily to our part in God's plans. No wonder Jesus taught us to pray, 'Our Father in heaven, hallowed be your name, your kingdom come, your will be done . . .' A concrete example of prayer in Jesus' name is found in Acts 4:29–31, where the early Jerusalem church, threatened by their Jewish leaders, prayed, 'Now, Lord, consider their threats and enable your servants to speak your word with great bold-ness. Stretch out your hand to heal and perform miraculous signs and wonders through the name of your holy servant Jesus.' This was a prayer to the sovereign Lord for Jesus' sake, and was answered forthwith: 'After they prayed, the place where they were meeting was shaken. And they were all filled with the Holy Spirit and spoke the word of God boldly' (Acts 4:31).

14. This verse makes explicit what was only implicit in 14:13, *viz.* prayer in Jesus' name in these verses is prayer directed towards Jesus himself: *You may ask me for anything in my name, and I will do it*. This repeats the promise made in 14:13. Prayer in Jesus' name is prayer for Jesus' sake, and when Jesus answers the prayer, as he promised, he brings glory to his Father.

Additional Note: 'In my name / in his name'

In a number of places in the Fourth Gospel the name clearly stands for the person. So to believe 'in his name' means to believe in him/Jesus (1:12; 2:23; 3:18), and to 'glorify someone's name' or 'make someone's name known' means to glorify that person or make him/her known (12:28; 17:6, 26 NRSV). 'Because of someone's name' means because of an association with that person (15:21), and 'to come in someone's name' means to represent that person (5:43; 12:13; 14:26). 'In the name of someone' can also mean using that person's power or authority (10:25; 17:11–12).

When it comes to 'asking in someone's name', an expression found six times in the Fourth Gospel (13, 14; 15:16; 16:23, 24, 26), the meaning is a little more difficult to ascertain. However we interpret it, it must make sense of 14:13, 14, where Jesus says he will do what we ask in his name, and that 'you may ask me for anything in my name and I will do it'. Clearly, then, to ask in his name is not using his name to gain favourable access to someone else. To ask in his name might mean to ask in a way that is in accordance with his character (in biblical times people's names reflected their characters). However, a more straightforward interpretation is that 'in Jesus' name' means for Jesus' sake, *i.e.* in line with his desire and purpose to bring glory to his Father. Thus 14:13–14 would read, 'And I will do whatever you ask for my sake, so that the Son may bring glory to the Father. You may ask me for anything for my sake, and I will do it.'

5. The first promise of the Counsellor (14:15–21)

In the light of his imminent departure Jesus promised not to leave his disciples desolate, but to come to them again in the person of the Counsellor, the Holy Spirit. The first promise of the Counsellor appears in this passage and is bracketed by two statements by Jesus that those who keep his commands are those who love him (15, 21).

15. Jesus prefaced his promise of the Counsellor with the words *If you love me, you will obey what I command* (lit. 'keep my commands'). Love for Jesus is not sentimental, but is expressed by keeping his commands, *i.e.* by responding to all he taught, with faith and obedience. In other passages Jesus' teaching is described as his word (*logos*), referring to his teaching as a whole, which people need to accept and obey (8:31, 51–52; 12:48; 14:23–24; 15:20; 17:6).

16–17a. To those who love and obey him Jesus promised, *And I will ask the Father, and he will give you another Counsellor to be with you for ever – the Spirit of truth*. The word translated 'Counsellor' (*paraklētos*) occurs here for the first time in the Fourth Gospel. It is not a common NT term and needs some clarification before we proceed.

Additional Note: The *Paraklētos*

Paraklētos is found four times in the Fourth Gospel (16, 26; 15:26; 16:7) and once in the First Letter of John (1 Jn. 2:1), but nowhere else in the NT, and not at all in the LXX. In the Fourth Gospel *paraklētos* consistently denotes the Holy Spirit sent to be with the disciples after Jesus' return to the Father. In 1 John *paraklētos* denotes Jesus himself as an advocate for believers (not surprising since Jesus described the Holy Spirit as 'another' *paraklētos*, implying that he also is a *paraklētos*).

Paraklētos in ancient Hellenistic texts consistently denotes an 'advocate', one who speaks on behalf of the accused (not in the professional sense in which we use 'advocate' today, but meaning a friend or patron who speaks up in favour of the accused). In the Fourth Gospel one of the functions of the *paraklētos* is to testify in favour of Jesus over against a hostile world (16:7–11).

However, the meaning of *paraklētos* cannot be determined by Hellenistic usage alone. This needs to be supplemented by information gleaned from its use in the Fourth Gospel itself and the functions ascribed to the *paraklētos* in the various contexts where the word is found. These functions include comforting the disciples after Jesus' departure (16–17), teaching them (26), testifying on behalf of Jesus (15:26), convincing the world of sin, righteousness and judgment (16:7–11), guiding the disciples into all truth, and telling them about things to come (16:13). It is understandable, then, that *paraklētos* has been variously translated as 'comforter', 'teacher', 'advocate', 'counsellor', 'helper' and 'guide'. None of these terms on its own satisfactorily represents all the functions of the *paraklētos*, and for that reason some people prefer to leave it untranslated, and use an anglicized form of the transliteration, 'Paraclete'.

Returning now to the commentary on 14:16–17a, we need to note several things about Jesus' promise of the Counsellor/*paraklētos*. First, the gift of the Counsellor is made by the Father to those who love and obey his Son. This must not be taken to mean that our love and obedience somehow merit this gift; rather, it is to those who are so related to his Son that the Father gives the Counsellor. It is also important to note that while obedience to Jesus is the key on the human side to receiving the gift of the Counsellor, we must not turn it into some sort of superspiritual obedience that only extraordinary Christians can achieve. What is meant by obedience is belief in Jesus and a commitment to follow him. Jesus' first disciples were not superdisciples deserving the gift of the Spirit because of their extraordinary faith and obedience. They didn't understand things; their thoughts were often the thoughts of mere humans, not the thoughts of God. At the time of Jesus' greatest need, they forsook him and fled, and Peter even denied that he knew Jesus at all. But in contrast to those of the world, who did not love and obey Jesus, they did love him and in their own imperfect way they did obey him. It was to disciples like these Jesus promised the Counsellor.

Second, the gift of the Counsellor is made by the Father to the disciples at Jesus' request. In 7:37–39 the evangelist says the bestowal of the Spirit was dependent upon the 'glorification' of Jesus (through his death, resurrection and exaltation). Having been 'glorified', Jesus would ask the Father to give the Spirit to his disciples.

Third, it was in the context of his departure that Jesus promised to send 'another'[1] Counsellor so that his disciples would not be left as orphans (14:18). This suggests that the coming of the Counsellor was to replace Jesus' physical presence, and the Counsellor would do for the disciples after Jesus' departure what Jesus had done for them before it. This is confirmed by the fact that the ministry of the Counsellor parallels the ministry of Jesus. Like him, the Counsellor comforts and teaches the disciples, proves the world wrong in regard to sin, righteousness and judgment, guides the disciples into truth, and tells them about things to come.

Fourth, Jesus promised his disciples that the Counsellor would be with them 'for ever'. The gift of the Holy Spirit once given is never taken away. This was so because the gift would be given, not because of the piety of the disciples, but in answer to Jesus' prayer, and be made possible by his death, resurrection and exaltation. The gift of the Spirit to Jesus' disciples differs from the working of the Spirit in OT times in two ways: (1) once given, the Spirit stays for ever; (2) the Spirit is given to all believers without exception, not just special people.

Fifth, the Counsellor is described as 'the Spirit of truth' here and in two other places in this Gospel (15:26; 16:13). In this respect, also, the Counsellor is like Jesus, who revealed the truth (8:31–36,

---

[1]There are two Greek words meaning 'other', *allos* and *heteros*. It is sometimes argued that the first means another of a similar kind, the second another of a different kind, and because *allos* is used in 14:16 the other Counsellor is of the same kind as Jesus himself. However, the way *allos* and *heteros* are used in the Fourth Gospel and the NT as a whole does not support this distinction. That the Counsellor is another one like Jesus is determined by the context, not the meaning of the word *allos*.

40, 45–46; 16:7; 18:37) and embodied the truth of God (1:14, 17; 14:6).[1]

17b. Jesus promised the Holy Spirit would be given to his disciples, but explained, *The world cannot accept him, because it neither sees him nor knows him.* The 'world' here refers to people who reject Jesus and the revelation he brings. They cannot receive the gift of the Counsellor, because they neither see him nor know him. We might wonder how anyone could 'see' and 'know' the Counsellor before Jesus' departure, since the Counsellor was to come only after Jesus' departure. What Jesus meant became clear when he added, *But you know him, for he lives with you and will be in you.*[2] We can understand this if we recognize that when the Counsellor came to the disciples, Jesus himself came to them as well (14:18). It is because the disciples knew Jesus that he could say they already knew the Counsellor and that he now lived 'with' them. It is also clear why the world did not 'know' the Counsellor. It was because they, unlike the disciples, did not 'know' Jesus.

What did Jesus mean when he said the Counsellor will be 'in you'. The words the NIV translates as 'in you' (*en hymin*) may also be rendered 'among you', seeing that the pronoun 'you' here is plural. However, just a few verses later, Jesus individualized this promise when he said (when the Spirit comes) the Father and the Son would make their home with the individual believer (21–23). In the light of this later statement it is best to interpret the promise that the Counsellor will 'be in you' to include an indwelling of individual believers as well as his presence among them as a group.

18. Jesus promised his disciples, *I will not leave you as orphans; I will come to you.* The word 'orphan' is a rare one in the NT. It is found only here and in James 1:27 ('Religion that God our Father

---

[1]The expression 'the spirit of truth' was current in Jesus' time and is found in the Pseudepigrapha (*Testament of Judah* 20:1–5) and the Dead Sea Scrolls (1QS3:18–21). However, it is used dualistically in these contexts to contrast 'the spirit of truth' with 'the spirit of perversity', a notion absent from the Fourth Gospel.

[2]There are two other variant readings for this verse, in which the tenses of the key verbs differ from those in the variant represented by the NIV translation. The first would read, 'he will live with you and will be in you', and the second, 'he lives with you and is in you'. The variant adopted in the NIV makes good sense, and is also adopted in the NEB, NRSV, AV.

306

accepts as pure and faultless is this: to look after orphans and widows in their distress') where the orphan's distress is highlighted. There are two ways in which Jesus' coming to his disciples in this verse has been interpreted. First, he came to them following his resurrection, turned their sorrow into joy and thus overcame their distress. However, these appearances were spasmodic, and afterwards the resurrected Jesus did leave them. Second, he came to them in the person of the Counsellor. At a time when Jesus was preparing his disciples for his return to the Father and promised that the Counsellor would replace his physical presence, Jesus' coming to them is best interpreted as his coming in the person of the Counsellor (23, 28).

With the coming of the Counsellor the exalted Jesus would make himself present to his disciples in the here and now. This is a reminder that the function of the Holy Spirit is not restricted to the bestowal of spiritual gifts, or the production of Christian character, but includes the creation of a sense of intimacy with Jesus himself as well.

19. Jesus promised his disciples that he would come to them again in the person of the Counsellor. However, this would not be the case with the 'world', those who did not believe in him: *Before long, the world will not see me any more*. The resurrected Jesus would not reveal himself to the world. Things would be different in the case of the disciples: *but you will see me*. They would see the resurrected Jesus. He then added, *Because I live, you also will live*. On first reading, this appears to mean that because Jesus was to be raised from death, so too would his disciples. But in a context where the role of the Counsellor is being stressed, it is better interpreted to mean that because Jesus is to be raised from death, and will ask his Father to give the Spirit to his disciples, they will experience life through the Spirit in the here and now. This is confirmed in the following verses (20–24).

20. Continuing this theme, Jesus said, *On that day you will realize that I am in my Father, and you are in me, and I am in you*. The day when the disciples would realize these things was the day when the Spirit came. Then they would realize two things. First, they would understand what they had not hitherto been able to comprehend (7–11), that Jesus and the Father are one and to see Jesus is to see the Father. Second, they would understand something new: with the coming of the Spirit they would be 'in' Jesus, and Jesus 'in' them. This concept of (mutual) indwelling is found in several places in the Fourth Gospel (6:56; 14:17, 20; 15:4–6, 7). What it means for Christ to dwell in believers is clear enough: with the coming of the Spirit to dwell in believers, Jesus also may be said to dwell 'in' them because of the unity of the Spirit and the Son. However, what it means for believers to dwell 'in' Christ is more difficult to explain. At one level it appears to be a metaphor for loyalty and obedience to Christ – at least this is what Jesus stressed about believers abiding in him. The key text is 15:4–10, where, describing the disciples' relationship to him in terms of branches in the vine, Jesus says the disciples/branches 'remain' in him / the vine by allowing his words to 'remain' in them (15:7), and implies that this is the same as abiding in his love by obeying his commands (15:10). However, more than loyalty and obedience is involved in their being 'in' Jesus, as his prayer in 17:21 indicates: 'Father, just as you are in me and I am in you. May they also be in us'. It is perhaps best understood in terms of a union brought about by the coming of the Holy Spirit.

21. The final verse in this passage (15–21), where the first promise of the Counsellor is found, returns to the theme of love and obedience with which the passage begins: *Whoever has my commands and obeys them, he is the one who loves me*. Love for Christ does involve heartfelt appreciation of him (*cf.* 21:15–17; Luke 7:36–50) and should express itself in concern for his pleasure (28), but what Jesus himself stressed was that those who love him are those who obey his commands. This means responding to his teaching with obedience and faith.

Jesus promised that *He who loves me will be loved by my Father, and I too will love him and show myself to him*. Our love for Jesus, imperfect though it is, is rewarded in two related ways. First, we become the objects of the Father's own love, and second, we become the objects of Jesus' love and self-revelation. Love for Jesus does not end in stoic obedience to his will. Obedience is involved, but it leads to an experience of the love of the Father and the Son, and the revelation of the Son to the believer – surely the greatest incentive to express our love for Christ by obedience to his will.

6. Jesus does not reveal himself to the world (14:22–24)

22. Many first-century Jews were waiting for the Messiah to come and reveal himself in power to the world. The disciples recognized Jesus as the Messiah, so when he spoke of 'showing himself' to them (21), *Judas (not Judas Iscariot) said, 'But, Lord, why do you intend to show yourself to us and not to the world?'* Judas (not Iscariot) was one of the Twelve chosen by Jesus (Lk. 6:13–16). Like many of their fellow Jews the disciples longed for the manifestation of the Messiah to the world. Jesus' promise to show himself to his disciples was not enough for Judas, so he asked why he was not going to show himself to the world as well.

23–24. Responding to this question, Jesus began, *If anyone loves me, he will obey my teaching. My Father will love him, and we will come to him and make our home with him.* Revelation would be made initially only to those who loved Jesus and obeyed his teaching. It was these whom the Father would love and with these Jesus and the Father would 'make their home'. According to Jewish expectation, God will dwell among his people in the age to come (Ezk. 37:26–27; *cf.* Rev. 21:3). Jesus promised that what was expected at the end time would be experienced (in part) in the present time. It would occur through the coming of the Spirit, whereby the Father and the Son would make their home with believers. It is worth noting that this promise applies to individual believers. It is to 'anyone' (*tis*) who loves and obeys Jesus that this promise is made. When Jesus spoke of the Father and the Son making their 'home' with the believer, he used the same word (*monē*) used in 14:2, where he said that in his Father's house there are many rooms (*monai*). As the disciples looked forward to a place in these 'rooms'/ in God's presence in the future, the Father and the Son would make their home (*monē*) with them in the here and now by the coming of the Spirit.

Continuing his response to Judas' question, Jesus said, *He who does not love me will not obey my teaching.* This is the reason he would not show himself to the world when he showed himself to his disciples. At the end of the age, of course, he will reveal himself to all as the judge of the living and the dead (5:28–29). Jesus concluded his response to Judas' question by saying, *These words you hear are not my own; they belong to the Father who sent me.* On a number of occasions Jesus emphasized that he spoke the Father's words: what the Father commanded him to say (7:16–17; 12:49–50; 17:14). He highlighted this fact again so that the disciples would know with certainty that the promise of the coming of the Father and the Son to make their home with the believer was entirely trustworthy.

7. *Jesus speaks of his departure again (14:25–31)*

This passage brings to a close the first part (13:31 – 14:31) of the farewell discourse in which Jesus prepared his disciples for his departure, and for their continued life in the world without his physical presence.

25–26. Referring to his teaching found in 13:31 – 14:24, Jesus said, *All this I have spoken while still with you,* and then, referring to the time after his departure, he added, *But the Counsellor, the Holy Spirit, whom the Father will send in my name, will teach you all things and will remind you of everything I have said to you.* This is the second of four references to the Counsellor (*paraklētos*) in the farewell discourse (16, 26; 15:26; 16:7), but the only one in which the Counsellor is explicitly identified as 'the Holy Spirit'.

On this occasion Jesus said the Father would send the Counsellor (also implied in 14:16). On other occasions he said he himself would send the Counsellor (15:26; 16:7). We should not make too much of these variations, because Jesus stressed repeatedly that in his incarnate state he did only what the Father commanded him to do, and that the Father carried out his work through him. We can safely assume the same unity of action and purpose between Father and Son in the sending of the Counsellor after the return of the Son to the Father.

Jesus said he would send the Counsellor 'in my name'. In this context 'in my name' means 'representing me' (see Additional Note: 'In my name / in his name', pp. 302–303). In 14:16–19 Jesus said the Counsellor's role would be to represent him to his disciples so they would not feel destitute after his departure. In fact, Jesus said he himself would come to them in the person of the Counsellor.

The role of the Counsellor emphasized here is teaching. He will teach the disciples 'all things'. 'All things' does not mean everything that it is possible to know, but all that Jesus himself taught them: he 'will remind you of everything I have said to you'. This promise is very important for today because it provides assurance from the Lord himself that the first witnesses, whose testimony is preserved in the New Testament, would be instructed by the Spirit regarding the truths that Jesus taught them, even though at the time he taught them they often did not understand.

27. Jesus promised, in addition to the coming of the Counsellor, the gift of his peace: *Peace I leave with you; my peace I give you. I do not give to you as the world gives.* The peace Jesus gives is not like the peace the world gives. In the OT false prophets proclaimed peace when there was no peace (Je. 6:13–14). In NT times the *Pax Romana*, the Roman peace, was won and maintained by force. When people of the world say, 'Peace be with you,' it is an expression of hope and goodwill. When Jesus said he would give his peace to his disciples, much more was involved. He bequeathed to them a peace of mind in the midst of trials and persecutions, a peace they would experience with the coming of the Counsellor (*cf.* Gal. 5:22). On these grounds Jesus could say, *Do not let your hearts be troubled and do not be afraid.* He was repeating what he had said earlier (1). Then his exhortation was connected with faith in God, but now with his gift of peace.

28. After promising his peace, Jesus reminded his disciples of his imminent departure, but also the promise of his return: *You heard me say, 'I am going away and I am coming back to you.'* There are two ways in which Jesus returned to his disciples after his departure: he came to them as the resurrected Christ, and he came to them in the person of the Spirit. Here in 14:28 he referred to the second of these comings. We know this because his departure meant his return to the Father. Once Jesus returned to the Father there were no more post-resurrection appearances, but he did come to his disciples in the person of the Spirit. The words that follow, *If you loved me, you would be glad that I am going to the Father*, enable us to see how much the return to the Father meant to Jesus himself, and sadly, how little the disciples recognized this. They were so preoccupied with their own problems they were unable rejoice with him in this matter.

Jesus looked forward to his return to the Father, for, he said, *the Father is greater than I*. This text has been the subject of much controversy in debates concerning the divinity of Christ and the relationships within the Trinity. However, it is unlikely that in the context of the Last Supper, as Jesus prepared his disciples for life without his physical presence, he was making statements about trinitarian or Christological matters. It is probably better to interpret this text in the light of the general statement that a messenger is not greater than the one who sends him (13:16). It was the Father who sent the Son into the world, and the Son who willingly obeyed. It was the Son who, as the incarnate Jesus, died on the cross, and it was the Father who raised him from the dead. As the sent one, Jesus could say the Father who sent him was greater than he was, but later he would ask to be restored to the full glory he had with the Father before the world began (17:5). For this he was returning to the Father, and in this he hoped his disciples might rejoice with him.

29. Jesus spoke only briefly about what his departure would mean for him, before giving his attention again to what it would mean for his disciples: *I have told you now before it happens, so that when it does happen you will believe*. He knew events soon to unfold would come as a shock to them. By telling them beforehand what was to happen, he was ensuring these events would not take them completely by surprise, and therefore their faith would not be destroyed. In this way Jesus attended to the emotional distress his disciples were to experience and made sure they would not be overwhelmed by it.

30. The time for preparation of the disciples for Jesus' departure was now growing short. He said, *I will not speak with you much longer for the prince of this world is coming*. This is the second of three references to 'the prince of this world' (12:31; 14:30; 16:11), Satan, whose coming was to occur through the actions of Judas

Iscariot (13:2, 27) and the Jewish leaders to whom Judas betrayed Jesus. While Jesus acknowledged that the machinations of the prince of this world meant that he would not speak with his disciples for much longer, he made it clear that *He has no hold on me*. Humanity apart from Christ is held in thraldom by the prince of the world (1 Jn. 5:19) because of their sin, but Jesus was without sin (8:46), and therefore the prince of this world had no hold on him.

31. Jesus said *the world must learn that I love the Father and that I do exactly what my Father has commanded me*. Jesus' impending passion and death was not a defeat suffered at the hands of the prince of this world, but an act of obedience to the Father. The peoples of the world must learn this, and if they do they may cease to be the 'world' and be numbered among Jesus' disciples. We often and rightly see Jesus' death on the cross as the demonstration of God's love for the world (3:16; Rom. 5:8) and of Jesus' special love for believers (15:13; Gal. 2:20), but this verse reminds us that his death was first and foremost a demonstration to the world of his love and obedience to the Father. It is a timely reminder that everything does not revolve around us, but around God.

Jesus concluded the first part of his farewell discourse by saying, *Come now; let us leave*. This statement is puzzling because it is not followed by a departure from the room where the Last Supper was eaten, but by the second part of the farewell discourse (15:1 – 16:33) and Jesus' prayer (17:1–26). It is only after these things that the evangelist says Jesus 'left with his disciples and crossed the Kidron Valley' (18:1). Various explanations have been offered to explain this: (1) Having urged his disciples to leave the room with him, Jesus gave further instructions and prayed before doing so – just as today people will signal their intention to leave, but then engage in further conversation before actually doing so. (2) This rough transition in the middle of the farewell discourse indicates the evangelist's use of two sources of tradition. (3) The second part of the farewell discourse and Jesus' prayer (15:1 – 17:26) were in fact spoken after departure from the room and on the way to the olive grove where the betrayal took place, but before they left the city of Jerusalem itself.[1] If we adopt this approach we could interpret 18:1 as a reference to Jesus and his disciples leaving, not the room where the Last Supper was held, but the city of Jerusalem *en route* to the olive grove on the other side of the Kidron valley.

C. THE SECOND PART OF THE FAREWELL DISCOURSE (15:1 – 16:33)

The second part of Jesus' farewell discourse runs from 15:1 to 16:33, and comprises the following sections.

1. The true vine and its branches (15:1–17)

In the time of Jesus a great golden vine hung over the entrance to the Jerusalem temple. Josephus describes it: 'The gate opening into the building was, as I said, completely overlaid with gold, as was the whole wall around it. It had, moreover, above it those golden vines, from which depended grape-clusters as tall as a man' (*Jewish War* v.210–212). If the second part of Jesus' farewell discourse was given *en route* from the Last Supper venue to the Garden where he was betrayed, his teaching on the true vine may have been given in the temple courtyard with the great golden vine glinting in the light of the Passover moon.

The OT depiction of Israel as a vine (Ps. 80:8–19; Is. 5:1–8; Je. 2:21; 6:8–9; Ezk. 17:6–8; 19:10–14; Ho. 10:1–2) provides important background information for understanding Jesus' teaching about the true vine. Most significant of the OT passages is Isaiah 5:1–8. Israel is represented as a vineyard planted by the Lord, from which he expected good grapes, but which produced only bad grapes and therefore had to be destroyed. The key verse is Isaiah 5:7:

> The vineyard of the Lord Almighty
>   is the house of Israel,
> and the men of Judah
>   are the garden of his delight.

[1]In favour of this last explanation it is noted that when Jesus begins to pray in 17:1, 'he looked towards heaven and prayed' – a statement that fits better with prayer outdoors than indoors.

> And he looked for justice, but saw bloodshed;
>   for righteousness, but heard cries of distress.

Ancient viticultural practices also provide important background information. Two processes were involved, the training of the vines and the pruning of the branches. Vines were trained in one of two ways: (1) they were allowed to trail along the ground and then the fruit-bearing branches were lifted up by placing rocks or poles under them to allow aeration in order to ensure better grapes, or (2) they were trained from the outset on to poles or trellises, the branches being lifted on to these to improve their fruit-bearing potential.

Pruning was also an essential part of first-century viticultural practice, as it is today. The first pruning occurred in spring when vines were in the flowering stage. This involved four operations: (1) the removal of the growing tips of vigorous shoots so that they would not grow too rapidly; (2) cutting off one or two feet from the end of growing shoots to prevent entire shoots being snapped off by the wind; (3) the removal of some flower or grape clusters so that those left could produce more and better-quality fruit; and (4) the removal of suckers that arose from below the ground or from the trunk and main branches so that the strength of the vine was not tapped by the suckers. Spring pruning did not involve the removal of wooden branches or their subsequent burning.

The second pruning occurred in autumn after the grapes were harvested and the vines were dormant. This involved the removal of unwanted branches, those that had produced fruit in the previous season but would not produce fruit in the ensuing season. It also involved cutting back the desired branches (the shoots from the year-old branches that would produce fruit in the coming year) to ensure maximum fruit production. After the autumn pruning the cuttings, including many wooden branches, were gathered up and burned.[1]

1. Against the OT background of Israel as the vine that failed to produce good fruit Jesus said, *I am the true vine, and my Father is*

---

[1]The important sources for our understanding of ancient practice are the Oxyrhnchus Papyrus 1631, 'Contract for Labour in a Vineyard' (dated around AD 280), and Pliny (the Elder), *Natural History* xvii.35. See Derickson, pp. 44–48.

the gardener. This is the last of the seven different 'I am' sayings with predicates in the Fourth Gospel (6:35, 48, 51; 8:12; 10:7, 9; 10:11, 14; 11:25; 14:6; 15:1, 5). Jesus used the word 'true' (*alēthinos*) several times to denote what is true or genuine (4:23: 'true worshippers', 6:32: 'true bread', 15:1: 'true vine', 17:3: 'the true God'). He used it on this occasion to indicate that, as the true vine, he produced what the nation Israel failed to produce: fruit for which the gardener (the Father) was looking. What Jesus meant by 'fruit' is discussed below in the commentary on 15:4. By depicting the Father as the gardener/vinedresser, Jesus indicated that the Father was in control of both his ministry (as the vine) and that of his disciples (as the branches).

2–3. Jesus' use of the metaphor of the vine not only enabled him to depict himself as the true vine and his Father as the gardener, but also to depict his disciples as branches of that vine and his Father's work as the pruning of the branches to increase their 'fruit-bearing'. Jesus began, *He cuts off every branch in me that bears no fruit*. The Father, as the gardener, Jesus said, cuts off those branches 'in me' that fail to produce fruit.[1] In the context of the Last Supper, just after Judas Iscariot went out to betray his master, the branch that is cut off would have as its primary reference the betrayer. Jesus referred to the removal of Judas later when he said, 'None has been lost except the one doomed to destruction so that Scripture would be fulfilled' (17:12). Jesus added, *while every branch that does bear fruit he prunes so that it will be even more fruitful*. This is an allusion to the spring pruning of the vines during the flowering stage so that fruit-bearing is maximized. The word translated 'to prune' (*kathairō*) can also mean 'to clean' or 'to purify'. It is found only here in the NT, but the cognate word 'clean/pure' (*katharos*) is found twenty-seven times in the NT, and four times in the Fourth Gospel (13:10 [2×], 11; 15:3). In 13:10–11 the word is used to describe the disciples (excluding Judas Iscariot) as 'clean', and here in 15:3 Jesus says of the Eleven, *You are already clean because of the word I have spoken to you*. In 15:2–3, then, there is a play on the words *kathairō* and *katharos* ('to clean' and 'clean'). The disciples have already been rendered 'clean' through the word Jesus spoke to

---

[1]Elsewhere in the NT the cutting off of branches denotes the rejection of unbelieving Israelites (Rom. 11:17–21), but here it refers to apostate Christians ('branches *in me*').

them. Now the Father also cleansed/pruned the disciples/branches so that they would bear more fruit. He 'pruned/cleansed' them through 'the word' Jesus spoke to them. It is as we hear and respond to the teaching of Jesus that we become more fruitful.[1]

4. Continuing to speak of his disciples as branches, Jesus said, *Remain in me, and I will remain in you. No branch can bear fruit by itself; it must remain in the vine. Neither can you bear fruit unless you remain in me.* In 15:3 the disciples bear fruit as they respond to the teaching of Jesus. In 15:4 Jesus emphasizes that, just as a branch cannot bear grapes unless it remains in the vine, so too the disciples cannot bear fruit unless they remain in him. A number of things in this verse call for explanation or comment.

First, what does it mean for disciples to 'remain' in Jesus? Because of the vine/branches metaphor this has often been interpreted as an organic union between Jesus and his disciples. It is unlikely that the disciples who listened to Jesus that night thought of their connection with him in that way. They probably thought of it in terms of loyalty and fellowship that would continue as they obeyed his word. There are two other places in the Fourth Gospel where Jesus speaks of his disciples 'remaining' in him or in his love, and each case involves keeping his word (7, 10). If 'remaining' in Jesus were a matter of organic union (whatever that means), it would be a given, not something dependent upon obedience. However, if 'remaining' in Jesus is a metaphor for continuing in fellowship with and loyalty to him, then obedience to his commands is clearly important.

Second, what does it mean for Jesus to 'remain' in the disciples? Again, we should think in terms of continuing fellowship; this time of Jesus with his disciples. The means by which Jesus remains in fellowship with his disciples cannot be the same as the means by which the disciples remain in fellowship with him. Jesus does not keep his disciples' commands! While physically present with his disciples, Jesus remained in fellowship with them by committing himself to be with them and for them. When he returned to the

---

[1] It has been suggested, the Father might clean/prune the disciples/branches by allowing them to experience trials and suffering, so that through this sort of 'discipline' they might come to share in his holiness (Heb. 12:4–11). However, there is no support for this interpretation of 15:3 in its immediate context.

Father, he did not leave them alone (see 14:15–18). He came to them again in the person of the Spirit, and then his remaining in them took on a deeper meaning. Today it is the combination of the disciples' remaining in fellowship with Jesus by obeying his word and Jesus' remaining in his disciples through the coming of the Spirit which produces 'fruit' that pleases the Father.

Third, what is the nature of the fruit produced when the disciples 'remain' in Jesus? There are two common interpretations: (1) righteous living (as required of Israel in Is. 5:1–8), or (2) the results of preaching the gospel, *i.e.* new converts. However, to choose one, or even both of these, is to narrow the meaning too much. The context, which stresses that 'fruit' is produced as the disciples maintain their fellowship with Jesus by keeping his word and when Jesus continues to fellowship with them by the Spirit, suggests that 'fruit' refers to the entire life and ministry of those who follow Jesus' teaching and experience his presence in their lives through the Spirit.

5. Until this point Jesus had only implied that his disciples are branches in the true vine; now he stated this quite explicitly – *I am the vine; you are the branches* – and then reiterated the teaching of 15:4: *If a man remains in me and I in him, he will bear much fruit.* If the disciples remained in fellowship with Jesus by observing his teaching, and he remained in fellowship with them through the coming of the Spirit, the disciples would produce much 'fruit' in their lives, fruit that would please the Father. However, if they did not remain in fellowship with Jesus, there would be no fruit, as Jesus said, *apart from me you can do nothing*.

6. Concerning those who do not 'remain' in him, Jesus said, *If anyone does not remain in me, he is like a branch that is thrown away and withers; such branches are picked up, thrown into the fire and burned*. The allusion is to the autumn pruning, when branches that cannot bear fruit any longer are cut off, thrown into the fire and burned. The implication is that those who do not obey Jesus will experience judgment (3:18; 8:21, 24; 12:25, 48; 17:12). The primary reference was probably to Judas Iscariot. The use of the passive voice in this verse ('thrown away', 'picked up', 'thrown into the fire', 'burned') indicates that God is the one who implements the judgment.

7. Explaining further the blessings attending those who do remain in him, Jesus said, *If you remain in me and my words remain in you, ask whatever you wish, and it will be given you.* To those who 'remain' in fellowship with Jesus by observing his teaching, he promised they may ask whatever they wish and it will be given to them. The passive voice ('it will be given to you') indicates God is the one who responds to the disciples' request. In 14:13–14 Jesus gave a similar promise concerning prayer, saying he will do whatever his disciples ask him in his name. Such promises are conditional upon prayer being in his name (*i.e.* for his sake – see Additional Note: 'In my name / in his name', pp. 302–303) and in line with his teaching (*i.e.* as his words remain in the petitioners).

8. *This is to my Father's glory, that you bear much fruit.* Disciples bring glory to God by bearing 'much fruit'. The 'fruit' is most likely the outcome of their entire life and ministry as they remain in fellowship with Jesus by keeping his commands and experiencing his presence with them through the Spirit (see commentary on 15:4). In their lives and ministry, then, they reflect the character of God and he is glorified as people catch glimpses of what he is truly like. As they bear this 'fruit', Jesus said to them, you are *showing yourselves to be my disciples.*

9–10. It looks, at first, as though 15:9 begins a new section (9–17) dealing primarily with Jesus' love for his disciples and his command that they love one another. However, in 15:16 the notion of fruit-bearing reappears, suggesting that this subsection dealing with love is also related to fruit-bearing. It begins with the amazing statement *As the Father has loved me, so have I loved you.* Just as Jesus is the recipient of the Father's love, so the disciples are the recipients of his love. Jesus' statement that he 'loved' his disciples employs the aorist tense, depicting his love as a complete action, denoting perhaps the entire demonstration of Jesus' love for his disciples throughout his time with them and culminating in his death for them.

We need to recognize there are some significant differences between the Father's love for the Son and the Son's love for his disciples. The Father's love for the Son predates creation and is the reason he gave glory to the Son (17:24). The Father's love for the Son expresses itself in placing everything in the Son's hands (3:35), and is drawn out further by the Son's willingness to lay down his life only to take it up again (10:17). In none of these ways can it be said that Jesus' love for his disciples is just the same as the Father's love for him.

While there are some differences, it still remains an immense privilege for disciples of Jesus to be brought into the community of love that exists between the Father and the Son. Jesus' purpose in telling his disciples this was to provide a basis for the exhortation that follows: *Now remain in my love, i.e.* remain in fellowship with me so that you may continue to experience my love for you. How they are to do this is then spelled out: *If you obey my commands, you will remain in my love, just as I have obeyed my Father's commands and remain in his love.* Remaining in the Father's love was not for Jesus a passive thing; it involved obedience to his commands. The same is true for Jesus' disciples. They remain in Jesus' love by keeping his commands.

11–13. While obedience is demanding, it is the pathway of true joy: *I have told you this so that my joy may be in you and that your joy may be complete.* Earlier Jesus told his puzzled disciples, 'I have food to eat that you know nothing about . . . My food is to do the will of him who sent me and to finish his work' (4:32–34). Jesus' joy came from doing the Father's will, and the joy of disciples will come from doing what Jesus commands them; and he said, *My command is this: Love each other as I have loved you.* The model for the disciples' love for one another is Jesus' love for them; and speaking of his love for them, he said, *Greater love has no-one than this, that he lay down his life for his friends.* In the ancient world friendship was very important, and operated at a number of levels: *political friendship,* in which certain people were known as friends of the king (friends of Caesar); *benefactor–client friendship,* in which a wealthy person would become the patron of someone less well-off; and *mutual friendship* among equals. Especially in this last category friendship involved sharing of confidences, possessions, and, in extreme cases, laying down one's life for one's friend. Jesus' love for his disciples was of this extreme form: he would lay down his life for his friends. The evangelist alluded to the extreme form of Jesus' love when he introduced the footwashing in 13:1: 'Having loved his own who were in the world, he now showed them the full extent of his love.' The footwashing symbolized Jesus' laying down his life on the cross for his disciples. It is noteworthy that earlier in the Gospel laying down his life was described as part of Jesus' obedience to his Father (10:18), while here it is described as an expression of his love for his disciples. Jesus expected his disciples to express the same sort of self-sacrificing love for one another.

14. Jesus explicitly identified his disciples as his friends (for whom he gave his life): *You are my friends*. Abraham and Moses were described as 'friends of God' (Ex. 33:11; 2 Ch. 20:7; Is. 41:8; Jas. 2:23) and Jesus spoke of his disciples in the same way, but he also pointed out that this friendship was conditional: *if you do what I command*. Jesus' giving of his life for his disciples showed his friendship was like that between intimate mutual friends, but the fact that he expected obedience to what he commanded reminds us that there were significant differences as well. Accordingly, while the disciples are called Jesus' friends (11:11; 15:13–15), Jesus is never called their friend.[1] This is because the nature of their friendship is not mutual in the same way as human friendships usually are. On Jesus' side it involved giving commands, and on the disciples' side it involved obedience; and, as becomes apparent in 15:16, the disciples were his friends, not because they chose him but because he chose them.

15. Jesus explained another aspect of what it means to be his friends: *I no longer call you servants, because a servant does not know his master's business. Instead, I have called you friends, for everything that I learned from my Father I have made known to you.* One important aspect of ancient friendship was the sharing of information and confidences. Jesus called his disciples his friends because he disclosed to them everything he had learned from the Father, by which he probably meant all that the Father commanded him to say (12:49–50). This included the teaching he gave to his disciples

[1] In the Synoptic Gospels the Jews describe Jesus disparagingly as 'a friend of tax collectors and "sinners"' (Mt. 11:19; Lk. 7:34); however, the implication is not that tax collectors and sinners can claim him as their friend on a reciprocal basis, but that Jesus befriended them.

concerning God's plan of salvation and, in particular, the instructions he gave them in the farewell discourses.

16. This verse does a number of things. First, it underlines the fact that the friendship between Jesus and his disciples was not a result of the disciples' choice: *You did not choose me, but I chose you and appointed you.* Jesus' initiative was the basis of this friendship, and his choice of the disciples as his friends involved an appointment or a commission. Second, it clarifies the purpose of this appointment: *to go and bear fruit.* With these words, Jesus returned to the theme of the earlier part of the chapter, the vine and the branches, and the function of the branches to bear fruit for the gardener. The nature of the fruit expected was discussed in the commentary on 15:4. It was concluded there that fruit is the entire outcome of the life and ministry of the disciples carried out in obedience to Christ and enjoying his presence through the Spirit. When Jesus said the disciples were to 'go' and bear fruit, the 'going' most likely refers to their missionary endeavours.[1] The 'fruit' they were to bear in their going would be new believers.

This fruit is described as *fruit that will last.* The word 'last' translates *menē.* The same word is used to speak of three other things that last: the 'food' that the Son of Man will give, which endures (*menousan*) to eternal life (6:27); the son, not the slave, who has a permanent place (*menei*) in the family (8:35); and the Christ who remains (*menei*) for ever and does not die (12:34). Noting these parallels, we can say 'fruit that will last' denotes the eternal significance of life and ministry carried out in obedience to Jesus,[2] and here in particular new believers.

Jesus made this promise to those who go and bear fruit: *Then the Father will give you whatever you ask in my name.* This is the third of four remarkable promises Jesus made concerning prayer (14:13–14; 15:7–8, 16–17; 16:23–24). In each case the promise is conditional. In 15:16 the promise is conditional upon two things: the disciples carrying out their commission to go and bear fruit, and

---

[1] Mk. 3:14–15 speaks of Jesus' appointment and sending of the disciples: 'He appointed twelve – designating them apostles – that they might be with him and that he might send them out to preach and to have authority to drive out demons.'

[2] In 1 Cor. 3:10–15 Paul speaks about the works of Christian ministers being tested, and where those works survive the testing the ministers are rewarded.

prayer being made in Jesus' name (see Additional Note: 'In my name / in his name', pp. 302–303).

17. This section, 15:1–17, on the true vine and the branches concludes with the words *This is my command: Love each other*. The means by which disciples (branches) remain in Jesus (the vine), *i.e.* remain in fellowship with him, is through obedience, something emphasized again and again throughout this section (7, 10, 12, 14, 17). The aspect of obedience Jesus stressed is that his disciples had to love one another. It is stated explicitly in 15:12 and again here in 15:17. In 13:35 Jesus made it clear that their love for one another was related to their mission in the world: 'By this all men will know that you are my disciples, if you love one another.' It is a crucial reminder to all Christians to love one another, for, unless they do, their mission activities will be largely negated. The apostle Paul told his Corinthian converts that no matter what ministry they exercised, if it was not carried out with love it counted for nothing in God's sight (1 Cor. 13:1–3).

2. The world's hatred of Jesus and his followers (15:18 – 16:4)

18. Jesus said, *If the world hates you, keep in mind that it hated me first*. In this context, the 'world' stands for those among the Jewish leadership who were antagonistic towards Jesus – not all his kinsfolk were antagonistic towards him, any more than all Jews since have been antagonistic towards his followers. In the following verses Jesus spells out the reasons for the world's hatred.

19. Jesus explained to his disciples that *If you belonged to the world, it would love you as its own*. If they were in league with those who opposed Jesus they would be embraced by them, but *as it is, you do not belong to the world, but I have chosen you out of the world*. Once they belonged to the world, but because Jesus chose them out of the world they could no longer identify with it, and Jesus explained, *That is why the world hates you*. This placed the disciples in a situation of tension (and it is the same for believers today). On the one hand, they were called upon to love the world and to seek its salvation, but the world rejected and persecuted them. The temptation might be to withdraw from contact with the world into a Christian ghetto, but this they could not do, because Jesus had sent them into the world to share the good news with its people (4:38; 17:18; 20:21).

20. However, Jesus did not want this hatred to take his disciples by surprise, so he said, *Remember the words I spoke to you: 'No servant is greater than his master.'* Jesus reminded the disciples of what he had said after washing their feet: 'I tell you the truth, no servant is greater than his master, nor is a messenger greater than the one who sent him' (13:16). Jesus uses the same truth here to explain why his disciples would experience the hatred of the world: *If they persecuted me, they will persecute you also.* But this is not the whole story, for not all their fellow Jews would hate and persecute them; many would receive their message as they had received Jesus' message; so he added, *If they obeyed my teaching, they will obey yours also.* The story of the early preaching of the apostles in Jerusalem in the Acts of the Apostles illustrates this.

21. Referring to the persecution his followers would experience, Jesus said, *They will treat you this way because of my name*. The 'name' stands for the person, so in effect Jesus was saying, 'they will treat you in this way because of me'. It is because they identified themselves with Jesus instead of their leaders that the disciples became objects of persecution. The ultimate reason, however, for this persecution, Jesus said, is *they do not know the One who sent me*. Even though the persecutors would think they were doing God a service by persecuting believers (16:2), Jesus insisted they did not really know God at all.

22–23. Jesus explained that this ignorance was culpable: *If I had not come and spoken to them, they would not be guilty of sin. Now, however, they have no excuse for their sin*. If he had not come into the world, and spoken the words God gave him to speak, people would not be guilty of rejecting this revelation. But Jesus had spoken God's words (3:34; 7:17; 8:28, 38, 40; 12:49–50; 14:10) and yet the majority of the Jewish leaders rejected his testimony, and so they had no excuse for their sin.

Jesus rejected his opponents' claim that they were true worshippers of God who opposed Jesus because of their faithfulness to God: *He who hates me hates my Father as well*. They could not claim to love

God while hating Jesus. Those who hate Jesus hate the Father as well, because Jesus and the Father are one (10:30; *cf.* 14:7–11).

24. Jesus expanded the reason for the guilt of his opponents: *If I had not done among them what no-one else did, they would not be guilty of sin.* It was not only what he said, but the works/miracles he performed that constituted the revelation from God which his opponents had rejected. These miracles were the works the Father had given him to do (5:36; 10:25, 32, 37–38; 17:4). His opponents had seen these works, but because their own privileged position was threatened, they rejected the revelation offered them through these works and plotted to kill him (11:45–53). Jesus said, *But now they have seen these miracles, and yet they have hated both me and my Father.* Though Jesus' opponents had seen his miracles, they still rejected his claims and hated him. But because Jesus and the Father are one, their hatred of Jesus was hatred of God also.

25. Their hatred came as no surprise to him. He told his disciples, *But this is to fulfil what is written in their Law: 'They hated me without reason.'* The 'Law' here means the whole OT, including Psalms 35:19; 69:4, to which Jesus alluded. The psalmist, using similar terminology, lamented the unfair persecution he experienced. Jesus saw scriptures such as these finding fulfilment in the opposition he experienced. Such a reading of Scripture rests upon the conviction that God's dealings with his people, and many of their experiences in OT times, foreshadow his dealings with his people, and their experiences in NT times (see 1 Cor. 10:1–11). It is a sad fact, not limited to the followers of Jesus, that good people who struggle for truth and righteousness often attract the anger of those who feel threatened by their goodness.

26. During his lifetime, Jesus himself bore testimony to the world. After his return to the Father, the Holy spirit would take up this task: *When the Counsellor comes, whom I will send to you from the Father, the Spirit of truth who goes out from the Father, he will testify about me.* This is the third of four references (14:16, 26; 15:26; 16:7) to the Counsellor (*paraklētos*) in the Fourth Gospel (see Additional Note: The *Paraklētos*, pp. 303–306). Each succeeding reference adds a little more to our understanding of the role of the Counsellor. In this context his role is to give testimony in favour of Jesus in a hostile world. He would do this when he was sent to the disciples, and, as the next verse indicates, he does it through their witness.

A number of things call for comment in this verse. First, Jesus said *he* would send the Counsellor to his disciples, and this is repeated in 16:7. However, in 14:16, 26 the Counsellor is sent by the Father. As mentioned in the commentary on 14:26, these variations are not significant, because the Father and the Son are united in their actions, and this is reinforced by the fact that the Counsellor sent by Jesus 'goes out from the Father'.

Second, the Western Text makes an addition to this verse so that the Counsellor is described as one who goes out from the Father 'and the Son' (Lat. *filioque*). This textual variant gave rise to the fourth-century trinitarian debates. Does the Spirit proceed from the Father only, or does he proceed also from the Son? And what is the ontological significance of these options, and what are the implications for the doctrine of the Trinity? The whole debate was probably misguided, as in context the proceeding of the Spirit relates to the sending of the Spirit to the disciples after Jesus' return to the Father. It does not relate to the inner workings of the Trinity, to some eternal procession of the Spirit from the Father (and the Son).

Third, in this verse the Counsellor is described as 'the Spirit of truth', as he is in two other places in this Gospel (14:16–17; 16:13). In this respect the Counsellor is like Jesus, who is himself frequently said to speak the truth (8:31–36, 40, 45–46; 16:7; 18:37) and embody the truth (1:14, 17; 14:6).

Fourth, when the Counsellor comes 'he' (*ekeinos*: masculine pronoun implying the personhood of the Counsellor/Holy Spirit) will testify to the truth about Jesus. Such testimony is largely a defence of Jesus in a hostile world, a world that hated Jesus because he told it the truth it did not want to hear. In this action the Counsellor functions in the standard way a *paraklētos* operated in the ancient world, providing testimony in favour of an accused friend.

27. The Counsellor's testimony would be given alongside the testimony of the disciples: *And you also must testify, for you have been with me from the beginning.* Because of the juxtaposition of the statement about the Counsellor's testimony (26) and the disciples' testimony to Jesus (27), it is probable that the Counsellor's testimony is to be understood as effected through the witness of the disciples. While the NIV translates the first clause of this sentence as an imperative, 'and you also must testify', it is, in fact, a simple indicative statement, 'and you also bear witness' (cf. RSV: 'and you also are witnesses'). The basis of the disciples' witness is their own experience of Jesus from 'from the beginning', *i.e.* from the time he first called them to follow him.

16:1. Referring to all he had said about the world's hatred of himself and the hatred his disciples would likewise experience, Jesus said, *All this I have told you so that you will not go astray.* If the disciples, after Jesus' return to the Father, were taken by surprise by the animosity of the world, they could 'go astray'. The verb translated 'go astray' (*skandalizō*) means 'to cause to stumble, or fall (into sin)'. Jesus was concerned that the intensity of the opposition his disciples were to experience might, if they were not prepared for it, cause them to stumble and fall away from their faith in him. So he warned them in advance. To be forewarned is to be forearmed.

2. In this verse the nature of the opposition the disciples would experience is described in some detail. Jesus said, *They will put you out of the synagogue.* This includes the third and final use of the word meaning 'put out of the synagogue' (*aposynagōgos*) in the Fourth Gospel. The word is found nowhere else in the NT (nor in the LXX). 'The Jews' had already decided to put out of the synagogue anyone who acknowledged that Jesus was the Christ (9:22), and many Jewish leaders who believed in Jesus were afraid to confess this openly lest they too be put out of the synagogue (12:42). Now Jesus warned his disciples that they would soon be excluded from the synagogue because they were his followers. This warning would resonate with Jewish readers of the Gospel if they feared or had suffered a similar fate.

But even worse was to happen. Jesus added, *in fact, a time is coming when anyone who kills you will think he is offering a service to God.* One has only to turn to the Acts of the Apostles to see this occurring: Stephen was stoned to death (Acts 7:57–60), Saul of Tarsus sought to destroy the church by making murderous threats against the disciples (Acts 8:3; 9:1–2), and Herod had James put to death with the sword (Acts 12:1–2). Saul/Paul saw his persecution of the church before his conversion as evidence of his zeal for God (Phil. 3:4–6).

3. While the Jewish leaders would persecute and kill both Jesus and some of his followers because they thought they were doing God a service, Jesus said, *They will do such things because they have not known the Father or me.* Far from rendering true service to God, Jesus said, they did not even know God. The evidence that they did not know God was that they did not recognize Jesus whom God sent, and in whom God was made known (5:23).

4. Reiterating what he had said earlier, Jesus informed his disciples, *I have told you this, so that when the time comes you will remember that I warned you.* When these persecutions befell the disciples, they would remember Jesus had warned them beforehand, and they would not think that everything had gone awry. It was what Jesus had said would happen. Knowing this, the persecutions would not cause them to stumble and fall.

Jesus then said to his disciples, *I did not tell you this at first because I was with you.* It was apparently not necessary for them to know these things before. It may have been too much for them to bear in the early days of their discipleship. But the real reason, Jesus said, was because 'I was with you'. While he remained with them he was the 'lightning rod' that attracted the flashes of persecution. But after he returned to the Father, his disciples would experience it themselves. That was why Jesus did not tell them at first, and why as he prepared them for his departure he told them now.

3. The work of the Counsellor (16:5–15)

This passage contains further explanations of the work of the Holy Spirit, including the last of the four references to the *paraklētos* (14:16, 26; 15:26; 16:7). Each succeeding reference adds more to our understanding of his role.

5. Referring again to his imminent departure, Jesus said, *Now I am going to him who sent me, yet none of you asks me, 'Where are you going?'* Earlier Peter asked this very question (13:36), and the same question was implied in Thomas' complaint (14:5). Some see this as evidence for two versions of Jesus' farewell discourse (13:31 – 14:31 and 15:1 – 16:33), which the evangelist combined without bothering about contradictions. Others suggest that Jesus was not saying the question had not been asked before, but that *now* no-one was asking it. However, the 'now' in this text does not qualify the asking, but Jesus' going. Another suggestion is that although his disciples had formally asked this question before, in reality they were less interested in where Jesus was going than in the effect his departure upon them. So Jesus could say none of them had (really) asked this question before.

6–7. Jesus, recognizing how his disciples were feeling, continued, *Because I have said these things, you are filled with grief*. It must have been disappointing for Jesus that his disciples showed no interest in his imminent sufferings and future vindication (*cf.* 14:28), because they were filled with grief at the prospect of their own loss; nevertheless, he responded to their sense of loss by saying, *But I tell you the truth: It is for your good that I am going away. Unless I go away, the Counsellor will not come to you; but if I go, I will send him to you*. In 7:39 the evangelist told his readers that the Spirit would not come until Jesus was glorified (through death, resurrection and exaltation). Thus Jesus' 'going away' would be for the disciples' good, because he would then be able to send the Counsellor/Spirit to them. The coming of the Counsellor would overcome the disciples' feeling of desolation. But he would do more. He would have a role *vis-à-vis* the world as well, as 16:8–11 makes clear.

8. A general description of the Counsellor's role *vis-à-vis* the world is given in 16:8: *When he comes, he will convict the world of guilt in regard to sin and righteousness and judgment*. The word the NIV translates as 'convict of guilt' (*elenchō*), was used by Greek moralists in relation to the conscience, and in the LXX with forensic overtones,[1] as it has here. When the Counsellor proves the

---

[1] It is found in two other places in the Gospel of John: in 3:20, where evildoers do not come to the light lest their deeds be 'exposed', and in 8:46, where Jesus asks who can 'prove him guilty' of sin. Elsewhere in the NT it is used with a range of similar meanings: 'to show or expose' (Mt. 18:15; Eph. 5:11, 13), 'to rebuke' (Lk. 3:19; 1 Tim. 5:20; 2 Tim. 4:2; Tit. 1:13; 2:15; Heb. 12:5; Rev. 3:19), 'to prove guilty or convict' (Jas. 2:9; Jude 15); 'to convince' (1 Cor. 14:24), and 'to refute' (Tit 1:9).

world wrong 'in regard to sin and righteousness and judgment' it could lead either to repentance and salvation or hardening of heart and condemnation, depending upon the response of those proved wrong. The Spirit's conviction would be effected through the ministry of the disciples (*cf.* 1 Cor. 14:24–25).

9. The Counsellor, Jesus said, would convict the world *in regard to sin, because men do not believe in me*. The 'world' in the Fourth Gospel, when in opposition to Jesus, refers to unbelieving Jews, often unbelieving Jewish leaders. On several occasions Jesus gave them dire warnings about their sins (8:21, 24; 9:41; 15:22, 24; 19:11). Particularly ominous were warnings like that in 8:24: 'I told you that you would die in your sins; if you do not believe that I am [the one I claim to be], you will indeed die in your sins.' The Counsellor, when he came, would likewise convict them of their sin of unbelief, just as Jesus himself had done. The sin of unbelief, refusing to accept Jesus and his revelation, is extremely serious, because it is a rejection of the one God sent, his one and only Son (3:18). It is tantamount to a rejection of God himself.

10. The Counsellor, Jesus said, will also convict the world *in regard to righteousness, because I am going to the Father, where you can see me no longer*. The word 'righteousness' (*dikaiosynē*) is found only in 16:8, 10 in the Fourth Gospel, so its meaning for the evangelist is not easy to determine. Our best way forward is to ask in what way the world would be proved guilty 'in regard to righteousness' by Jesus' return to the Father. Applying their standards of righteousness, 'the Jews' concluded Jesus was a sinful man (9:24), but they were wrong because their standards were wrong. The one they declared sinful was vindicated by God when he raised him from the dead and exalted him to his right hand. The Counsellor will convict the world of its false standards of righteousness.

11. The Counsellor will also convict the world *in regard to judgment*. This is best understood along the same lines as the Counsellor's convicting role in relation to righteousness. Just as the standards of righteousness by which 'the Jews' operated were mistaken, so also were their judgments about Jesus. During his ministry Jesus said to them, 'Stop judging by mere appearances, and make a right judgment' (7:24). After Jesus' return to the Father, the Counsellor would continue to prove them wrong 'in regard to judgment', *because the prince of this world now stands condemned*. Earlier in the Gospel Jesus described the devil (= prince of this world) as 'a liar and the father of lies' (8:44). He is the source of all false judgment. As the time for Jesus' death and exaltation drew near, he said, 'Now is the time for judgment on this world; now the prince of this world will be driven out' (12:31). The prince of this world, the distorter of true judgment, stands condemned, and the role of the Counsellor will be to prove wrong those of the world who likewise distort true judgment, particularly in relation to Jesus.

12. Focusing his attention back upon his disciples, Jesus said, *I have much more to say to you, more than you can now bear*. He understood their emotional state, and recognized they were not ready to hear more, probably meaning more about the terrible events soon to befall him and them. He had given some warnings beforehand about what was to happen (13:19; 14:29–30; 16:4), but more than this he judged they could not bear.

13. What they could not bear then, they would need to understand afterwards. Therefore, Jesus promised, *But when he, the Spirit of truth, comes, he will guide you into all truth*. The Spirit is here referred to with the masculine pronoun 'he' (*ekeinos*), underlining again (*cf.* 15:26) the personhood of the Spirit – he is not just a force. He has already been twice described as 'the Spirit of truth' (14:17; 15:26). The Spirit would guide Jesus' disciples 'into all truth'. This is not to be interpreted absolutely as if the Counsellor will teach them all that can be known, but rather that he will interpret to them afterwards the truth about the death, resurrection and exaltation of Jesus. His role is to testify to Jesus: *He will not speak on his own; he will speak only what he hears, and he will tell you what is yet to come*. As Jesus did not speak independently of the Father, so the Counsellor will not speak independently of Jesus. What he hears from the Son he will tell the disciples: the significance of the things 'yet to come', *i.e.* the significance of the events soon to befall Jesus, and perhaps his return at the end of the age.

331

14–15. Underlining that the Counsellor does not act independently, Jesus said, *He will bring glory to me by taking from what is mine and making it known to you.* Just as Jesus' purpose was to bring glory to the Father, so the Counsellor's role is to bring glory to Jesus. This he will do by taking what belongs to Jesus and making it known to his disciples. Jesus then explained, *All that belongs to the Father is mine.* In several other places it is made clear that all that belongs to the Father belongs to Jesus (3:35; 13:3; 17:7, 10). However, here the emphasis is upon the knowledge the Father has, for Jesus went on to say, *That is why I said the Spirit will take from what is mine and make it known to you.* The knowledge the Father has also belongs to Jesus (*cf.* 15:15), and the Counsellor will take that knowledge and make it known to the disciples. Once again, this is not an absolute statement, meaning everything God knows will be revealed to the disciples. It relates to the significance of the great saving events that were about to unfold in the death and resurrection of Jesus.

4. The disciples' grief will give way to joy (16:16–24)

16–19. In these verses Jesus begins to deal directly with the effect of his departure upon his disciples: *In a little while you will see me no more, and then after a little while you will see me.* This puzzled them, so *some of his disciples said to one another, 'What does he mean by saying, "In a little while you will see me no more, and then after a little while you will see me," and "Because I am going to the Father"?'* In 16:16 Jesus makes no mention of his 'going to the Father', but this was and continued to be an important theme in his teaching (13:1; 14:12, 28; 16:10, 28; 20:17). It is probably earlier references to this theme to which the disciples' question alludes. Clearly, this whole matter was a great puzzle to them, for in 16:18 the evangelist adds, *They kept asking, 'What does he mean by "a little while"? We don't understand what he is saying.'* As the disciples persisted in asking themselves what this meant, *Jesus saw that they wanted to ask him about this, so he said to them, 'Are you asking one another what I meant when I said, "In a little while you will see me no more, and then after a little while you will see me"?'* He knew they wanted to ask him what he meant but were reticent to do so (he knew what was in people; 2:25), perhaps because they did not

want to reveal their lack of comprehension. In the next verses
Jesus answers the question they were not prepared to ask.

20. Jesus continued, *I tell you the truth, you will weep and mourn
while the world rejoices. You will grieve, but your grief will turn to joy.*
The disciples would weep and mourn as they saw events unfold:
Jesus' betrayal at the hands of Judas Iscariot, his being handed
over by the Jewish Sanhedrin to the Roman governor, and it all
culminating in his crucifixion. Sadly, they would grieve for their
own loss, rather than feel outrage at the miscarriage of justice
that brought Jesus to his death. But their grief would last but a
few days, for Jesus would be raised from death, and appear to his
disciples again, and then their grief would be turned to joy. The
'little while' of the previous verse after which the disciples would
see Jesus no more was the brief period between the time of speaking and his crucifixion, and the 'little while' after which they
would see him again was the three days between his crucifixion
and resurrection.

21–22. Jesus used an analogy to reinforce his statement about
grief turning into joy: *A woman giving birth to a child has pain because
her time has come; but when her baby is born she forgets the anguish
because of her joy that a child is born into the world.* The pain of childbirth can be excruciating, but afterwards the joy of a child born
into the world completely overshadows the pain. Jesus said to his
disciples, *So with you: Now is your time of grief, but I will see you again
and you will rejoice, and no-one will take away your joy.* Grief would
engulf the disciples as they saw Jesus betrayed, handed over to
the Roman governor and crucified, just as the pains of childbirth
engulf a woman in labour. But when Jesus met his disciples again
as the resurrected one their grief would turn to exultant joy, just
as joy floods a new mother at the birth of her child.

Jewish people believed the age of the Messiah would be
brought in only after a time of distress, the so-called 'birth pangs
of the Messiah', the tribulations that preceded the end of this age
and ushered in the new age. Perhaps the words of 16:21–22 allude
to this belief, and, if so, indicate that the death and resurrection of
Jesus would inaugurate, though not consummate, the new age.
Other NT writings also speak of tribulation before the end of the

age (*e.g.* Mk. 13:19; Mt. 24:21; Acts 14:22; Rev. 7:14). But Jesus' use of the birth-pains analogy may simply have been an illustration of the point he wished to make.

23. Jesus continued, *In that day you will no longer ask me anything. I tell you the truth, my Father will give you whatever you ask in my name.* Different words are used for asking Jesus anything (*erōtaō*) and asking the Father for something (*aiteō*). *Erōtaō* usually means to ask *about* something, but can also mean to ask *for* something. *Aiteō* means to ask *for* something. Here in 16:23 the two verbs are used synonymously, meaning to ask *for* something. The disciples' relationship with Jesus after his resurrection, exaltation and the coming of the Spirit would be different from his relationship with them before these events. Then, instead of asking him for things, they would be able to ask the Father and he would give them whatever they asked. This was a solemn promise, introduced with the words 'I tell you the truth' (*amēn amēn legō hymin*).

This is the last of four places in the farewell discourses (14:13-14; 15:7, 16; 16:23-26) where Jesus makes promises to his disciples concerning prayer. In every case but one the answer to the prayer is conditional upon asking 'in his name'. The exception is 15:7, where the condition is that the disciples 'remain' in him and his words 'remain' in them. Here in 16:23 it is again prayer in Jesus' name that is guaranteed a positive answer. As suggested above (see Additional Note: 'In my name / in his name', pp. 302–303), to pray in Jesus' name means to pray for things 'for his sake', or in line with his purposes. So in this verse Jesus is saying that after his resurrection, the disciples will begin approaching the Father directly in their prayers, and whatever they ask the Father, which is in line with Jesus' purposes for humankind and the glory of God, will be given to them.

24. To encourage his disciples further to begin praying in this way, Jesus said, *Until now you have not asked for anything in my name. Ask and you will receive, and your joy will be complete.* They had not yet learned to ask in Jesus' name. Jesus now told them to ask in his name, promising that if they did, they would receive what they asked for, and then they would know complete joy.

5. Jesus speaks plainly to his disciples (16:25–33)

25. Jesus began, *Though I have been speaking figuratively*. Earlier, in 10:6, the evangelist says the same sort of thing about Jesus' teaching concerning the good shepherd: 'Jesus used this figure of speech, but they did not understand what he was telling them.' Throughout the farewell speeches Jesus used figurative speech, for example, in regard to the footwashing, when speaking of the 'way' to the Father, in the metaphor of the vine and the branches, and finally, in his cryptic comments about 'a little while'. Jesus continued, *a time is coming when I will no longer use this kind of language but will tell you plainly about my Father*. The time for plain speech was now close at hand.

26–27. Referring to this time, Jesus said, *In that day you will ask in my name*. To ask in Jesus' name is to ask 'for his sake' or in line with his purpose to bring glory to God (see Additional Note: 'In my name / in his name', pp. 302–303). In 16:23 Jesus spoke about 'that day' as a time when his disciples would make their requests to the Father and he would give them what they asked. Repeating this statement, he expanded it with the words *I am not saying that I will ask the Father on your behalf*. Following Jesus' resurrection, ascension and the coming of the Spirit, the disciples would no longer have access to Jesus' physical presence, but this would not prove to be a loss, because they would have direct access to the Father. They would not need Jesus to ask the Father on their behalf. To encourage them to make use of their access to the Father, Jesus added, *No, the Father himself loves you because you have loved me and have believed that I came from God*. The disciples knew something of Jesus' love for them and had grown in their love for him and in their belief that he had come from God. Jesus told them that because they loved him and believed in him the Father also loved them. This repeated earlier teaching (14:21, 23) about the Father's love for them and provided the basis upon which they could come to the Father and make their requests in Jesus' name.

28. Speaking now without figures of speech or enigmatic phrases, Jesus said, *I came from the Father and entered the world; now I am leaving the world and going back to the Father*. That Jesus came from God (3:2; 13:3; 16:27, 30; 17:8) into the world (1:9; 3:17, 19; 6:14, 33; 9:39; 10:36; 11:27; 12:46; 17:18) and was returning to God (13:1, 3; 14:12, 28; 16:10, 17, 28; 17:13; 20:17) are recurring themes in the Fourth Gospel. Here in 16:28 all three are brought together. It was as the Word made flesh (1:14) that Jesus entered the world, and it would be through betrayal, death, resurrection and exaltation that he would leave the world and go back to the Father.

29–30. Hearing him speak in this way, *Jesus' disciples said, 'Now you are speaking clearly and without figures of speech.'* They believed his promise to speak plainly to them 'in that day' had already been fulfilled. They felt emboldened to say, *Now we can see that you know all things and that you do not even need to have anyone ask you questions.* The disciples were now convinced that there need be no more interrogation of Jesus to test his knowledge or determine who he was. It was plain that he knew all things, and so they said, *This makes us believe that you came from God.* In confessing this they were picking up on what Jesus had told them in 16:28: 'I came from the Father'.

31–32. Jesus' response to the disciples' confession was far from enthusiastic. The NIV translates 16:31 as a statement, *'You believe at last!' Jesus answered,* but it may be translated equally well as a question, 'Do you now believe?' (NRSV). This is probably better, because what follows in 16:32 indicates that the disciples' belief was shallow at best and needed to be questioned. Jesus warned them, *But a time is coming, and has come, when you will be scattered, each to his own home.* Whatever the nature of their belief, it was not enough to sustain them in the time of crisis that was about to overtake them. When Jesus was betrayed and handed over to the Roman governor, they would be scattered and flee to their homes (Mt. 26:56; Mk. 14:50). Jesus added, *You will leave me all alone. Yet I am not alone, for my Father is with me.* Though he was to be deserted by his disciples, the Father would stand by him through all his trials.

Some have asked if there is not a contradiction in this Gospel. It says here that all the disciples would be scattered and Jesus would be left alone, yet 18:15 says Peter and John followed him to the high priest's courtyard. Perhaps we should recognize that their first reaction was to flee and they did so, but later they pulled themselves together and followed Jesus to the high priest's house. Another thing that has puzzled readers is that here Jesus says that though his disciples would leave him alone the Father would be with him. How does this square with his cry of dereliction, 'My God, my God, why have you forsaken me?' recorded in the Synoptic Gospels (Mt. 27:46; Mk. 15:34)? But there is no contradiction here. We recognize that God was with Jesus through all his sufferings: the betrayal, Jewish and Roman trials, and crucifixion. It was only as he bore the sins of the world in the darkness that covered the land that he was abandoned by the Father.

33. Jesus' words to his disciples informing them of their desertion would have troubled them deeply. But it would have been even more troubling for them to be overtaken by these events and to think that Jesus himself was also taken by surprise. So Jesus said, *I have told you these things, so that in me you may have peace.* When afterwards the disciples felt ashamed and remorseful because they deserted Jesus in his time of need, they would be able to recall that he knew about these things beforehand and was still committed to them and still loved them. In this knowledge they could have peace in their relationship with him.

Jesus knew that after his return to the Father the disciples too would be persecuted. He warned them that the Jewish leaders would hate them as they had hated him, that they would put the disciples out of the synagogue and would even think they did God a service by putting them to death (15:18 – 16:4). They had already felt something of the world's hatred (*cf.* 17:14). He now warned them of further persecution: *In this world you will have trouble.*[1] It was another reminder that their lives would not be easy. In this world, *i.e.* in their relationships with a hostile world (in particular, unbelieving Jews), they would have trouble. To balance this, Jesus promised that in their relationship with him, even in the midst of their troubles, they would know peace.

Even though they would have trouble in the world, Jesus said,

---

[1] The word for 'trouble' is *thlipsis*, also used in 16:21 when Jesus referred to the 'anguish' of a woman in childbirth to depict the anguish the disciples would experience when he was betrayed and crucified; an anguish that would soon turn to joy when he was raised from the dead.

But take heart! I have overcome the world. This is ironic, for it would appear that the world overcame Jesus; after all, the Jewish leaders did succeed in having him crucified by the Romans. Yet Jesus insisted that he had overcome the world. In what sense? In that all its opposition did not succeed in turning him aside from what he came to do: to reveal the truth about God and the human condition, and to give his life that the world might be saved.

In 1 John believers also are said to overcome the world, and this they did by resisting all pressures to turn aside from the message about Jesus that they had heard from the eyewitnesses in the beginning (1 Jn. 5:4–5). They were enabled to do so because the word of God remained in them (1 Jn. 2:13–14) and because the one who was in them (the Spirit of truth) is stronger than the one who is in the world (the spirit of antichrist) (1 Jn. 4:4).

Jesus' words 'But take heart! I have overcome the world' would strengthen the disciples when they faced the full onslaught from the world after he returned to the Father.

D. JESUS' PRAYER (17:1–26)

After the farewell discourse, in which Jesus prepared his disciples for life without him (13:31 – 16:33), he turned to his Father in prayer (17:1–26). This is the third prayer of Jesus recorded by the evangelist. Earlier prayers were uttered at the tomb of Lazarus (11:41–42) and when Jesus was approached by the Greeks (12:27–28). The prayer of 17:1–26 has four parts.

1. Jesus prays for himself (17:1–5)

1–2. The evangelist commences his account, *After Jesus said this, he looked towards heaven and prayed.* After 'this' refers to the farewell discourses in 13:1 – 16:33 in which Jesus' prepared his disciples for his departure. 'He looked up to heaven' could mean Jesus was outdoors, possibly *en route* from the Last Supper venue to the olive grove on the other side of the Kidron valley (see commentary on 14:31; 18:1). The actual prayer begins, *Father, the time has come.* The expression 'the time has come' includes the last of nine references to Jesus' 'hour/time' (see commentary on 7:30).

The first three say that Jesus' hour had not yet come; the last six indicate that his hour had come. The 'hour' to which Jesus had now come was the hour of his glorification to take place through his death, and subsequent exaltation. Coming to this hour, Jesus asked the Father to *glorify your Son*. This could mean two things: (1) that the glory of his love and compassion for others might be revealed through his death (12:23–24, 28); and (2) that following his death he would be reinstated to the glory he enjoyed with the Father before the world began (5). Jesus' purpose in praying that the Father might glorify his Son was *that your Son may glorify you*. How the son would glorify the Father is spelled out in the following words, which should follow on without a sentence break, *For* (lit. 'just as') *you granted him authority over all people that he might give eternal life to all those you have given him*. The Son glorifies the Father by exercising the authority the Father granted him to bestow eternal life upon those the Father has given to him (*cf.* 5:19–30). This brings glory to the Father because it reveals the love and compassion the Father has for human beings. In Exodus 34:5–7, when Moses asked to see God's glory, God revealed his compassion, grace, love and faithfulness. All these things were revealed again and supremely in the death of Jesus, as the Father gave his one and only Son so that those who believe might have eternal life (3:16).

The recipients of eternal life are described as those the Father has 'given him', something repeated again and again in Jesus' prayer (6, 9, 24). This shows that, viewed from the divine side, it is God's choice that is determinative. However, this must be held together with Jesus' teaching that people's response of belief or unbelief determines whether or not they receive eternal life.

3. Jesus defined eternal life, *Now this is eternal life: that they may know you, the only true God, and Jesus Christ, whom you have sent.* Eternal life is knowing God, but, as in the OT, this knowledge is not simply information about God; it is a relationship with him. Under the terms of the new covenant, all God's children are to know him personally (Je. 31:34). This verse makes clear that knowing God and therefore experiencing eternal life is inseparable from knowing Jesus Christ whom God sent (*cf.* 3:36; 5:39–40; 14:6; 20:31). Viewed from the human side a person's relationship with God is established by acceptance of and obedience to Jesus' teaching (see Additional Note: Eternal life, pp. 111–113).

4. Jesus mentioned another way in which he glorified the Father: *I have brought you glory on earth by completing the work you gave me to do.* He came into the world to carry out the work God gave him to do (*cf.* 4:34; 5:36; 9:3–4) and the Father was glorified when this work was completed. This work, which involved revealing the Father through his life and ministry, and culminated in giving himself on the cross, glorified the Father by revealing his character to the world.

5. Coming now to the end of this work, Jesus prayed, *And now, Father, glorify me in your presence with the glory I had with you before the world began.* The work of revealing the Father through his life and ministry had come to an end. The final act of revelation would take place through his death and exaltation, and this would also be the means of his return to the Father and to the glory he had with the Father before the world began. In the Prologue Jesus is introduced as the Word who 'was with God in the beginning' (1:2), and he prayed now to be restored to that place and the glory attaching to it, a prayer that would most certainly be answered.

2. Jesus prays for his disciples (17:6–19)

In this section of the prayer Jesus speaks about those whom the Father gave him, and prays for their protection as they remain in the world when he returns to the Father.

6–8. Jesus spoke of his ministry to his disciples: *I have revealed you to those whom you gave me out of the world.* Jesus, the only one who has ever seen God (1:18), made him known to his disciples through his words and actions (2:11; 8:38; 15:15) and his person (14:7–11). Jesus described the disciples as those 'you gave me out of the world'. Once they, like everyone else, were part of the world, but were chosen out of the world by God. Of these chosen ones, Jesus said, *They were yours; you gave them to me and they have obeyed your word.* They belonged to the Father because he chose them, but he entrusted them to the Son so that he might convey his word to them. They showed they belonged to God by obeying that word. As a result, Jesus said, *Now they know that everything you have given me comes from you. For I gave them the words you gave me and they accepted them.* The words Jesus spoke were the words his Father gave him to speak (*cf.* 7:16–17; 8:28, 38, 40; 12:49–50). His disciples accepted these words, and so distinguished themselves from those of the world who disputed Jesus' claim to speak the words of God, saying instead that Jesus was demon-possessed (7:20; 8:48–49, 52; 10:20). Jesus then said of his disciples, *They knew with certainty that I came from you, and they believed that you sent me.* Their faith was certainly not exemplary, as subsequent events reveal, but they did believe in Jesus and accepted the revelation he brought. This was enough to show that they belonged to God.

9–11. Jesus continued, *I pray for them. I am not praying for the world, but for those you have given me, for they are yours.* Those of 'the world' were excluded from Jesus' prayer because they rejected him and the revelation he brought. If they accepted Jesus, they would cease to be 'the world' and be included among those who belong to God.

Before articulating his actual petition for his disciples, Jesus said to the Father, *All I have is yours, and all you have is mine.* The words translated 'all' here are neuter plurals, indicting that 'all' here refers not just to the disciples but to all things. It is a general statement to the effect that everything the Son has belongs to the Father, and everything that belongs to the Father has been given to the Son. Included in the 'all' that belongs to the Father and which he has given to the Son are the people whom the Father gave to the Son. Of these Jesus said, *And glory has come to me through them.* On no other occasion did Jesus speak of his disciples bringing glory to him. He did speak of the disciples bringing glory to God by bearing 'much fruit' (15:8), and in Peter's case by the kind of death he would die (21:19). It was primarily by believing in him, accepting and obeying his words, and carrying out his commission that the disciples brought glory to Jesus.

Jesus' prayer was prompted by his imminent departure: *I will remain in the world no longer, but they are still in the world, and I am coming to you.* His departure would occur through his death, resurrection and exaltation. When he left this world, his disciples would

341

remain in it and therefore Jesus' first actual petition was, *Holy Father, protect them by the power of your name – the name you gave me*. Jesus' form of address to God, 'Holy Father', is unique in the NT. It combines reference to God's transcendence ('holy') and Jesus' intimacy with God ('Father'). Jesus asked the Father to protect his disciples 'by the power of your name' (lit. 'by your name'). The 'name' stands for the person, and so Jesus asked the Father to protect them by his power, to protect them from the power of the evil one.

Jesus' prayer for the protection of the disciples was *so that they may be one as we are one*. It seems their oneness, especially, would be under threat after Jesus' departure. The oneness Jesus wanted for his disciples was the oneness he and the Father have, something he spoke of in 10:30. The context of 10:30 makes it clear that the Father and the Son are one in what they say and do; it is a oneness in mission (*cf.* 10:27–30). It is likely, therefore, that the oneness Jesus requested for his disciples here was the same. And in fact, Jesus' prayers for the oneness of his disciples in other places (11, 21–23) all include references to the world, and express the desire that, because of his disciples' oneness, the world might believe that God had sent his Son into the world. Unity among disciples is unity for the sake of mission. If we allow 10:27–30 to guide us, we would also say that it is unity in mission as well as unity for the sake of mission. However, as 17:21–23 makes clear, this unity in mission is rooted in the disciples' unity/relationship with the Father and the Son.

12. Jesus continued, *While I was with them, I protected them and kept them safe by that name you gave me*. The NIV's 'by that name' renders the expression *en tō onomati sou*, which is better translated 'in the name'. During his ministry Jesus kept the disciples safe in the revelation of the Father embodied in Jesus himself so that they did not turn aside from it, and, he said, *None has been lost except the one doomed to destruction* (lit. 'the son of destruction') *so that Scripture would be fulfilled*. 'Son of destruction' can denote either a person's character or destiny or both. The reference is to Judas Iscariot, one of the Twelve, who did not remain loyal and who had already gone out to betray Jesus (13:27–30). The evangelist does not say here which Scripture was fulfilled by Judas' act of betrayal, but in 13:18 Jesus cited Psalm 41:9 in reference to Judas:

'But this is to fulfil the scripture: "He who shares my bread has lifted up his heel against me."'

The word 'destruction' (*apōleia*) when used in the NT of human beings or the 'beast' in Revelation always denotes eternal destruction (Mt. 7:13; Jn. 17:12; Rom. 9:22; Phil. 1:28; 3:19; 2 Thes. 2:3; 1 Tim. 6:9; Heb. 10:39; 2 Pet. 2:1, 3; 3:7, 16; Rev. 17:8, 11). That Jesus said that Judas was doomed to destruction 'so that Scripture would be fulfilled' is another reminder of the sovereignty of God in all things. However, once again it must be stressed that teaching about God's sovereignty is always to be held together with the equally clear teaching about human responsibility. In the case of Judas it was the devil who put it into his mind to betray Jesus (13:2, 27; *cf.* Lk. 22:3) and it was Judas himself who willingly carried it through (13:30; 18:2–3, 5; *cf.* Mt. 26:14, 25, 47; Mk. 14:10, 43; Lk. 22:48).

13–14. Still having the disciples in mind, Jesus said, *I am coming to you now, but I say these things while I am still in the world, so that they may have the full measure of my joy within them*. What Jesus said was spoken in the hearing of his disciples, so that hearing it they might share in Jesus' own joy. There is only one other place where Jesus speaks of his disciples sharing in his joy (15:9–11). There he speaks of the need for his disciples to continue in his love as he continued in the Father's love by obedience to his commands, and concludes, 'I have told you this so that my joy may be in you and that your joy may be complete' (15:11). In another place, without using the word 'joy' Jesus says something similar about himself: 'I have food to eat that you know nothing about . . . My food . . . is to do the will of him who sent me and to finish his work (4:32–34). Jesus' joy came from doing the Father's will, and the joy of the disciples would come from doing what Jesus commanded (see Acts 5:41).

Speaking further of his disciples, Jesus said, *I have given them your word and the world has hated them, for they are not of the world any more than I am of the world*. By receiving the word of God that Jesus gave them, they, like Jesus himself, were now 'not of the world'. The world did not accept Jesus' word and hated those who did, just as it hated him (7:7; 15:18–19, 24–25). In the Fourth Gospel very often the 'world', when it appears in opposition to

Jesus as it does here, stands for those elements of the Jewish leadership who were antagonistic towards him, who sought to arrest him (7:30, 32, 44; 8:20; 10:39; 11:57) and wished to put him to death (5:18; 7:1, 19, 25; 8:37, 40; 11:53).

15–16. We come now to the second actual petition made by Jesus for his disciples: *My prayer is not that you take them out of the world but that you protect them from the evil one*. Despite the world's hatred for his disciples, Jesus did not pray that they be taken out of the world. They were to remain in the world as his witnesses (*cf.* 15:26–27). Jesus prayed that the Father would protect them from 'the evil one'. In each place in the Fourth Gospel where the activity of the evil one (or the devil or Satan) is mentioned up to this point it was directed against Jesus to bring about his death (6:70; 8:44; 13:2, 27). Once Jesus was removed from the scene, this activity would be directed against his disciples. Jesus prayed, therefore, that the Father would protect them from the evil one. After praying for their protection Jesus added, *They are not of the world, even as I am not of it*, repeating what he had said earlier (14). Because they were not of the world, yet must remain in the world and bear witness to Jesus, they would need the Father's protection.

17. We come now to Jesus' third petition for his disciples: *Sanctify them by the truth; your word is truth*. Jesus' prayer here is related to what he said to his disciples in 15:3: 'You are already clean because of the word I have spoken to you.' But if his disciples were 'already clean' because they had accepted Jesus' word, why did he now pray that they be sanctified by God's word? Perhaps he was praying not so much for their purification but that they be set apart for God's use. The disciples were distinguished from the world by their acceptance of God's word (14). Stated negatively, God's word separated them *from* the world. Stated positively it set them apart *for* God. What this entailed is explained in the next verse.

18. Jesus indicated what the disciples were to be set apart for: *As you sent me into the world, I have sent them into the world*. There are many references in the Fourth Gospel to Jesus having been sent by the Father (3:17, 34; 5:36, 38; 6:38, 57; 7:29; 8:42; 10:36; 11:42;

17:3, 8, 18, 21, 23, 25; 20:21). Others speak of what he was sent to do: to save the world (3:17), to speak the words of God (3:34; 14:10), and to display the work of God through miracles (9:3–4; 10:25, 32, 37–38; 14:11). Putting it in general terms, Jesus was sent to carry out the work the Father gave him to do (5:36; 17:4). Apart from the unique work of saving the world through his atoning death, all that Jesus was sent to do he in turn sent his disciples to do. In brief, they were to carry on Jesus' ministry after his departure. What the Father sent him into the world to do, he sent them into the world to do (*cf.* 20:21).

19. Jesus concluded his prayer for his disciples by saying, *For them I sanctify myself, that they too may be truly sanctified*. Jesus sanctified himself by setting himself apart to do the Father's will, which included bringing the knowledge of God and eternal life to all who believe, and laying down his life for them. By laying down his life he also sanctified them, *i.e.* he cleansed them from sin, separated them from the world, and set them apart as his witnesses in the world.

3. *Jesus prays for all who are to believe (17:20–24)*

20–21. This last section of Jesus' prayer embraced all who are to believe: *My prayer is not for them alone. I pray also for those who will believe in me through their message, that all of them may be one*. His prayer was that all disciples, present and future, might be one, a oneness modelled upon his own oneness with the Father. Thus he prayed, *Father, just as you are in me and I am in you. May they also be in us*. Jesus spoke much of his unity with the Father, especially as it related to what he said and did in the world (5:19; 8:28; 10:25, 32, 37; 12:50). But here it is a unity of being, not only of purpose and action. The unity of Father and Son exists because, as Jesus said, 'you [Father] are in me and I am in you' (*cf.* 10:38; 14:9–11). This unity of being is extended to the disciples: 'that all of them may be one, Father, just as you are in me and I am in you, may they also be in us'. This relationship between believers and the Father and Jesus would be brought about through the ministry of the Counsellor, the Holy Spirit, sent to the disciples after Jesus' return to the Father (15:26; 16:7). Because the Holy Spirit comes to dwell within them, the Father and the Son dwell within them also, and they dwell in the Father and the Son (14:15–20).

The reason Jesus prayed that the disciples might be in the Father and the Son was *so that the world may believe that you have sent me*. Their living relationship with the Father and the Son through the Spirit would give credibility to their message about Jesus, and lead many in the world to believe in Jesus. When those of the world believe, they cease to be 'the world' and join the number of Jesus' disciples.

22–23. Jesus continued, *I have given them the glory that you gave me, that they may be one as we are one: I in them and you in me*. In this context the glory the Father gave Jesus is the revelation of himself that Jesus was to communicate to his disciples. By receiving that revelation they came to share in the glory of oneness like that existing between Father and Son. The disciples share this oneness because the Father is in Jesus, and Jesus will be in his disciples by his Spirit. The glory the Father gave the Son found expression in the love between them (15:10; 17:23, 26), the signs Jesus performed (2:11; 11:4), in the honour the Father bestowed upon Jesus (8:50, 54), and in the exaltation of Jesus after he laid down his life (5, 24). The glory Jesus would give to his disciples is similar. It is the glory of oneness with the Father and the Son mediated by the Spirit. It likewise finds expression in love between them and the Father (14:21, 23; 17:23, 26), in the signs they are to perform (14:12), in the honour the Father bestows upon them (12:26) and in their share in future glory (24).

Jesus continued his prayer, *May they be brought to complete unity to let the world know that you sent me and have loved them even as you have loved me*. Although the NIV renders this as an independent sentence, it actually consists of two purpose clauses indicating the purpose for which Jesus gave the disciples the glory the Father gave him, *i.e.* their unity with the Father and the Son. Literally translated this text would read, '*in order that* they may be perfected in one, *in order that* the world may know that you sent me and that you loved them as you loved me'. It is the unity of the disciples one with another (based on their common oneness with the Father and the Son) that functions as a powerful witness to the world. And although Jesus did not say so, the converse is also sadly true. The lack of unity among his disciples undermines their witness to him.

The unity of the disciples not only testifies to the fact that Jesus was sent into the world by the Father; it is also a testimony to the fact that the Father loves the disciples as he has loved his Son. They are recognized as God's people by their unity and love for one another. Jesus said previously, 'By this all men will know that you are my disciples, if you love one another' (13:35). As they are marked out as God's people by their unity and mutual love, their witness to Jesus will have credibility.

It is amazing that Jesus should say the Father has loved them even as the Father loved him. We can only understand this in terms of the disciples' privilege of being drawn into the circle of love in which the Father and the Son exist.

24. This verse contains another of Jesus' petitions on behalf of all his disciples: *Father, I want those you have given me to be with me where I am, and to see my glory, the glory you have given me because you loved me before the creation of the world.* The petition itself is in two parts. First, Jesus asked that his disciples (those whom the Father had given him) might be with him where he would be. In 14:2–3 he told his disciples that by his departure he would prepare places for them in his Father's house and that he would return to take them to be with him there. In this first part of the petition he told the Father that he wanted this to happen.

Second, Jesus asked that his disciples might see his glory, the glory the Father had given him, as the pre-existent Logos. Earlier, Jesus said that the Father loved him because of his obedience in laying down his life (10:17), but that is only part of the story. The Father loved the Son even before the creation of the world, before time as we know it began. Even then the Father had bestowed glory upon his Son. It is this glory Jesus prayed that his disciples might see. The ultimate goal for the disciples is not participation in the mission to which Jesus called them, vital though that is, but to see the glory of their exalted Redeemer in the presence of the Father.

4. Jesus concludes his prayer (17:25–26)

25–26. Jesus concluded his prayer by focusing upon his relationship with the Father: *Righteous Father, though the world does not* *know you, I know you.* He addressed God as 'Righteous Father'. This is the only place in the NT where God is addressed or spoken of in this way, although on three occasions Jesus himself is referred to as 'the Righteous One' (Acts 7:52; 22:14; 1 Jn. 2:1). Nevertheless, God is frequently described as righteous/just in his person (1 Jn. 2:29; 3:7), his ways (Rev. 15:3), his judgments (2 Thes. 1:5–6; Rev. 16:5, 7; 19:2) and forgiveness (1 Jn. 1:9).

In saying 'the world does not know you' Jesus was reflecting the fact that, despite protestations to the contrary, the world ('the Jews') did not know God. The evidence for this was that they did not accept the one sent by God (8:42). Jesus, however, does know God, and, referring to his disciples, he added, *and they know that you have sent me.* The disciples distinguished themselves from the world by recognizing that Jesus was sent by God. Of them, Jesus said, *I have made you known to them, and will continue to make you known.* Literally rendered, the first clause would read, 'I have made your name known to them'. To make known a person's name is to make known the person, so the NIV's translation/interpretation is appropriate. Earlier in his prayer Jesus said, 'I have revealed you to those whom you gave me out of the world' (6). This he did through his person (14:9), his teaching and his miracles (14:10–11). In 17:26 Jesus said he would continue to make the Father known to his disciples. Given he spoke on the eve of his betrayal and crucifixion, this future revelation of the Father would take place either through the very events of the passion itself, or the coming of the Spirit after his exaltation, or both.

Jesus said the purpose of the revelation of the Father to his disciples was *in order that the love you have for me may be in them and that I myself may be in them.* When Jesus reveals the Father to those who accept him as Messiah, he introduces them at the same time to the love of the Father. One of the things Jesus taught his disciples in the Last Supper discourses was that the Father himself loved them, and therefore they could bring their prayers directly to him (16:26–27). Also, he taught them that he himself would dwell with/in those who accepted his teaching and obeyed him (14:23). The ongoing presence of Jesus among his people ('I myself may be in/among them') is the unique feature of the Christian community (*cf.* Mt. 18:20; 1 Cor. 14:24–25).

E. THE PASSION NARRATIVE (18:1 – 19:42)

1. Jesus is betrayed and arrested in the olive grove (18:1–11)

Following the description of Jesus' Last Supper discourses (13:31 – 16:33) and his prayer for himself and his disciples (17:1–26), the evangelist provides an account of Jesus' arrest, trials, crucifixion and burial (18:1 – 19:42).

1–2. The evangelist begins with a comment about the timing of the arrest: *When he had finished praying, Jesus left with his disciples and crossed the Kidron Valley.* In 14:31, following the first part of the farewell discourse, Jesus said to his disciples, 'Come now; let us leave.' The second part of the farewell discourse then followed, and it is not until 18:1 that Jesus and his disciples actually leave and cross the Kidron valley. There are various ways of explaining this (see commentary on 14:31). One suggestion is that Jesus and his disciples did leave the room where the Last Supper was held when he said, 'Come now; let us leave,' and that the second part of his farewell discourse was delivered as they walked through the streets of Jerusalem. If this were case, the prayers of 17:1–26 could have been uttered on the Temple Mount and then 18:1 would mark the time they left the Temple Mount and crossed the Kidron valley, which separates the city of Jerusalem from the Mount of Olives.

The evangelist describes the setting of the arrest: *On the other side there was an olive grove, and he and his disciples went into it.* In the Synoptic Gospels this olive grove is identified as 'a place called Gethsemane' (Mt. 26:36; Mk. 14:32). The evangelist adds, *Now Judas, who betrayed him, knew the place, because Jesus had often met there with his disciples.* It is only in the Fourth Gospel we learn that Jesus and his disciples frequented this place, and therefore Judas knew where to find him.

3. Having described the time and setting, the evangelist begins his description of the arrest: *So Judas came to the grove, guiding a detachment of soldiers* (speiran) *and some officials* (hypēretas) *from the chief priests and Pharisees.* The NT, including the Fourth Gospel, always uses *speira* for Roman soldiers, and *hypēretēs* is used mostly for Jewish temple officials. So the chief priests and Pharisees to whom Judas had betrayed Jesus not only sent temple officials to arrest him but asked Pilate for a detachment of Roman soldiers as well.[1] *They were carrying torches, lanterns and weapons.* The torches and lanterns were needed because it was night (13:30), though being Passover time the full moon might have been visible. Weapons were normally carried by Roman soldiers and needed in this case to deal with possible resistance on the part of Jesus or his followers.

4-5. Then the evangelist says, *Jesus, knowing all that was going to happen to him, went out and asked them, 'Who is it you want?'* Here we see Jesus taking the initiative. He was no victim of circumstance. His arrest and subsequent death did not take him by surprise. In fact, he insisted that he would lay down his life of his own accord, and that no-one would take it from him (10:17-18).

To be arrested was a matter of shame, but by taking the initiative himself Jesus showed that he was not accepting the shame. He stepped forward and asked, 'Who is it you want'? *'Jesus of Nazareth,' they replied. 'I am he,' Jesus said.* The words translated 'Jesus of Nazareth', literally rendered would be 'Jesus the Nazarene', which is the way he is also described in 18:7; 19:19. A Nazarene is someone from Nazareth (Mt. 2:23), so either rendering is acceptable.

When the soldiers and temple officials said who they were looking for, Jesus replied, 'I am he' (*egō eimi*). This is one of the many uses of *egō eimi* in the Fourth Gospel, construed here by the NIV as having an implied predicate: 'I am [he]', by which Jesus simply identifies himself. In parenthesis the evangelist notes that as this took place, *Judas the traitor was standing there with them.* The evangelist does not include the details of Judas' betrayal of Jesus, either the arrangements made with the chief priests and Pharisees beforehand (Mt. 26:14-16; Mk. 14:10-11; Lk. 22:3-6) or the kiss with which he identified Jesus for the arresting party (Mt. 26:48-49; Mk. 14:44-45; Lk. 22:47-48).

6. The response to Jesus' self-identification was dramatic: *When Jesus said, 'I am he,' they drew back and fell to the ground.* In the light

---

[1] *Speira* normally denoted a cohort consisting of 480 soldiers, but here it is probably used less precisely to denote a smaller group of soldiers provided at the request of the Jewish leaders in case their temple officials encountered resistance when seeking to arrest Jesus.

of this remarkable reaction, it is possible that Jesus' use of *egō eimi*, as well as being a means of self-identification ('I am he') involved the application of the divine name to himself – a claim to be one with God (see Additional Note: *Egō eimi*, p. 138). Whether or not the Roman soldiers and temple officials understood Jesus' words in this way, it is clear some revelation of his power and authority must have occurred to make them draw back and fall to the ground.

7–9. Jesus took the initiative: *Again he asked them, 'Who is it you want?'* Once more they answered, *Jesus of Nazareth*. Once more Jesus identified himself, *I told you that I am he* (*egō eimi*). His authority in this situation was revealed again when he gave orders to the arresting party: *If you are looking for me, then let these men go*. Jesus did not accept the shame of arrest – having his personal liberty curtailed by others. On the contrary, he remained in control. His command to the Roman soldiers and the temple officials with their torches and weapons was, 'let these men go'. He was referring to the disciples. The evangelist adds, *This happened so that the words he had spoken would be fulfilled: 'I have not lost one of those you gave me.'* In his prayer to the Father for his disciples Jesus said, 'While I was with them, I protected them and kept them safe by that name you gave me. None has been lost except the one doomed to destruction so that Scripture would be fulfilled' (17:12; *cf.* 6:39). The evangelist sees a fulfilment of these words in Jesus' action to prevent the arrest of his disciples.

10–11. Seeing Jesus about to be arrested, *Simon Peter, who had a sword, drew it and struck the high priest's servant, cutting off his right ear. (The servant's name was Malchus.)* In Luke 22:35–38 we learn that at the Last Supper the disciples had two swords among them, and now the evangelist tells us that Peter stepped forward with one of them to defend his master's honour against the shame of arrest. *Jesus commanded Peter, 'Put your sword away!'* Jesus was not to be shamed by the impending arrest. He had already shown he was in control of the situation. He asked Peter, *Shall I not drink the cup the Father has given me?* This was an allusion to Jesus' prayer in Gethsemane in which he prayed first that if it were possible the cup of suffering might pass from him, but, above all, that the

Father's will might be done (Mt. 26:39; Mk. 14:36; Lk. 22:42). He did not need his disciples to fight to defend his honour (36), for he was determined now to 'drink the cup' of suffering.

The other three Gospels also record the fact that one of the disciples cut off the ear of the high priest's servant with a sword (Mt. 26:51; Mk. 14:47; Lk. 22:49–50), but only the Fourth Gospel names Simon Peter as the disciple who did so, and Luke alone records the fact that Jesus healed the man (Lk. 22:51).

2. *Jesus taken to Annas (18:12–14)*

12–14. Jesus' determination to drink the cup his Father gave him led him to reject the efforts of his disciples to defend him. *Then the detachment of soldiers with its commander and the Jewish officials arrested Jesus. They bound him and brought him first to Annas, who was the father-in-law of Caiaphas, the high priest that year.* 'Commander' translates *chiliarchos*, meaning 'tribune' or 'commander of a thousand', underlining the fact that Roman soldiers were involved, but certainly not their number. After delivering Jesus to Annas they would have returned to their barracks in the Antonia fortress.

Although Caiaphas was high priest that year, they took Jesus first to Caiaphas' father-in-law, Annas. He had been high priest from AD 5 to 15. He was succeeded over time by five sons and by his son-in-law, Caiaphas. While the Romans appointed and replaced the high priests, the Jewish people regarded high priesthood as a life office. While Caiaphas was high priest from AD 18 to 36, Luke, describing John the Baptist's ministry, which took place during Caiaphas' term of office, says it began 'during the high priesthood of Annas and Caiaphas' (Lk. 3:2). Annas continued to be regarded as high priest well after his official term of office and continued to function *de facto* as high priest and was regarded as such by many Jews.[1] The evangelist

---

[1] The Mishnah says, 'A High Priest in office differs from the priest that is passed [from his high priesthood] only in the bullock that is offered on the Day of Atonement and the Tenth of the Ephah. Both are equal in the [Temple-]service of the Day of Atonement; and both are subject to the commandment to marry only a virgin, and both are forbidden to marry a widow, and neither may contract uncleanness because of their near of kin [that have died]; neither may unbind their hair or rend their clothes [in token of mourning]; and both [when they die] serve to bring back the manslayer [from the cities of refuge]' (*Horayot* 3:4).

reminds his readers, *Caiaphas was the one who had advised the Jews that it would be good if one man died for the people*. This is a reference back to 11:47–53, where Caiaphas said to members of the Sanhedrin who were at a loss to know what to do about Jesus, 'You do not realize that it is better for you that one man die for the people than that the whole nation perish' (11:50).

3. Peter's first denial (18:15–18)

15–16a. Following Jesus' arrest, *Simon Peter and another disciple were following Jesus* as he was lead away to Annas the high priest. The other disciple is not identified, but in the only other passage where the evangelist refers to 'the other disciple' he is identified as 'the one Jesus loved' (20:1–8). The fact that the beloved disciple and Peter are frequently associated with one another supports this identification (13:23–24; 20:3–8; 21:20–22). *Because this disciple was known to the high priest, he went with Jesus into the high priest's courtyard, but Peter had to wait outside at the door*. The word 'known' (*gnōstos*) denotes not just acquaintance but personal knowledge and friendship (*cf.* Luke 2:44; 23:49). The 'other disciple' must have known the high priest well to gain immediate unchallenged access to the courtyard. It was to Annas' house (and not the temple) that Jesus was taken, and the 'courtyard' would be the atrium of his house. This is confirmed by the description of the doorkeeper as 'the girl on duty' (16), rather than a temple official.

If the other disciple was the beloved disciple, and if the beloved disciple is identified as John the son of Zebedee, how do we account for him, as a Galilean fisherman, being 'known' to the high priest? In Jewish society there was not the same division between manual labourers and others as there was in the Hellenistic world (rabbis were expected to have a trade – the apostle Paul was a leatherworker). Someone in the fishing industry could have friends among the chief priests. Also, it should be remembered that Zebedee was prosperous enough to employ hired hands alongside his sons in his fishing business (see Mk. 1:20), indicating that the family was reasonably well off.

16b–17. When the other disciple went into the courtyard, Peter was left standing outside, but then *the other disciple, who was* *known to the high priest, came back, spoke to the girl on duty there and brought Peter in*. This confirms the other disciple was well known in the household of the high priest. As he led Peter in, *the girl at the door asked Peter, 'You are not one of his disciples, are you?'* The girl's question is more accurately translated by the NRSV, 'You are not *also* one of this man's disciples, are you?' This implies she knew the other disciple was one of Jesus' disciples and now asked whether Peter was his disciple as well. It was not necessarily a hostile question. Nevertheless, Peter was thrown off balance. *He replied, 'I am not.'* Why Peter should deny any association with Jesus at this point is hard to explain. After all, it seems the other disciple was known to be a disciple and was admitted without any problem, and he was the one bringing Peter into the courtyard. Perhaps Peter felt guilty and vulnerable because he had attacked the high priest's servant with a sword (10). Peter's response was the first of his three denials (17, 25, 27) predicted by Jesus (13:38).

18. After his first denial, Peter was admitted to the courtyard. *It was cold, and the servants and officials stood round a fire they had made to keep warm. Peter also was standing with them, warming himself.* While daytime temperatures during Passover (spring time to March/April) were quite warm, the nights could be cold; hence Peter joined the servants and the officials warming themselves around the charcoal fire.

4. The high priest questions Jesus (18:19–24)

19. Peter and the other disciple remained in the courtyard. *Meanwhile, the high priest questioned Jesus about his disciples and his teaching.* When he was arrested, Jesus told his captors to let his disciples go, so they were not arrested along with Jesus. The high priest now questioned Jesus about his disciples and also his teaching.

20–21. Jesus did not answer the question about his disciples, but responded to Annas' question about his teaching with a bold riposte: *'I have spoken openly to the world,'* Jesus replied. *'I always taught in synagogues or at the temple, where all the Jews come together.*

354

I said nothing in secret. Why question me? Ask those who heard me. Surely they know what I said.' Jesus claimed to have acted in an honourable way, giving his teaching in the public arena openly and boldly. Jesus refused to be cowed by Annas' interrogation. He had nothing to hide. Annas could ask those who heard his public teaching if he wanted to know about it. In fact, this is what he should have done, because, in official proceedings at least, it was not the accused who was interrogated, but the witnesses for and against the accused. Jesus' response, then, appears to have been a rebuke to Annas, for which he had no answer.

22–23. Jesus' response to Annas' question was clearly understood as a rebuke: *When Jesus said this, one of the officials near by struck him in the face. 'Is this the way you answer the high priest?' he demanded.* This was a counter-challenge accompanied by a slap in the face intended to humiliate Jesus. But once again Jesus refused to be cowed, and challenged the action of the official: *'If I said something wrong,' Jesus replied, 'testify as to what is wrong. But if I spoke the truth, why did you strike me?'* The apostle Paul was later to be struck on the mouth by order of the high priest Ananias, and he responded in much stronger terms, 'God will strike you, you whitewashed wall! You sit there to judge me according to the law, yet you yourself violate the law by commanding that I be struck!' However, when challenged for insulting the high priest, Paul acknowledged that he was wrong in speaking evil of the ruler of the people (Acts 23:1–5). Jesus, for his part, did not insult the high priest, but he did challenge the illegality of both the action of his official in striking him and his interrogation of the accused instead of witnesses – there appear to have been no witnesses in this 'trial'. Jesus demanded an explanation for the actions taken against him.

24. Annas had no answer to Jesus' challenge to the legality of the treatment meted out to him, and therefore Jesus emerged as the winner in this episode of challenge and riposte – he had not been shamed by Annas or his officials. *Then Annas sent him, still bound, to Caiaphas the high priest.* This appears to be a tacit recognition that they had no case against him.

5. Peter's second and third denials (18:25–27)

25. The evangelist switches scenes back to the courtyard: *As Simon Peter stood warming himself, he was asked, 'You are not one of his disciples, are you?' He denied it, saying, 'I am not.'* Peter, feeling more threatened, denied for a second time that he was one of Jesus' disciples.

26–27. The third and final challenge to Peter was the most threatening: *One of the high priest's servants, a relative of the man whose ear Peter had cut off, challenged him, 'Didn't I see you with him in the olive grove?'* The one who now challenged Peter was not only a member of the arresting party; he was also a relative of the man Peter attacked. *Again Peter denied it, and at that moment a cock began to crow.* In the Gospels of Matthew and Mark we are told when Peter uttered this third denial he swore that he did not know Jesus, invoking curses upon himself if this were not true (Mt. 26:74; Mk. 14:71). Despite protestations earlier in the evening that he was prepared to lay down his life for Jesus' sake (13:37), Peter's fear led him to deny him three times, and so fulfilled Jesus' prediction that before the cock crowed Peter would deny him three times (13:38). This was not the end of Peter's discipleship, for following the resurrection he was restored to fellowship with Jesus and recommissioned for service (21:15–17) – an encouragement to all subsequent disciples that their Lord is willing to forgive, restore and employ them in his service even after the most serious lapses.

6. Jesus' trial before Pilate (18:28 – 19:16a)

This long passage provides, first, the setting for Jesus' trial before Pilate (18:28), and then presents the actual trial in eight scenes in which Pilate repeatedly goes out to talk with 'the Jews' and comes back in to the Praetorium to speak with Jesus (18:29 – 19:16a).

28. In 18:24 we are told that Jesus was sent bound by Annas to Caiaphas. The evangelist provides no account of Jesus' trial before the high priest Caiaphas in the Sanhedrin recorded in the other Gospels (Mt. 26:57–68; Mk. 14:53–65; Lk. 22:54–55, 63–71). From the very earliest times this has been seen as problematic. In a few manuscripts verses 13–27 have been rearranged to overcome this problem.[1] However, such rearrangements are not supported by the best or the majority of manuscripts.

Omitting any description of the trial before Caiaphas, the evangelist says, *Then the Jews led Jesus from Caiaphas to the palace of the Roman governor*. The word translated 'palace' (*praitōrion*) is a Greek transliteration of the Latin (*praetorium*), which was the term used for a military headquarters, or in Pilate's case the residence of the military governor. Pilate normally resided in Caesarea Maritima, but during major Jewish festivals he would take up residence in Jerusalem. The actual location of the praetorium in Jerusalem is debated. It could have been either the Antonia fortress abutting the north-west corner of the temple complex, or what was previously Herod's palace on the western wall of Jerusalem (the ruins of which may be seen near the present-day Jaffa Gate).

By now it was early morning. 'Early morning' translates *prōi*, which denoted the fourth watch (3.00 a.m. to 6.00 a.m.) according to the Roman division of the night. If we interpret *prōi* strictly according to the Roman division it would mean that Jesus was brought to Pilate before 6.00 a.m. It was not unusual for Roman governors to begin their duties very early in the morning.

Bringing Jesus to Pilate's praetorium involved problems for 'the Jews': *to avoid ceremonial uncleanness the Jews did not enter the palace; they wanted to be able to eat the Passover*. To enter a Gentile house was believed to cause ritual uncleanness, which would prevent them eating Passover.[2] The Mishnah says, 'the dwelling places of gentiles are unclean', a footnote adding 'because they throw abortions down their drains' ('*Ohalot* 18:7). To enter a Gentile house, then, could mean contamination because of a dead body. Contamination of this sort rendered one unclean for seven days, and would prevent 'the Jews' participating in Passover that evening. For this reason they did not enter the palace/praetorium.

---

[1] *E.g.* the Old Sinaitic Syriac version arranges the verses in the following order: 13, 24, 14–15, 19–23, 16–18, 25b–27.

[2] For the implications of this statement for the question of whether Jesus ate Passover with his disciples and the apparent discrepancy between the Fourth Gospel and the Synoptics, see Marshall, *Last Supper*, pp. 57–75.

There is a terrible irony here. 'The Jews' were being scrupulously careful not to contract ritual uncleanness, while making themselves guilty of a far worse crime: seeking the death of an innocent man.

29–31. These verses form the first of the eight scenes of the trial: Pilate and 'the Jews'. Because 'the Jews' would not enter the palace, *Pilate came out to them.* He opened proceedings with the formal question *What charges are you bringing against this man?* The whole exchange between Pilate and 'the Jews' that followed took the form of challenge and riposte. Pilate's demand to know what charges they were bringing was met with a riposte from 'the Jews': *'If he were not a criminal,' they replied, 'we would not have handed him over to you.'* Apparently they expected Pilate to confirm their decision about Jesus (that he was a criminal) without their advancing any specific charges, and so they answered Pilate in this insolent way. Not accepting their insolent response, and challenging them instead, *Pilate said, 'Take him yourselves and judge him by your own law.'* In effect he was saying, you have decided in the light of your own law, without any need of my judgment, that he is a criminal, so judge and execute him yourselves. Pilate knew the Jews did not have the authority to do this, and so in this first exchange he prevailed, as 'the Jews' were forced to acknowledge, *we have no right to execute anyone.* The only exception to this rule was the authority given to 'the Jews' to execute Gentiles, even Roman soldiers, who ignored the prohibition excluding Gentiles from the Court of Women and the Court of Israel in the temple (see commentary on 2:14–16). Other instances of people being put to death by 'the Jews' appear to have been either a stoning in the case of Stephen, (Acts 7:54–60) or an execution during an interregnum (between rules of the procurators Festus and Albinus), in the case of James (Acts 12:1–4).

32. Commenting on the inability of 'the Jews' to carry out the death penalty, the evangelist says, *This happened so that the words Jesus had spoken indicating the kind of death he was going to die would be fulfilled.* If 'the Jews' carried out the execution, it would have been by stoning, but Jesus had already said he was to be 'lifted up', a reference to crucifixion (3:14; 8:28; 12:32–33). This would occur only if the death penalty were carried out by the Romans. It may be that 'the Jews' wanted Jesus crucified to show he was under the curse of God (Dt. 21:23).

33–38a. These verses form the second trial scene: Pilate and Jesus. *Pilate then went back inside the palace, summoned Jesus and asked him, 'Are you the king of the Jews?'* Up until this point in the narrative no formal charge has been mentioned. Pilate's question 'Are you the king of the Jews?' presumed that 'the Jews' had brought the charge of treason against Jesus, *i.e.* they represented him as a rival to Caesar. Jesus' response was to ask, *Is that your own idea or did others talk to you about me?* As Jesus was not intimidated by the arresting party (4–9) or by the high priest Annas (20–23), neither was he intimidated by Pilate. Jesus questioned the governor about the source of his information and therefore the nature of kingship he had in mind. Pilate's first reaction showed his disdain for the Jewish people: *'Am I a Jew?' Pilate replied.* Next he pointed out the shameful situation in which Jesus found himself, shunned by his own people: *It was your people and your chief priests who handed you over to me.* Finally, reflecting a judicial system that presumed guilt rather than innocence, he asked, *What is it you have done?*

Jesus rejected the shame Pilate heaped upon him and the assumption that he had done wrong, and replied, *My kingdom is not of this world. If it were, my servants would fight to prevent my arrest by the Jews. But now my kingdom is from another place.* Jesus continued to control the direction of the exchange by returning to the question of kingship and claiming that he did have a kingdom, but not one of this world. In 3:3, 5 Jesus spoke of the kingdom of God to Nicodemus but refused to be made a king by the crowds, following the feeding of the five thousand (6:15). Because his kingdom is not of this world, Jesus rejected the attempt by Peter to prevent his arrest (10–11). His kingdom is 'from another place' (lit. 'not from here'). His kingdom is given by God, not established by human struggle. His kingdom is active in this world, and will one day come with power, but its power is not of this world; it is of God.

Pilate played a reactive role as Jesus continued to determine the direction of their exchange. Seizing upon Jesus' reference to 'my kingdom', Pilate said, *You are a king, then!* If Jesus acknowledged he was a king, Pilate would have something substantial to deal with. Jesus responded directly this time: *You are right in saying I am a king. In fact, for this reason I was born, and for this I came into the world, to testify to the truth.* Here the NIV translation obscures the thrust of what Jesus said. Rendered literally it would read, *'You* say I am a king. *I* was born and came into the world for this, to bear witness to the truth.' Pilate wanted an acknowledgment from Jesus that he was a claimant to worldly kingship. Jesus refused to be pinned down in this way. Instead, he said he came as a witness to God's truth, a witness to the coming kingdom of God, and informed Pilate that *Everyone on the side of truth listens to me*. Thus he challenged Pilate to stop listening to the manufactured charges of his accusers and start listening to him. In this exchange of challenge and riposte Jesus emerged as victor and Pilate was reduced to confusion: *'What is truth?' Pilate asked.*

38b–40. These verses form the third trial scene: Pilate and 'the Jews'. Leaving Jesus in the praetorium, Pilate *went out again to the Jews and said, 'I find no basis for a charge against him.'* This should have been the end of the matter, but Pilate wanted both to release Jesus and to placate 'the Jews'. He reminded them, *But it is your custom for me to release to you one prisoner at the time of the Passover.* This is the only place we learn of such a custom; there are no extra-biblical references to it. Having come off second best in his preliminary interrogation of Jesus, Pilate was in no frame of mind to be bested by 'the Jews'. He planned to use the custom of freeing one prisoner at Passover to release Jesus, and chose to needle 'the Jews' by asking, *Do you want me to release 'the king of the Jews'?* The reference to Jesus as 'the king of the Jews' would make them angry. Pilate's plan to use the custom to release Jesus backfired, for *they shouted back, 'No, not him! Give us Barabbas!'* The evangelist explains, *Now Barabbas had taken part in a rebellion.* In Matthew 27:16 Barabbas is described as a 'notorious prisoner' and in Mark 15:7 as one who 'was in prison with the insurrectionists who had committed murder in the uprising'. Pilate probably thought the crowd would choose Jesus over Barabbas, and so he could release Jesus and be finished with the matter. But as Matthew 27:20/Mark

15:11 points out, the chief priests and the elders incited the crowd to ask for Barabbas, not Jesus. This is ironic, for the chief priests and elders had no sympathy for insurrectionists, because they jeopardized the *status quo* with the Romans; yet still they asked for Barabbas instead of Jesus. Having come off second best in this episode of challenge and riposte with 'the Jews', Pilate was left with the problem of Jesus.

19:1-3. These verses form the fourth trial scene: Pilate has Jesus scourged. *Then Pilate took Jesus and had him flogged.* Flogging was a way of heaping shame upon a person. Flogging by the Romans took one of three forms: *fustes* (a light beating administered as a warning), *flagella* and *verbera* (severe beatings associated with other punishments, *e.g.* crucifixion). It is difficult to know to which sort of beating the evangelist refers here. It is possible that Pilate ordered a lighter beating (*fustes*) as a warning, hoping it would be enough to satisfy 'the Jews', and then he would release him. Luke indicates that this was Pilate's intention at least at one stage when he has him say to 'the Jews' that he will punish Jesus and then release him (Lk. 23:16, 22). However, references in Mt. 27:26/Mk. 15:15 which say that Pilate had Jesus flogged and handed over to be crucified suggest that Jesus may (also) have been subjected to the severe beating (*verbera*) associated with crucifixion.

Pilate had taunted 'the Jews' by referring to Jesus as 'the king of the Jews' (18:39), and taking their cue from this, *The soldiers twisted together a crown of thorns and put it on his head. They clothed him in a purple robe and went up to him again and again, saying, 'Hail, king of the Jews!' And they struck him in the face.* In these ways they sought to humiliate Jesus and ridicule his claims to have a kingdom. Striking people in the face was another way of shaming them.

4-7. These verses form the fifth trial scene: Pilate and 'the Jews'. *Once more Pilate came out and said to the Jews, 'Look, I am bringing him out to you to let you know that I find no basis for a charge against him.'* Pilate brought Jesus out to the crowd, and publicly declared that he found no basis for a charge against him. *Jesus came out wearing the crown of thorns and the purple robe.* Jesus was still wearing the crown of thorns and the purple robe the soldiers had put on him to mock him after they had flogged him. He would have been a sorry sight. As he stood there before the crowd, *Pilate said to them, 'Here is the man!'* (Lat. *Ecce homo!*). It may be that Pilate thought the crowd, having seen that Jesus had been flogged and humiliated, would be satisfied, and then he could release him. However, this was not to be. *As soon as the chief priests and their officials saw him, they shouted, 'Crucify! Crucify!'* It appears that Pilate was frustrated, but he was not ready to be dictated to by the chief priests and their officials. *Pilate answered, 'You take him and crucify him. As for me, I find no basis for a charge against him.'* Once again Pilate publicly declared Jesus' innocence and taunted 'the Jews', telling them to crucify him, knowing of course that they could not do so (*cf.* 18:31). For the moment the Jews had failed in their attempt to have Jesus condemned according to the laws by which the governor worked, so *the Jews insisted, 'We have a law, and according to that law he must die, because he claimed to be the Son of God.'* This appears to be an echo of the trial before Caiaphas (assumed but not described in this Gospel) in which Jesus was accused of blasphemy (Mk. 14:61–64). From the Jewish point of view, Jesus' claim to be the Son of God was tantamount to a claim to be God, which they regarded as blasphemy, and therefore rendered him liable to death by stoning (see commentary on 10:33). Pilate was under no obligation to implement Jewish law, but that Jesus claimed to be the Son of God caused him to reconsider his position.

8–11. These verses form the sixth trial scene: Pilate and Jesus. *When Pilate heard this, he was even more afraid, and he went back inside the palace.* The evangelist implies that Pilate was fearful in his dealings with Jesus, and hearing that he claimed to be the Son of God he became 'even more afraid', wondering perhaps whether the gods had come down to earth in this man whom he had just had flogged (*cf.* Acts 14:11). Pilate took Jesus with him back into the praetorium. *'Where do you come from?' he asked Jesus.* In the first century a person's identity and honour were closely related to his/her place of origin (as well as family ties). For example, the apostle Paul said of himself, 'I am a Jew, from Tarsus in Cilicia, a citizen of no ordinary city' (Acts 21:39). In seeking to understand Jesus, then, Pilate asked, 'Where do you come from?', wondering perhaps whether he was from heaven, seeing that he claimed to be the Son of God. Readers of the Fourth Gospel know Jesus came down from heaven (see 3:13, 31; 6:33, 38, 41–42, 50–51). To Pilate's consternation, *Jesus gave him no answer*. Normally, to fail to answer a challenge about one's origins was to accept shame, but this does not seem to have been the case with Jesus, for throughout his exchanges with Pilate he called the tune. Perhaps Jesus, having borne his witness to Pilate only to have it set aside (18:33–38) and then be handed over to be flogged (1), refused to accommodate him further. Pilate interpreted Jesus' silence as a challenge to his authority. *'Do you refuse to speak to me?' Pilate said. 'Don't you realize I have power either to free you or to crucify you?'* Pilate reminded Jesus of the powers invested in him by his appointment as procurator of Judea, powers of life and death over provincials like him. *Jesus answered, 'You would have no power over me if it were not given to you from above.'* Pilate believed his power originated from the Roman emperor. Humanly speaking, this was true, but Jesus told Pilate that all power comes 'from above', from God. He raises up kings and emperors and deposes them as he wills (*cf.* Dn. 2:20–21; 4:25, 32). Therefore, Pilate had no power over Jesus, except that given him by God. Jesus recognized that Pilate was carrying out a God-given responsibility (even though he was not doing so with justice and courage), and said to him, *Therefore the one who handed me over to you is guilty of a greater sin*. It was Caiaphas who handed Jesus over to Pilate (18:28–30) and Jesus said his culpability was greater than Pilate's. It is true that Pilate did not administer justice without fear or favour when Jesus was handed over, but Caiaphas was chief among those responsible for vigorously seeking the death of an innocent man.

12. This verse forms the seventh trial scene: Pilate and 'the Jews'. Hearing Jesus place the greater blame upon 'the Jews' and not on him, *From then on* (lit. 'from this' or 'because of this', referring to what Jesus said about the greater sin), *Pilate tried to set Jesus free, but the Jews kept shouting, 'If you let this man go, you are no friend of Caesar.'* This is the second time Pilate sought to release Jesus (*cf.* 18:38b–40) but once again he was vehemently opposed by 'the Jews'. They shouted that if he released Jesus he would be no 'friend of Caesar'. This title could reflect a political client–patron relationship between Pilate and Tiberius Caesar (*amicus Caesaris*). Pilate's appointment as procurator of Judea was probably a benefice received from Tiberius and he would be required always to act with the honour of his benefactor in mind and deal with any threats to his position. 'The Jews' had brought to Pilate one they claimed was presenting himself as a king, and they reminded Pilate that *Anyone who claims to be a king opposes Caesar*. If Pilate failed to act against one the Jewish hierarchy believed was a threat to the emperor, the suspicions of the paranoid Tiberius could easily be aroused, and Pilate would suffer for it.

13–16a. These verses form the eighth and final scene of the trial: Pilate brings Jesus out and hands him over to be crucified. When 'the Jews' told Pilate that if he released Jesus he was no 'friend of Caesar', they were playing their trump card. There was probably an implied threat: if you release him we will make sure Caesar finds out. *When Pilate heard this, he brought Jesus out and sat down on the judge's seat at a place known as the Stone Pavement (which in Aramaic is Gabbatha).* Taking his place on the judge's seat (*bēma*) signalled he was about to give judgment in the case. The judge's seat was set up on a stone pavement (*lithostrotōs*) outside the praetorium, which in Aramaic was called 'Gabbatha'. The evangelist does not say 'Gabbatha' is a translation of *lithostrotos*, but simply that this was what the pavement was called in Aramaic. Many suggestions have been made concerning the meaning of 'Gabbatha' (*e.g.* 'elevated place') but we do not know for sure what it meant.

The evangelist notes that *It was the day of Preparation of Passover Week, about the sixth hour* when Pilate brought Jesus out and took his place on the judgment seat. Preparation day was not the day of preparation for Passover but for the sabbath, which followed Passover (*cf.* Mt. 27:62; Mk. 15:42; Lk. 23:54). It was a special sabbath because it fell in Passover week. *'Here is your king,' Pilate said to the Jews.* Pilate was seeking to shame 'the Jews' by presenting Jesus as their king for the second time (*cf.* 18:39). *But they shouted, 'Take him away! Take him away! Crucify him!'* Jesus suffered the shame of public rejection by his own people as they engaged in challenge and riposte with Pilate. *'Shall I crucify your king?' Pilate asked,* presenting Jesus to 'the Jews' as their king (*cf.* 18:39;

19:14). To their everlasting shame *the chief priests answered, 'We have no king but Caesar.'* In the OT the Lord is the true king of Israel:

> O LORD, our God, other lords besides you have ruled
>> over us,
> but your name alone do we honour. (Is. 26:13)

Jewish people concluded the great Hallel (the recital of Pss. 113 – 118) with the prayer 'From everlasting to everlasting thou art God; beside thee we have no king, redeemer, or saviour; no liberator, deliverer, provider; none who takes pity in every time of distress or trouble. We have no king but thee.' When God gave the Israelites the kings they wanted, they were seen as exercising kingship in the name of the Lord (see 1 Ch. 29:23). For the chief priests to say 'We have no king but Caesar' was both a travesty of the Jewish faith as well as a renunciation of Jesus, their true Messiah. Indeed, 'He came to that which was his own, but his own did not receive him' (1:11).

In the face of the intransigence of the chief priests, *Finally Pilate handed him over to them to be crucified*. Pilate was not handing Jesus over to the chief priests to carry out the crucifixion. That was done by Roman soldiers (23–24). He was handing him over to the chief priests in the sense that he was yielding to their pressure to have Jesus crucified. As Luke 23:24 has it, 'Pilate decided to grant their demand.'

7. Jesus is crucified (19:16b–22)

16b–18. After Pilate handed him over to 'them' *the soldiers took charge of Jesus*. Four Roman soldiers were commissioned to carry out the crucifixion (23). *Carrying his own cross, he went out to the place of the Skull (which in Aramaic is called Golgotha)*. Condemned criminals carried the cross beam to the place of crucifixion. Jesus carried his cross at least as far as the gate of the city, where, according to the Synoptic Gospels, Simon from Cyrene, who was coming into the city at the time, was forced to carry it for him (Mt. 27:32/Mk. 15:21/Lk. 23:26). This gave rise to the tradition that Jesus fell under the weight of the cross because of weakness and loss of blood brought about by the flogging he had received. The execution party made its way towards 'the place of the Skull'

(Gk. *kranion*, the Aramaic equivalent being *gulgoltâ*, *i.e.* Golgotha). The site of Golgotha today is to be found in the Church of the Holy Sepulchre. Gordon's Calvary[1] near the bus station is not the site, though its appearance may be more like the first-century site of the crucifixion in appearance than what can be seen in the Church of the Holy Sepulchre today.[2] *Here they crucified him, and with him two others – one on each side and Jesus in the middle.* Because his primary focus is upon Jesus, the evangelist says nothing more about the other two. The Synoptic Gospels describe them as robbers/criminals (Mt. 27:38/Mk. 15:27/Lk. 23:32), being justly executed for their crimes (Lk. 23:39–41).

19–20. In a gesture that was to antagonize the chief priests, *Pilate had a notice prepared and fastened to the cross. It read:* JESUS OF NAZARETH, THE KING OF THE JEWS. Pilate felt forced, under the implied threat from the chief priests of reporting him to Caesar, to condemn a man he believed was innocent of any capital offence. Now, it seems, he attached this notice to the cross of the condemned man to aggravate the chief priests. Two factors ensured the aggravation. First, *Many of the Jews read this sign, for the place where Jesus was crucified was near the city.* Jesus was crucified just outside the city of Jerusalem in a place where people would pass by and read the notice. (Although the site of Golgotha, within the Church of the Holy Sepulchre, is inside the walls of Jerusalem today, it was outside the walls of first-century Jerusalem.) Second, *the sign was written in Aramaic, Latin and Greek*, and could therefore be read by all – by Judean Jews, Romans, Jews of the Diaspora and Gentile God-fearers and proselytes.

21–22. Pilate aggravated the chief priests by describing Jesus as 'the King of the Jews'. Their response was not long coming. *The chief priests of the Jews protested to Pilate, 'Do not write "The King of the Jews", but that this man claimed to be king of the Jews.'* The chief priests had rejected Jesus as their king, declaring, 'We have no king but Caesar' (15), but Pilate was declaring this crucified person to be their king. Having been forced to back down and

---

[1]'Calvary' derives from the Latin *calvaria*, which translates Golgotha in the Vulgate.
[2]See Murphy-O'Connor, pp. 36–42, 104–106.

hand Jesus over for crucifixion under the implied threat from the chief priests that they would report him to Caesar (see commentary on 19:13–16a), Pilate was in no mood to listen to their protest. *Pilate answered, 'What I have written, I have written.'* He was determined to let the affront stand.

8. The soldiers divide Jesus' garments (19:23–24)

23–24. Following the ancient custom that allowed executioners to take the garments of the condemned person as a perquisite, *When the soldiers crucified Jesus, they took his clothes, dividing them into four shares, one for each of them, with the undergarment remaining.* Jesus' outer garment was apparently torn along the seams and the cloth divided among the four soldiers. However, they did not tear the undergarment (*chitōn* – a long tunic worn next to the skin) because *This garment was seamless, woven in one piece from top to bottom.*[1] Seeing the garment was seamless, the soldiers said to one another, *Let's not tear it. Let's decide by lot who will get it.* This was a pragmatic action on the part of the soldiers, but the evangelist believed that *This happened that the scripture might be fulfilled which said,*

> 'They divided my garments among them
> and cast lots for my clothing.'

The quotation is from Psalm 22:18 (from which Jesus' cry of dereliction was also drawn; *cf.* Mt. 27:46; Mk. 15:34). The evangelist includes it here to show that Jesus' passion and death occurred in accordance with the will of God, something he does repeatedly in this Gospel (2:19–22; 13:18; 19:24, 28, 36, 37). *So this is what the soldiers did.* That Jesus' clothing was appropriated by the soldiers meant he was left naked, which underlines the extent of humiliation heaped upon him when he was crucified.

9. Jesus makes provision for his mother (19:25–27)

25. All of the Gospels make mention of the women who stood around the cross of Jesus (25–27; *cf.* Mt. 27:55–56; Mk. 15:40–41;

---

[1] Some have seen in this an allusion to the unity of the Christian community for which Jesus prayed in ch. 17, but this is unlikely to have been in the evangelist's mind when he recorded this event.

Lk. 23:49), but only the Fourth Gospel makes specific mention of the mother of Jesus: *Near the cross of Jesus stood his mother, his mother's sister, Mary the wife of Clopas, and Mary Magdalene.* The NIV editors have added the words 'the wife' in the phrase 'Mary the wife of Clopas'. Literally rendered it would read simply, 'Mary of Clopas', which could mean that Mary was either the wife or daughter of Clopas. The list of women is then susceptible to three interpretations involving two, three or four women: (1) *two women*, *i.e.* Jesus' mother (daughter of Clopas) and her sister (Mary Magdalene) – unlikely because the two sisters would have the same name (Mary); (2) *three women*, *i.e.* Jesus' mother, his mother's sister (Mary of Clopas), and Mary Magdalene – again unlikely because the two sisters would have the same name; or the most likely (3) *four women*, comprising two pairs, one unnamed pair (Jesus' mother and her sister) and a named pair (Mary of Clopas and Mary Magdalene). Mary the wife of Clopas appears only here in the NT. Mary Magdalene features prominently in all Gospels, not only at the foot of the cross, but also in the resurrection stories (20:1, 18; *cf.* Mt. 28:1; Mk. 16:1, 9; Lk. 24:10), and is described as the one from whom Jesus drove out seven demons (Mk. 16:9; Lk. 8:2).

26–27. What follows is remarkable. Though experiencing the agonies of crucifixion, *When Jesus saw his mother there, and the disciple whom he loved standing near by, he said to his mother, 'Dear woman, here is your son,' and to the disciple, 'Here is your mother.'* The mother of Jesus appears only twice in the Fourth Gospel: in 2:1–11 at the wedding in Cana and here in 19:25–27 at the foot of the cross. At Cana she demonstrated exemplary faith in Jesus, telling the servants to do whatever he told them. Here we see Jesus, in extremity, acting as an exemplary son, making provision for his mother by entrusting her to the care of the disciple whom he loved. His mother was henceforth to regard this disciple as her son, and the disciple was to regard her as his mother, thus taking over the responsibility that had belonged to Jesus during his lifetime. The reason why he entrusted her to the beloved disciple instead of one of his own brothers was probably because at that time they did not believe in him as his mother did (7:2–5) and were not present at the crucifixion. The beloved disciple proved to be an exemplary disciple: *From that time on, this disciple took her into his home*. Tradition has it that the beloved disciple, identified as the apostle John, came to live in Ephesus, and accordingly the traditional sites of the tombs of Mary and John are both in Ephesus.

Some see in Jesus' words to the beloved disciple 'Here is your mother' the elevation of Mary as the mother of all disciples, but this goes well beyond the intention of the evangelist, and ignores the significance of the evangelist's final words, 'From that time on, this disciple took her into his home,' which suggest that Jesus' mother was placed in the disciple's care and not *vice versa*.

10. The death of Jesus (19:28–30)

28. Jesus had taken care of his mother, and *Later, knowing that all was now completed, and so that the Scripture would be fulfilled, Jesus said, 'I am thirsty.'* As he hung now upon the cross Jesus knew that he had completed the works God had sent him into the world to do (*cf.* 4:34; 5:36; 17:4).

The evangelist saw in Jesus' words 'I am thirsty' a fulfilment of something foreshadowed in Scripture. The allusion may be to Psalm 22:15, where the sufferer says:

> My strength is dried up like a potsherd,
> and my tongue sticks to the roof of my mouth.

The evangelist cited this psalm earlier in relation to the dividing of Jesus' clothes among the Roman soldiers (23–24). By drawing attention to the way Scripture was being fulfilled in what took place during Jesus' crucifixion, the evangelist shows again that all was being accomplished in accordance with the divine plan.

29–30. The evangelist describes the response to Jesus' thirst: *A jar of wine vinegar was there, so they soaked a sponge in it, put the sponge on a stalk of the hyssop plant, and lifted it to Jesus' lips*. There may be an allusion here to Psalm 69:21:

> They put gall in my food
> and gave me vinegar for my thirst.

Wine vinegar was cheap wine for the soldiers, and was probably diluted with water. Most likely it was one of the soldiers who offered Jesus the wine vinegar, an unusually kind gesture suggesting that this soldier might have been the one who later confessed Jesus as the Son of God (Mk. 15:39). The wine vinegar was offered to Jesus in a sponge placed on (a stalk of) hyssop (*hyssōpō*). Roman crosses were not tall and the stalk of hyssop, which was weak, would not need to be very long to accomplish the task. Only the Fourth Gospel identifies hyssop; the other Gospels simply refer to a stick (*kalamos*).[1] There may be here an allusion to the hyssop used to daub the lintels and doorposts with blood to protect the Israelites when the angel of death 'passed over' at the time of the Exodus, thus connecting Jesus' death with the death of the Passover lamb.

While Jesus refused the wine mixed with myrrh (which would have deadened somewhat the pain of crucifixion) offered to him on the way to the cross (Mt. 27:34/Mk. 15:23), he accepted the wine vinegar offered now. *When he had received the drink, Jesus said, 'It is finished.'* Earlier, when Jesus knew his work had been completed, he said, 'I am thirsty' (28). Now he said, 'It is finished.' To understand the significance of these words we need to remember that in Matthew and Mark the offer of wine vinegar followed Jesus' cry of dereliction, 'My God, my God, why have you forsaken me?' (Mt. 27:46–49; Mk. 15:33–37), which signalled the fact that he was bearing in his own person the awful consequences of human sin. When, in the Fourth Gospel, having received the drink, Jesus said, 'It is finished,' he was referring, not only to the work of revelation through word and sign, but also to the great work of redemption. *With that, he bowed his head and gave up his spirit.* In 10:18 Jesus insisted that no-one would take his life from him and that he would lay it down of his own accord, and here he did just that – bowing his head, he gave up his spirit. He had finished the work he came to do. He had given his flesh for the life of the world (6:51), as the good shepherd he had laid down his life for the sheep (10:11, 14), he became the one man who died for the nation (11:50), he was the seed that had fallen into the ground, and

[1] The suggestion that *hyssōpō* ('on hyssop') should be replaced with *hyssō* ('on a javelin'), though attractive, is supported only by one eleventh-century manuscript (476). It is rendered less likely by the evangelist's use of *lonchē*, not *hyssos*, for 'javelin' or 'spear' at 19:34.

would now produce many seeds (12:24), and he had shown the love greater than any other – he had laid down his life for his friends (15:13).

11. Jesus' side is pierced (19:31–37)

31. What follows Jesus' death is understandable, but deeply ironic. The evangelist first explains, *Now it was the day of Preparation, and the next day was to be a special Sabbath.* Preparation day, as already mentioned, was not the day of preparation for the Passover meal but for the ensuing sabbath (*cf.* Mt. 27:62; Mk. 15:42; Lk. 23:54). It was a special sabbath because it fell in Passover week. The evangelist adds, *Because the Jews did not want the bodies left on the crosses during the Sabbath, they asked Pilate to have the legs broken and the bodies taken down.* According to Deuteronomy 21:22–23, to leave the dead body of an executed man hanging on a tree over-night desecrated the land. 'The Jews' wanted to have the bodies of Jesus and those crucified with him removed before sunset, which would usher in the sabbath. Breaking the legs of those crucified hastened death by preventing the victims supporting themselves with their legs; the arms alone cannot take the weight for long and the victims soon die of asphyxiation. The irony was that 'the Jews', rightly seeking to ensure no desecration of the land, were at the same time desecrating themselves by pursuing to death an inno-cent man, their true Messiah.

32–34. With orders from Pilate, *The soldiers therefore came and broke the legs of the first man who had been crucified with Jesus, and then those of the other. But when they came to Jesus and found that he was already dead, they did not break his legs.* Jesus had already given up his spirit (30), so when the soldiers came to break his legs they found him dead. Instead of breaking his legs, *one of the soldiers pierced Jesus' side with a spear.* Presumably, the spear thrust was to ensure that Jesus was dead, but the spear penetrated quite a way, *bringing a sudden flow of blood and water.* Medical experts have sug-gested a couple of explanations for this phenomenon. One is that the spear penetrated Jesus' heart and the flow was made up of fluid (like water) from the pericardial sac and blood from the heart itself. Another explanation is that severe injury to the chest can result in haemorrhagic fluid gathering between the rib cage and the lung. This can separate into clear serum and red fluid, both of which flow out when the chest cavity is pierced.[1]

35. No matter how we understand the physical explanation for the flow of blood and water, the phenomenon itself was regarded as very important: *The man who saw it has given testimony, and his testimony is true. He knows that he tells the truth, and he testifies so that you also may believe.* Here we encounter either a claim to be a truthful witness on the part of the one testifying, or an editorial comment supporting the veracity of the testimony of the one who witnessed this event. His testimony is intended, like the whole of the Gospel (20:31), to engender faith on the part of the reader. It would appear the flow of blood and water was seen as evidence for the reality of Jesus' death, something that was soon to be questioned (*cf.* 1 Jn. 5:6–8).[2]

Some regard the reference to the blood and water flowing from Jesus' side as an allusion to the sacraments of the Lord's Supper (blood) and baptism (water). While it is easy to see how later Christians might make such a connection, it is more likely that the evangelist mentions the blood and water to emphasize the reality of Jesus' death at a time when this was being questioned.

36–37. Reflecting upon the significance of Jesus' legs not being broken but his side being pierced with a spear instead, the evangelist says, *These things happened so that the scripture would be fulfilled: 'Not one of his bones will be broken,' and, as another scripture says, 'They will look on the one they have pierced.'* The first quotation is from Psalm 34:20, with possible allusions to the Passover lamb, whose bones were not to be broken (Ex. 12:46; Nu. 9:12). The second quotation is from Zechariah 12:10, and drawn from a passage that speaks of the mourning of Israel preceding their restoration. The evangelist probably had in mind the last day, when the tribes of the earth will look on the one who was pierced and lament (Rev. 1:7). For the evangelist, the fact that Jesus' sufferings were foreshadowed in the Scriptures shows that all this took place

[1]Carson, p. 623, provides details and documentation.
[2]See commentary on 1 Jn. 5:6–8 in Kruse, pp. 174–180.

in accordance with the divine plan; it was not simply a terrible miscarriage of justice.

12. The burial of Jesus (19:38–42)

38. According to Roman custom, the bodies of executed criminals were not buried, but left to be devoured by vultures. The Mishnah indicates that it was Jewish custom to bury criminals' bodies in common graves provided by the Sanhedrin (*Sanhedrin* 6:5). Neither was to be the fate of Jesus' body. *Later, Joseph of Arimathea asked Pilate for the body of Jesus. Now Joseph was a disciple of Jesus, but secretly because he feared the Jews. With Pilate's permission, he came and took the body away.* Joseph of Arimathea is described elsewhere as 'a rich man' (Mt. 27:57), 'a prominent member of the Council' [Sanhedrin] and one who was 'waiting for the kingdom of God' (Mk. 15:43). Only the Fourth Gospel says he was a secret disciple of Jesus, one of those many leaders who believed in Jesus but were afraid to confess him openly lest they be put out of the synagogue (12:42). But that was about to change. When he went to Pilate and asked for the body of Jesus to give it an honourable burial, this would certainly become known to the other members of the Sanhedrin, and he would then bear the reproach of being a disciple of Jesus. We cannot be sure why Pilate granted his request. Perhaps it was because Joseph was a prominent member of the Sanhedrin; perhaps because Pilate still felt that Jesus did not deserve to die as a criminal, and therefore his body deserved better treatment than that of a criminal.

39. Only the Fourth Gospel says that Joseph had assistance: *He was accompanied by Nicodemus, the man who earlier had visited Jesus at night. Nicodemus brought a mixture of myrrh and aloes, about seventy-five pounds.* Nicodemus was also one of those members of the Sanhedrin (3:1; 12:42) who was a secret disciple. He had come to Jesus at first by night (3:1–15), and then courageously raised a point of law in Jesus' favour in the Sanhedrin (7:50–51). Now, with Joseph, he was making his discipleship public, as together they ensured Jesus' body received an honourable burial. As the Fourth Gospel unfolds, therefore, we see Nicodemus, an influential teacher of Israel, moving gradually but surely from inquiry through tentative support to public confession of faith in Jesus. He functions as another example of the sort of belief that the evangelist hoped his Gospel would evoke in readers.

Nicodemus brought with him a large amount of spices, 'a mixture of myrrh and aloes'. In the OT, myrrh was used as a perfume (Ps. 45:8; Song 3:6; 4:6, 14; 5:1, 5, 13) and as one of the ingredients in the anointing oil produced by the perfumer for use in the tabernacle (Ex. 30:23). Its only other mention in the NT is for one of the gifts brought to the Christ child by the Magi (Mt. 2:11). While there is no evidence in the Bible for the use of myrrh as a burial perfume, there is in extra-biblical sources (*e.g.* Herodotus, *History* ii.86). Aloes is mentioned only here in the NT. In the OT, like myrrh, it was used as a perfume (Ps. 45:8; Pr. 7:17; Song 4:14), but there is no mention of its use for burials. Seventy-five pounds of myrrh and aloes is a very large amount, sufficient for a royal burial.

40–42. *Taking Jesus' body, the two of them wrapped it, with the spices, in strips of linen.* Joseph and Nicodemus wrapped Jesus' body with strips of linen, applying the mixture of spices as they did so. The evangelist explains, for the benefit of non-Jewish readers, *This was in accordance with Jewish burial customs.* Then he adds, *At the place where Jesus was crucified, there was a garden, and in the garden a new tomb, in which no-one had ever been laid.* The mention of a 'new tomb' heightens the sense of the honour being paid to Jesus' body, as did the large amount of spices used. All this served to counteract the humiliation involved in his crucifixion.

The reason for the use of this tomb was quite pragmatic: *Because it was the Jewish day of Preparation and since the tomb was near by, they laid Jesus there.* It was necessary to get Jesus' body into the tomb hastily because evening would usher in the sabbath. Hence a nearby tomb was used. Matthew 27:60 explains that it was Joseph's own new tomb into which Jesus' body was placed.

F. THE RESURRECTION NARRATIVE (20:1–31)

1. The morning of the first day of the week (20:1–18)

1–3. Jesus' body was placed in the tomb on the evening of the day of preparation for the sabbath, and it remained there during the sabbath; and then, *Early on the first day of the week, while it was still dark, Mary Magdalene went to the tomb and saw that the stone had been removed from the entrance.* The Fourth Gospel says nothing about a stone being placed across the entrance of the tomb, though the mention of its removal here presupposes that. The passive form of the clause 'the stone had been removed' suggests divine intervention. Seeing the stone removed (and the tomb empty), Mary Magdalene was distraught: *She came running to Simon Peter and the other disciple, the one Jesus loved, and said, 'They have taken the Lord out of the tomb, and we don't know where they have put him!'* There are earlier references to 'the other disciple' (18:15, 16), but only here he is identified as 'the one Jesus loved' (*cf.* 13:23; 19:26; 21:7, 20), who, as already mentioned, is traditionally identified with the apostle John. Finding these two disciples, Mary Magdalene expressed her distress: 'we don't know where they have put him'. The first-person plural 'we' suggests Mary Magdalene was not alone in her early morning visit to the tomb, though her companions are not mentioned (*cf.* Mt. 28:1; Mk. 16:1; Lk. 24:1). Seeing the tomb empty, she assumed 'they' (probably Jesus' enemies) had taken his body. Stealing bodies from tombs was a serious offence. An inscription found at Nazareth records a decree by the emperor Claudius making it a capital offence. Hearing Mary Magdalene's report, *Peter and the other disciple started for the tomb.*

4–5. They set out together: *Both were running, but the other disciple outran Peter and reached the tomb first.* On arrival, the other disciple *bent over and looked in at the strips of linen lying there but did not go in.* Jesus' body had been wrapped in strips of linen by Joseph of Arimathea and Nicodemus (19:40) and placed in the tomb. When the other disciple looked in, all he could see was the strips of linen, but no body. For some reason he did not enter the tomb for closer inspection.

6-7. Peter showed no such reticence: *Then Simon Peter, who was behind him, arrived and went into the tomb. He saw the strips of linen lying there, as well as the burial cloth that had been around Jesus' head. The cloth was folded up by itself, separate from the linen.* No mention is made of the burial cloth in the account of the burial (19:38–41), but it was common to use one for the face of the deceased (11:44). The main point is that the linen strips were just lying there with no body, and the burial cloth was folded by itself, no longer covering the face of Jesus' body. Clearly, the body of Jesus had not been stolen by his enemies, nor removed by his friends. In either case, the linen strips and the burial cloth would not have been removed at the tomb.

It has been suggested, but cannot be proved, that Jesus' resurrected body simply passed through the linen strips, leaving them still in the shape of his body, though somewhat collapsed. Perhaps attentive readers of John are meant to note the difference between Lazarus' restoration to life and Jesus' resurrection. Lazarus emerged from the tomb still 'wrapped with strips of linen, and a cloth around his face' and he had to be released by others (11:44), whereas in the case of Jesus the linen strips and burial cloth were simply left behind when he rose from the dead.

8-9. Following Peter's example, *Finally the other disciple, who had reached the tomb first, also went inside.* When he had a closer look at the linen strips and the facial burial cloth just lying there without any trace of Jesus' body, *He saw and believed.* This must mean that he believed that Jesus had been raised from the dead, even though, the evangelist adds in parenthesis, *They still did not understand from Scripture that Jesus had to rise from the dead.* It was to take some time before even 'the other disciple' understood that Scripture foreshadowed the resurrection of Christ. According to Luke, the risen Jesus himself opened the eyes of his disciples to understand the Scriptures, *i.e.* what was written about him 'in the Law of Moses, the Prophets and the Psalms' (Lk. 24:25–27, 44–46).

It is important to note the emphasis John and other NT writers place upon the importance of the empty tomb. For them the resurrection of Jesus was certainly not just 'spiritual' survival after death; it involved a real resurrection of the body.

10–12. The reaction of these two disciples is puzzling: *Then the disciples went back to their homes*. Presumably, Peter did not understand the significance of what he had seen, but the other disciple did understand, yet for some reason kept it largely to himself, though he must surely have told Mary the mother of Jesus whom he had taken into his own home (19:26–27).

Like Peter, Mary Magdalene did not understand the significance of the empty tomb. She was still grief-stricken, so when they returned to their homes, *Mary stood outside the tomb crying. As she wept, she bent over to look into the tomb and saw two angels in white, seated where Jesus' body had been, one at the head and the other at the foot*. Mark mentions 'a young man dressed in a white robe' (Mk. 16:5), Luke refers to 'two men in clothes that gleamed like lightning' (Lk. 24:4), Matthew speaks of 'an angel of the Lord' whose 'clothes were white as snow' (Mt. 28:2–3) and John here refers to 'two angels in white'. The overall impression is of angels in appearance like men stationed at the place where Jesus' body had lain, the first at one end of the rock ledge in the tomb where the head of Jesus' body had been, the second at the other end where the feet had been. The presence of angels at the tomb testifies to the fact that the disappearance of Jesus' body has been caused by divine, not human, intervention.

13. The two angels asked Mary, *Woman, why are you crying?* Mary, not yet understanding the significance of the empty tomb, replied, *They have taken my Lord away, and I don't know where they have put him*. She had already spoken to Peter and the other disciple, and clearly they knew nothing about any of Jesus' disciples removing the body. This confirms that the 'they' she supposed had removed the body must be Jesus' enemies; hence the compounding of her grief. The other Gospels say that Mary (with others) came with spices to anoint Jesus' body (Mk. 16:1; Lk. 23:56; 24:1), doing what was expected to honour him and at the same time to express grief. But even this activity had been denied her by what she supposed was the removal of his body by enemies.

14. Having said this, and apparently aware there was now someone outside the tomb, *she turned round and saw Jesus standing there, but she did not realize that it was Jesus*. Perhaps she did not immediately recognize him because her eyes were filled with tears, and the last person she expected to see was Jesus, and so she did not realize it was him, or perhaps there was something about Jesus' resurrection body that hindered immediate recognition.

15. Jesus addressed Mary Magdalene, *'Woman,' he said, 'why are you crying? Who is it you are looking for?'* Still she did not recognize him, and *thinking he was the gardener, she said, 'Sir, if you have carried him away, tell me where you have put him, and I will get him.'* Now she wondered whether this 'gardener' had removed Jesus' body from its garden tomb, and not his enemies. She wanted to know where he had put it so she could ensure that it received a proper burial. This suggests, as Luke 8:2–3 confirms, that Mary Magdalene was a woman of substance.

16–17. In response, *Jesus said to her, 'Mary.'* Once she heard him utter her name she recognized him immediately. The shepherd had called his sheep by name and she recognized his voice (*cf.* 10:3–4). *She turned towards him and cried out in Aramaic, 'Rabboni!'* The only other place in the NT where the expression 'Rabboni' is found is Mark 10:51, where blind Bartimaeus says to Jesus, 'Rabboni, I want to see.' The evangelist explains for readers who do not speak Aramaic that 'Rabboni' *means Teacher*.

Jesus' next words to Mary Magdalene are difficult to understand. *Jesus said, 'Do not hold on to me'*. Why should Jesus not want Mary Magdalene to touch him? It is unlikely that it was a rejection of natural affection. Prior to his death and resurrection Jesus showed no reticence about being touched or receiving affection. He allowed Mary, the sister of Martha and Lazarus, to anoint his feet with perfume and wipe them with her hair (12:3). After his resurrection he encouraged Thomas to put his finger in the nail prints in his hands and his hand into the spear wound in his side (27). In Matthew 28:9, when Jesus met Mary Magdalene and 'the other Mary', he did not discourage them when they 'clasped his feet and worshipped him'.

The reason Jesus gave Mary Magdalene for not touching him on this occasion was, *for I have not yet returned to the Father.* Two related things beg explanation: what did Jesus mean here by saying he had not yet returned to the Father, and why was that a reason for Mary

Magdalene not to touch him? In his farewell discourse Jesus spoke repeatedly of his return to the Father (13:1, 3; 14:28; 16:17, 28; 17:1, 5, 11) and this invariably meant his return to the Father's presence through death, resurrection and exaltation. Now, after his death and resurrection, Jesus said, 'I have not yet returned to the Father,' meaning apparently that he had not yet finally left this world in which he was appearing to his disciples to return to the Father.

Why was this a reason for Mary not to touch him? Perhaps the reason is to be found in the next thing Jesus said to her: *Go instead to my brothers and tell them, 'I am returning to my Father and your Father, to my God and your God.'* Mary Magdalene had an immediate task to perform. She had to inform Jesus' 'brothers', *i.e.* Jesus' disciples (*cf.* 20:18), that he was now returning to the Father. This was not a time to be dwelling in Jesus' presence, touching or holding him; there was a job to do. When Jesus said, 'I am returning to my Father,' it did not mean he was at that precise moment actually departing to the Father, but rather that the process of his return to the Father was under way. In fact, that process began with the betrayal and continued through the cross and resurrection and would culminate in his exaltation.

By referring to God as 'my Father and your Father' Jesus not only implied some distinction between his relationship with the Father and his disciples' relationship with the Father, but also included them with himself as children of God.

18. Accepting the commission Jesus gave her, *Mary Magdalene went to the disciples with the news: 'I have seen the Lord!' And she told them that he had said these things to her*. She told them first the amazing news that she had seen the Lord, and then communicated his message to them. In the course of just a few verses (11–18), the evangelist has chronicled Mary Magdalene's movement from grief to joyous belief. The evangelist does not say how the disciples received her message, but according to Mark 16:10–11/Luke 24:9–11 they regarded it as an idle tale.

2. The evening of the first day of the week (20:19–23)

19–20. The events described in the previous section (1–18) took place at the tomb in the early morning of the first day of the week.

The evangelist begins his account of what happened later that day, *On the evening of that first day of the week, when the disciples were together, with the doors locked for fear of the Jews.* He does not tell us how many disciples were present on this occasion, though the statement in 20:24 that 'Thomas (called Didymus), one of the Twelve, was not with the disciples when Jesus came' suggests 'the disciples' included at least the Twelve less Thomas and Judas Iscariot.

Peter and 'the other disciple' had seen the empty tomb, and Mary Magdalene had seen the Lord and passed on his message to the disciples that he was soon to return to the Father. Nevertheless, the disciples (with the exception of 'the other disciple') had not yet realized that Jesus had risen from the dead. They were still afraid of what 'the Jews' might do to them as his followers, and secluded themselves behind locked doors. These locked doors might keep out the prying eyes of 'the Jews', but they could not exclude the risen Lord: *Jesus came and stood among them and said, 'Peace be with you!'* Jesus' sudden appearance to his disciples behind locked doors, like his emergence from the tomb, demonstrated that in his resurrected state he was no longer bound by earthly limitations.

Prior to his death, Jesus told his disciples they would all be scattered and leave him alone (16:32). When he was arrested he told the soldiers to let his disciples go (18:8–9), and he was taken alone to the high priest and eventually to Pilate to be condemned to death. The disciples, and especially Peter who had denied him three times (18:17–18, 25–27), would have felt deeply ashamed that they had abandoned Jesus in his hour of need. When Jesus appeared to them behind locked doors, his greeting of 'Peace be with you!' showed he was not holding their failures against them; rather, he was offering a restored relationship.

After he said this, he showed them his hands and side. By showing them the nail prints in his hands and the spear wound in his side Jesus removed any doubt they had that the one who stood before them in that locked room was Jesus crucified but now risen from the dead. He predicted that the disciples' sorrow at his death would be turned to joy following his resurrection (16:20–22), and now *the disciples were overjoyed when they saw the Lord.*

21. Jesus repeated his greeting *Peace be with you!* This time it came with a commission for his disciples. Instead of reproaching them for their failures, he recommissioned them as his emissaries: *As the Father has sent me, I am sending you.* To express Jesus' being sent by the Father, here the evangelist uses the verb *apostellō*, while for the disciples' sending by Jesus he uses the verb *pempō*. However, nothing should be made of this, as the words are used synonymously in the Fourth Gospel for the sending of Jesus by the Father (*e.g.* 3:17; 5:36/4:34; 5:23), the disciples by Jesus (*e.g.* 4:38/20:21), John the Baptist by God (*e.g.* 1:6; 3:34/1:33), and various people sent by the Jewish leaders (*e.g.* 1:19, 24/1:22).

The Fourth Gospel speaks often of Jesus being sent into the world by the Father: to do his will (6:38–39; 8:29), to speak his words (3:34; 8:28; 12:49; 14:24; 17:8), to perform his works (4:34; 5:36; 9:4) and win salvation for all who believe (3:16–17). That the disciples were sent to continue the words and works of Jesus is foreshadowed at various places in the Gospel: Jesus urged them to lift up their eyes and see fields ripe for harvest, and told them he had sent them to reap where others had laboured (4:35–38), he said those who believed in him would do the works he had done and greater works than these because he was returning to the Father (14:12); he told them, 'I chose you and appointed you to go and bear fruit – fruit that will last' (15:16), saying that when the Counsellor comes 'he will testify about me. And you also must testify, for you have been with me from the beginning' (15:26–27), and when he prayed for his disciples he said to the Father, 'As you sent me into the world, I have sent them into the world' (17:18). This last text, which parallels 20:21, confirms that the sending of the disciples was 'into the world', *i.e.* with a mission to the world. The other texts reveal the essential content of their mission was to 'harvest' men and women for the kingdom by their witness to Jesus by word and deed, alongside the ongoing witness of the Spirit.

While Jesus' words about sending his disciples as the Father sent him applied primarily to the Twelve (Mk. 3:13–19), there is a sense in which all believers are privileged to share in this commission in so far as they all are recipients of the Spirit whom he bequeathed to his disciples (see 20:22). With the particular enabling that Spirit provides, each plays a part in continuing the work and witness of Jesus.

22. Following Jesus' words of recommissioning, the evangelist says, *And with that he breathed on them and said, 'Receive the Holy Spirit.'* The words 'on them' are missing in the Greek text, being supplied by the NIV translators. So the text could simply read, 'he breathed and said . . .' However, the word used for 'breathe' is *emphusaō*, which, though found only here in the NT, occurs several times in the LXX, where it refers to God breathing life into the man formed from the dust (Gn. 2:7; *cf.* Wisdom 15:11), Elijah breathing into the nostrils of the widow's dead son while calling upon the Lord to restore his life (1 Ki. 17:21 LXX), and Ezekiel prophesying to the wind to breathe life into the slain in the valley of dry bones (Ezk. 37:9). It is therefore probably legitimate to add 'on them' in 20:22, and perhaps to see in it allusions to the life-giving work of God in creation.

In many places in the Fourth Gospel the promise of the Spirit is foreshadowed (1:33; 4:10, 13–14; 7:37–39; 14:16–17, 26, 28; 15:26–27; 16:7–15). The clearest of these is 7:39, where, following Jesus' promise of streams of living water for those who believe in him, the evangelist adds, 'By this he meant the Spirit, whom those who believed in him were later to receive. Up to that time the Spirit had not been given, since Jesus had not yet been glorified.' What we read here in 20:22 looks like the fulfilment of these promises.

Accordingly, some have identified 20:22 as the Fourth Gospel's equivalent of Pentecost, but there are problems with such a view. Thomas was not included (20:24), nor was there any great change in the disciples' behaviour – they were still meeting behind closed doors when Jesus next appeared to them (26). Others have suggested it constituted a lesser bestowal of the Spirit to be supplemented with a greater endowment at Pentecost, or that what Jesus was bestowing was not the personal Holy Spirit (the promised Counsellor) but some impersonal power/breath from God. There is little to support either of these views in the Fourth Gospel. Another view is that there was a real impartation of the personal Spirit on this occasion, but that the Spirit was only experienced as the Counsellor, the one who replaced Jesus' earthly presence, after Jesus' final post-resurrection appearance and ascension. Finally, there is the view that Jesus' action was symbolic, foreshadowing the bestowal of the Spirit to take place on the Day of Pentecost.

Either of the last two explanations create the least problems, especially for those who accept the Acts account of Pentecost as historical.

23. After breathing (on his disciples) and saying, 'Receive the Holy spirit, Jesus said, *If you forgive anyone his sins, they are forgiven; if you do not forgive them, they are not forgiven.* These words have affinities with teaching of Jesus in the Gospel of Matthew. Jesus said to Peter, 'I will give you the keys of the kingdom of heaven; whatever you bind on earth will be bound in heaven, and whatever you loose on earth will be loosed in heaven' (Mt. 16:19). It also has affinities to what he said to the disciples generally in relation to those who would not heed admonition who must be treated as pagans or tax collectors: 'I tell you the truth, whatever you bind on earth will be bound in heaven, and whatever you loose on earth will be loosed in heaven' (Mt. 18:18). Both these texts have their own contexts in Matthew's Gospel, and we must not jump to the conclusion that what we find here in 20:23 means the same. This text must be interpreted in the context of the Fourth Gospel.

This is the only place in the Fourth Gospel where forgiveness of sins is spoken about, though the idea of sins remaining unforgiven is mentioned a number of times (8:24; 9:41; 15:22, 24; 16:8–9; 19:11). The non-forgiveness of sins is always related to refusal to believe in Jesus, suggesting that forgiveness of sins comes through belief in him. It is noteworthy that Jesus' statement 'If you forgive anyone his sins, they are forgiven; if you do not forgive them, they are not forgiven' is intimately connected with the (symbolic) bestowal of the Spirit (22–23), which is in turn related to the disciples' being sent into the world as his witnesses (21–22; *cf.* 15:26–27). This supports the view that the way in which the disciples forgive sins and retain sins is by preaching the good news and declaring the effects of believing it (forgiveness) and rejecting it (no forgiveness). It is important to notice the passive voice used in the statements in this verse regarding the forgiveness and non-forgiveness of sins. They function as divine passives reminding us that God alone forgives sin (*cf.* Mk. 2:3–12; Lk. 5:17–26) and Jesus' disciples declare what God does.

3. *The following Sunday (20:24–29)*

24–25. Continuing his account of the appearances of the risen Jesus, the evangelist says, *Now Thomas (called Didymus), one of the Twelve, was not with the disciples when Jesus came.* Thomas is called 'Didymus' three times in the Fourth Gospel (11:16; 20:24; 21:2), but never in the Synoptic Gospels. 'Didymus' means 'twin', suggesting he had a twin brother or sister, of whom no mention is made in any of the Gospels. We would not have known Thomas was absent on the previous occasion except that the evangelist explains that this was the case here. *So the other disciples told him, 'We have seen the Lord!' But he said to them, 'Unless I see the nail marks in his hands and put my finger where the nails were, and put my hand into his side, I will not believe it.'* Thomas' refusal to believe is expressed using the double negative (*ou mē*), showing he was adamant about this matter. The same double negative is used describing Peter's refusal to allow Jesus to wash his feet (13:8). At first reading it looks like Thomas was more unbelieving than the other disciples, but this was not necessarily the case. They do not seem to have believed Mary Magdalene when she said she had seen the Lord – it was not until Jesus appeared to them that they were filled with joy (20). Earlier references to Thomas reveal one who was dogged in his commitment to Jesus (11:16) and honest about his doubts (14:5). He refused to believe that Jesus had risen from the dead unless he actually saw the prints of the nails and spear wound for himself. By the way, this shows that the disciples and the evangelist were talking about a bodily resurrection of Jesus, not some spiritual survival beyond death.

26–27. Quite some time elapsed before Thomas' doubts were dealt with: *A week later his disciples were in the house again, and Thomas was with them. Though the doors were locked, Jesus came and stood among them and said, 'Peace be with you!'* Once again Jesus found his disciples behind locked doors, presumably still afraid of 'the Jews'. Once again he greeted them, 'Peace be with you!' *Then he said to Thomas, 'Put your finger here; see my hands. Reach out your hand and put it into my side.'* Without being told, Jesus knew of the conditions Thomas had placed upon his acceptance of the reality of his resurrection and invited him to touch him. Jesus' resurrection body, though it could pass through locked doors, was physically real.

It is not good to demand proofs from the Lord before one will believe, but the one 'who knew what was in a person' met Thomas where he was, inviting him to touch the nail prints in his hands and the spear wound in his side. But he also had a word of rebuke for Thomas: *Stop doubting and believe*. Presumably, Thomas had heard the witness of Mary Magdalene and his fellow disciples, but still refused to believe. Now confronted by the risen Jesus he was rebuked for doubting and encouraged to believe. Jesus' word to Thomas is similar to his word to the royal official who asked him to come down from Cana to Capernaum and cure his son: 'Unless you people see miraculous signs and wonders you will never believe' (4:48).

28. The effect of Jesus' words was immediate: *Thomas said to him, 'My Lord and my God!'* Thomas no longer needed to place his finger in the nail prints or his hand in Jesus' side; seeing him was enough (*cf.* 20:29). This is the last of a series of confessions of Jesus found in the Fourth Gospel. John the Baptist testified that Jesus is the Son of God (1:34), Nathanael declared, 'Rabbi, you are the Son of God; you are the King of Israel' (1:49), the Samaritans said, 'we know this man really is the Saviour of the world' (4:42), the man born blind said, 'If this man were not from God he could do nothing,' and later worshipped him as the Son of Man (9:33, 35–38), Martha said, 'I believe that you are the Christ, the Son of God, who was to come into the world' (11:27), and the disciples said, 'This makes us believe that you came from God' (16:30). Thomas' confession is not only the last; it is also the climactic confession of the Fourth Gospel. He confessed Jesus not only as *his* Lord, but *his* God. It was a strongly personal confession. By recording it the evangelist brings his readers back to the opening verse of the Prologue: 'In the beginning was the Word, and the Word was with God, and the Word was God.'

It has been noted that the emperor Domitian required worship of himself as Lord and God (*Dominus et Deus*). Readers of the Gospel may have recognized a polemic against such demands in Thomas' confession of Jesus as his 'Lord and God'.

29. In response, Jesus told Thomas, *Because you have seen me, you have believed; blessed are those who have not seen and yet have believed.* Thomas came to believe because he saw the risen Lord, but Jesus did not praise Thomas' pathway to faith; rather, he pronounced a blessing upon those who have not seen the risen Jesus yet have believed in him nevertheless. These are those who hear or read the witness to Jesus borne by the disciples and confirmed by the Spirit (15:26–27). This is the second pronunciation of blessing by Jesus in the form of a beatitude in the Fourth Gospel (*cf.* 13:17: 'Now that you know these things, you will be blessed if you do them').

4. Concluding statement of purpose (20:30–31)

30–31. The account of Thomas' climactic confession leads naturally into the statement of purpose for the writing of the Fourth Gospel. It begins with a reference to the many signs Jesus performed: *Jesus did many other miraculous signs in the presence of his disciples, which are not recorded in this book.* In the first part of the Gospel, the Book of Signs, the evangelist records seven signs performed by Jesus: turning water to wine in Cana (2:1–11), raising the royal official's son (4:46–54), healing the lame man at the Pool of Bethesda (5:1–9), feeding the five thousand (6:1–14); walking on the sea (6:16–21), healing the man born blind (9:1–7) and raising Lazarus (11:1–44). These were, as the evangelist says, but a selection from a far greater number of signs Jesus performed in the presence of this disciples (25).

While he included only a selection of the signs Jesus performed, the evangelist says, *But these are written that you may believe that Jesus is the Christ, the Son of God, and that by believing you may have life in his name.* The purpose of the Fourth Gospel is that people might recognize Jesus of Nazareth as the Christ (Messiah), the Son of God and put their faith in him.[1] In fact, the whole Gospel points

---

[1] As mentioned earlier, the debate about the purpose of the Fourth Gospel has often been discussed in relation to the textual variant in 20:31, whether the better reading is the aorist subjunctive (*pisteusēte* – taken to mean 'begin to believe') or the present subjunctive (*pisteuēte* – taken to mean 'continue to believe'). The former is believed to support an evangelistic purpose for the Gospel, the latter, an edificatory purpose. However, this is to read too much into the choice of tense, because elsewhere in this Gospel the aorist tense can denote both initial faith (1:7; 4:48; 6:30; 8:24; 9:36; 11:42; 19:35) and ongoing faith (11:15, 40; 13:19; 14:29), and the present tense is used to denote both initial faith (6:29; 10:38; 17:21) and continuing faith (6:35).

in this direction. Time and again the evangelist provides examples of people who have made this confession: Nathanael (1:49); the Samaritans (4:42); the man born blind (9:33, 35–38); Martha (11:27); the disciples themselves (16:30) and Thomas (28).

The title 'Son of God' was not a common designation for the Messiah among first-century Jews, but it is used in some texts in this way (see commentary on 1:34). Its use here is the last of a long line of explicit (1:34, 49; 5:25; 10:36; 11:4, 27; 19:7; 20:31) or implicit (3:16, 17, 18, 35, 36; 5:19, 20, 21, 22, 23, 26; 6:40; 14:13; 17:1) references to Jesus as the Son of God.

The people for whom the Fourth Gospel was primarily intended were the evangelist's fellow Jews or proselytes/God-fearers, those who still needed to believe that Jesus of Nazareth was the true Messiah. Of course, the Fourth Gospel was intended for a wider audience as well, including Samaritans (4:42) and Gentiles (10:16; 12:20–26). While the primary purpose of the Gospel was to help people recognize Jesus of Nazareth as the Messiah, the Son of God, this does not exclude secondary purposes, chief among which is encouragement and equipping of those who already believe (see pp. 20–23). Chapters 13 – 17, including the footwashing (13:1–17), the farewell speeches (13:31 – 16:33) and Jesus' prayers (17:1–26) particularly serve this purpose.

Many have observed that 20:30–31 would constitute a very appropriate conclusion to the Fourth Gospel. It follows the climactic confession of faith made by Thomas, the last in a long line of confessions, and also refers back to the seven signs recounted in the Book of Signs, and then urges the readers to reflect upon the signs recorded and come to the same faith in Jesus as the Messiah, the Son of God. There is, then, some merit in the view that an earlier form of the Gospel did conclude at 20:31, and 21:1–25 was added later as an epilogue.

IV. EPILOGUE (21:1–25)

A. JESUS APPEARS TO SEVEN DISCIPLES (21:1–14)

1–3. The epilogue begins with another post-resurrection appearance: *Afterwards Jesus appeared again to his disciples, by the Sea* *of Tiberias.* The Sea of Tiberias is another name for the Sea of Galilee (*cf.* 6:1). Beginning his account, the evangelist lists the seven disciples involved: *It happened this way: Simon Peter, Thomas (called Didymus), Nathanael from Cana in Galilee, the sons of Zebedee, and two other disciples were together.* Peter, Thomas and Nathanael all appear earlier in the Gospel, but the sons of Zebedee, James and John (*cf.* Mk. 1:19), have not been mentioned by name. We are not told who the 'two other disciples' were. Thomas is again said to be called 'Didymus', which means 'twin', suggesting he had a twin brother or sister, of whom no mention is made in any of the Gospels (*cf.* 11:16; 20:24).

First, the setting for the resurrection appearance is given: *'I'm going out to fish,' Simon Peter told them, and they said, 'We'll go with you.' So they went out and got into the boat, but that night they caught nothing.* Some have seen in this activity evidence of ongoing disorientation or a dereliction of duty on the part of disciples re-commissioned in 20:21–23, but there is no hint of that in the way the story is told. Others have suggested that chapter 21, added later to the Gospel, may report events that took place earlier than the recommissioning of 20:21–23. In this way the anomaly of the disciples returning to their former occupation after their recommissioning is overcome. However, it seems unnecessary to defend the disciples' actions. According to Mark 14:28; 16:7, Jesus himself had told them to return to Galilee, and he would see them there. It is natural they would occupy themselves fishing while they waited for him. Though night-time is the best time for fishing, the disciples caught nothing that night. Such an experience was not without precedent for them (*cf.* Lk. 5:5).

4–6. Next, Jesus' appearance is described: *Early in the morning, Jesus stood on the shore, but the disciples did not realize that it was Jesus.* The boat was about one hundred yards off shore (*cf.* 21:8), and in the early light of morning it would not have been clear who it was standing on the shore. *He called out to them, 'Friends,* (lit. 'children'), *haven't you any fish?'* The word translated 'fish' (*prosphag-ion*) was used for a relish used with bread, often small pieces of fish. *'No,' they answered. He said, 'Throw your net on the right side of the boat and you will find some.'* They followed his command and when they did, they were unable to haul the net in because of the large *number of fish*. In some ways this was similar to the experience of Simon Peter and his partners recorded in Luke 5:4–9. In both cases the authority of Jesus over nature is implied.

7–8. It is not surprising that then *the disciple whom Jesus loved said to Peter, 'It is the Lord!'* If 'the disciple whom Jesus loved' is identified as John the son of Zebedee, then he was also a fisherman, and very probably one of the partners involved with Peter on that earlier occasion recorded in Luke 5:4–9. When he saw a similar series of events unfold, he realized the person on the shore was none other than Jesus. Then *as soon as Simon Peter heard him say, 'It is the Lord,' he wrapped his outer garment around him (for he had taken it off) and jumped into the water*. The word the NIV translates as 'outer garment' (*ependytēs*) is found only here in the NT and may need to be rendered differently in the light of its context. The words the NIV translates, 'for he had taken it off' (*ēn gar gymnos*), literally rendered would be 'for he was naked'. Ancient art and literature indicate that cast-net fisherman worked naked, and it is likely that Peter, being naked, wrapped not a full 'outer garment' but a simple loincloth around him to show respect for Jesus before jumping into the water to make his way to the shore to meet him. (The verb *diazōnnymi*, translated 'wrapped', can also mean 'hitch up'. It is possible, therefore, that Peter was not completely naked and did not put on a garment at all, but hitched up the simple garment he was wearing so it would not impede him in the water as he made his way towards Jesus.) While Peter led the way to the shore and to Jesus, *The other disciples followed in the boat, towing the net full of fish, for they were not far from shore, about a hundred yards.*

9–11. There was a welcome surprise awaiting them on the shore: *When they landed, they saw a fire of burning coals there with fish on it, and some bread*. How the risen Jesus procured the fish he was cooking or the bread is not explained. He did not ignore the fruits of their labours: *Jesus said to them, 'Bring some of the fish you have just caught.'* Jesus addressed the seven disciples ('them') but it was Peter who responded first: *Simon Peter climbed aboard and dragged the net ashore. It was full of large fish, 153, but even with so many the net was not torn.* The evangelist's reference to the number of fish was probably not meant to be symbolic, as some have suggested,[1] but rather to emphasize the miraculous nature of the catch – there was a large number of fish (153), they were large fish, and even so the net was not torn.

12–13. Following the landing of the fish, *Jesus said to them, 'Come and have breakfast.'* The next statement is puzzling: *None of the disciples dared ask him, 'Who are you?' They knew it was the Lord.* It reflects some lingering doubts. Despite these lingering doubts, they did not dare ask, 'Who are you?' Intuitively they knew it was the Lord. What Jesus did next would have removed any last traces of doubt: *Jesus came, took the bread and gave it to them, and did the same with the fish.* They had seen him do this before for a multitude (6:1–13), just as they had heard him tell them on a previous occasion where to net many fish (Lk. 5:4–9). Together these things removed any doubt that it was the Lord they were encountering.

14. This episode concludes with the explanation *This was now the third time Jesus appeared to his disciples after he was raised from the dead.* The first of the previous occasions was when Jesus appeared to the disciples when Thomas was absent (20:19–23), the second, when Thomas was present (20:26–29). This reference in chapter 21 back to events in chapter 20 indicates that if this chapter was added later as an epilogue, it was intended to link in with what had been previously written.

B. JESUS AND PETER (21:15–19)

15. This section reports Jesus' questioning and recommissioning of Simon Peter. It begins, *When they had finished eating, Jesus said to Simon Peter, 'Simon son of John, do you truly love me more than these?'* After sharing breakfast with all seven disciples, Jesus singled Peter out and asked him whether he loved him more than 'these'. Jesus could have been asking whether Peter loved him (1) more than the other disciples who were present did; (2) more than

---

[1] Jerome noted that Greek authors believed there existed 153 species of fish, the allusion to the entire range of species of fish symbolizes the universality of the Christian mission.

he loved those other disciples; (3) more than the large catch of fish, the boats and fishing gear. The second is unlikely because there is no mention elsewhere of Peter's love for the other disciples. The third is possible if one thinks that Peter's decision to go fishing (21:3) represented a turning away from Jesus to go back to his old trade. If this is unlikely, then the first option is to be preferred, remembering that Peter had been the most forward in asserting his dedication to Jesus (13:37–38; *cf.* Mt. 26:33). In answer to Jesus' question, Peter said, *Yes, Lord, you know that I love you.* Peter's response was positive, but involved no bold claims like those he had made previously. He simply said that his Lord knew the truth about his love for him. In response to Peter's affirmation of love for him, *Jesus said, 'Feed my lambs.'* His commission to Peter was to feed (*boske*) his 'lambs' (*arnia*), meaning he was to provide spiritual nourishment for new believers.

16. In this verse Jesus repeats his question, and receives the same answer: *Again Jesus said, 'Simon son of John, do you truly love me?' He answered, 'Yes, Lord, you know that I love you.' Jesus said, 'Take care of my sheep.'* The only differences are that Jesus' commission to Peter is to take care of (*poimaine*) his 'sheep' (*probata*) implying pastoral care of believers generally (*cf.* 10:1–27).

17. Then for *the third time he said to him, 'Simon son of John, do you love me?'* It has often been noted that the verb 'to love' (*agapaō*) used in Jesus' first two questions is different from the verb 'to love' (*phileō*) used in Peter's first two answers, but that in the third question and answer *phileō* is used in both Jesus' question and Peter's answer. Sometimes a lot has been made of these differences, but the fact is that *agapaō* and *phileō* are used synonymously in the Fourth Gospel. For example, both *agapaō* and *phileō* are used of the Father's love for the Son (10:17; 15:9; 17:23, 24, 26/5:20), Jesus' love for Lazarus (11:5/11:3, 36), the disciple whom Jesus loved (13:23; 19:26; 21:7, 20/20:2), and the Father's love for the disciples (14:23/16:27).

One significant difference is the insertion of the editorial comment that *Peter was hurt because Jesus asked him the third time, 'Do you love me?'* Why he was hurt is not explained. Perhaps he felt Jesus was not satisfied with his previous answers. In response, *He said, 'Lord, you know all things; you know that I love you.'* Peter's answer was the same as before, except that he prefaced it with the words 'you know all things' to stress that he really meant it when he said 'you know that I love you', and that Jesus who knew all things knew the state of Peter's heart. In response, *Jesus said, 'Feed my sheep.'* This time Peter was charged with the responsibility to feed (*boske*) my sheep (*probata*), meaning he was to provide spiritual nourishment for believers generally.

Jesus may have given Peter three opportunities to re-express his love for him and recommissioned him three times as well because of his threefold denial (18:15–17, 25–27). The record of Peter's reinstatement stands as an encouragement for all who might crack under pressure and deny their Lord. This is not the same as cold-blooded apostasy, and is not regarded as such by the Lord.

Two other things call for comment. First, Jesus' reference to 'my sheep' has a parallel in 10:27, where Jesus refers to believers as 'my sheep'. Here, then, Jesus was giving Peter a pastoral role towards the believers. Second, similar terminology is used in 1 Peter 5:1–4 and Acts 20:28–29 to urge elders to shepherd God's flock, suggesting that Jesus' commission to Peter to feed his sheep here in 20:15–17 was not understood to be restricted to Peter in an exclusive way. More recent Roman Catholic scholars rightly point out that it is inappropriate to import questions of the Petrine office in Roman Christianity into the exegesis of this text.[1]

18–19. Following the reinstatement of Peter, Jesus said to him, *I tell you the truth, when you were younger you dressed yourself and went where you wanted; but when you are old you will stretch out your hands, and someone else will dress you and lead you where you do not want to go.* This enigmatic statement contrasts Peter's experience during his youth when he dressed himself and went wherever he pleased, with what was to happen to him when he grew old. His independence would be stripped away. He would be forced to stretch out his hands and others would 'clothe' him and lead him to a place he would not wish to go. Stretching out the hands is an allusion to the way those to be crucified were

---

[1]Schnackenburg, vol. 3, p. 336; Moloney, p. 555.

forced to stretch out their arms and bear the cross beam to the place of execution (*cf.* Barnabas 12:4; Justin, *I Apology*, 35). The evangelist leaves us in no doubt about the intention of this saying: *Jesus said this to indicate the kind of death by which Peter would glorify God*. Peter is known to have suffered a violent death (1 Clement 5:4) by crucifixion (Tertullian, *Scorpiace* xv.3), and 21:18–19 is the earliest testimony to his martyrdom by this means. Jesus' next words to Peter were most apt: *Then he said to him, 'Follow me!'* Peter was to take up his cross literally and follow Jesus.

C. JESUS AND THE BELOVED DISCIPLE (21:20–24)

20–21. After hearing Jesus' prediction concerning his own fate, *Peter turned and saw that the disciple whom Jesus loved was following them*. This disciple is further identified as *the one who had leaned back against Jesus at the supper and had said, 'Lord, who is going to betray you?'* (13:22–26). *When Peter saw him, he asked, 'Lord, what about him?'* It is not surprising that Peter, having heard of his own fate, wanted to know what was to happen to this other disciple with whom he was so closely associated.[1]

22. In response to Peter's question, *Jesus answered, 'If I want him to remain alive until I return, what is that to you? You must follow me.'* Essentially, Jesus' answer to Peter was a reminder that he was to 'follow' him (19); the fate of the beloved disciple was not his concern. While Peter was to encounter a violent death, the beloved disciple might survive until Jesus himself returned (*cf.* 14:3). It is worth noting that in the Fourth Gospel the hope of the second coming of Jesus is still assumed, despite the emphasis on the present experience of eternal life and the coming of the Counsellor (*cf.* also 1 Jn. 2:28; 3:2).

23. These words of Jesus to Peter were misunderstood by some of the followers of Jesus. *Because of this, the rumour spread*

---

[1] When 'the disciple whom Jesus loved' is mentioned in the Fourth Gospel, it is with only one exception (19:26) in contexts where Peter is involved also (13:23–24; 21:7, 20).

among the brothers that this disciple would not die. People believed
that Jesus would return during the lifetime of the beloved disciple. It seems that the death of the beloved disciple caused a
crisis of faith among these people, so the final editors of the
Fourth Gospel explained that *Jesus did not say that he would not
die; he only said, 'If I want him to remain alive until I return, what is
that to you?'* The purpose of this statement was to correct misunderstanding by pointing out that Jesus' statement was prefaced by the words 'if I want him to remain'. It was not a
prediction that the beloved disciple would not die. By dealing
with the misunderstanding the editors also dealt with the crisis
of faith it had produced.

24. This verse contains an endorsement of the beloved disciple's testimony by the final editors of the Fourth Gospel. Who
these editors were cannot be determined with certainty. One
viable suggestion is that they were elders in the church at
Ephesus. Referring back to Jesus' reference to the beloved disciple, the editors say, *This is the disciple who testifies to these things
and who wrote them down. We*[1] *know that his testimony is true.* 'These
things' refers to the content of the whole Gospel, not just the
events recorded in chapter 21, much less Jesus' words to Peter in
21:23. What is implied here is that the basic testimony preserved
in the Fourth Gospel came from the beloved disciple, and that he
was also responsible for writing it down. Then the editors added
their own endorsement to the validity of his testimony. This, of
course, was intended to reassure readers that what they are
reading is worthy of acceptance.

D. CONCLUSION (21:25)

25. The epilogue concludes with words reminiscent of, though
not the same as, those found in 20:30: *Jesus did many other things as
well. If every one of them were written down, I suppose that even the*

---

[1] Some suggest the 'we' in this verse is a literary plural employed by the writer as an individual self-reference, but the use of a literary 'we' in antiquity is open to serious question.
Jackson, pp. 1–34, puts forward another view – that 'we' means the author (the beloved disciple) and his readers, *i.e.* 'you and I'.

whole world would not have room for the books that would be written. The use of such hyperboles was common.[1] It functions here as a reminder that the works of Jesus recorded in this Gospel are but a small selection of all those he performed. But, as 20:31 indicates, they are sufficient to provide a basis of faith that Jesus is the Christ, which will bring readers into the experience of eternal life.

[1]Johanan ben Zakkai (*d.* AD 80, making him a contemporary of the beloved disciple) said something similar: 'If all heaven were parchment and all trees were pens and all seas were ink, it would not be enough to write down my wisdom which I have learnt from my teacher' (*Soperim* 16:8; cited in Str-B 2, 587).